Lydia
and
Maynard

Lydia and Maynard

Letters between Lydia Lopokova and John Maynard Keynes

Edited by
Polly Hill and Richard Keynes

ANDRE DEUTSCH

First published 1989 by
André Deutsch Limited
105–106 Great Russell Street, London WC1B 3LJ

The letters of John Maynard Keynes and Lydia Lopokova
copyright © 1989 King's College, Cambridge
Introduction, editorial work, notes and all other matter
copyright © 1989 Polly Hill and Richard Keynes
All rights reserved

ISBN 233 98283 3

Photoset by Rowland Phototypesetting Limited
Printed in Great Britain by
St Edmundsbury Press Limited, Bury St Edmunds, Suffolk

Contents

List of Illustrations

Acknowledgments: Photographs not specifically acknowledged are from the Keynes family archives. Thanks are due to King's College, Cambridge for permission to reproduce numbers 6, 16, 19, 22, 26 and 41; to the Marshall Library, Cambridge, for numbers 27 and 44; to the BBC Hulton Picture Library for number 30; to the Courtauld Institute of Art for number 40; to *The Times* for number 42; to Mrs Clarissa Heald for numbers 36 and 37; to Mrs Laura Phillips for number 38; to Oleg Polunin for number 34. Number 18 is from a private collection, photograph by Christopher Dalton.

Editors' Preface

As a niece and a nephew of Maynard Keynes, we both have the advantage of having known our uncle and aunt well. It is our affectionate belief that the publication of these letters, written during the period of their court-ship in 1922–25, will be of value and interest and will not offend their ghosts.

Our decision not to present the letters in full was necessitated by their great length, which no publisher of a popular edition could possibly contemplate. From 1922 to 1937 Lydia wrote over 200,000 words to Maynard, and his preserved correspondence for the same period runs to around 150,000 words. So both sets of letters have had to be cut.

Lydia's letters presented special problems of incomprehensibility during April 1922 to August 1923, when very few of the letters from Maynard, which she was often answering, have survived. More generally, her letters often contain passages which are repetitious, misleadingly inaccurate, trivial, or lacking in general interest, as when she lists the contents of *The Nation* – they are, also, occasionally illegible. Fortunately Polly Hill, the editor of Lydia's letters, believes that they can be made more charming and true to their original purpose by a little careful, sensitive excision, provided certain guide lines are observed. As for Maynard's letters, although almost always clear and legible, they are often somewhat over-burdened with references to unexciting college gossip and business, and to domestic affairs of no lasting interest.

Judicious cuts, indicated thus . . . , have therefore been made to both sides of the correspondence. Also, 62 letters (forty-four Lydia's and eighteen Maynard's), which are mostly short, have been omitted altogether. Our primary aim throughout has been to serve the general reader by omitting only material that is unimportant or difficult to understand. Nearly everything connected with the relationship of the lovers, with ballet, theatre and art in London, and with the important activities of mutual friends within and outside the Bloomsbury circle, has been faithfully retained, and Maynard's primary concern with economics features largely.

For four years, from 1983, Polly Hill was partly occupied in personally transcribing Lydia's entire text from greatly enlarged photo-copies; in the final stages she received invaluable help from her daughter, Susannah Burn, who read all the letters aloud, with particular attention to punctuation and spelling, as a check on the transcription. The final transcripts have been deposited in the Modern Archives of King's College, Cambridge, so that they will be available to scholars after the publication of the edited version. Maynard's letters, which have been edited by Richard Keynes, were transcribed with impeccable accuracy by Miss Rosemary Graham, except for the first one hundred transcribed by the editor; these transcripts, also, are in the King's Archives.

Nearly all Lydia's letters bear no more than the day of the week at their head and the editor was greatly helped by the meticulous research on the sorting and dating of the originals in the King's Archives that had been carried out by Lady (Margaret) Lintott. Fortunately an appreciable number of postmarked envelopes had been preserved, for sets of letters of around the same date had been thrust into them by an unknown hand. But although this was a great help, there were inevitably some letters for which the dates had to be deduced from the contents, whether or not they contained reference to Maynard's fully dated letters. It seems that it is only in October 1922, when Maynard's letters were missing, that everyone's detective work has, briefly, failed. Accordingly, both the day of the week and the date are given at the head of nearly all the published letters, though in most cases they did not appear on the original.

Just as Lydia's letters seldom bore complete dates, so they rarely bore an address, unless she was away from home. Inferred addresses, which are reasonably reliable, are shown in brackets.

Lydia's spelling and punctuation were apt to be very haphazard. She adored dictionaries, often carrying them with her on her travels, but she used them to enlarge and poeticise her vocabulary rather than to check her spelling, so that they may have been the source of some of her endless fund of new and original endearments which terminate so many of her letters. It seemed important to retain most of her mis-spellings so as to convey something of the quality of her conversational personality, which delighted her friends because of her deliberate mispronunciations; so her mis-spellings have been preserved unless they hopelessly impair comprehension or are obvious slips of the pen. But proper names are a different case. It would have been confusing if Lydia's different renderings, even sometimes in the same letter, of names such as Florrie (Florie, Flory) or Massine (Massin, Miassin, Miassine) had been retained. So the spelling of nearly all proper names has been silently standardised where necessary, using accepted modern Western spellings in the case of the names of Russian ballet people – thus Diaghilev not Diaghileff. The same treatment has been adopted for street names, which were often spelt inconsistently.

Further inconsistencies affected Lydia's abbreviations of first names to initial letters or first syllables, such as V. and D., or Van. and Dun., with or without a full stop, for Vanessa Bell and Duncan Grant. When first names alone are used, the surname is added in square brackets on its first appearance in the correspondence, but not subsequently, and an identifying list of first names and nicknames is provided on pp. 356–57. When an initial is used, we substitute the first name on its first appearance in any letter, but not subsequently in the same letter. The confusion over the plethora of Vs has been avoided: Vanessa, Vera and Virginia are distinguished.

In accordance with modern practice the names of newspapers, and the titles of ballets, plays and book, have been italicised in both sets of letters. Where words were underlined for emphasis, italics are also used.

When it came to punctuation, Lydia was quite good with full stops and a dab hand with the colon, but her commas were often omitted or displaced and what should have been separate sentences were sometimes run together. Her paragraphing was particularly unreliable and unclear, suffering from the small size of the paper on which she wrote; here it has been necessary to compromise between fidelity to an uncertain text and the interests of intelligibility, with preference for the latter. One liberty which has often been taken is the separation of her concluding endearments from the preceding text, since they deserve to stand on their own.

Many editors are uncertain how to treat their author's deletions, but this does not apply to Lydia. She evidently went over her letters after writing them, for bold deletions, which were applied with some broad instrument other than a pen, fairly abound – they are deletions indeed!

Most of the people who feature significantly in the correspondence (other than the few we have failed to identify and public figures who are still well known) are included in the list of Dramatis Personae on pp. 340–55. In compiling the list long entries have been given to people, such as Vera Bowen, who are important personalities in the letters about whom little is known, but not to those like Vanessa Bell who feature largely in the literature. Many ballet personalities are included. In general, but not always, later careers, after 1925, are ignored in this volume.

In interleaving the two sets of letters, Lydia's letter of any date, irrespective of when it was posted, has been placed before Maynard's of the same date. The speed and reliability of the postal service of the time, which made it possible for a letter posted in London to be delivered in Cambridge the same evening, seem almost inconceivable today, but even so a late collection might be missed, thus delaying the reply to a letter until after the next one was on its way. So the correspondence was far from being an orderly exchange, and neither writer waited to hear from the other before making the latest report. In terms of the trouble taken in the choice of topics, and in the frequency of letters, Lydia was the better correspondent of the two: thus between 13th

January and 14th March 1924 she wrote forty-five letters as against Maynard's twenty-five.

During the lengthy Cambridge vacations the two were often together in Gordon Square, when no letters were written, and events which were important to them went unrecorded. It is partly to maintain the continuity of the correspondence that brief interpolations between batches of letters have been provided.

Finally a note on pronunciation. Maynard traced his descent from the Norman family of Cahagnes (finding to his pleasure that William de Cahagnes is named in Domesday Book as holder of the land at his Sussex house, Tilton). The family name came to be attached to several of the places in England that belonged to its various branches, and in the Middle Ages was normally spelled 'Kaynes', pronounced as 'canes'. Later the spelling changed uniformly to Keynes, but the original pronunciation was always retained, not only for the surname but also for the place names, with the exception of the new city of Milton Keynes where officialdom, ignorant of etymology and influenced by the pronunciation of 'key', has recently decided otherwise. The name Maynard ought to be stressed in the same way as Edward, but nowadays most people put the stress on the second syllable – May*nard* – which happens to be how Lydia pronounced it except that she omitted the final letter: May*nar*. She pronounced her own name in an English way, with four more or less equally stressed syllables: Lo-po-ko-vah, not *Lop-* okova, even though Loppy was her nickname.

Acknowledgments

Our chief debt is to the Provost and Fellows of King's College, Cambridge, owners both of the letters themselves and the copyright, who have given us every encouragement to publish this volume. We are particularly grateful to Dr Michael Halls, Modern Archivist of King's College, for his invaluable help in finding our way about the relevant papers in his charge, and in elucidating references to College business and its members in Maynard's letters. We must also express our gratitude to the staff of the Cambridge University Library for their unfailing assistance.

In editing Lydia's letters, constant reference has been made to the volume of essays entitled *Lydia Lopokova*, edited by Dr Milo Keynes and published in 1983. This excellent compilation was based on much research into several aspects of her career, and Dr Keynes has been especially helpful in searching for additional information related to the Lopukhov family. We are also indebted to him as the source of some of our illustrations.

In the task of identifying the numerous people mentioned in the letters, we have drawn heavily on the biographical sketches provided in Anne Olivier Bell's immaculate edition of *The Diary of Virginia Woolf*, which was outstandingly helpful.

Special thanks are also due to Mrs Clarissa Heald, daughter of Vera and Harold Bowen, for providing much information about her parents, who were Lydia's closest friends in 1922–25. It was very exciting to be given access to Harold Bowen's unpublished diary for 1923–24, and we are most grateful to Mrs Heald for looking out all the references to Lydia in the diary, and for permission to quote from it. We thank her in addition for providing photographs and other material. We are fortunate that descendants of Lydia's other greatest friends, Florrie Grenfell and Sam and Lil Courtauld, were also able to help us. They are Mrs Laura Phillips, grand-daughter of Florrie, and the Rt. Hon. Sir Adam Butler, son of the Courtaulds' only daughter.

The assistance of Miss Mary Clarke, editor of the *Dancing Times* and author of many books on dance, was much appreciated.

Apart from Professor Lord Kahn, who does not enter the scene until our next volume, the foremost living experts on the life of Maynard Keynes are

Professor Sir Austin Robinson and Professor Donald Moggridge, managing editors of the thirty volumes of his collected works, and Professor Robert Skidelsky, the first volume of whose biography *John Maynard Keynes* was published in 1983. All have responded most kindly to our requests for help on a variety of details, and Professor Skidelsky graciously provided a copy of his unpublished lecture 'The Wooing of Lydia'.

That historic, though reticent, figure Dr George ('Dadie') Rylands, who was well acquainted with Bloomsbury and still resides in King's College, successfully identified Lydia's 'platonic lover' as Basil Maine, thereby saving us in the nick of time from making a serious error. We are greatly indebted to him.

Lastly, Polly Hill wishes to express her thanks to Miss Diana Athill of André Deutsch, Mrs Susannah Burn and Professor Martin Robertson, who were her three literary advisers in this work.

P.H.
R.K.

Introduction

The love affair between Lydia Lopokova and John Maynard Keynes, which is so poignantly recorded in these letters, appalled their Bloomsbury friends and when it culminated in marriage in 1925 caused widespread surprise. But it should not surprise us.

Although Maynard was a world-famous economist much of his time was devoted to other activities, for he needed to be involved in literature and the arts, as well as in financial and public affairs and in journalism, in order to flourish intellectually. He also needed Lydia who was, as these letters reveal, uncommonly honest, generous and original, as well as being a sensitive reader of literature and a poetic and witty writer. Indeed, he could hardly have found a more suitable companion.

Lydia, for her part, needed Maynard: she was a Russian emigrée who had been unhappily married, and in 1922, when their affair began, she yearned for the kind of emotional sustenance which was provided by the capacious and indeed leisurely love which was Maynard's style. Besides, the collapse of Diaghilev's ballet company at that time had made her financial situation precarious.

In 1922 both Maynard and Lydia were at turning points in their lives, though neither of them may have been fully aware of this. Maynard needed a break with the past, especially as he could not continue indefinitely to find satisfactory refuge at Charleston, the unsettled and often unoccupied house of his 'Bloomsbury mother' Vanessa Bell; and the numerous more or less ephemeral homosexual affairs or encounters which had succeeded his passionate relationship with Duncan Grant in 1908 were proving less satisfying, though in 1922 he was still presumably enjoying a mild affair with the young Cambridge man, Sebastian Sprott. As for Lydia, she had a curiously unambitious side to her nature, which was shown by the earlier discontinuities in her professional career. While retaining her enormous capacity for friendship, and her taste for cosmopolitan life, she, like Maynard, was not averse to settling down in surprisingly conventional married happiness.

Maynard and Lydia were alike in having parents to whom they were devoted. Maynard could hardly do any wrong in the eyes of his parents, who were of course ignorant of the nature of his emotional life. His doting father, a cautious and charming man, had actually helped him out with money in 1920 when Maynard's financial recklessness in the money market, coupled with the slump, had driven him into debt. Quite exceptionally for Bloomsbury, Maynard enjoyed very close relationships with his parents, visiting them weekly during full term, and constantly seeking his mother's advice on matters of health; he actually predeceased them both.

But he gradually fell into unexpressed intellectual revolt against his kind and demure father, who had been an eminent Cambridge moral scientist and political economist before he turned to university administration; and his devotion to his mother was tempered by the fact that she somehow represented the sort of Newnham woman, and public figure, who had never appealed to him. Lydia liberated him from his somewhat stifling, though agreeable, Cambridge background; as a poet *manqué*, who had no real artistic outlets, he found her more intelligently artistic than he had any right to expect; he often deferred to her judgement.

Lydia adored her widowed mother and often longed to see her. But by long residence, since 1910, she was irrevocably committed to the West and would never have contemplated returning to live for any length of time in her post-revolutionary homeland – in which Diaghilev's ballet company had never performed.

In January 1922, when his serious courtship of Lydia began, Maynard was in his thirty-ninth year. Since leaving his parental home in 1902, on going up to King's College, he had never really settled anywhere for long, and he was now in constant oscillation between King's and his Bloomsbury house, 46 Gordon Square. Although Lydia was only in her thirtieth year, she had been in perpetual motion as a dancer, and occasionally as an actress, for some twelve years – except that we know hardly anything of what she was doing during her disappearance for about nineteen months in 1919–1921. Both Maynard and Lydia needed a still centre.

This applied more to her than to him since King's College, to which he had returned in 1908, was often such a centre for Maynard. But although his devotion to his college resembled his love for his parents and friends, and was equally indestructible, he always lost all taste for college life during the three vacations which lasted altogether for more than half the year; and despite his many bursarial and other college duties, he always spent regular days in London in term time.

It is this oscillation between London and Cambridge which accounts for the existence of these letters at a time when the use of private telephones for long-distance calls was not usual. During the Cambridge term Lydia was deprived of Maynard's company in London for much more than half the week, including the weekend; he usually spent only two full days there, most often Wednesdays and Thursdays. So while leading her own busy social life, and sometimes dancing, she courted him assiduously in her letters. Understanding his craving for private flattery, she perspicaciously set about studying his economic journalism and even his *Tract on Monetary Reform*, which almost began to interest her.

The charm of Lydia as a correspondent is obvious. Maynard's letters are usually those of a busy man, signalling his affection without having the time to say much, so that the impression gained of *his* charm is at first difficult to understand. It comes partly from his attentiveness to Lydia's needs, both material and psychological, which never fails in its sensitivity, and partly from one's realisation that she could not have indulged her own idiosyncratic style so freely had she not trusted him implicitly. An atmosphere of mutual affection, trust, understanding and amusement prevails throughout.

So it is all the more remarkable that there is not a single sentence in any of Lydia's letters in which she criticises, even by implication, any of Maynard's Bloomsbury friends, though she was well aware of their hostility, which was often overt. Contrary to all appearances, she was endowed with a strong sense of discretion, for use when required. By using this sense, when it was indeed required, she outwitted Bloomsbury in their attempts to dissuade Maynard from his love.

It yet remains mysterious that they should, for some years, have remained so oblivious to the sincerity of her well-cultivated literary and artistic tastes, though Virginia Woolf partly explains this:

> 'Maynard is very heavy and rather portentous; Maynard is passionately and pathetically in love, because he sees very well that he's dished if he marries her, and she has him by the snout. You can't argue solidly when Lydia's there, and as we set now to the decline, and prefer reason to any amount of high spirits, Lydia's pranks put us all on edge; and Bloomsbury steals off to its dens, leaving Maynard with Lydia on his knee, a sublime but heartrending spectacle.' (From a letter to Jacques Raverat, 8th June, 1924, in Nicolson, ed., 1977.)

As for Lydia's pranks, it is true that, as Harold Bowen's unpublished diary makes clear, she was occasionally apt to make a fool of herself in public, talking loudly to draw the attention of strangers and so on. But in earlier times members of Bloomsbury had been pranksters themselves, and they were certainly not elderly or conformist in the 1920s. Far from disapproving, Maynard found Lydia's showing-off and the spectacle of other people's disapproval amusing. No doubt he appreciated that when she was mischievous it was partly due to her frustrated need to perform on the stage; and he himself had an underground streak of mischief that answered to hers. He was not the only person to be amused: Lydia's chic appearance, with her rounded, diminutive figure topped by one of the hats so carefully chosen at the Galeries Lafayette in Regent Street, enabled her to get away with anything in most circles. The members of Bloomsbury mutually cultivated their jealousy – and it was the last straw when they were outclassed as performers.

Harold Bowen's diary has revealed that, in 1922 and 1923, Vera Bowen was Lydia's safety valve in whom she confided her secret fears; in 1923 it is even possible, as readers will learn, that she was so much troubled by Bloomsbury's hostility that she was temporarily testing the idea of facing a future without Maynard.

Maynard's appearance (though in earlier life) has been best described by Paul Levy:

'Keynes had a certain sense of his physical presence, which was magnetic and seductive, though he never considered himself attractive. This was not the presence of someone . . . who was aware of his physical beauty, but of someone who was used to his own appearance and comfortable with his body. This last was shown by the economy with which Keynes used his hands, which he was capable of keeping perfectly at rest throughout a conversation, save when his talk demanded him to strike a deliberate attitude. He was capable of a physical repose that is the complement of a confident attitude, and his voice was silky and well-modulated. Though not good-looking in any conventional sense save for his eyes, these formidable attributes made Keynes attractive both to men and to women.' Keynes, ed., 1975, pp. 64–5.

Basking in Lydia's love, and also in his increased wealth, Maynard's appearance in 1922–25 underwent great change. He who had previously been notably thin and lanky, began to resemble certain of his mother's portly brothers, and he was troubled by his baldness.

Maynard had never enjoyed very vigorous health and like so many people in the inter-war period, and earlier, he was often a victim of minor ailments, which feature largely in his letters, so that Lydia gave much advice about warm clothing and draught-avoidance. Unfortunately he was to become seriously ill in 1937, after which he led a semi-invalid life, though this did not prevent his full activity in the Treasury during the war.

He was fated to die of a coronary thrombosis in 1946, aged only sixty-two – Lydia surviving him, in dogged rural widowhood, for over a quarter of a century.

A full account of Maynard's life up to 1920 is given in Robert Skidelsky's biography (1983) so only a few basic facts need be provided here (see, also, pages 25–28). Born on 5th June 1883, he was the eldest child of a middle-class Cambridge couple, who enjoyed a standard of living more or less typical of that comfortable time; he was his parents' favourite and benefited from gaining a scholarship to Eton College in 1897, where he excelled both at mathematics and classics, finally being awarded an open scholarship at King's College, Cambridge, in 1902, in both subjects. Having decided, somewhat reluctantly, to read mathematics, he was placed twelfth in the university in his final examinations in 1905; he then instantly switched his mind to economics. In 1906 he was placed second, out of 104 candidates, in the Civil Service Examination. Unable to enter the Treasury owing to his failure to come first, he followed convention by choosing the India Office, where he found he had insufficient work so that he was able to devote his spare time to his philosophical thesis on probability. Despite his failure to obtain a Fellowship at King's College with that thesis at his first attempt in 1908, he resigned from the India Office in July to take up an ill-paid Cambridge lectureship in economics, and was fortunately rewarded with a Fellowship in 1909.

Such was his reputation as a largely self-taught economist, that he was summoned to advise the Treasury at the outbreak of war; after an interval he was appointed to an official position there in January 1915, at the high annual salary of £600. Very deeply distressed by the high rate of war casualties (of the 774 Kingsmen who served in that war, in all capacities, as many as twenty-two per cent lost their lives), Maynard sought to justify his own comfortable existence by working extremely hard and by giving moral support to his pacifist friends; sanguine, as ever, he had no doubt as to the outcome of the war. He first met Lydia at the end of 1918 before proceeding, as a Treasury delegate, to the Paris Peace Conference which opened in January 1919.

Lydia Lopukhova was born in St Petersburg on 21st October 1892, the third child of Vasili and Constanza Karlovna Douglas Lopukhov (see p. 348 below). As Vasili was an attendant at the Imperial Alexandrinsky Theatre, four of his five children (two sons and two daughters) were educated free, after qualifying for entry, at the Imperial Ballet School, where they received an excellent education; all of them became distinguished dancers. Lydia entered the school in 1901 – Karsavina was one of her teachers – and graduated from it in April 1909, soon joining the corps de ballet at the Maryinsky Theatre. In 1910 she first displayed the restlessness which was to distinguish her career until she settled down with Maynard, by becoming the first Russian dancer to break her agreement with the Maryinsky by going abroad. She then joined Diaghilev's company in Paris; as Karsavina reported (1930, p. 262), she fainted at the lovely sight of the Gare du Nord on her arrival.

Lydia's brother Fedor described (see Keynes, ed. 1983, pp. 50–53) her 'remarkable leap', which he regarded as unprecedented, from the ranks of the corps de ballet to ballerina status as soon as she reached Paris, when she was under eighteen years old. 'Her success was such that Diaghilev already began to base his box office calculations on her appearances.' Often partnered by Nijinsky, she brought great success to Fokine's ballets, *Firebird*, *Carnaval* and *Petrushka*, and also danced in *Giselle*, *Les Sylphides* and *Prince Igor*.

Fedor sought to explain the fascination of his young sister who had taken Paris by storm:

'Her cheerful nature, the optimistic, youthful *joie de vivre* of her interpretations, infected audiences; any number that she danced ended with thunderous applause. Her pirouette technique was unremarkable, but her running on points was infectiously gay and light, as if she was tripping on air, without any boards beneath her feet ... Her flight through the air – or hovering in mid-air – was delicate and typically feminine, as was her landing. It was the kind of leap of which Nijinsky was capable, but whereas his leap reminded one of the jump and flight of a grasshopper, Lydia's resembled rather the wafting and descent of dandelion down, and thus the alighting upon earth of the little angels of quattrocento painters.'

Although, after going to Brussels, the members of the troupe dispersed in July, the prospects of further work with Diaghilev were good. But Lydia needed to travel further and, accompanied by her brother Fedor, her elder sister Eugenia (known as Lopukhova I, Lydia being II), and by the dancer Alexander Volinin, she sailed for America, where she arrived on 3rd August 1910, to fulfil an eight month contract with the vaudeville producer Charles Frohman.

Lydia's life in America, which lasted until 1917, is fairly well documented by F. W. Ries – 'Lydia Lopokova in America' in Keynes ed. (1983). After working with Frohman she joined Gertrude Hoffmann in a kind of pirated Ballets Russes. Then she was in the more respectable 'All-Star Russian Ballet'; when Mordkin later joined that troupe, he became jealous of her popularity, as was Massine in 1922, and actually cancelled her appearance in the course of the evening performance, a matter which led to a prolonged legal case, which she won.

In 1912 articles began to appear in the newspapers emphasising Lydia's desire to become an American citizen. In the summer and winter of 1913–14 she vanished from public view (as was to happen again in 1919–21) and it was not revealed until years later that, desirous of becoming an actress, she had been in the Catskill Mountains, studying English and taking drama lessons. To celebrate her new identity she legally changed her name to Lopokova in April 1914. But the bad play in which she was to appear closed within a week when it reached Broadway and she was forced back into revue. Then, changing her mind again, and turning down dancing offers of between one and two thousand dollars weekly, she took an acting engagement at a hundred dollars monthly. As a result, a drama and sports critic called

Heywood Broun fell in love with her, while watching her performances, as Maynard was to do in 1921, and she consented to become engaged to him.

But 'within the week another startling announcement was made about Miss Lopokova': the Diaghilev ballet, which was due to tour America, would welcome her back into the fold. So on 19th January, 1916, Lydia again appeared in *Carnaval*, this time in New York. Later, while the company was on tour, Lydia is supposed to have become attached to Randolfo Barocchi, Diaghilev's business manager, and to have agreed to marry him. Ries now states that application for a marriage licence was made on 2nd March in Minneapolis – which is odd because when the marriage was annulled in London, in 1925, it emerged that the place was the county of Westchester, New York State, and the date 22nd October, 1916. Perhaps the couple went through a form of ceremony twice? Alternatively, as Ries suggests, the Minneapolis ceremony never actually occurred.

Anyway, in April 1916 the company returned to New York for a brief appearance, only to leave for Spain on 6th May – when it was revealed, according to Buckle (1979, p. 311) that Lydia had married Barocchi, having jettisoned Broun. The company left Spain for the United States on 8th September, in time to perform in New York – and to arrange a marriage? Nijinsky was so jealous of Lydia when he partnered her, that he would not allow her to take separate curtain calls, but Lydia made allowances for his bad state of health. The tour finally ended at Albany, New York State, on 24th February, 1917, when Lydia danced Blue Bird with Nijinsky. The company then embarked on the dangerous wartime voyage to Europe.

In April 1917 the company performed in Rome, when Lydia was in the première of *Good-Humoured Ladies*; they then went on to Paris where she was in *Parade*. In early June they were in Madrid, when Lydia danced *Spectre de la rose* with Nijinsky; in late June they were in Barcelona. On 4th July the troupe sailed to South America, where it stayed until late September. On their return to Spain, Diaghilev told them that, beyond a few performances there and in Portugal, there were no engagements. When 1918 dawned 'the company were cold, hungry, bored and hopeless for the first time since the war began.' (Buckle, 1979, p. 341). And, owing to the Soviet revolution, Diaghilev, like most of his dancers, had become a stateless exile.

But the worst was over, as Diaghilev had secured a touring engagement in Spain; this ended in Barcelona, where nobody had any money. But Diaghilev had already been in touch with Oswald Stoll of the London Coliseum who sent him travel funds, and the King of Spain, who was a great friend of the dancers, personally arranged their journey through France to England. Lydia's passport shows that she was in Paris on 14th August, where the company was delayed through 'loss of boxes', and that she arrived in Southampton two days later. Thus it was that Lydia, presumably accompanied by Barocchi, arrived in war-time London.

Although Lydia was unknown in London, she very soon enjoyed enormous success at the Coliseum, where she first danced *Good-Humoured Ladies* in September. She also appeared in *Carnaval*, *Prince Igor*, *Papillons* and the Blue Bird *pas de deux* . . . Soon it would be Armistice Day.

Just as Bloomsbury over-denigrated Lydia (often for the wrong reasons), so we must not over-praise her, especially as her letters to Maynard were particularly designed to conceal her weaknesses in a bed of wit. She was not charming in any conventional sense, and could be very rude, though she might leave no hurt:

> 'She [Lydia] has an earnest, at times almost pathetic, manner that can allow her to say the rudest or most argumentative things in such a way that the truth of them only dawns upon one some considerable time after, and then leaves no hurt.' (Haskell, 1934, p. 184)

Capable of being logical, she cultivated the illogic. She was profoundly obstinate, as many of those who vainly endeavoured to visit her in her prolonged widowhood experienced to their cost. Her minor public pranks and escapades embarrassed some people, even the delightful and sophisticated Harold Bowen. She loved to run away (to vanish without trace) – though not, as it turned out, from Maynard. She affected to be bored by intellectual conversation. She was wayward and impetuous. She chattered too much and interrupted Vanessa Bell's work with scandalous disregard for its importance; nor did she understand why she exasperated her, though she may have realised that poor Vanessa was embroiled, as it were, in an archetypal mother-in-law fix. The fact is that exhausted by flattering Maynard, Lydia lacked the strength to flatter his Bloomsbury friends, though when she had married Maynard she proved to be a perfect daughter-in-law to his actual parents.

Turning to Lydia's numerous virtues of character, which have been extolled by so many writers, her luminous sincerity had an absolute quality and her lack of jealousy of other dancers was renowned. Thus, Anton Dolin:

> 'I do not remember in all my career and with all the knowledge I possess of my fellow artists that I have known anyone who has shown more love and open-hearted appreciation for the work of other dancers than Lydia Lopokova has.' (1938, p. 53)

> 'Just before the interval [at a performance in memory of Pavlova] Lydia Lopokova made one of the most beautifully spoken speeches in appreciation of Pavlova it has been my privilege to hear. So simple, yet with a depth of sincere feeling and poignancy. I shall not forget that memory.' (p. 126)

Introduction

And Lydia Sokolova:

> 'In all the years of my friendship with Lydia Lopokova, I have never known her say or do an unkind thing either in the theatre or out of it. She was sweet to everybody, never jealous and never coveting another dancer's roles; but she always seemed to be hopping off somewhere, and obviously valued her private life as much as her life in ballet. She had a quick brain and was very witty, and her best friends were often intellectuals . . . She never sold her soul to Diaghilev, fond of him as she was.' (1960, p. 73)

Then, on Lydia's charming naughtiness, which is so evident from these letters, here is Sokolova again, referring to a performance of *Sylphides* in 1918:

> 'Her raised leg fell lower and lower; then to everyone's surprise, she stopped, tucked her hand under her costume and stepped out of a pair of tarlatan drawers. She threw them into the wings, picked up her music where she had left off and carried on as if nothing had happened.' (pp. 132–3)

As for Lydia's dancing, let Osbert Sitwell's famous praise of her performance in Massine's *Good-Humoured Ladies* in 1918 be cited again:

> 'In this work it was the grace, pathos, entrancing cleverness, the true comic genius and liveliness of a dancer new to this country, Lydia Lopokova, which made the chief impression . . .
>
> 'Her face, too, was appealing, inquisitive, bird-like, that of a mask of comedy, while, being an artist in everything, she comprehended exactly the span and the limits of her capacities: the personification of gaiety, of spontaneity, and of that particular pathos which is its complement, the movements of her hands and arms in a way that hitherto no dancer had attempted, thereby achieving a new step forward in technique. Her wit entered into every gesture, into everything she did. Moreover this great ballerina, fair, with the plump, greenish pallor of arctic flowers, formed the perfect foil to the dark, grotesque quality which Massine instilled into his masterpieces of satiric dancing and choreography.' (1949, p. 14)

'Sam likes to feed me with lobsters and other preciositys, but I like poetry.' Lydia's letter to Maynard, 5th June, 1924.

P.H.

Letters from
December 1918 to December 1921

Perhaps Maynard first met Lydia at the Sitwells' house on 10th October 1918 but, as Skidelsky notes (1983, p. 352), he was not then enchanted by her dancing with Diaghilev's Ballets Russes, having remarked to a friend 'She is a rotten dancer – she has such a stiff bottom.' On November 11th Lydia and Maynard were both at an Armistice Day party at the Adelphi, off the Strand, and later Lydia was present at a larger supper party given for the Diaghilev company by Maynard and Clive Bell at 46 Gordon Square.

Lydia's first known letter to Maynard is dated 28th December, 1918; it was written at the Savoy Hotel, where she was living with Randolfo Barocchi. Lydia then believed herself to have been married to Barocchi, Diaghilev's business manager, for just over two years. Beaumont (1940, p. 114) describes him as having been 'a dapper Italian in the thirties' – an unusually small man, who boasted of a beard and whiskers. He spoke English, French, Italian, Russian, Spanish and possibly German. 'In a flash he would compress his mouth into a certain shape, place an imaginary eye-glass in his eye, and give you Diaghilev to the life . . .' (ibid, p. 117).

Had Diaghilev arranged their marriage in order to capture Lydia at a time when she was twenty-four years and two days old? Maybe. But in fact it was not legally valid since Barocchi had only just received his decree nisi of divorce from Mary E. Hargreaves from an American court and did not wait for the decree absolute. (Thus it was that, in 1925, the marriage was finally annulled, allowing Lydia and Maynard to marry.) The likelihood is that Maynard did not set eyes on Lydia again until May 1921 (at the earliest), when she was again dancing with Diaghilev. He had gone to Paris on 10th January 1919, as the chief Treasury representative of the British delegation to the Peace Conference, and was to be there until June when, out of misery and frustration, he resigned, reaching London on 8th June, before the signing of the Treaty of Versailles on 28th June. He fled to the peace of Vanessa Bell's Sussex house, Charleston, where, on 23rd June, he started writing his *most famous polemical book,* The Economic Consequences of the Peace, *which was published as soon as 12th December. Lydia, meanwhile, had sensationally disappeared, the newsvendors' hoardings of 10th July 1919 announcing 'Famous Ballerina Vanishes'. So both Maynard and Lydia had resigned within the space of a little more than a month.*

Lydia had abandoned both her husband and Diaghilev. In a letter of resignation to Diaghilev, 10th July 1919, Lydia said that she had had a serious nervous breakdown, 'for reasons of a personal nature', so that it had only been with great difficulty that she had been able to get through recent performances. On the same day she had written to Barocchi saying – 'It is very hard for me to continue the life I led lately. I decided to go away from it. If you really want to help me you will send me the necessary [divorce] papers . . . Excuse me, if I trouble you, but I can't do otherwise.' (King's Archives). Barocchi fled to Italy but, as he later returned to Diaghilev, he must have become reacquainted with Lydia on her reappearance in 1921.

Until shortly before this volume went to press, nothing whatever was known about Lydia's whereabouts after her disappearance, until she surfaced as a dancer in New York in a show called The Rose Girl. *The only hypothesis mentioned in the literature was that she had first eloped no further than St John's Wood, in London, with a Russian officer, who was never identified. Certainly, this correspondence includes several tantalising references to a general, who seems to have been the officer involved – evidently Lydia had told Maynard her past secrets. But he, like Lydia, never gave any indication of how such a conspicuous personality had contrived to vanish without trace. It had even seemed unlikely that Lydia had gone abroad before sailing for America in 1921, for at the hearing of her divorce case, when she was much concerned to be on her best behaviour, she said that she had lived in London since July 1919 except for two months in the United States.*

But Lydia's passport, which was discovered in September 1987, reveals that she planned to go abroad in 1919 even if she did not in fact do so. On 17th June, over three weeks before her disappearance, she was granted a visa for Spain. Much more excitingly, on 13th August the Italian Consulate in London (she was an Italian citizen by marriage) granted her permission to travel to Batum in Russia by way of Taranto in Italy. Batum is a most insalubrious naval base on the Black Sea near the Turkish frontier: why should the mysterious general have wanted to take her there, of all places? But, unfortunately, we do not know if she ever reached the Black Sea for no dates of arrival at any destination are recorded in her passport.

However, the passport does establish that Lydia was in London both in August 1920 when permission to go to St Germain en Laye (by way of Boulogne) was granted to her, and in January 1921 when she visited the

Aliens Registration Office at Bow St before going to the United States. So even if she had spent some time abroad, this conspicuous personality was living incognito in London at times.

In Paris in May 1921 Lydia rejoined Diaghilev, for the second time in her life, where she danced in The Firebird, Les Sylphides and Petrushka. The company soon transferred to London, where it opened on 26th May at the Prince's theatre. There Lydia added leading roles in Parade, Prince Igor and La Boutique Fantasque to her Paris repertory. She was a great box office draw, especially when appearing with Massine as the can-can dancer in Boutique. The season ended in a burst of enthusiasm on 30th July 'with a kind of apotheosis for the popular Lopokova', who had been paid as much as £100 weekly throughout the season (Buckle, 1979, p. 387). Sam Courtauld, who was later to become a close friend, was there on the last night on 30th July. He wrote to Lydia inviting her to join him and his wife in Scotland, an invitation she declined, saying that she was going to Biarritz. Sam wrote that 'All the parts you danced, ending with your lovely delicate "abandon" and touch of pathos in La Boutique, and then your sweet little speech, and then your impulsive greeting in your dressing room made us love you more than ever.' (King's Archives).

Balletomania being in the air, like opera today, Diaghilev then decided to risk everything by presenting the five-act ballet The Sleeping Princess (formerly The Sleeping Beauty) in a revised version, which he edited himself, of Petipa's original, with most lavish decor and costumes by Bakst. Oswald Stoll agreed to put up £10,000, followed by further sums, for the production at the Alhambra, although he accorded Diaghilev complete artistic control. Lydia and Nijinska alternated as the Lilac Fairy, and Lydia occasionally took over Spessiva's primary role as Princess Aurora; her Blue Bird pas de deux with Idzikovsky, in the final scene, has passed into legend.

A few weeks after the opening, audiences began to dwindle alarmingly and Maynard was provided with a good opportunity to court Lydia by sitting conspicuously in the thinly-occupied stalls. Although they had evidently not become intimate by 26th December, when Lydia addressed him in a letter from the Waldorf Hotel (p. 29 below) as 'Mr Keynes', she had lunched with him on 11th December and on 16th December he had taken her to the Savoy after the ballet where they had chatted until 1 a.m. (See Bell in Keynes, ed. 1983, p. 85). On 22nd December he had written to Vanessa that he found Lydia 'perfect in every way' – one of her new charms being 'the most knowing and judicious use of English words' (King's Archives). Then, on 28th December, before he had had tea with Lydia at the Waldorf, he had asked Vanessa 'What is to be done about it? I am getting terrified'; to which Vanessa had replied '. . . don't marry her . . . However charming she is, she'd be a very *expensive wife and would give up dancing and is altogether to be preferred as a mistress.'*

The two little letters from the Waldorf are also intriguing because Maynard had taken Sebastian Sprott to stay with Lytton Strachey at Tidmarsh over Christmas, and did not leave until 28th December, so that he would have had to have telegraphed his refusal to have tea with her on 27th December. However, there can be no doubt about when these letters were written for, by an extraordinary chance, they actually bear the dates 26th and 28th December, whereas virtually all her other letters in this volume of correspondence, before March 1925, show the day of the week only. Perhaps the romance, which up to that time had mainly blossomed in the theatre, exploded into a full passion on the afternoon of 30th December, 1921, in the Waldorf Hotel, for by 6th January, 1922, Maynard had written to Vanessa — 'You needn't be afraid of marriage, but the affair is very serious and I don't know in the least what to do about it.' He added that 'I begin to think it's a good thing I'm going to India' — an expedition which was about to be cancelled for well-established reasons which were quite unconnected with Lydia. Anyway, in characteristic fashion, Maynard had suddenly moved with great speed and determination and would never look back.

Soon after this Stoll's patience came to an end and he cancelled The Sleeping Princess from 4th February, impounding the valuable decor and costumes, which rotted in storage, against payment of a debt of £1,000. Diaghilev fled to Paris, where he ate in a cab-drivers' restaurant, leaving many of the dancers, including Lydia, stranded in London. So Lydia's affair with Maynard began, in a sense, just at the time that her career had ended, for she was never to have long-term engagements again. But Duncan Grant was wrong in forecasting, in a letter of 15th January to Vanessa, that an out of work artist would be 'a terrible problem and very unsuited to a man of Maynard's tastes' (King's Archives), for Lydia had a creative taste for ordinary day-to-day living, as these letters so well reveal.

Savoy Hotel, Saturday 28th December, 1918

Dear J. M. Keynes

The book was most welcomed, and I appreciate indeed your charming thought. I wish you a most happy New-Year in which wish my husband joins me heartily.

Lydia Lopokova

Waldorf Hotel, Monday 26th December, 1921[1]

Dear Mr Keynes

It will be nice if you can come and have tea with me about 5½ o'clock to-morrow.

Yours sincerely
L. Lopokova

---

1   As Lydia is known to have been living in the Waldorf Hotel before moving to Gordon Square early in 1922, this letter dated only '26th December' must have been written in 1921.

Waldorf Hotel, Wednesday 28th December, 1921

Dear Mr Keynes

Do come then Friday about 5 o'clock if it is possible.

Yours sincerely
L. Lopokova

Letters from
8th April 1922 to 1st May 1922

When Lydia's long-term correspondence with Maynard started on 8th April 1922 (or earlier if some letters have been lost), he had recently installed her in vacant rooms at 50 Gordon Square, a house where Vanessa Bell and others of his friends were living, so that she would be near him at his house, number 46. He assumed responsibility for her financial affairs, (it is always said that she had previously 'banked' with the hall porter at the Waldorf) and he gradually began to involve himself in her ballet affairs.

When Maynard was away, Lydia was a very regular, indeed punctilious, correspondent; although Maynard evidently wrote to her quite often, hardly any of his letters before September 1923 have been preserved; this unfortunate fact leads to some obscurities in Lydia's correspondence.

On 8th April Maynard had left England, it being the Cambridge Easter vacation, to attend the international Genoa conference, which included representatives of Germany and the Soviet Union. As the special correspondent of the Manchester Guardian, he was to write a series of articles over three weeks. He and his companions stayed at Santa Margherita and often went to the Casino at Rapallo in the evenings, though Maynard's interest in gambling was waning. Lydia made great efforts to keep in touch with Maynard through his writings, which she eagerly refers to in her letters; she wanted to show that she was an intellectual woman and besides – 'When I read what you write somehow I feel bigger than I am.'

In April 1932, when she was still under thirty, the days of Lydia's great fame and fortune, which had depended on Diaghilev, lay behind her. Unable, and presumably anyway unwilling, to follow Diaghilev to Paris, from April 3rd she had joined company with Massine, who happened to have come to London – he had not been in the Sleeping Princess. Their dances were mere insertions in twice-daily variety programmes at Covent Garden. The list of ballets is hard to establish, for they were mainly petty divertissements which were short-lived; but they included Lydia's Scottish reel (for which Duncan

Grant was the designer), The Cockatoo's Holiday *(in which Lydia had to paint herself black),* Stravinsky's Ragtime *and a golf dance. Just before Maynard's return home, Lydia referred to Massine's lack of finance and appealed for his advice.*

(50 Gordon Square), Saturday 8th April, 1922

It is very empty Maynard,[1] without your walk of life in 46 or 50 [Gordon Square].

I just have arrived after the theatre,[2] I expect to drink tea, now Grace[3] comes in – stop –

I had tulips this afternoon, besides other things I also received 100 pounds. Very nice!

You shall not have a cold I put my vows. I send you my very best, and I know you will achieve splendidly wondrous results with the Genoa Conference.

L.

1   He had left for the Genoa Conference on 8th April.
2   Covent Garden, where Lydia was in Massine's company.
3   Vanessa Bell's servant.

(50 Gordon Square), Monday 10th April, 1922

I gobble you my dear Maynard.

I am not like you talented in idea put into words, I express myself better in impulses to you.

. . .

Saturday night I had an automobile luxurious indeed, somehow I felt a different being, and thought that I would not like to have it as a permanent article around me.

I re-gobble you.

L.

Vanessa [Bell], Duncan [Grant], Clive [Bell] and Mary [Hutchinson] are going to witness my Scotch flicker[1] to-night. Instead of stockings I have socks of the same clan as the dress, quite suitable.

1   Lydia wore a kilt in this divertissement, which had choreography by Massine and music by Grainger, each of whom had been advised by Duncan Grant.

(50 Gordon Square), Tuesday 11th April, 1922

How is your mood? Are you pleased how things move?[1]

I am very anxious to see your articles printed: to-day I went to three news stands, but not one did satisfy me as they did not produce *Manchester Guardian*. I complained to Vanessa, so now I am going to have it every day. This important matter is settled. I am so glad! It stood in my head all day.

Last night Clive, Mary, Duncan, Vanessa, went to Covent Garden – to-day Vanessa gave me the drawing by Duncan[2] of me – I look like a Scotch whirlwind, so much activity, and not only in the legs – everywhere.

. . .

I lead simple working man's life, and you – do you go in the evenings to dissipated houses?

I am very fond of you, dear Maynard.
L.

1 At the Genoa Conference.
2 In her Scottish attire (there is also an oil painting of the Scotch whirlwind by Duncan).

(50 Gordon Square), Wednesday 12th April, 1922

Nice Maynard – I wish to be on speaking terms with any bird to oblige me with a pair of wings . . .

Today's *Daily Express* publishes 'Obstacles overcome'.

I notice that you take an optimistic point of view. L.G. [Lloyd George] and Chicherin,[1] very clever indeed.

I like to have more of your articles – it is not enough. You are also copyright in *N.Y. World*. So very famous. Of all three newspapers,[2] only one desires to have *my* picture in a Scotch attire, and that is your respectable *Daily Express*. Not so bad.

I have been to Sam's [Courtauld] house after the performance, supper in the dining room – Sam wants me to play tragic parts. I disagree, I say I have comic elements in me. The conversation ends with an explanation from you 'what is tragedy?'

Good night, my very nice Maynard.
L.

1 The Russian foreign minister.
2 *Manchester Guardian*, *Daily Express* and *N.Y. World*.

(50 Gordon Square), Thursday 13th April, 1922

It is late night – all day's work is done.

I feel we are so near each other.

Vanessa came in. Sat a few moments – I told her your impressions on the conference.

To-morrow I go to 46 [Gordon Square, Maynard's house]. I have not been there yet, since you went away. No performance to-morrow. I am glad about it to have a stop for one day, otherwise I fear I may become a very good metronom.

Your expressions in the end give me nice tremblings.

I kiss.
L.

(50 Gordon Square), Friday 14th April, 1922

At last I had time to look through *Manchester Guardian*.

The first one, the one you have read to me, is the best, so full in everything, the others finish too soon. I do think you must enjoy your conference life, if I be a man I take your place at the present moment.

To-day spring is so strong that gives me spring-fluids, I feel weakness in the body.

I lunched with Barrie[1] in the Savoy grill-room, although it is well filled it seems as a restoran passée and people come just because they have heard a few years ago that it was a good restoran. However I had serious food after my work.

Barrie flattered me, he said the way I conducted myself on the opening night when I came out with Massine, stood apart, then brought Massine forward and again put myself in the back ground, put the people in the mood to like everything that was done that evening.

Very complimentary indeed. To-morrow he will go and see my Scotch conception.

I am inexhaustibly fond of you, Maynard.
L.

1   J. M. Barrie, the playwright.

(50 Gordon Square), Saturday 15th April, 1922

To-night I feel so exhilarating – I want so much [to] step into your dwelling, if you feel intelectual I would produce just opposite for instance my negress dance.[1] It might amuse you.

33

I had bouquets from female admirers, sweets, Easter eggs. My 'mobile vulgas.'

Today *Manchester Guardian* publishes your currency reform in Genoa; it is very good what you say, specially 'time ripe for much more than generalities', you always go in advance of all the others although how confusing must it be – commissions, sub-commissions, amendments etc.

. . .

You are *very nice* dear Maynard I kiss you.

L.

1　*The Cockatoo's Holiday.*

(50 Gordon Square), [Easter] Sunday 16th April, 1922

'Christ is risen' I say, you answer yes indeed, and we give at once three kisses. That is a Russian custom.[1] Chicherin and Krassin might offer it to you.

I stayed in bed till 12 o'clock, such a desired sleep, I longed for it just as you long for a holiday sometime.

I went to 46 for dinner. I was full of speaking spirits, tonight I invite Vanessa, Duncan and Clive to go out for supper, the rest of the evening in the cinema. I like you to see more spectacalar horses.

It is regretful that you are not here. I wish to invite you to go out, I am so richly independent with two weeks salary.

The day looks dull but I feel bright, it is like when it rains you say you feel brisk.

I am so much in your sphere of influence. I do wait for you, how I would come into your study sit on the couch and you speak simple words to me, peacefully joyful.

L.

1　At Easter.

(50 Gordon Square), Monday 17th April, 1922

To-days article in M.G. [*Manchester Guardian*] and D.E. [*Daily Express*] and your letter give me much satisfaction. What you write now is dry and serious, influencing the conference and a little later I see U.S. stepping into it by your idea.

You are very famous, Maynard.

I work very hard specially with the dark paint,[1] it so hard to get it off I have a feeling that I ought not wash myself for a week then easily I become the incarnation of a nigger.

To-night Vanessa and Duncan and Mrs [Lady] Strachey go to the theatre. Now it is almost 9 o'clock, I feel tired in the head, but legs are quite cheerful like an independent body. My being is not independent, I have not the free will in my heart – it stretches a link towards you . . .

L.

1   Still *The Cockatoo's Holiday.*

(50 Gordon Square), Tuesday 18th April, 1922

It is very good *rubbish about milliards.*[1] I had big pleasure out of it.

I see you have sympathy for Russia, when Chicherin reads it he will follow your direction and answer not with milliards.

The newspapers make a very grave sitiation out of R.G. Treaty.[2] It is not so serious, I see with you that Germans are wise . . .

I was to tea to-day to Mr Maine's[3] house and met his two sisters, rather pleasant creatures. He showed me photos of Cambridge, where he lived, where his rooms were, etc. He is Irish, he finds so much resemblance with the Russians. I do not think there is a nation on earth that does not remind of Russia. I have met many nationalities – they all think the same. Flattering!

Is there any resemblance between you and me. No! So different that it becomes attractive. I want to wrap up around you and give the abundance of my feeling. For this specially designed word I had to look into the dictionary. I did not know how this process spoke in English.

L.

1   The title of Maynard's article, *Manchester Guardian*, 18th April.
2   Russian/German Agreement.
3   The musician Basil Maine, later to be known as Lydia's 'platonic lover'.

(50 Gordon Square), Wednesday 19th April, 1922

To-night I go to Goossens' [Eugene III] party.[1] I do not wish it, but I cannot refuse it. So I am in the evening dress already, at the same time with you, when you prepare probably be an honorary guest, in very inteligent circles.

Your article for the Russian settlement can be only approved.[2] I do want it to be adopted. It is clever.

When I read what you write somehow I feel bigger than I am.

It is very nice for me.

I blend my mouth and heart to yours.

L.

1   He was their conductor.
2   *Manchester Guardian*, 19th April.

(50 Gordon Square), Thursday 20th April, 1922

I have so many surprises about you, Maynard: two letters at once. I see how much you are involved in intelectual excitement, but the main point is tremendous work you do, although you say it is fatiguing to you, the result is beneficent and beneficial to the world.

Another surprise – you in M.G. [*Manchester Guardian*] quite a big photo. Very famous! I did show to Vanessa to Q. [Quentin Bell] to Grace. Very nice!

Vanessa went away this afternoon, she told me to take care of myself – I said I shall control myself, because sometimes after the performance I feel I could destroy this house and build a new instead. I suppose it is animalistic energy, but in the morning and the day I am like a dead stone.

I kiss your eyes. I see they look at me just now.

L.

(50 Gordon Square), Friday 21st April, 1922

Oh! Maynard I lead such a dirty life this and next week – the brown powder does not come off very well, it stabilises in me, halph of my body is not pure quality these days, and when I put a good deal of cold cream, to have easier after, Massine complaints that he cannot grasp me as I slide from him like a frog.

Last night I had such a laughter I thought I could not finish from it – Massine while dancing lost halph of his shirt, collar, hat, when I saw that I immediately thought to have a decidedly funny disaster is to lose his trousers.

To-day there is no article in M.G.[1] [*Manchester Guardian*] so I wait for a complete one to-morrow, it is very nice to meet your articles they *breathe* to me.

I gobble you from head to foot.

L.

1 Perhaps she had the wrong edition, as there was one.

(50 Gordon Square), Saturday 22nd April, 1922

It is really your sense of imagination that sees expressing myself in words. Super thyroid gland is not in my mind only in the body.

Do not speak against your articles in jornalism – just think how many peoples read, understand and remember it; and when you go to bed have the feeling of the work you have done with mind and inspiration.

What a splendid answer from Gorky.[1] I am glad you have send it to me.

His hand writing is curious, like hieroglyph.
It is nice to hear that you have intelectual and domestic comforts.
I embrace you, and so add one more comfort if you can bear it.

L.

1   Maynard had written to him on 10th April.

(50 Gordon Square), Sunday 23rd April, 1922

All morning in bed pure delight! Duncan and I had Sunday dinner together
– Vanessa, Clive, are away, Angelica [Bell] is not.
I showed your photo to Duncan, the letter from Gorky and all the
important news you tell me.
Russians came out very well in this conference, they are wise, but you are
the wisest. I imagine how much they admire and appreciate you.
2½ o'clock I had to go to have *my* pictures taken with Massine for a stylish
magasine *Vogue*. Massine likes to speak to me, he asked me for tea, but I have
promised to another house, one of our dancers her 21 birthday. I am almost
10 years older, but I felt I was very young in conversation and that helps.
Came home, writing to you now and then again to bed.

My boundless caresses to you.
L.

(50 Gordon Square), Monday 24th April, 1922

Being in such near relation with Gorky through you, I acquired his
recollections of L. Tolstoy. I know you have read it and liked it so well. How
very well it is written.
I have ordered the M.G. [*Manchester Guardian*] your edition. It did not
come yet. I signed myself for 12 months. I am very serious dealing with
everything you write. Your plans or your suggestions or your advice are like
clear compact buildings, for instance to-days article on the reparation
problem is very energetic, when the conference experts read it they will adopt
the right course.
I riddle you with the words that are blackened with so much ink,[1] again it is
simply foxiness just to enigmatise you.
I detain infinitely your warm wet kisses.

L.

1   She is referring to her habit of deleting words with very thick black strokes.

37

Genoa[1], Monday 24th April, 1922

Dearest Lydi,

You work me too hard in complaining if there is not an article every day (as bad as Mary)! However I expect you found *two* articles in to-day's paper to make up for there being none on Friday or Saturday.

To-day I have stayed at home, quietly hard at work, and have written on The Financial System of the Bolsheviks, which is the most interesting I have written so far, in my own opinion.

Shall I find you with a holiday and all the brown paint washed off when I come back? (Did you see in *The Times* that Diaghilev announces a Paris season?)

I want to be foxed and gobbled abundantly. It is only half a life here, says the fountain pen to the metronome.

JMK

1   He was actually staying at a hotel in nearby Santa Margherita.

(50 Gordon Square), Tuesday 25th April, 1922

Dearest Maynard

Yes, I do get your letters every day – almost always every morning with the breakfast, and I open it with enlivened fingers. Very nice!

About my plans I cannot tell something absolume, but probably soon we will appear at the Coliseum, most appropriate for our programme. Soon Massine wants to introduce a golf dance – very modern indeed. Goossens' music, and costumes he wants to ask Duncan.

Curious is it not? Can I seduce you in golf clothes – as I have failed in masculine clothes perhaps I may win in masculine game?

Vanessa has come back. I was glad to see her, even if I do not see her it is pleasant to know she is here.

I love my sleep, but the sleep turns away from me third night, however I slept a little in the afternoon after the performance.

To-day nothing of your mind in M.G. I wish it would every day. I am fond of it.

. . .

I think you must stay as long as conference stays, put them all into proper atmosphere for reconstruction of the world.

I cover you with kisses full of flame.

L.

Genoa, Tuesday 25th April, 1922

Another quiet day; but the weather has recovered and I can now sit working on my balcony.

I begin to think a good deal about coming home; I have already written as much as my contract; and the Conference moves very slowly. They talk about ending on Saturday week but it is impossible that they should really settle things by then. The Conference is going badly again and I don't now see much prospect of anything coming out of it. I feel that I should like to be back home again. My present idea is to leave here on Tuesday or Wednesday of next week.

I want to see you again. I don't do much good here.

Good night.

Your Maynard

(50 Gordon Square), Wednesday 26th April, 1922

Only this morning I have received *Reconstruction in Europe.*[1] It does look well, there lies strength in it because it is your production. In your work to-day, financially speaking, Russia has only pessimistic roubles to offer of no value. But your 'a possible surprise'[2] sounds very nice and after reading your article they must stabilise money.

Last night Elisabeth B. [Bibesco], Clive, Mary came into dressing room to express their delight but I think E. wanted also to see how I look very near. She is thiner and it becomes her. Mrs Asquith could not come into the dressing room, too tired, but waved her handkerchief while I danced. (I did not see such details but I was told so to believe.) We finished this Saturday. After is not decided yet.

The differing at the Coliseum is very little and Massine wants to wait, and here also financial question is a problem to keep these few artists as they have nothing. Also Massine wants to produce a new ballet, but how without finance? When you have a few minutes free wouldn't you suggest a thought to improve the sitiation. I know it will be wise and substantial.

With caresses large as sea I stretch out to you.

L.

1 The title of his collected articles for the Genoa Conference.
2 A paragraph in Maynard's 'The Financial System of the Bolsheviks' (*Manchester Guardian*, 26th April, 1922) is headed 'A possible surprise' and includes the words 'Who knows but that Russia may not give us a final surprise by being the first of the European belligerents to stabilise her money?'

(50 Gordon Square), Thursday 27th April, 1922

I am in such good spirits – yesterday it was otherwise – the consequences, I bought a veil to wear and cover my face; to-day I want pyjama, so I went into a female big store, and so the pyjamas were all too big, to-morrow I shall visit an especial masculine pyjama's store, and I shall find something suitable.

I like so much your letter Maynard, you are so very nice.

Yes, it is very good about the bolsheviks financial sistem[1], and also you do want and do help to the 'children of steppes'.

What a description of Litvinoff, and Jews are Jews, very funny.

It is annoying that financial experts do not want stablisation, but I also understand they cannot be Maynards (there is only *one* Maynard), that is why delays happen.

I warm my lips to yours, they feel very red.

L.

1 'The Financial System of the Bolsheviks', *Manchester Guardian*, 26th April.

(50 Gordon Square), Friday 28th April, 1922

As bad as Mary. Oh so funny.

Maynard I am so *fond* of you.

The difference between me and Mary – I think she is pleading for *her* personal cause, but with you I know you produce every day new works and they ought to be known to the whole world. I do not speak individially but collectively, the voice from majority.

Maynard you are so brilliant I think sometimes I say things not as bright as you expect. Anyhow I try to develop my mind.

Your fountain pen speaks such delightful things, when I read it I have a smile inside and outside of me. But tonight's letter of yours is in another spirit – spirit of contradiction. You say you don't do much good. It is not true and you must stay there till the Conference lasts.[1] Do you not see how they need you? Perhaps you don't see but I, as an outside person, observe clearly how necessary you are.

Very tender at same time exotic kisses.

L.

1 He left after the three weeks required by the *Manchester Guardian*.

(50 Gordon Square), Saturday 29th April, 1922

Our last night [at Covent Garden], after I am asked to go to Goossens's party, I may and again I may not.

I do not remember if I have told you about the scent Goossens presented me with. It is very ancient may be 100 years old, he received from a friend who visited Arabia, so everyone who comes into my dressing room obtains a part of it.

Vanessa, Duncan, Volkoff, Mrs Grenfell had a touch of it.

I had another wild passion and bought another pair of pyjama. I am relieved.

. . .

I place melodious strokes all over you. Maynard, you are very nice.

L.

(50 Gordon Square), Sunday 1st May, 1922

You are very nice Maynard . . .

. . .

I visited B. [Boris] Anrep saw his wife, children, his sister. No harmony, that is why he searches for persons to whom he can pour his lyric qualities.

To-night I was in the company of the new M.P. Both are delighted, I welcomed their delight. For the super ocassion, we drank champagne. Feeling dry in general towards you – liquid.

L.

Letters from
24th May 1922 to 6th September 1922

Maynard must have proceeded at once to Cambridge after his return from Genoa, but during the three weeks or so before 24th May Lydia's letters to him are missing – and there are, also, later gaps. She went on tour with Massine to Bournemouth and then danced at the Coliseum. At the end of the Cambridge term Maynard took a holiday at Lindisfarne Castle, on Holy Island in Northumbria, and Lydia briefly joined him there at the end of June, en route for a dancing engagement in Glasgow, where Massine's boastful publicity angered her.

For a week, from 17th July, Lydia (with Massine, Sokolova and Woizi-kovsky) performed at the Coliseum; Lydia and Massine danced the Can-Can to music by Rossini and Lydia again performed the Scottish reel. In the following week a Tarantella, as well as a Variation with music by Gounod, were added, all the choreography being by Massine. In mid-August Maynard visited the McKennas in Cornwall. On 22nd August, when he was about to attend a conference in Hamburg, Lydia wrote deploring his 'wild passions for other people'. After dining with his friend Melchior on 25th August, Maynard gave a public address on 26th August, which was received with great enthusiasm: 'I can imagine dominant sentiment taking such a turn amongst Germans as to render restored Germany a bulwark of the peace of Europe.'

Lydia was very lonely when she returned to Gordon Square on 24th August. On 19th August Vanessa Bell had written to Maynard extending a haughty invitation to Lydia to stay at Charleston – '. . . tell her I hope very much [she] shall come here and not put us off vaguely at the last moment. English households can't be treated like that.' (King's Archives) (Earlier, on 19th May, apropos of Charleston, she had written that Maynard might be 'forced to choose between us and Lydia.') Presumably Lydia did refuse at the last moment for Maynard went to Charleston alone on returning from Germany, by which time Lydia had taken refuge, perhaps impulsively, with her great friends Vera and Harold Bowen in Bedfordshire, when she is known

to have confided in Vera over her affair with Maynard. After they had
returned to Gordon Square both Maynard and Lydia went to Parsonage
House at Oare in Wiltshire for three weeks; while she was there Lydia wrote
(22nd September) to Mr Croxton of the Coliseum saying 'I am in country
with horse as dancing partner.' (King's Archives)

Central Hotel, Bournemouth, Wednesday 24th May, 1922

Here I am in a respectable house[1] – windows, bed, pictures, soap, breakfast
is due to-morrow morning. The train was extremely jumping.

I put quiet kisses, the others I keep in reserve.

L.

1   On tour with Massine.

Central Hotel, Bournemouth, Thursday 25th May, 1922

Maynard – you are correct it is not exactly a theatre it is called Winter
Garden.

This afternoon we had big enthousiasm – small income, very small indeed,
situation improved in the evening: I hear Lady Tree and other titles visited the
theatre. The air here is warm and it does smell so very well everywhere.

We did work. Dear Lord I am tired.

How is your mood?

From me I am supplying enthousiastic embrases for you.

L.

Central Hotel, Bournemouth, Friday 26th May, 1922

Oh! I have a stiff neck; it had been so warm I rested on the draft, I bought
embrocation I shall rub on myself.

I have had another funny misfortune. Last night while undressing somehow I upset the cup with the ink, so halph of my body is a study in white and
black, it does not come off with water, I went into salt water (the ocean was
glorious even with stiff neck), but still I think traces will be noticed for a good
while.

. . .

Good night. True gobbler for you.

L.

(50 Gordon Square), Friday 9th June, 1922

I am very fond of you, Maynard.

I dreamt that I have been on a Chinese ship, which had a form of a lantern. I had only a pair of turkish trousers on, and I searched for you everywhere . . . The best arrived when I opened my eyes I knew your destination.

I am going to see Vera [Bowen]. She has received both letters, and she is filled with delight to do something for me.

I gobble you extravagantly.

Lydia

(50 Gordon Square), Sunday 11th June, 1922

All day long I have been with Vera; the costume[1] is going to be artisticaly striking. I shall be in it quite interesting; and you Maynard, how is your mood? How are your odds and ends?

I lick you tenderly.
Lydia

I write very little because it is late, I don't want to miss the mail.

1 Presumably for Vera's ballet *Masquerade*.

(50 Gordon Square), Monday 12th June, 1922

Clive gave a tea party – iced coffee was tasty; as usual great many boring persons, including Ottoline [Morrell], Mary, J. H. Smith and others.

We danced rather well, academically speaking, we are in a better atmosphere than at the Covent Garden. Coliseum is an 'organisation' so when I danced I thought I was an organisation myself. It is not a disadvantage.

I do have a stormy affection for you. 'Maynard' crosses my mind early in the morning into late night.

Lydia

(50 Gordon Square), Thursday 22nd June, 1922

I came back from the Rothermere party in a Rolls Roys like you last night – kisses excluded. Everybody danced so did I, met various English and foreign subjects, including black Aga Khan. It is nice to be back home and write to you.

We go to Glasgow on the 3rd July, otherwise plans are all the same.

I was so tired this morning – lesson was missed. Maynard's influence. Massine's wife[1] danced this afternoon. I gave her a kiss – pity asked me to do it, she kissed my hand.

At last you have the *holiday*, is it cold over there[2] as it is here? In case being such, I warm you with my thoughtful feelings.

Lydia

1 Vera Savina, whom Massine was soon to divorce.
2 Maynard and O. T. Falk, the financier, were staying at Lindisfarne Castle, which Sir Edwin Lutyens had restored for Edward Hudson, founder of *Country Life*.

(50 Gordon Square), Friday 23rd June, 1922

To-day before the performance we all had to go to a theatrical garden party – a charitable cause. I think every theatrical person does it for the sake of a réclame. That is what prompted me to do it, when I was asked. I had my green trousers on, I was offering my own photos for a shilling, but did not refuse 2s 6d. Altogether I was rather cheap. I had 7s 6d, true it was too early, people would be ready for all sorts of sports about tea time. I also had to perform a few skipping steps with a Scotch pipe treatment to get people into the theatre; those who were caught had to pay a shilling for the inside performance, stars like C. Loftus appeared there.

In the evening Vanessa, Duncan, Roger [Fry], Clive, Mary, Vera [Bowen], Garia [Bowen], *leech* [sic] all came in. Vanessa said I was 'extraordinary'. I came home with her, we spoke a little, almost no gossip. We thought you were discussing finance on Holy Island.

Good night

I taste your buttons.
Lydia

(50 Gordon Square), Saturday 24th June, 1922

I also want to see the town of birds and to be in friendly terms with them[1]. It sounds fascinating your new surroundings, the island – rock – castle, suggests space.

We had plenty of flowers to-night and applause, somehow I feel soon, very soon, we must do better things.

. . .

Slavinsky also [is] another Pole in a depressed sitiation, I gave 5 pounds to the Pole, he will change it into Polish marks and stabilise his position in

Poland. I asked Slavinsky to come on Monday? We go away next Sunday *positively*, it is not changed.

I have a passion for an omelette that Grace prepares; today I had it twice.

I am sleepy, but I see the light of your eyes.
Lydia

1   There was a colony of puffins on Holy Island.

(50 Gordon Square), Sunday 25th June, 1922

. . .

I find letters unanswered since Alhambra season. Do they need a reply? I would like to know your opinion.

The evening brings such sweet smell in the air; I contemplate you.

Lydia

(50 Gordon Square), Monday 26th June, 1922

Virginia [Woolf] sais she would like to see you, I took her to the omnibus after Roger's lecture. I saw a great deal of Poussin, heard less; altogether this lecture was a big success. I did not understand everything, but the main idea of his *inventivness*, continuity, unity, his styles like dorik and ionic in different periods rest in my head.

. . .

How is your mood? I suppose you work in your recreation. I like to hear it.

Maynard I am fond of you, full of electricity towards your thoughts and yourself.

Lydia

(50 Gordon Square), Tuesday 27th June, 1922

I am in a state of excitement; when I read your telegramme I had a feeling of jumping, so I did plunge myself into a bath. I do like to come [to Holy Island], but I do not know your friend, perhaps he does not desire me, it is only in relation with you.

I saw to-day Barrie, one of the questions – 'How is Mr Keynes'? I said I probably will see you on my way to Glasgow, described the island: 'didn't you ever meet him?'. He said he did not, but thought highly of you.

I said you were *very nice*. Later I went to Cecchetti's to bid au-revoir.[1]

I wait for your letter. All your descriptions about the island: the puffins – the seals and the nature of it – quite alluring.

I have so much intensity for you.
Lydia

1   The renowned ballet teacher, always known as Maestro, was retiring and going to Italy.

(50 Gordon Square), Wednesday 28th June, 1922

Yes, I thank you very much for the explanation in to-day's letter. I think I am rather English – everything is thought out by you for my journey. I hope to have the ticket to-morrow . . . I told Massine about my going away before,[1] I became practical and asked to reverse the money for the ticket. He thought it would be better to give it in Glasgow, as they had little money with them just now, what a stingy insect! I had tea with Miss Naylor[2] and her oncle, they asked me to come with them to Swiss soil on the lakes and mountains.

In the evening I was at the Café Royal with Anglo-Russian friends – so popular for to-day! Maynard – you ever surprise me I never know what is in your head, so much petuatry gland.

L.

1   *En route* for Glasgow to join him.
2   Not identified.

Central Station Hotel, Glasgow, Sunday 2nd July, 1922

How is your head, dear Maynard? The theatre is situated on the other side – faces the hotel. I went to the theatre – closed – I was surprised by a [poster]

Leonide Massine's quintette
Lydia Lopokova
Lydia Sokolova
Vera Savina
Leonid Massine
Leon [Woizikowsky]

I do not care if Massine calls it quintette, sextette, or quadre, but as a name my should be on the same paralell. Again, dirty insect!
I saw again the wonderful castle on my way here. Unforgettable.
In Newcastle I walked on the streets, the high wind picked up my skirts,

47

people did look at my silk stockings I suppose; feeling shy I returned to the station, had a desire of sleep, wooden benches so hard . . .

How lovely the time was spent with you in the castle.

I kiss especially the head, and lick your hands.

Your dog
Lydia

Central Station Hotel, Glasgow, Monday 3rd July, 1922

We begin about 7 o'clock, also later about 9 – the theatre is not bad. Glasgow looks industrious.

I spoke to Massine [about the poster]. I thought of you, your rightness. 'I want my name the same as yours, do not bring me any arguments, because within yourself you know you are wrong.' He had silly remarks that it was his choreography. I said he should be happy to have such material. He did look dissatisfied after . . .

I do like to sit in your intelectual room occupied with your sound of the fountain pen.

Lydia

Central Station Hotel, Glasgow, Tuesday 4th July, 1922

Our latest plans are: after Coliseum one week Edinburgh and one week Manchester and no more. I think in September Massine will go to America[1] with Vera; therefore shall end short lived Massiniana. About his American engagement he has not mentioned to anyone – so everyone knows.

Glasgow audiences are content with Leonide Massine's quintette and also with Hetty King[2] if you should see her – at once you would acknowledge that she knows how to wear male trousers. She has acquired all man's habits to perfection. Clever, indeed. I rather like her!

It rains to perfection in Glasgow also, makes fisherman's fortune (my father used to fish when it rained). It is almost 6 o'clock, I am going to show my healthy mechanism to the healthy crowd.

Wet lips towards you.
Lydia

My room N is 365. Salutations to 46 and 50 [Gordon Square] from me.

1   He did not go.
2   The male impersonator in music hall.

48

Central Station Hotel, Glasgow, Wednesday 5th July, 1922

We do not go to Edinburgh next week!

. . . I cannot understand from where you have an invitation and that you will arrive late, but the birth control reception should be exceedingly interesting. What you shall say will prove a healthy and clear outlook of present day and after. Will you send me your speech?

. . .

Your dog (I am not mad at all)
Lydia

Central Station Hotel, Glasgow, Thursday 6th July, 1922

My privilege is to be adored by waiters, so it happens also here. I have an old boy who is very good to me. He inquires not only about feeding questions, but builds a general conversation.

I can have a Jewish adventure with a man called Max Darevsky, he is on the same programme with us in the same hotel and almost opposite to my room. Yes, yes, I can dine with you on that day.

I have not learned a new sonnet because I have not taken a bath, but when I return I hope to have more than one organised in my mind.

L.

. . .

Central Station Hotel, Glasgow, Friday 7th July, 1922

Splendid poster. Looking at it I find myself in close communication with the world.

Is it the new réclame after your influence.

I could not call Barrie 'Jim' – I never adress him 'Sir' either.

Maynard, Edinburgh after all is not yet decided *positively*.

It is a pity you cannot have Miss Rees.[1] I think she has had too long a holiday.

I put holding kisses on you.
L.

1 His secretary.

Midland Hotel, Manchester, Monday 14th August, 1922

How are you impressed with the country? Did it stimulate to produce precious bricks for your active buildings?

Last night I was met by Slavinsky at the station, 'the theatrical husband'. He attends to my odds and ends in Manchester.

Damnation: Three performances to-day.

I write between performances in the dressing room. Do you feel the scent of it?

Massine's mouth full of sugar for me, Oh, he is foxy. It is worth listening to.

He wants to take a big house in Bloomsbury, too big for him he offers part to me and also, as the sum is 1400 pounds to pay advance, he wants not *me* but *my friends* to help him and as a garantie he will stage things for me what I require. I told him for present I did put him out of my head, then he asked me to think, I said 'very well' not to be rude. He wants to rebambuzle me, but I am not tipsy at all with him.

Why did you choose *Winter's Tale* for me to read?

I put my mental and organic feelings on you.

Lydia

Midland Hotel, Manchester, Tuesday 15th August, 1922

Here are the news to tell you; I am going to Harrogate on Wednesday morning and evening performance . . .

I see you are definite about the house,[1] but we are not there yet. I do not mind W.C. with earth: in the country one does not expect anything else.

Lindisfarne is remarkable from the North and South West. Such nice remembrances.

Do not be 'gloomy' . . . To be a Don is *your* destination.

In truth I am so fond of you, Maynard.
Lydia

P.S. It is dreadful to dance in Manchester, no athmospere. I think I dance not well, orchestra is bad also.

1 Parsonage House, at Oare in Wiltshire.

Midland Hotel, Manchester, Wednesday 16th August, 1922

You shall not be bored any more, as you start to-day for your visit in Cornwall[1]. The sound of the train, the activity in your brain, the movement itself, there is not a tiny place left for boredom.

. . .

The letter you sent is from my Indian friend. If you like to read it I offer it to you. He is rather cultured, but culture sometimes breeds animosity. Now, if I would be in a university I would be able to build a report on it, and I would satisfy you mentally. What a pity I have not the gift of words.

I am going to the theatre, I know I have there a telegramme from Sickert, I was told on the telephone. What is it about?

I wrote a letter home, it is better than the one before – which I did tear. I also wrote to Vera. My pen has been flinging . . .

If it is cold where you are, as it is here, I warm you with my foxy licks.

Lydia

1 Where he was visiting the McKennas.

Midland Hotel, Manchester, Thursday 17th August, 1922

I am going to buy your 'reconstruction'[1]. It is out to-day.

When I woke up this morning sun was stepping into the room and your letter that I had for breakfast was penetrated with the rays of the same. I mean your mood = wine = grapes = sun. Is it clear?

Poor Sheppard.[2] 'Hinky inky lacrime.'[3] I think if Manchester would open a gambling house I would be one of enthusiasts.

I know Cornwall will breathe into you *new* life's forces as open nature always does.

I kiss you outside inside.

L.

1 *Reconstruction in Europe.*
2 J.T. Sheppard, Fellow of King's College, Cambridge. He had presumably suffered gambling losses, as he often did.
3 I.e. Cicero's *Hinc illae lacrimae,* from the *Pro Caelio* ('So that's the cause of all this how-d'ye do!'); presumably Lydia had learnt a schoolboy version of this well-known catch phrase from Maynard or his friends.

Midland Hotel, Manchester, Friday 18th August, 1922

It was very nice, Maynard, to hear from your *Express* this morning.

You posess so much dynamite, please lend me part of it; as you know, Manchester in almost a week being decent, still becomes dull.

Yesterday I went to the picture gallery I wanted to see Sickerts, unfortunately they are in other places, and I, although with artistic sympathies, have not enough energy to try once more, besides it is rather far.

The manager of this theatre remembers me from Alhambra 1919 (he was manager there). He advertises me with all his might. I being a 'parlamentarian darling' (that is how Sickert calls me) shall ask him for tea to-morrow. To-day I asked Slavinsky. I want him to show certain dancing steps. The artists in the theatre think he is 'my husband', often he carries my bag and we go out of the theatre together – so the rumour spreads! Only in Manchester.

Primitive love kisses to you.
Lydia

Crown Hotel, Harrogate, Tuesday 22nd August, 1922

The moment I have arrived I find that it is much easier to see me advertised than to have a place for myself to sleep, I even thought I have the new ballet's skirts for pillows, cab as a bed, and the driver as a cerber [cerberus?], but patience, now I am in a luxirious place, (probably all the Lords and Ladies living here). Please, notice the Crown! [on her letter paper].

Oh! Maynard. Do not have wild passions for other people.

Your dog
L.

Crown Hotel, Harrogate, Wednesday 23rd August, 1922

Life in this place seems to be quiet and even. Change does not occur here, I mean in the hotel – on the contrary the Royal Hall is one of the best I have seen. It is tremendously big; if every seat is occupied Massine will be able to buy a ticket for Italy in the first class and might buy another villa near Neapol [Naples] the sky and the sea do not ask for rent, as for the walls he could choose ancient ruins. Orchestra is ultra splendid. Sun is beaming everywhere. People here are very old or just babies that came out, so tiny.

You are already greatly entertained?[1] Admirateurs – trice in a line. In what mood are you? I put so many strong embrases for your well being and for mine as well.

I am your dog
Lydia

1 Maynard was at a conference in Hamburg convened to discuss the economic situation.

(50 Gordon Square), Thursday 24th August, 1922

I tremble – I sit at *your* table without your permission. I do not touch anything, occasionally I glance my eyes over it. I think of you so very much – your activities.

Last night we had a splendid reception. I have 15 pounds, Massine I think 20 or 25. In the day time the theatre empty, in the evening all the rhematic people of Harrogate assembled to watch us in can-can I suppose. I performed a duty to humanity. I am almost convinced while they watched our legs their legs became active also.

I brought you from Harrogate a bottle of iron. Not bad, I drank myself and another bottle, but that is also for me I mean 50–50, I thought it was very valuable to have from the source, perhaps we would'nt need it, it is called – magnesia. Looks nice in the bottle.

. . .

Is your speech ready? I want to hear and see it. Lucky those who dwell in Hamburg while you are there.

I gobble you enormously.
Lydia

50 Gordon Square, Friday 25th August, 1922

The house is big – I am all by myself. I did not go to sleep till 5 o'clock. I am wretched. Even my hands shake. I am a thousand years old. I might try and drink iron I brought for you.

To-morrow I know you – your voice will carry out brilliantly, because you are *you*. In it lies everything.

Tender dog
L.

Colworth, Sharnbrook, Bedfordshire, Monday 28th August, 1922

You were Royally entertained. I think it is very nice. Vera [Bowen] translated the cutting. I imagine how over populated the place was. As for R. Strauss and supper after really it is touching.[1]

I arrive to-morrow a little after 5 o'clock. I want to see you so very much.

Your gobbling dog
Lydia

53

I brought here your 'reconstruction', Vera and Garia find it splendid and the Malthus Island[2] delights them enormously.

1   Richard Strauss had conducted a rare revival of his ballet *Josephslegende* in Hamburg during Maynard's visit there; Lydia was interested because Diaghilev had first recruited Massine for the title role in this work.

2   Effectively the first version of his essay on the economist T. R. Malthus, not published until 1933.

Colworth, Sharnbrook, Friday 1st September, 1922

Mieli[1] Maynard – One contemplates, being in the country, rather well. Do you for reconstruction N 7?[2] I concentrate my attention on malborougs [mulberries] they are improving almost black since last I have tasted them. I never have seen such beautiful cones on fir trees, from the distance they look like birds that kind that sold as inseparables. They also crack in the fire. Sounds nice. It rains just now but I see comfort at this moment. I told Vera and Garia about our theatrical proceedings, how talented you were to avert the catastrophe.[3] She thought it was lucky for me to go with you. The idea of a divertissement seems to her dull for me, and we continue to work as before.

I just remind you I am *very fond* of you.

Lydia

1   *Mieli* is Russian for dear.
2   On the financial system of the Bolsheviks.
3   Maynard was proposing to help Lydia to become her own producer so that she would 'employ' Massine.

Colworth, Sharnbrook, Saturday 2nd September, 1922

This house is full with guests: Garia's eldest brother, his spouse, 3 children. Vera keeps up the conversation especially at general meetings such as lunch, dinner etc. The brother is a soldier, reduction of the army one of the topics; the wife belongs to the warring nation: her motto preparedness, poor French, the Germans are going to swallow us in 3 years time.

As for myself I work a little and gossip with Vera, only not so abundantly about Mary, as I do with Vanessa. She thinks my riding habit being blue in color is rather funny.

In one of Chekof's stories I met Malthus, I *was* pleased, if I would not have met you I would be ignorant about him – now I swell with pride.

Lydia

Colworth, Sharnbrook, Sunday 3rd September, 1922

The neighbors called to tea this afternoon. What a boring affaire. 'We have witnessed your triumphs': I say it is my sister. 'Exactly like a butterfly': I say I prefer to resemble a duck. At last Vera comes to rescue and tells the audience that I being frail (oh funny!) would like to rest. I nod sadly and run like a wild fox back to the house. It is so nice to be all by myself. I would like to go for a long long walk and meet you.

Last night 'Daddy'[1] arrived. He brought caviar from Volga. I become greedy in the country and have an endless appetite. How was the hair?

Greedy gobbles.
L.

1 Presumably Garia's father, Sir Albert Bowen.

Colworth, Sharnbrook, Monday 4th September, 1922

. . .

The house is quiet. The relations went to Bedford to cut children's hair. At lunch we spoke about ghosts. Vera and Garia looked into one of the houses, where Garia's brother used to live with his family. The wife said that she heard often the steps advancing even towards bed and then descending. I said 'Why didn't you leave the house?' 'I paid the rent already,' she answered. So you can see she is not spiritual rather practical, still she heard the steps and the dog howled – I prefer to see the ghost than hear him. How is about 41?[1]

I like your photo. I kiss it. I am going to put to bed with me. After that I am to be called the person with vice – vestiare, is it not?

Lydia

Salutations to everyone belonging to Charleston.[2]

1 Gordon Square, to which she was to remove.
2 Vanessa's house in Sussex, where he was staying.

Colworth, Sharnbrook, Tuesday 5th September, 1922

Now I know why Mr Harland[1] did not make my bed. A man never arranges a female bed. It is 'comprometant'. Weeding exercise is a wholesome one an advantage in doing it.

How is your mood? Is the next 'reconstruction' in good order? I am ashamed but in the country I am inclined not to do anything, but then I am a weak creature. You are the opposite.

I kiss you and your strenth and every inch of you.
Lydia

I shall arrive Thursday morning – decisively.

1   Maynard's manservant. His house was looked after by Mr and Mrs Harland.

Colworth, Sharnbrook, Wednesday 6th September, 1922

I also have two letters from you. Very nice. Vera and Garia left this morning for London to meet a German professor (Orientalist), I expect them back to tea. In a few moments I will go and play Mozart, while no one hears me.

I kiss your heart.
L.

Letters from
29th September 1922 to 6th December 1922

While they had been at Oare, Maynard and Lydia had been making plans for her to become a ballet producer and Lydia got a letter from her agent saying that Oswald Stoll had agreed that her salary should be £300. Although the agent thought that the ballet, Vera's Masquerade, *should be able to play the Coliseum for an indefinite period, it actually ran only from 20th November to 9th December, when Lydia became unemployed again. Maynard had written to the agent on 30th September making suggestions for performances of various divertissements, for the three weeks starting 16th October, adding that 'Madame Lopokova apologises for being so tiresome and she can only make the excuse that she is a beginner at the game of producing for herself . . .' (King's Archives). Other, somewhat obscure, details are given in Lydia's letter of 29th September. Unfortunately, as Maynard's letters are missing, some of Lydia's October letters cannot be dated, or even ordered with confidence.*

On or before 20th October Maynard was obliged to transfer Lydia from 50 to 41 Gordon Square at the request of Vanessa Bell, who had found her presence in Number 50 very disturbing. At the Coliseum Mr Dove strongly objected (from 25th October) to the proposed use of Mozart's music for Masquerade, *but Lydia staunchly held out and finally, on 17th November, the music was accepted. Maynard accepted an invitation from the German government to go to Berlin on 2nd November to discuss the stabilisation of the mark; on 31st October he travelled there, in advance, to meet his old friend Carl Melchior.*

Bailey's Hotel, London, sw7, Friday 29th September, 1922

Maynarochka I stepped in Queens Gate place just for lunch, now I have stepped out and find myself in a respectable hotel, I put a virginal mask. Garia's relations are all in the house, besides some of them in strained

57

relations to each other (so Vera told me), that is why V. arranged a room for me here. I can be with her most of the time.

The programme arranged by us should be changed as it does not give me time enough to have rest and dance afresh with sparkle, besides three girls[1] are much more decorative than a solo dancer.

1) Russian dance[2] (about the costume I must pay 300 franks for the rights to Goncharova).

2) Arlekinada London (Slavinsky).[3]

3) Three girls Grecian dance.

4) Pas de deux from *Sleeping Princess*, which includes also the variation, but as a whole makes more of a climax and will last about 6 minutes.

Three girls are more important to me than Leon [Woizikovsky] or Ninette [de Valois] or any solo, and it is easier to do a dance for them as it is going to be on Grecian lines.

I want Morton Coxon and Margot Astafieva. It is no influence of Vera but it is in reality better for the whole effect. She went to buy for me music, and in the evening we shall work.

I prefer to have less for myself but to have three girls, Vera sais the costumes will not be expencive – less than you think. Do you agree to it? Please do. For next week, *Les Elegantes*, it is a ready feature, as it was danced before. I need three girls again much more than Leon. I sent the contract with the messenger boy. I put kisses to you than only canter [?] can cover[4] in space and swiftness.

Lydia.

P.S. I have only to arrange two dances for the first week.

1   De Valois, Astafieva and Dorothy Coxon.
2   It was to music by Tchaikovsky, Lydia being the soloist.
3   This was *Arabesques*, danced by Sokolova and Slavinsky.
4   That only a cantering horse could overtake?

(50 Gordon Square), possibly Saturday 14th October, 1922

I kiss you deeply.

Just borrowed a pound from Vanessa. I have 2 pounds 10 shillings, I thought it was not enough for lunch with Mr Croxton. I would have more money of what you gave me, you see, have I [not] paid for the ballet skirts, but this afternoon Ah . . .

Sickert came last night, so pleased with your choosing[1] and so am I. I introduced him to the Duncans. One day they will let him know and pose for him.

Tomorrow I am going to spend with Vera in her house working.

. . .

Cambridge must be beautiful, just now autumn glory reigns in Gordon Square. Oh! Maynarochka I am fond of you.

Lydia

1 Presumably the painting *The Bar Parlour*, which in 1922 was exhibited by the London Group and acquired by Maynard.

(50 Gordon Square), possibly Sunday 15th October, 1922

I was in bed till 11 o'clock, it was true rest for my poor legs. I jumped into the bath and after jumped into the taxi and worked with Vera till this evening. I went to see Vanessa just now, Anrep and another painter are there, so I came here [46?], it is much better for my present state of head and body.

What is your state of mind? Have you built up your lectures? When you do your 'odds and ends' I like to come and sit with you, miely Maynard.

L.

P.S. L. George's speech is like a miscarriage, but still he might go on 'forever'.[1]

1 Lloyd George, who had been prime minister since 1916, was to resign on 19th October.

(50 Gordon Square), probably Monday 16th October, 1922

If you come to-morrow 8.33 you must ask for the ticket in the box office on your name. I have not taken off the blue boots nor put back the few bars, so you might be dissapointed about my salary. This morning I had to purchase something for myself. Vera told me when I go to the Savoy and have diplomatic lunches I must be dressed well, more than that. She sais from it depends the price of my salary. So I have a new hat and a new coat for the day wear. All is worth about 20 [pounds]. Extravagant? Up till now I have paid all the salaries and gave Vera 40 pounds for costumes. I wait for you to send money to the agents. I put in the book you gave me all expences.

I stand on my knees and kiss you.
L.

P.S. If you have a free moment could you let me say something funny especially about the bridge and being a Prime Minister for a day. It is going to be printed in the programmes.

To-morrow I go to have tea with Barrie.

(50 Gordon Square), Thursday 19th October, 1922

To-morrow is your first night,[1] no your first second night in the day time. Coliseum – Cambridge, both begin with C, and no more resemblance.

While in the taxi I saw L.G. resigns. I suppose appetites of politicians are growing fast at this tremulous moment.

After the performance I tried on the costume for next week, then I visited dentist. He has a new light, so strong that all peoples' teeth must appear like diamonds.

I came home so hungry I swalowed almost all of the chicken, oh so greedy but I can't help it. Inside of me demands it.

I think of Africa,[2] you will have a horse and a dog. With [? damaged] now and then.

Lydia

1 As a Cambridge lecturer; he was lecturing once a week on Money.
2 He was thinking of going on holiday in north Africa.

(Gordon Square), unknown date in October, 1922

To-morrow I shall have my salary, is it not a pleasant thought? I am such a calculatrice nowadays.

Vera and I went to Duncan's studio, we had lunch and explanation of Mozart's ballet [see 3rd November]. Duncan and Vanessa I thought were pleased of the sceleton idea. Polunin is rejected. Vera calls him 'a hanger on', besides he would require much finance for a special studio, whereas the real scene-painters, such as she knows, would not need anything but to copy skilfully under supervision from time to time by Duncan.

Last night I had flowers from Vera and Garia to suit my pink costumes – very big and dark pink astres, and the relations thought it was 'fine art' only too little of it.

The taxi man who drove me home said when I was searching for silver in my purse 'Lots of money,' I said 'Very little earned with my work.' 'What do you do?' 'I dance'. 'Are you French?' 'I am a Russian'. 'Have you parents with you?' 'No.' 'Well, miss, I wish you good luck, and if I may say so be wise.' 'It is difficult', I said and we parted.

Maynarochka, how are you?

I see yôu now ever. Kisses, kisses. Your dog
L.

(41 Gordon Square), Friday 20th October, 1922

Very nice, Maynarochka, I thank you for the book. It can be useful.

You seem to be full of progressive energy, so I do not believe in the cycle, and when you say you will put up with discomfort the meaning is that 'discomfort' does not exist.

Volkoff came in to see me. Asked if I still lived in Gordon Square . . . I said *when* I have order in the appartement[1] I will ask him for tea.

Then after the young man you remember from Pall Mall. I also said when I have order in my rooms I will ask him to tea. Very funny.

He also asked was I not married to a well known Englishman? Oh! Those journalists do like gossip just as much as women.

How did your lecture come out? I put kisses on your lectures.

L.

. . .

1 She had just removed from 50 to the ground floor of 41 Gordon Square; Vanessa (who lived in No. 50) as well as Clive Bell (who was in 46) had asked Maynard to arrange this; she had dining rights at No. 46.

(41 Gordon Square), Sunday 22nd October, 1922

I have stolen from you halph dosen envelopes just now. I returned from Vera, went to Vanessa's drawing room, met miss [Ethel] Sands and Oliver Strachey, stayed a moment, came to your study. Sighed a while to be there without you.

I did not work hard, only a small rehearsal in the afternoon.

I think I might look like a 'poupsie' in my new dress. It hides my true age and makes me look naughty innocent in *Les elegantes*.[1]

I am excited for tomorrow.

Kisses of devotion to you.
Lydia

1 A ballet she was to perform for a week at the Coliseum beginning 23rd October; also performed were a variation from the *Sleeping Princess* and her Scottish reel.

(41 Gordon Square), Monday 23rd October, 1922

I am mad mad with excitement. It did come out very well in the afternoon, yet we do not know about the evening.

We end the first part of the programme it is about 9 o'clock, perhaps a little later. It is a good thing that Vera's baby has not formed in these few months otherwise dangerous indeed[1]. I have a seat for you to-morrow. Vanessa and Duncan are coming tonight.

It is nice very nice to have crosses from you, dearest Maynarochka.

Kisses from your dog.

L.

1   He was born on 30th April, 1923.

(41 Gordon Square), Wednesday 25th October, 1922

Oh! Maynard! more troubles! To-night Mr Dove came in, he looked at the Mozart's music, and said 'it will not do for Coliseum it is too quiet, and besides it was tried at the Coliseum and did not go, I as a friend advise you *not to do it*'[1]. I agree – he knows Coliseum point of vue. We must change. Distressing. Duncan said about Oliver Strachey, that he knows a good deal of that epoch in music.

. . .

I see that we must do something else, the only choice. To put myself in better mood I watched little Tich.[2] I told him after he was a joy. He is tiny in comparison with me.

Lil and Sam [Courtauld] came in. Lil was on her knees before me. Probably I looked tired. Vanessa and Duncan and I came together. Spoke about your miraculous speculations. You and the speech? I expect to see it in *Manchester Guardian*. Crosses for your other speech.

Lydia

[In brackets at the side] (Touch wood or spit 3 times behind your shoulder. I always do it in such cases.)

1   The music proposed for Vera Bowen's ballet *The Masquerade* was Mozart's Serenade in G.
2   The 'great little comedian' (otherwise Harry Relph, 1868–1928) who was also appearing at the Coliseum.

(41 Gordon Square), Thursday 26th October, 1922

I have read the *speech* and the editorial about you. Maynard, you are famous, but apart from it the speech [which was evidently political] is very good, alive and constructive; and also good taste about L.G., the measure is right in action and words.

I myself a little better tonight. Mr Dove is going to give me an orchestra rehearsal Monday afternoon and we shall see how it sounds there. If it is not

62

successful (still I think it ought to be) I am inclined at this moment to do nothing instead, but ride Oops over the forests.

I caress you with words and kisses dearest Maynarochka.

Lydia

(41 Gordon Square), Friday 27th October, 1922

[In Vanessa's hand] Dearest Maynard,

[In Duncan's hand] We are all absolutely crazy drunk.

[The rest in Lydia's hand] We are slightly tipsy. Duncan invited Vanessa and me to a big jug of beer at Gatti's.[1] We all drank your health and we kiss you, and I too more than anybody.

Lydia

If you think the money is safe,[2] Duncan wishes to go on further and if wobbly stop in instanter. I kiss you outrageslously.

PS [On flap of envelope] The blue bells are ringing
No more can I wait
I must join my mate

1   Gatti's restaurant and café was on the Strand.
2   This presumably refers to the syndicate, formed in 1920, whereby Maynard and his friend the financier Oswald Toynbee Falk might use their own capital, plus that of their friends, for speculative purposes.

(41 Gordon Square), Saturday 28th October, 1922

I was going to write to you in the dressing room, but Vera came in and asked why did I look so serious. My contemplation was broken.

It is nice of the German Chancellor to ask you to help them,[1] only it is so very difficult to raise the mark when it goes down and down, but you *will* help them.

Vanessa asked me to tell you that they have looked [for] furniture for you in Tottenham Court Road, it is very nice italien, when you come to London you must see for yourself. That is the message. I invited Mr Croxton to lunch with me one day next week. Vera said he hesitated because he did not know I really acquired a new primadonna coat.

. . .

To-night I shall be rich, I invite you to dinner when you come to London, it is impossible for me to accept your invitation because it was in my mind long time ago, only I did not mention it.

I am so fond of you dearest Maynarochka.

Kisses on your finger tips.

L.

1   To discuss measures for the stabilisation of the mark.

(41 Gordon Square), Tuesday 31st October, 1922

I thought the crossing was not very strong, and that you would be comfortable,[1] dearest Maynard.

From to-morrow on I shall look so much forward to see the mark standing up. It will be very nice.

Shall I tell you my troubles? They are the same of yesterday. I could not convince Vera with my approval of Duncan nor, what is much more, I did repeat what you said, noble failure is preferable to cheap success, that financial ruin was not so desperately important. Her reply ever the same: 'I do not believe in these decor and I have no enthousiasm for it so I can't work on it.' I told her I could not work without her, and after I repeated the conversation to Vanessa. She understood, as you did with me – there is no halph ways. It is not easy for me, and for all of us.

Crosses on your *stabilisation* [of the mark].

Kisses into you.

Lydia

P.S. I hurry to mail it for 11.50.

1   Maynard was on his way to Germany.

(41 Gordon Square), Wednesday 1st November, 1922

How nice it ought to be for you by now, after the journey, in a comfortable house with Melchior and secretary surrounding you.

I impatiently wait to see the outcome of your ideas.

My work goes on with Vera, but in me I am still troubled with what has happened. Tonight I shall put [on] the new dress, I might look nice in it. Mrs Grenfell will come after me and we shall go together.

I touch you with warm feelings.

Your dog.

Lydia

64

(41 Gordon Square), Thursday 2nd November, 1922

Miely, miely Maynard,

Who do you think sleeps in your bed to night? It is objecting, but Vanessa assured that it is only for a night as the person is elderly she could not put him in the attic. Sickert's ceiling is falling, he tried to find a room in my house, then Vanessa offered yours.

. . .

I saw your name in *The Times* to-day, and nothing else, I have been out all day long. Had lunch with Mr and Mrs Croxton, diplomatically friendly. He is not convinced about Mozart, but I can't help it. I can't do anything else, although I am offered to do another thing from Coliseum. Dreadful, I shall not do it.

I embrase you tenderly.
Lydia

(41 Gordon Square), Friday 3rd November, 1922

I have your letter. It is so very nice. I kiss you much. You build up my existence.

At the Coliseum spirit is absolutely anti-Mozart. Mr Stoll, Mr Dove still do not like music and offer me to do a cheap act instead with the expences covered. I said to-night 'Mozart or nothing', what am I to do? So difficult indeed! Vanessa and Duncan think the same. I wait for your decision. Maynard I am so fond of you. I caress your slender fingers.

Lydia

(41 Gordon Square), Saturday 4th November, 1922

I feel like putting crosses all over you. May I?

Hilda [Sokolova] has arrived for two days; we lunched at Florrie's [Florence Grenfell] and dined at Vera's house, Garia's birthday passed with champagne, Hilda sends her love to you. I work hard and very tired to-morrow also.

Your licking dog.
Lydia

Sunday. It was too late to mail it last night. Dearest, miely Maynard, what I do see from the newspapers to-day [is] that sitiation is very complex. The Germans do not seem to have one opinion . . . I wish they would agree at once on all what you say and be wise.

I spent halph of the day with Vera working; and now evening, I am home – shall go to bed early, first will see Vanessa for 5 minutes.

I palpitate in my head for you and otherwise.

Lydia

Oh! Woe to me. I came to see Vanessa, she is out, coming down I saw your hand writing with your Berlin adress it is *Bellevue* Strasse, and I all my letters adressed Belleme, perhaps you still have received them?

(41 Gordon Square), Friday 10th November, 1922

How do you regard editorial in *The Times*? I see a victory for your document.

Did your pupils profered interesting works as if they were going to Berlin instead of you?

Did you rest in the train and afterwards?

Dearest Maynard I put restful quiet strokes all over you.

Lydia

P.S. Vera vomited for the first time, I gave her my handkerchief.

(41 Gordon Square), Saturday 11th November, 1922

I regretted so much that I could not be on the street at 11 o'clock this morning to see life stopped for two minutes,[1] instead I stood nude in the dressing room of maestro [Cecchetti]. It is a spirited idea. Every one will remember each year that war is terrible and should be no more.

I tried to rehearse on the stage, but could not obtain it as Sir Oswald [Stoll] tried a new lamp. . . .

I am going to dinner to maestro, doing so I keep in friendly terms.

I have tickings and acheings in my heart for you.

L.

P.S. In the dictionary is only *ache* but to me sounds not literary with tickings.

---

1 The two-minute silence on Armistice Day, observed to commemorate those who fell in The First World War, which for many years was all but absolute throughout the country.

(41 Gordon Square), Sunday 12th November, 1922

Fog. Truly it was so beautiful (in the park on the way to Vera), I believe all the fogs are made for Sundays, especially last season when we had our meetings, except one to Hampton Court. Do you remember?

Last night at maestro's house, even after supper, I was not scolded as it happened on the previous visit. Mme Cecchetti was really too sweet when she explained how intelligent was the cat whose name is 'Mammy' and how Mme Cecchetti, knowing that in the night Mammy might wake her for W.C. purposes, before going to bed she takes Mammy in her hand goes with her to W.C. and murmurs 'make some water Mammy'. Mammy obeys most of the time, except rare occasions when she can't produce any water but even then, being inteligent, she pours one drop out of her to please Mme Cecchetti.

I embrase you deeply.
Lydia

(41 Gordon Square), Monday 13th November, 1922

. . .

I do not like fog to-day, uncomfortable to work.

News papers yesterday to-day, with 'keen fight at Dover' or 'practical politicks at Stepney', fill me with spleen.[1] I suspect you like them truly only for the speculating curiosity sake.

Leisure? Next year for you? But when you posess the gift for work you can't have the opposite. For instance, *I* have the gift for leisure, but this is another question.

Till to-morrow Maynarochka.
Lydia

1 A general election was to be held on 15th November.

(41 Gordon Square), Friday 17th November, 1922

One of the difficulties in my theatrical life is solved. Mr Dove brought an olive branch, he said 'he never expected it [the Mozart ballet] so nice and will do all he can for to-morrow rehearsal with the orchestra.' I must confess I feel relieved: I believe Vera seduced him sitting shoulder to shoulder in stalls.

Vanessa and Duncan saw it, liked it, Duncan still desires to be one of the conspirators. I shall ask them to-morrow in Gordon Square what do they think outside of the theatre, that means the *inside* opinion.

. . .

9 o'clock beats just now, I am so exhasted, shall relax my body by your method.

Lydia

(41 Gordon Square), Saturday 18th November, 1922

. . .

The rehearsal [of *Masquerade*[1]] was very difficult. Mr Dove in the beginning took such a quick tempo that we couldn't dance, and also said I did not know how Mozart should be played, I agreed at once musically speaking, but choreographically speaking I asked for 'moderation' in tempo. The second time he took so slow that again we couldn't dance, but we made a compromise, that on Monday he will do a little quicker and so the dancers . . . Mr Croxton said to Vera that I looked 'care worn'. So Vera answered '*they* make so many obstacles' etc.

My devotion to you.
L.

1   This 'ballet comique' was set in 18th century Venice; it consisted of one act and two tableaux. Lydia was the wife, Slavinsky the lover, and Woizikovsky the husband. Other performers were de Valois, Coxon and Astafieva. The Coliseum advertisements for the performance referred to 'Lopokova and Co.'

(41 Gordon Square), Monday 20th November, 1922[1]

Masquerade did go well except the lights in the second scene they were too dark, but the applause was genuine, much more appreciation than for the divertisement. Mr Dove was excelent.

I do not know where am I, I do not exist fully.

Mr Crocker told me that Sir Oswald and Lady Stoll said 'what a nice little show.' Is it not cheerful?

I shall try to sleep, as last night was a nightmare for me. How is your article? By now it is probably well written without a holiday. I expect to listen to it when you come to London.

. . . It will be very nice to see you when you arrive to-morrow.

Lydia

. . .

1   Presumably written after the first performance of *Masquerade* which must have been a matinée as the postmark was 7.15 p.m.

(41 Gordon Square), Thursday 23rd November, 1922

After the lesson I go to bed, so after lunch, so after the performance and so indefinitely I go to bed. I also dreamt that Garia had a child (from another woman) and Vera did not show any signs of annoyance.

I mentioned to her your idea.[1] She spoke out quite a few words with a great deal of heat in them. Perhaps I ought not have mentioned in her present sitiation?

I bought a Russian *Economist*. I know without looking in there must be much about you, but what and how interests me.

I am so fond of you.

Lydia

1   See Lydia's letter of 25th November.

(41 Gordon Square), Friday 24th November, 1922

. . .

I lunched with Lil [Courtauld]. To start a conversation about you she began 'Are you interested in economics?' I said 'not particularly, less than in other things.' Lil is funny. I believe she wants to put monkey gland into herself, and she knows by now just as much as I 'petuatry, thymos, etc.'

8 o'clock beats now, I shall go and see Vanessa for a few minutes, I did not see her since Monday.

I put crosses on you without reason.

Lydia

(41 Gordon Square), Saturday 25th November, 1922

No! How could I repeat what you have said. By 'your idea'[1] I mean the costumes and décor by Duncan. That is where the flame of her tongue was flying.

. . .

I do want to listen to your article. They are also so rare lately.

Lydia

1   Letter of 23rd November.

(41 Gordon Square), Sunday 26th November, 1922

I *had* my salary, a good deal is out, but I have yet a few nice papers [bank notes]. Leon [Woizikowsky] told Vera as he's to pay 10 pounds to Cochran; it is too small a summe for him the rest, so I am to add 10 pounds now, he said he thought he ought to receive 25 and also Sokolova, I think I ought to satisfy him in that. Do you?

It was a nasty Sunday, about the fire is the only comfort. I sit most of the time and do not move.

. . .

With firm affection to you, (after mailing this) I go to bed.

Lydia

(41 Gordon Square), Monday 27th November, 1922

Send the cold to me I will dance it off.

I am in the theatre, and after the performance am going to sit a little in Barrie's house . . . I have so many things to tell you. I hope you can come to-morrow.

L.

. . .

(41 Gordon Square), Thursday 30th November, 1922

I have had so many visitors: Volkoff, Florrie, Naylor with the young man, Garia, Vera, Florrie's father with his wife Mrs Kennington. I lend Volkoff the cape, hat and the mask for to-night's Albert Hall Ball and I have asked him to make an intrigue with Lil, he said it was so dull with Lil but promised to do it for me. Vera mocks at me and calls me 'the obedient wife'.

I spoke to-night with one of my fidele female friends about Massine. She went to see his class, and it seems that a difficulty might arise for Massine to dance with me as then he would have to give up his class, so I think of your original idea of Massine's only producing a ballet . . .

I believe your cold has had the crisis and to-morrow you will give a palpitating lecture.

Lydia

(41 Gordon Square), Friday 1st December, 1922

Lunch with Sickert – what a splendid cook, I was full of hunger. We read some criticism on Jewish players he wrote for M.G. The Jews will be enthousiastic, I am not yet one of them. The pictures looked interesting. Altogether it was pleasant.

. . .

I know you are better with your cold, I make it evaporate with my warmth towards you.

Lydia

(41 Gordon Square), Saturday 2nd December, 1922

. . .

To-day also is maestro's and Mme 44 years of marriage. Maestro sais it is such a long time to wait for a golden one, 6 years more.

In the end of the ballet I thought how nice it is to have salary on Saturday, but just now I belong to the 'unemployed' in that sense. We are advertised as *last* week,[1] most of the artists want to know the future, but my agents keep silent.

The development of your cold is logic, next week you shall be free from it.

I am very fond of you.
Lydia

1 The run ended on 9th December.

(41 Gordon Square), Sunday 3rd December, 1922

My Sunday at your house.

Vanessa, Duncan, Clive, Quentin and last but not the least Angelica, had more life in her than in most of us. To-night I go with them to cinema. It was a good offer for Vanessa to make.

Last night when I gave away almost all my salary I felt discouraged, but Vera while sympathysing with me said that after all it was a rare thing to pay all my expences in three [actually two] weeks, so I did not ask her how much would be the bills, it fulfilled an answer for you although I suspect it might be a little more than three.

I have read this morning a Russian novel: the ideal of the hero; full indiference toward everything. Beauty can be bought, Might be expensive, not more expensive than money, and so to sell and to buy, except contempt.

I want to bury my head in your knees.

Lydia

(41 Gordon Square), Monday 4th December, 1922

How delicious! I laughed loud in the morning. Later in the day I read it [M's letter] to Florrie and Vera. I could not keep within myself. Maynard, you are talented.

We have not yet the answer for the Coliseum. I myself think that they will give 1 or 2 weeks rest and than an 'extraordinary engagement' again at the Coliseum.

I am full of apples. Did you send? It is very nice. I thank you.

Lydia

King's College, Cambridge, Monday 4th December, 1922

I have just found my old estimate. The figure for decor and costumes (including wigs and shoes) was £260.

Did you see in the papers that a medium called Munnings had been arrested for burglary? Surely it must be Sokolova's father!

JMK

(41 Gordon Square), Wednesday 6th December, 1922

Your feast ought to last till break of day, that is true feast not otherwise.

What you have read to me to-day was like sourse that flows and comes out with force. Big and simple. To be read everywhere in the world, that is so very nice. It is almost 11.

I hurry
Lydia

Letters from
17th January 1923 to 16th March 1923

Presumably Maynard and Lydia were both in Gordon Square from early December until they went to visit Lytton Strachey at Tidmarsh over Christmas. In the King's Archives there is a copy of an undated letter to Massine in Lydia's name, but in Maynard's handwriting, offering to pay him £50 weekly, both as dancer and choreographer, for an engagement starting on about 22nd January. Massine accepted the offer and Lydia presented his curious ballet Togo at the Coliseum, as a mere item in a distinctly unhappy variety show, You'd be Surprised.

From her letter of 25th January it seems likely that Lydia had expressed some doubt about the continuance of her affair with Maynard and had then wished she had stayed silent; maybe she was distressed by the thought of Maynard's projected holiday in Africa, a plan which came to nothing. At this time Maynard was much preoccupied by his plans to take over the Liberal weekly journal the Nation. His economic interests were beginning to turn away from reparations, and he started to compile his book A Tract on Monetary Reform, which was largely a re-working of newspaper articles of 1922. Lydia is concerned about the health of her pregnant friend Vera Bowen. There is a tantalising reference to 'the general' on 15th February, and Lydia's 'platonic lover', Basil Maine, calls on 23rd February. On 1st March there are hints of another emotional crisis. Soon after this Lydia made one of her rare visits to Cambridge; and on 16th March she reports having had Maynard's friend Sebastian Sprott to tea.

(41 Gordon Square), Wednesday 17th January, 1923

Reynolds, Bedini,[1] arrived to look and to see. Approved indeed, in fact so much that Bedini suggested after the end the men should drag us straight into the Wild Cat. I asked Reynolds to join me there.

Leon, Slavinsky both agreed to dance.[2] Massine is against it and so do I (not visibly).

73

We did not come to the understanding about our (Massine and I) coming in in the 'finale'.

I told Mr Reynolds 'I do all the good I can and yet everybody says I am such a disagreeable man [sic] and I can't think why.'

We saw Goossens after the rehearsal, we took a taxi and saw him in the intermission at the Kingsway.

Probably you are tired after *such such* activity in so many walks of life.

I apply my head into your knees.

L.

1 Producer of the 'Jazzaganga' *You'd be Surprised* – see 21st January.
2 In the forthcoming ballet *Togo*.

(41 Gordon Square), Thursday 18th January, 1923

I am in a state of a complete parasite. I did not drag my legs out of bed to maestro [Enrico Cecchetti].

The agents called me up. I was 'not in.'

This afternoon friend of Angus Davidson[1] (Webb [?]) came to ask me to dine with them and Bunny [Garnett] and Vanessa and Duncan. On the top of the buss he saw a sturgeon (a Russian fish), he bought it and it is going to be presented to us in a restoran on Saturday 7 o'clock, at 8 I must rehearse.

I read the women should be brothers to men, I have not progressed so much, I am only your brotherly dog.

Lydia

1 The art critic of the *Nation*.

(41 Gordon Square), Saturday 20th January, 1923

I came home exhasted, lunched, went to bed. Duncan came in so I, taking the advantage of him, asked him to go to Goossens at the theatre, because last night he was not in, away. I had to sleep. *Oh* such dream that you and I were soldiers and when the bullet went through me I did not die. . . .

Then another dream. I shall speak out that dream when I see you. . . .

Mucous membrances to you.

L.

(41 Gordon Square), Sunday 21st January, 1923

We tried on costumes for 3 solid hours, so much detail to attend to.[1] Vanessa, Duncan,[2] Massine all had something to say. My Mexican is very good, so is the cock with bushy tail . . . So tired we were that a rehearsal was out of question, the 'sturgeon' party was awaiting us at the 'Commercio'. About 20 peoples. Not all Bloomsbury, still sympathetic. I was tipsy, I was empty when I started, Vanessa and Duncan were also tipsy. People flirted with me. Bunny flirted in Russian phrases . . . The continuation of this party was carried into a place 'Cave of harmony'. I went to bed . . .

To-day all afternoon I did gossip with Vanessa, in doing so I rest my body.

I see in the newspapers Cambridge is much concentrated about the new buildings you spoke of, and more baths to two colleges. A vote of thanks to civilisation.

I suppose you find quiet moments for clear ideas, they become so warm in your head that you make words out of them and write it on paper, then you have nice feelings of life and I put crosses on them.

Lydia

1 From 22nd January Lydia, Massine, Sokolova, Woizikovsky, Slavinsky and de Valois were to perform Massine's ballet *Togo: or The Noble Savage* for eight weeks at Covent Garden as a number in Bedini's somewhat uninspired 'Jazzaganga' *You'd be Surprised*. Lydia and Woizikovsky were a Mexican couple on honeymoon and Massine was an Indian chief. 'The dancing is wild and curious, and all the time one is inclined to wonder whether Massine is not having a quiet little joke at our expense.' (*Dancing Times*, March, 1923.)
2 The costumes were from designs by Duncan Grant.

(41 Gordon Square), Thursday 25th January, 1923

I can't put myself yet to that state of wisdom when all is over happiness and unhappiness.

I am ashamed it came out. Forgive me. I am your servus-regi.

L.

(41 Gordon Square), Friday 26th January, 1923

This morning everlasting bore from 11 till 2 o'clock. *Oh*. The photos taking on the stage. I saw Sedova at the Coliseum – correct of the old school. I wanted to see the other numbers . . . When I reached Sedova's dressing room – too late, so I left a few civilised words.

Last night Duncan showed my costume, Empire suitable for my proportions, blue, simple not short, but when I move all the legs become very

75

visible. In a few moments I go to maestro-dinner, he must not trouble with lira in the near future, he might have better news.

Your pupils do they show intelect? If only I had intelect, could such a day arrive?

L.

(41 Gordon Square), Saturday 27th January, 1923

Oh! one of the important happenings! Our engagement is extended for 8 weeks. The *artists* rejoice. Massine especially. Salaries are paid. I thank you very much what you calculated for me. I believe Leon had to sit up all night long to count up the sum + extra 2/9. I am quite rich. I will write with tenderness all the expences in the book. Please tell me the arrangement with Vanessa-Duncan.

My chair in the theatre quite soothing for my back and halphs (the boiling water reminds of 'samovar' when it grumbles).

Please do not give up *The Nation*.[1] If you could only tell to the editor 'go out' instead of 'come in'.

Your words are so inteligent, you do not misunderstand me. The jolts from my heart for you.

L.

Sunday [same paper]

Last night too late it was to put in the [post] box.

This morning I have a slight neralgia on one side of the face; in the theatre too much draft. Probably you contemplate already on the construction for *Manchester Guardian*.

Did you feel spring this morning? The air was intoxicating. Vanessa, Quentin and I had lunch together. I mentioned what you have said about *The Nation*. She said everybody dislikes the man-editor.[2] I think he must be a 'disagreeable man' without even 'why'. Leonard Woolf, Virginia, were speaking to Vanessa about him. I see it is troublesome but, if you say, they must choose between you and him.

. . .

One of my theatrical complaints, when we finish the Mexican item [Togo] our applause is ruined by the noisy crowd that come. Could I write a letter to Sir Oswald that after dance we should have a pause? . . .

I had tea with Vera, she is afraid she might have twins so I mentioned the Siamese. I embrace into your neck.

Lydia

1 Which Maynard was taking over.
2 H. W. Massingham; when Maynard became chairman of the new Board he replaced him with Hubert Henderson.

(41 Gordon Square), Sunday 28th January, 1923

The mischief is done by me in your study. I broke the light. What a chance that you are not here, would cause you such *inconvinience*. Please pardon me.

I write with a candle and Quentin tells me I look like an early Victorian. We had supper together and discussed Mount Everest. He is more of a sportsman than I. It comes from Stephen's family.

I bought some more Sunday news papers to read about our performance. All except the *News of the World* pronounce it as a failure. All these criticisms are a sour medicine to Sir Oswald, Bedini, etc.

I have read a story about a boy 2½ who remembered great many things, and I told Vanessa that you remembered more than that when you felt the christening water sprinkled by your grandfather.

Angelica[1] asked me to draw. That was a hard task, I believe I could do it better with my toes. I still better could tell a tale.

Vanessa and Duncan went to the theatre. I shall go to bed now. I put enormous affections on you.

Lydia

1   Angelica Bell was four years old at that time.

(41 Gordon Square), Monday 29th January, 1923

I am rather uncomfortable. I have a cold. I try to stay in bed most of the time. Your book[1] sounds very interesting, of course in his [?] time women did not have an intelect but they have progressed since. The woman mathematician in Cambridge (I forget the name)[2] could she arrive only with sex. I claim 'egalité'.

. . .

All your Sunday letter is in humorous atmosphere, and I smile. It is very nice.

Lydia

1   *A Tract on Monetary Reform*, 1923.
2   Philippa Fawcett, who in 1890 was placed above the Senior Wrangler (the top mathematician) in the mathematical Tripos, when women were not eligible to take degrees.

(41 Gordon Square), Thursday 8th February, 1923

Was your intoxication noticeable, mine was by Vanessa and Duncan. We stayed in the theatre when everyone was out except Robey's[1] taxi. In our taxi we discussed my bed: I want one side (aspiring towards intelect) another side subject – love. It will make a pleasant atmosfere for going to bed.

Again one of the troubles. Sir Oswald wants to make *Togo* shorter in the size of three minutes (Bedini's influence). We shall try to cut some of the things that look monotonous but I do not know if it will be three minutes, before Monday also we can't change, we would also need a rehearsal. How tiresome! Oh!

Your creative conceptions? I do not know why, but I think you have much energy for it.

Lydia

1   The famous comedian George Robey who starred in *You'd be Surprised.*

(41 Gordon Square), Friday 9th February, 1923

. . .

I also heard from one of the pupils of maestro that to go to Africa[1] is very extravagant, sometimes one chicken is worth 10,000 franks or did I put too many ooo? Only one hotel composed of French origin that rob and rob foreigners. Very bad economically speaking and otherwise.

What a state of mind you are in, if you continue in that calmness with 'I want and I can' it will be very splendid for the work.

Your dog
L.

1   Evidently she was trying to dissuade Maynard from going there.

(41 Gordon Square), Sunday 11th February, 1923

My Turkish bath's desire is not fulfilled; after the performance Leon [Woizikovsky], Hilda [Sokolova] and I safely arrived to the place to find that at 8 o'clock Turkish delight is closed for women. I was dissapointed. I went to grieve over it to Vanessa . . .

This morning we were photographed for the *Vogue* (I am yet not so famous as to have my apartments be photographed, that would be much more comfortable), then to 46 . . . I made an attack on Vera because she does not allow Garia to love his Arabs, but we finished rather learnedly about glands, it's connection to nature-science etc. . . .

You develop your gifts and acquire more and more questions into your head.

I quietly think of you.
L.

(41 Gordon Square), Monday 12th February, 1923

To-day I have been seduced by the fur coat, perhaps it is wicked, it was so suitable, realising how big the price was I offered to pay in two instalments, halph to-day another next week, it is 55 pounds. I will be ready in it Wednesday as it has to be lined, but if I would buy in the season the price would be much more. Just like a woman.

. . . Personally you probably smile reading the last paragraf, you having been married to so many walks of life of which Cambridge is certainly not a divorce proposition.

Constructive kisses.
L.

(41 Gordon Square), Thursday 15th February, 1923

. . .
I have a letter from the general, also his 'tale' in the *Weekly Westminster Gazette*[1] and other American magazins, so I am to read and give the opinions.

The Nation so it seems is getting more and more harmonious from all sides. It is satisfactory . . .

You are very nice even if secretly married.
L.

1 No such 'tale' can be found in that weekly.

(41 Gordon Square), Saturday 17th February, 1923

I have a letter from home. I am so glad – they are all well, were disquietened about me, then finding me in the newspapers that I was dancing and alive my sister wrote to me and the letter was posted by somebody here. I answered back last night.

. . .
Poor Vera! I have a letter that she broke her foot where the ancle lies. 8 weeks in bed. I shall see her to-morrow. My sister asks me to come and see them. Oh. I also would like to.

This morning I go to a lesson at 12 o'clock. I hoped to stay in bed, but wretched man with the gas-stove drove me out, so the only thing I can do is to say these few words to you and kiss your eyes.
L.

(41 Gordon Square), Sunday 18th February, 1923

I visited Vera. God's did not want her to have so much activity. It is pitiful to see her helpless altogether. Night and day nurse, especial suffering at night. The accident happened without reason. Stepping off taxi. After that she might acquire a fat ancle for life . . .

To-morrow no more *Togo* . . . Last night Massine said as he is going to lose his lessons I must pay for it. I said 'We will see', I did not argue. Please come to help me.

. . .

I put red and white kisses on you.

Lydia

(41 Gordon Square), Thursday 22nd February, 1923

A huge bouquet arrived last night from B. [Berta] Ruck, I was supposed to give an answer on the card to allow her in, but that nuance I only noticed when I was home. I felt touched, I wrote an amiable letter. This morning I read to Vanessa and Duncan and Roger [Fry]. They said that I shall have, in future, volumes of novels about my eyes, mouth and various organs. I posted also. For once I was not dreamy and committed a fact . . .

I put crosses on your vigour for further intelectual aspirations.

Lydia

(41 Gordon Square), Friday 23rd February, 1923

Just a few minutes ago I had tea with my 'platonic lover.'[1] The theme in conversation is a 'natural' one: men-women. I certify for the first and he opposes me. He stays about an hour. 7 o'clock beats. Enough. He is out.

I lunched with Vanessa, Duncan and Roger. V. and D. 'ragged' R. for his love-adventures. I am asked from R. not to believe, so one day I will find myself as a sympathetic listener on that adventurous subject.

I looked by bed-panels. Delicious. Should I not entertain there instead of a drawing room? Love, intelect, abstract art, science, ally themselves in this bed.

I see your strength is regained. 'Holiday' was only a whim.[2] Your life balances very well without it (except in summer).

Balancing touches on and into your eyes.

Lydia

. . .

1   Basil Maine, often called 'Vaz' or 'Vasiline' (in Russian 'Basil' is 'Vasili') by Maynard and Lydia.
2   He had evidently cancelled his African holiday.

(41 Gordon Square), Saturday 24th February, 1923

Rich again; the papers [money] do arrive so rapidly every week; still the artists are rather anxious to know about future. Is it to-day that I should have a letter for further 4 weeks? They think it is, I am vague about it.

I have been again a model, Roger diverts me with scientific questions like nature and human nature. I thought that was one [and] the same. How terrific it is when one tries to think of it. If to go into it thoroughly the brains should get very well developed.

I am so glad that your brother is better. The 'bacilus' must be out by now. Human nature pushed nature. Send him my sympathies.

I had tea with Sedova. We were professional monkeys about our 'metier', also we discussed Serge, but what – I shall tell you to-morrow.

I am so fond of *you*.
Lydia

(41 Gordon Square), Monday 26th February, 1923

It is very well that you concentrate on your book,[1] but do not give up your various activities, as for holiday[2] it only comes once a year – summer time.

I was full of unintelectual machineries of life. I washed my head and sent packages home for my mother, sister, brothers. They shall touch it in 4–5 weeks.

. . .

The *Nation* I see progresses. You must be in a state of content about it even if you do not receive a 'holiday'. When you are at odds and ends I breath into you – comfortings.

Lydia

1   *A Tract on Monetary Reform.*
2   Another reference to his cancelled African holiday.

(41 Gordon Square), Friday 2nd March, 1923

I know you are relieved to-day from yesterday's mentally stormy happenings.

I struggle for sleep. I did not study this morning. I am a phisical invalid. Oh.

Before a rehearsal I have tea with Leon and Hilda. They asked me come on the underground, but the only action I am capable to have my halphes undisturbed.

. . .

I write an insipid letter.

You are very nice.

L.

(41 Gordon Square), Monday 5th March, 1923

This afternoon I slept, after I read the book you gave me from the pen of Jews. The one I remember most is a sexual, how an old father living in the same room with his 30 years of age daughter can't help going to bed with her, as she reminds him so much of his wife who is dead, but it is the daughter that seduces father. Ancient subject I suppose.

I kiss you deeply. It is very nice to see and speak with you to-morrow.

Lydia

(41 Gordon Square), Monday 12th March, 1923

I was just like a woman in the train – lost my ticket. Oh! then recovered it from my pocket book. Much colder here than in Cambridge.

I bought a curious book, the name '13 pipes'. The author does not like to write about objects, but a pipe such an irresistible one. Bitten, oversmoked, it is a life of a human being. I shall try to put more knowledge into your ashes from the cigarettes.

Your tender dog

L.

(41 Gordon Square), Friday 16th March, 1923

. . .

Then I had Sebastian [Sprott] for tea. He has more intelect than others and told me about electricity, and that each of us is a battery. He asked me for lunch . . .

How very nice that the term is ended. Blissful. Crosses to the termination.

Kisses to you.

Lydia

Letters from
25th March 1923 to 15th June 1923

As the Cambridge term was over, Maynard was evidently away somewhere else when Lydia wrote to him on 25th March; no more letters exist until he had returned to Cambridge before 20th April. In April he published a Memorandum on 'Stocks of Staple Commodities' – a subject in which he was becoming increasingly interested as a successful private investor. The first issue of the new Nation *appeared on 5th May, the price having come down from 9d to 6d. The* Nation *took up more of Maynard's time than was evident, for he wrote much that was unsigned – later even occupying the Editor's (Henderson's) chair at least once, when he was on holiday. Lydia read the* Nation *assiduously, often making detailed comments, as on 5th and 27th May.*

Although she was not currently performing, she continued her regular lessons with Maestro Cecchetti until his departure for Italy in June. She saw a good deal of Sam and Lil Courtauld. Vera Bowen's son was born. Florrie Grenfell begins to flit through the pages. On his own initiative Maynard saw Prime Minister Baldwin on 30th May, preparatory to visiting Berlin from 1st to 4th June, for discussions with Melchior and the German Chancellor. He was forty years old on 6th June.

On 15th June Lydia went to Paris for three nights to see the last performances of the Diaghilev ballet there; she vividly describes the mad Nijinsky in a box. On her return she was in 'a great state of excitement' (Harold Bowen's diary) because in her absence Maynard had arranged a three-week run for her at the Coliseum, starting on 23rd July, including a revival of Masquerade.

(41 Gordon Square), Sunday 25th March, 1923

. . .

Later I visited Vera in her new house.[1] She asked me how I liked the articles, I was enthousiastic about the wardrobe (17 century Italian lovely paintings) and another box (the same period I think), about the bed I said it ought to be in a museum (frank but not very polite). Poor Vera she is so active that she crawls on her 2 halphes to look into the other rooms. I mentioned your invitation to the King and Queen. Florrie arrived and said that K and Q wish to meet famous literary talents and Labour leaders, on the day of your appearance. Florrie just met them, her account of the King that he speaks out everything twice[2]. . . .

And you work, invent new bricks, ever marching.

I give you my pulsations.

L.

1 The Bowens had moved from 1 Spanish Place, Manchester Square, to a very large house in Bryanston Square.
2 He stuttered.

(41 Gordon Square), Friday 20th April, 1923

The freedom of Cambridge is more spacious than in London. Is it not so? I imagine after the circulation of activity there is an atmosphere of calm (in the night especially). How logic are my reasonings, I stroke myself with pride and look into mirroir. I am alone just now, the 'bizareries' of life descend on me also. I put crosses on your constructive forces of to-morrow.

Lydia

(41 Gordon Square), Saturday 21st April, 1923

Oh! I am in raptures over maestro. I saw two acts of *Coppelia* that he prepared for his pupil, and himself played the part of Dr Coppelius. Marvelous. 'I do want to play with you this ballet,' said I. Said he, 'Before I go away I could prepare it in less than 2 weeks, it is for you to make arrangements.' It is a very nice ballet.

. . . To breathe fresh air every day is my conception, as for you it is different, for instance you breathe the air to-day in Cambridge and the result might be in the main article for the *Nation*. Perhaps I shall meet it in your eyes like Shakespeare did in his sonnet 14.[1]

Lydia

1 'But from thine eyes my knowledge I derive.'

(41 Gordon Square), Sunday 22nd April, 1923

Sonnets [Shakespeare's] are repeated for the first part of to-day. In my head I would like to learn them all, but when in tongue it requires perseverance, I don't think I shall be able to accomplish many tasks after all, or perhaps it is Sunday that exists for tranquility . . .

I read two of Gorky's articles, it is interesting, inteligent, only one asks why is it not yet better?

Vera is not to be seen, but still in a state of pregnancy, her voice sounded not vital as of old; somehow I feel fear for her.

I go to see Sam-Lil. I hurt Sam I did not recognise his voice, so I asked Lil to let me speak to him, and then probably hurt her's as she did not allow?

I have no more news except that I must run around the square. It is full of sun. I think of you now, how I forgot the hooks for the boots in Marlborough [Oare], you state about it all to me very nice.

Lydia

(41 Gordon Square), Friday 27th April, 1923

I was arriving when Lil descended for dinner, even they thought I was punctual. . . .

The play *At Mrs Beans*[1] very amusing has also slacking moments. Subject: people whose life passes from morning till night in the bording house. All of them certainly have incomes. Very dangerous. I enjoyed it. Lil-Sam . . . simply abhored it. They do not approve of meeting in the theatre what they meet in life . . . However, I was asked to join them again in food after the theatre, I said impossible, this scribbling food to you is more sympathetic to me.

Lydia

1   By C. K. Munro.

(41 Gordon Square), Saturday 28th April, 1923

Vera thinks it [the baby] is coming, so to-morrow is the begining of an end. Garia went to see the London Group,[1] did not like it. I visited my dancing parents, Errol [Addison] was there too, maestro, as usual, was saying that Russian women were worse of all, because they did not care be good cooks and housekeepers . . . Everywhere is the same existence of dancing peoples, awful lack of work and hunger.

I bought two Russian weekly magasines from Moscow, many pictures also of Foreign nations, for instance how president Harding is the most unpopular president as he only salutes, walks with Mrs Harding, presides at dinners, but such an automaton is indispensable to the American bankers who rule the country.

Lydia

1   A group of artists formed in 1913.

(41 Gordon Square), Monday 30th April, 1923

I thank you very much for the objects in my habitation. The furniture for my water out, the jug for the water in and the chest to keep literature, shall be warmly received. Vera has a child Nicolas, came out with great pains 5 o'clock this morning, later she was progressing towards recovery. I knew about it from the telephone message. All is well that ends well.

Sebastian came to see me, after my platonic friend. Serious conversation with him, also about the theatre including [the ballet] *Coppelia*. He does want to help, made suggestions about the theatre.

The first *Nation* is complete! I am excited but not troubled. I shall be absolutely punctual for your dinner purpose, which is a double one for me.

Lydia

(41 Gordon Square), Friday 4th May, 1923

. . . The audience the high breed of Mayfair. Florrie was very excited, seeing all the bolsheviks coming to power. I told her she was a nice woman, so we shook hands and all went better.

So many women in the theatre were pregnant, one of them Lady Mosley the daughter of Lord Curzon. She had a very big head gear but I was not taken in and looked on her stomach of 9 months instead.

Your complete dog
L.

(41 Gordon Square), Saturday 5th May, 1923

With palpitations I demanded the *Nation*. The cover gives confidence of strength. The 'British Policy in Europe'[1] is powerful and reads with easiness, very nice. Sarah B.[2] is brilliant only I am confused how to take (I must read once more), serious or not serious and when? To Spain[3] is charming. The gossip, I mean the German students, birds, London Group, puppets, came out very well.

Others I did not read yet . . . I see that you must write every week for the beginning months at least.[4]

It is necessary. I am fond of you.

L.

1 By Maynard.
2 'Sarah Bernhardt' by Lytton Strachey.
3 By Virginia Woolf.
4 This was the first issue under the new management.

(41 Gordon Square), Saturday 5th May, 1923

The same Oah! I have had 7–8 perspirations. I can't walk, I ride in such a warm day . . .

Lil telephoned, Monday Sam's birthday, am I to offer something? Also Lil sais that Vera had one step from death only. Garia was not told how serious everything was.

With all my activity the day was not a necessary one, I shall find my peace in Shakspeare reading.

L.

(41 Gordon Square), Sunday 6th May, 1923

. . .

Sickert and Thérèse came in to take me for Simmond's puppets. Exquisite they were, the little fawn was my delight, I wanted to take him to bed, only he had too many strings, and also he is not without horns.

Calm true tenderness to you.
L.

(41 Gordon Square), Thursday 10th May, 1923

I am back, inclined to do some order in the box of Charles II. When that is done I should run on the Square and breathe the pure air. I did not communicate yet with Hilda [Bewicke][1] but I see something about Persians, female Persians, in silks are whipped. Behind that a mob of male Persians halph naked beat their own backs with iron chains and still behind that young and old in rows, marching rythimically, beat their faces with swords. Further they went, more blood they did produce. All for an idea! But Hilda will

87

protect her Hassan and shall not let even scrathch himself with a pin. East and West are so apart in culture.

Your uncultured but tender Asiat
Lydia

1   The Scottish dancer had married Hassan Arfa, a Persian.

(41 Gordon Square), Friday 11th May, 1923

To-day Vera did look spiritual the expression soft and calm, something of an Eastern Madonna, (not exactly a Buddha). The Child is healthy of English origin. (V. is secretly happy, such good luck.) Garia is ill – reaction of pregnancy. She wanted to write to you the enthusiasm she undergone while reading yours and two other stars. No criticism only admiration! While this conversation had it's moment we passed to Hilda . . .
. . .
I am of gossiping nature tonight.

Lydia

How does the hand feel, I touch it. Very nice.

(41 Gordon Square), Saturday 12th May, 1923

This week you are the only star,[1] but on the whole it looks interesting inside, I did not read the others yet (I am so very busy). It seems to me that the *ensemble* is progressing since last week. To-morrow I shall step into thoroughly.

By now you put bright letters into your book, your mental energy with this cold fresh atmosphere is of Vesuvian dimensions. I go and take a warm bath instead, as no mental powers exist in me.

Received letter from my brother. Very interesting, it is too long to write, quite intelectual. If you come to London you will help me to read it. To-night *Puss in Boots* with a dinner at 5½, maestro does not wish to be late in the theatre just now. *Oh.*

Touches on your pleasing complexion.

L.

1   In *The Nation*: his article was on 'The German offer and the French reply.'

(41 Gordon Square), Sunday 13th May, 1923

I was out almost till 7 o'clock with Florrie . . . Later as Lil is not well I visited her: 'It did me good to read Mr Keynes' article.' Sam: 'If he continues to be so unprejudiced he will lose readers.' Also a compliment, only from a different angle. All I see is that you become an idol of Mayfair community. *Oh* – I rubbed in to Sam and Lil that rich people ought to buy my portrait of London Group[1] . . .

Last night maestro and Mme were introduced to Sickert who sat a few rows behind with Thérèse. Both parties charmed, although of different schools.

Feelings of affection.

L.

1   This was, presumably, a missing portrait by Vanessa Bell – see Keynes, ed. 1983 p. 198.

(41 Gordon Square), Monday 14th May, 1923

I am 'high brow'. I saw *Electra*[1] this afternoon. Great intensities were in the play and continuity of drama was in existence, it is easier to say as well built. My platonic friend arranged a seat next to his lady friend with her son, but I as usual was late, my steps led me into balcony where I remained till the end. About 7 o'clock he came, he thought perhaps I met with an accident. Finding me in a good state he taught me a song 'I am poor but I am honest.' . . .

It is well to lay concentration on your book, but who is going to write next week in the *Nation*? I dare say it is all premeditated by you. So necessary in the art of intelect.

Unpremeditated kiss.

Lydia

1   Sheppard's production.

(41 Gordon Square), Sunday 20th May, 1923

I visited Hampton Court, would be more exilirating to come out with you; all the same how remarkable, we did not go inside, our steps were with nature among flower beds (some of them looked like French female lingerie, pink and blue). I watched with satisfaction the two courts, the houses are so well blend, the day was dark light blue-grey, the people looked as ugly 'Robots', they also spoke Volapice or Esperanto. We were the only English, not bad, after to the house of Sir Herbert Cook we galloped in the automobile, with

Flemise as the principal view from the windows, inside pictures of Florentine, Venetian, Flemish, Spanish, French (one room with pictures of Poussin only). I remember the 'Rape of Sabinians', very tumultous, vivid and next also bodies of humans but in a peaceful state, very good contrast from the same author in painting, *Oh*, there was so much to see, once is not enough.

I came home a dead body, however I looked into *The Nation*, quite a weight to read it all through; but the game in speculations / will add a few more patients / as the readers of the Nation's. You can drop 's' out of Nation. I used from a rhyme point of view.

L.

. . .

(41 Gordon Square), Monday 21st May, 1923

You progressed in big measure with your work, I see from your letter. I encouraged such means to an end, it is the right direction. Here to-day is peaceful silence, I recited all the sonnets I know, now I do not know to possess the unknown in learning, or to take Quentin to *Dr Mabuse*,[1] it has travelled from Regent Street to Tottenham [Court Road]. In the end I might do both or nothing at all.

The Nation is not as good as 2 others. Too much politicks and too many books. 'James' article is pleasing, makes comfortable reading, Clive is good, Virginia is wasted on Misses Wilson and Richardson, who are full of romance and the heart, but who cares about them? I have no more words to say, I speak with my eyes into yours.

L.

1   The German film directed by Fritz Lang.

(41 Gordon Square), Thursday 24th May, 1923

I bought apples and asparagus, Quentin and I feasted on it, after we ran in the taxi to the Charing Cross post office to send away the telegramme, I did not do it before, as I am a guilty man – *I simply lost the telegramme*. I went into your room I found the adress, and the rest I had it in my memory, only 2 words 'received, replying'. The same thing is done only 2 hours later, please accept all my apologising, otherwise I will remain sad for many months to come.

L.

(41 Gordon Square), Friday 25th May, 1923

I did not go to a lesson, although the cycle did not arrive yet, I was comfortable in bed, spoke with Emelie who cleaned the other room about her little niece and suggested bromide. If I have a pain in the right ear does it show that my left brain is wrong or that I have a cold? . . .

I invited Florrie to lunch. I had a chicken, substantial food indeed! We had it in our fingers, Florrie followed my example of a hostess, I did not ask you long time are your pupils marching ahead? With all the other activities this seems least mentioned in our conversations.

To you I send a chirp from under the left breast.

Lydia

(41 Gordon Square), Saturday 26th May, 1923

I pour out kisses on you. Ethousiasm! Your letters are [signature is] not at the end, but the writing on Bonar [Law] is of *your* artistic touch, those who read have no doubt.[1]

'The International Loan' is more of a dry cause, but is very instructive, and does not seem intelectual to read. The whole number [of the *Nation*] looks alive again, because it is touched by your flicker.

I am very hungry, it is almost 7 o'clock, my mouth was empty since this morning, maestro's last lesson, I had to listen to him for hours, and it is all funny and sad.

L.

1 'Mr Bonar Law: a Personal Appreciation', an unsigned article in *The Nation*, 26th May, 1923.

(41 Gordon Square), Sunday 27th May, 1923

I have been a 'social caller' twice. Vera and Garia are impressed indeed with your articles. Last night I looked thouroughly over into the *Nation*.

On 'Bonar Law' strikes me as one of your inspirational moments, it is a wave that does not come out every day. The articles of other people like Life and Politics, the teachers, Royal Academy, critisism of Forster's book[1] (very fine by Dickinson), all quite interesting, and your last phrase about finance and investment touched me, that is in the rise of the curve and decline of the curve 'anything can happen.'

I kiss you and am fond of you.

Platonic Basil payed me a visit, again I studied the other lines 'he seduced and then – left her, and she bore in a child by him.' Angus Davidson, with his brother, came in to ask me to a party to-morrow, I said 'perhaps'.

I saw how Vera gave milk to her child, I did not see how it was sucked (very simple I imagine) but the outline of bending was rather graceful.

L.

1   *Pharos and Pharillon.*

(41 Gordon Square), Monday 28th May, 1923

Bonnie and [Stephen] Tomlin have been special callers about to-night's party, so I could not refuse, it is going to be in the studio of Tomlin, but nor you or Vanessa or Duncan will be there. How strange I think of it now. It is palpitating about your going to Germany, you could help them more on the spot while action develops.

. . .

Oh! my belly aches very much. I take the strokes you sent me and concentrate them all on one place in the centre. I feel very sorry for myself, but not to the point of tears.

You are naughty, you write too often to me, instead the book could be already finished and you would not be bored with it even a little.

L.

(41 Gordon Square), Friday 1st June, 1923

This morning is stimulating. Your telegramme. I thank you. You are very nice.

Very much earlier I opened my eyes 'Maynard crosses Holland.' Suddenly 8 o'clock beat. Too late. How is that? I felt angry with myself in miscalculating the vibration of your arrival.

No doubt you are full and plenty of comfort in Melchior house,[1] it is such a good thing. All your time is filled with reconstructive elements I know, but in the evening do step into the world of 'poetry and beauty'.

Kisses on the results of your events.

L.

1   Maynard arrived in Berlin (not Hamburg where Melchior lived) on the evening of 1st June, where he was met by Melchior.

(41 Gordon Square), Saturday 2nd June, 1923

Oh emotions! When I arrived at the studio of maestro everybody's eyes were so red that mine felt purple. The [parting] present was already given, as poor maestro was quite exhasted by awaiting it (not a pin, nor buttons, but a bronze statue without anything on but an Italian tamborin, dancing). I said a few words and the end was such: '*C'est ne pas possible de vous dire adieu mais seulement au-revoir.*'

Then after I met Genée, it was good taste on her side to see maestro going away. She made me think of a marionette, very young[1] she looked, correct and stiff, or perhaps she was dressed (mentally) in late Victorians. I snatched the opportunity to be full of admiration (as her art was admirable), in reverse I might have appeared to her like a Robot. I am convinced that you are in intimacy with consultations, speeches, politics and progress of the World.

Your true underworld dog
Lydia

Last night I went with B.M. [presumably Basil Maine] to the Palladium. Nellie Wallace overwhelmed me as a sailor but she still had a pettycoat on.

[1] Adeline Genée was 45 years old.

(41 Gordon Square), Friday 8th June, 1923

The Note[1] is admirable. Well worded, simple, honest, there is no doubt that the public opinion for the first time will be touched toward German sitiation, it is a 'pure matter'. That is speaking seriously, but in lighter vein, I mean in the world of speculation, the Note shall improve the mark by great many points.

Vanessa arrives to-day, she sent a telegramme from Paris. I had a tremendous ride on the bus, because I have a heavy head and did not do my study but embrace myself in *Rosmersholm*. Very difficult to play Ibsen, only action in the mind . . .

I put such warm approval on you and the Note.

L.

[1] Presumably 'Finance and Investment: The Situation in Germany', *The Nation*, 9th June, 1923.

(41 Gordon Square), Saturday 9th June, 1923

Times editorial to-day clings to your Note[1] as a 'basis of settlement'. It will bear fruit when it comes to conference.

Poor Vanessa arrived all by her little self into an empty house, no one to meet, no one! We all thought telegramme meant 10 o'clock, 'tea time' what V. meant. When she came into my place I recompensated her with embracing

93

kisses etc. She cared for nothing in the world to bring but 'pottery', what I saw was charming but when your box arrives it probably will be astounding as the money you sent is of a greater value than V.

She is well glad to come back, not without humor about Roger, filled with beauty about pictures, churches and Spanich women, longs to go next time with a rich man (who can be responsible for an automobile to drive from one little place into another), might be your lot . . .

Tomorrow caressing current to you.

L.

1   See preceding letter.

(41 Gordon Square), Sunday 10th June, 1923

. . .

I liked on the 'inteligence',[1] I tested myself with bad result, the only excuse is that I am a foreigner, also I did not know what 'lofty' means. Quentin explained: he was not a foreigner . . .

. . . Last night on the door step returning, Clive asked me to go to his rooms with Vanessa. We gossiped a while, his place looks as of old, Vanessa's taste dwells in it. To-day after dinner Vanessa and Clive were educating Angelica, oxygenating her Cockney, as she is full of it, but she looks like a little Princess.

Florrie goes to Paris to-morrow, she thought I ought to come for a week end to see the last performances of the Ballet. I like to, and yet I don't know.

With peaceful embrace
Lydia

1   'What constitutes intelligence' by Bertrand Russell, *The Nation*, 9th June, 1923.

(41 Gordon Square), Monday 11th June, 1923

Lunch with Vera and Garia.[1] Leading conversation Duncan's exhibition.[2] Admiration for Bussy's critisism. I nodd 'very interesting indeed' in the company of experts. They wanted to buy what is already bought, my portrait is not liked but the drawing, yes. Each time I go there now I behold 'tableau, family happiness.' Vera is milking Nicholas, Garia gazing profoundly in the pasture.

I thank you very much, I found the package Frau Lopokova, 'Frau' sounds like a woman with numberless children, but the choice of books is praized, not intelect, but poetry and amusement. I kiss you with heat, yet tenderly. Tonight I go to see one of Shakespeare's children with Maine.

94

Splendid that you will write more for *The Nation*, and same about Lytton, it will be better and better for all times.

L.

1   After lunch they all went to Heal's in Tottenham Court Road where, according to Harold Bowen's diary, Lydia 'behaved absurdly'.
2   At the Independent Gallery.

(Written in the train, on Crown Hotel, Harrogate, paper, and posted at Dover), Friday 15th June, 1923

I thank you dearest Maynard for all the troubles I gave you for [my] going to Europe.[1] The country looks very ripe, but my neighbour (the man with an especially cut waistcoat that you noticed) is over-ripen with fat and money. I have no inclination to converse with him, but I doubt if he is a Jew . . .

The train is very comfortable and goes with a rythmical shaking, the profit I derive being in it.

The country sometimes looks to me like Charleston. I assossiate the paysages of Duncan with horses.

I cannot contemplate nor concentrate, my mechanism follows only the train in great haste.

My lips with love and thanks.

L.

1   She was en route for Paris to see Diaghilev's ballet. On 13th June Harold Bowen wrote in his diary that 'Loppie came to tea in a rage of excitement', having been to Bow Street over her passport.

(Paris), 15th June, 1923
Friday night after the theatre very late

I came back from the theatre worn out to the last degree. So many faces so many kisses, everything turned out à la Russe. Big Serge gave me outwardly affectionate embrace, then Boris [Kochno], then Picasso, then [Ida] Rubinstein, then most tragic of all Serge said: 'Nijinsky is [in] the box', to verify I went into the box and there I saw indeed Nijinsky but he did not know me, nor anybody, he does not recognise anyone, but being in a quiet state the doctors want to give him a thrill, so as to move him, and then perhaps he might be cured. His wife is with him. Who is so cruel to him? Terrible, terrible, yet it was forgotten when music played and dancers appeared.

The new ballet[1] is quite interesting: blue curtain at the back with a tiny window and black wings, dancers are dressed in black and white, just as the men look when they rehearse and so the women. It is built on groups, human waves doing the same dance, and when they are about 40 the wave becomes an ocean, primitive and Byzantine mixture, music is very intense with words that nobody understands, nor is there any need, altogether it is a well balanced madness in black and white. I go to see to-morrow another time. *Petrushka* was also played, that is immortal, because of the drama in music and action.

To-morrow I shall see Picasso and his family, also Hilda with Hassan, also Rubinstein, very buzy indeed. Florrie is charming and the hotel is very smart, room is worth 40 francs, but go out for food because it is more economic.

All the artists want to come to London for the months of holiday, I was not encouraging, so to say I could not boast with engagements. And you, Maynarochka, probably deligtfuly you spent your evening with your close in spirit friends.

So I in both spirit and body say good night to you.

L.

I come back on Monday.

1   *Les Noces*, devised by Stravinsky.

1 *Lydia as the Lilac Fairy in* The Sleeping Princess, *1921*

2   *Lydia by Laura Knight*

3   *Lydia as Princess Aurora in*
The Sleeping Princess

4   *Lydia in* Prince Igor *at the*
Maryinska Theatre, Leningrad,
in 1909

5   *Lydia with Nijinsky in*
Carnaval,
1916

6   *Maynard by Duncan Grant, 1917*

7   *Florence Ada Keynes,*
Maynard's mother, in about 1905

8   *John Neville Keynes,*
Maynard's father, in about 1905

9   *6 Harvey Road from the garden*

10 *Constanza Karlovna Douglas Lopukhova, Lydia's mother, with her sons Andrei (left) and Fedor, 1900*

11 *Lydia with two dancer friends, Leon Woizikovsky and Taddeus Slavinsky*

12 *Enrico Cecchetti ('Maestro') and his wife*

13 *Lydia and Massine dancing the can-can in* Boutique Fantasque, *1919*

14 *Lydia with Idzikovsky in*
    The Postman, *1925*

15 *Lydia with Massine in a Chinese*
    dance at the Coliseum, 1923

16 *Lydia by Duncan Grant,*
    1922–23

17 *Lydia with Massine in*
    Stravinsky's Ragtime, *1924*

18   *Lydia by Picasso, 1919*

Letters from
4th August 1923 to 8th August 1923

The long gap in the series of Lydia's letters between 15th June and 4th August, 1923, is mainly accounted for by their joint residence in Gordon Square. On 26th June, according to Harold Bowen's diary, Vera Bowen dined with Maynard and Lydia, the other guests being Virginia Woolf, Mr and Mrs Sinclair Lewis, Osbert Sitwell and Raymond Mortimer; Lydia wore an unrestored dress from the early eighteenth century. Soon afterwards trouble with Vera began, for on 26th July she proposed taking over the entire management of her Masquerade *from Lydia, to whom she would pay a weekly salary of £75. On 6th July Maynard made counter-proposals, pointing out that there had already been a deficit of £140. The Bowens were very angry, but after much thought they returned a politic reply. On 31st July, after performances of the* Masquerade *revival had begun, financial arrangements began to break down; the next day Vera spoke to Lydia in her dressing room and was treated as a stranger; negotiations continued; on 13th August the Bowens received an 'amazingly rude' letter from Maynard, which agitated them all day. How the matter ended is unknown, for Lydia's letter of 12th October is unclear.*

Maynard attended the Liberal Summer School in Cambridge in early August. He was writing his book and contributing much to the Nation, *especially on the matter of the impasse in the Ruhr. Later in August he and Lydia went to the Knoll, Studland, a rented house in Dorset. The Woolfs were with them from 7th to 10th September and other companions included Mortimer and Rylands. According to her* Diary *(Vol. 2, pp. 265–7), Virginia wanted to observe Lydia as a type for her character Rezia in* Mrs Dalloway, *and noted that 'she got cross, frowned, complained of the heat, seemed about to cry, precisely like a child of six.' At Bindon Abbey, after lying in a Bishop's tomb, Lydia acted death: 'What did she think about? About Maynard, & her death, & what would happen before.' 'Maynard had grown very gross and stout' and had 'a queer swollen eel like look, not very pleasant.' Then, on 4th*

November, 1923, Virginia wrote an extraordinarily disagreeable letter about Lydia's domestic habits at the Knoll to Jacques Raverat (Nicolson ed. 1977, p. 76).

(41 Gordon Square), Saturday 4th August, 1923

At last in peace by myself I am in 41, 12 o'clock night, after a thunder of words, most of the time of an unflattering character as to me in a Chinese costume, as to your letter she[1] said 'the polemics shall yet continue' in writing. I regretted. I boasted about your inventing the *Sylphides*[2] costumes especially about the double skirt, no unbounded enthousiasm from the respondent, of course it is in the nature of things. I understand, and thank her for the *Masquerade*. Cambridge[3] must be all pleasing at this moment well chosen for distinguished speeches and conversations.

Crosses on all of your activity.

L.

1 Vera Bowen, who was currently quarrelling with Lydia; she wrote a letter of protest to Maynard on 9th August.
2 Perhaps this was, in fact, a piece called *Les Élégantes* to the music of Chopin.
3 Where Maynard was attending the Liberal Summer School.

(41 Gordon Square), Monday 6th August, 1923

. . . Duncan came in this morning. I told him how pleased you were with costumes, everything promises to go with a big eclat in your garden party seasonal is it not? My troubles seem to be over, afternoon and evening performances went without hesitations, quite a good success.[1] Your costume[2] is a big success, even Vera admitted it to-night. The *Valse* and the Mexican go biggest, others less, but I feel confident about the general atmosphere in the audience, very friendly. V. and Garia took me home also very friendly, and although V. ridicules me I said I was kind and did not mind.

We are very early in the programme, last number before the interval, good place early finishing.

To-night I feel not one eyed but a hunded eyes cyclop[3] because to-morrow is so near 90 eyes for the speech, 10 for the party, and a kiss for you.

L.

1 In this, the third week of her three-week programme in variety at the Coliseum, the dances were: first, a Chopin waltz danced by Lydia and her partner; second, two solo dances, one of them a 'Chinese dance' by Lydia (*The Times*, 7th August, 1923); third, a *pavane* with de Valois, Dorothy Coxon and Astafieva; and fourth a *pas de*

deux danced by Lydia and Woizikovsky (Vera Bowen's *Masquerade* had been performed in the first fortnight.)
2   Presumably for the Chopin waltz.
3   See next letter.

(41 Gordon Square), Tuesday 7th August, 1923

Cyclops[1] had their chance, being in free open air with trees and grass as a background. At this moment the play is finished and you are receiving felicitations in your dressing room, a good moment to get people for *The Nation*, not you, but your aide de camps, Henderson and Leonard. I like the picture that is a paradox because to-day I had complete hunger and cannot abstain from ham, just now I look at a covered pot of jam, and how foxy even the fly is to situate herself under the paper. I do not kill her but let use her wings.

I thank you for *The New Statesman* . . . To-morrow I will buy *Manchester Guardian*, I want to know about your speech, where I expect to find it registered. My halphes ache, and Slavinsky probably wouldn't be able to lift me even if I look like a sylph.

I touch you.
L.

1   Sheppard's production of the Greek play, performed for the benefit of the Liberal Summer School at Cambridge.

(41 Gordon Square), Wednesday 8th August, 1923

So it seems there was enthosiasm for the production, I could not expect otherwise, but it is nice to state it as a fact. Tête à tête is disturbed, but perhaps you are not pleased? Your explanation of last night's idyl is very melodious up to the moment when you sang the only song you know and that is Four blue bottles or beetles.[1] Is it not correct? I made a mistake in calculating that your speech was on the same day, it is much better that it is apart . . .
. . .

I am fond of you.
L.

1   Maynard is recorded as having sung 'Three Blue Bottles' at Eton, with great gusto and entire indifference to tune.

Letters from
13th September 1923 to 9th December 1923

*After returning from Dorset, Maynard set off for Exmoor for a stag hunting
holiday with Macaulay, the Vice Provost of King's College, and it seems that
most of his letters thereafter have been preserved. Lydia had a weekend in
Deal with the Johnstons; went to St Albans with Sam Courtauld; and then on
19th September joined the Bowens at Colworth, where she stayed until 23rd
September. Owing to the row they had been having, the Bowens were
surprised to receive a telegram from Lydia inviting herself to stay, but were
relieved to find her 'very cordial' – 'although V. detected a slight strain.'
[Harold's diary]. Lydia desperately needed to confide in Vera, as she had in
the previous year, 'as if no cloud had darkened the horizon.' Harold Bowen's
report on what happened, while the two were closeted together for hours, is
tantalisingly brief: first, Vera 'ventured on the most outspoken criticism of
Bloomsbury and its ways'; then, 'Loppie looks on the end of her Maynard
attachment as inevitable and not even out of sight. She said significantly that
she has no money for her own productions, and that no offers seem to be
forthcoming. She is keen to act, but Vera discouraged her from essaying the
ordinary stage on account of her accent.'*

*What might this mean? On first reading it might be thought that Lydia was
predicting that (alas) Maynard's passion for her was subsiding and would
soon end; on the other hand, the words 'her Maynard attachment' suggest
that her own feelings were waning. The latter hypothesis is supported by an
inscription on a demure photograph of herself and Maynard, which she gave
to Vera on 31st December, 1927: 'Second thoughts are best. To Vera from
Lydia.' Considering the strength of Lydia's attachment which is revealed by
her letters, what could have happened? Was it that the bitchiness of 'Bloomsbury', and in particular of Virginia Woolf, during their holiday at the Knoll,
Studland, made the future seem intolerable? This seems a more reasonable
idea than that she was scared of a resumption of Maynard's homosexual*

behaviour for, given her Russian ballet background, homosexuality was (almost) to be taken for granted.

The only other discussion of the love affair in Bowen's diary was on 19th November when Lydia reduced Vera to tears by remaining almost until midnight 'discussing interminably the problem whether Maynard is to marry her or no.' Again there is ambiguity, for if it is thought that Lydia was forecasting Maynard's rejection of her, it should be remembered that she had met his mother for the first time about three days before, and had been kissed on her departure. Certainly, Lydia's letters provide no clue to her real state of mind; and Maynard's letters retain their unruffled, affectionate aloofness.

It is fascinating to reflect that had Lydia really decided to leave Maynard (which is admittedly fairly unlikely), she could hardly have fulfilled her intention without 'vanishing' yet again.

As a man of affairs, Maynard was as busy as ever. He was intensely dismayed by the German political situation and wrote reprimandingly to General Smuts on 21st October – however, Smuts' reaction pleased him. On the same day he completed the proofs of his book A Tract on Monetary Reform. *He was active on* The Nation. *He was endlessly concerned with the new buildings at King's. He was uninterested in standing for Parliament as Member for Cambridge University. He campaigned in Lancashire on behalf of the Liberals.*

Lydia was 32 years old on 19th October and, at the height of her powers, was unemployed. She took the opportunity of having her head sculpted by Dobson and she continued her Spanish lessons. She read The Nation *with assiduity and, as a passionate Free Trader, applauded the Liberal and Labour gains at the election. And Basil Maine sang to her.*

(41 Gordon Square), Thursday 13th September, 1923

Here I am with the fountain pen you gave me from Berlin, the little one, and although I want to say something to you, it is so difficult, the pen does not desire to collaborate. Do you notice it? . . . Wicked Mme Tussaud, already she includes the present prime-minister [Baldwin] in the 'chamber of horrors'. I always thought 'post mortem' was Tussaud affair . . .

Vasiline called me again, so I did it to him, I shall see him this Sunday, did not forget to ask the widow[1] with the boys, it is arranged they will come if it is possible but I doubt it.

I touch you and give my touchings for your successful hunting start. Your 'ridiculous apple.'

L.

1 Basil Maine's friend Mrs Martineau.

(41 Gordon Square), Friday 14th September, 1923

Is there such a thing as a 'hunting morale'? Have you acquired it? I suppose one sniffs it from the dogs. *Oh!* I worked to-day. Why? I cannot tell; in the morning exercise, then Mr Mrs Johnston[1] and at three I began to undress for the photos; remained in that situation about 3 hours. I asked the man to take me as a tragic, but he thought I had too much mobility instead of stability . . .

> There was Lydia's lack of stability
> only mobility
> and sometimes virility.
> Then J. M. Keyne's (you must pronounce your name in a foreign way)
> with international fameness
> swung her into the path of stability.
> (or instilled her with the root of stability.)

At the photographers they asked me to write a few words about myself and when I do next appear, I said I will write to them. Please, help me and write a few suitable words for me if you can spare time.

Last night Pavlova's performance was less interesting than first . . .

. . .

To-morrow morning I go away with Johnston family for a week end (*how English* to Dover cliffs or in that direction). I come back Sunday. I am fond, pro-fond and re-fond of you.

L.

P.S. Perhaps this is Better?

> Then J. M. Keynes
> with international brains

1 Mr and Mrs Johnston have not been identified, but she may be the woman who Harold Bowen mentions in his diary (31st October, 1923) as having an enormous collection of paintings by Augustus John and McEvoy.

Crown Hotel, Exford, Taunton, Friday 14th September, 1923

Dearest Lydochka,

I am in my bed sitting room in this tiny townlet in the middle of the moor, – rather high up and the clouds are low so that a thick wet blanket of water fills the air outside. But I have a fire and the room is large, so I am very happy and comfortable writing my letters and going to sit down with my proof sheets in a few minutes. But I must first of all tell you that I *got up* and had breakfast in the coffee-room at 8.30. I feel rather strange but it has not led to nervous breakdown yet.

Another old gentleman, a brother of Macaulay's, has turned up too. But he is not going to hunt, so I don't know what he'll do, – for there is no other occupation. Macaulay is delightful and very sweet – very much excited about the hunting, telling me old hunting stories of earlier years, and instructing me in the technical terms. I know now what 'tufters' are. He also tells me all the etiquette, and we look at the maps a great deal. My first hunt is to-morrow, and I am rather relieved to find that we shall motor to the meet which is twelve miles away and have the horses sent on. This afternoon we are going out for a quiet ride on the moor to stretch my legs.

I wonder how you liked Pavlova last night. My dear love to you. I am very fond of you. I kiss you and touch you.

M

(41 Gordon Square), Saturday 15th September, 1923

Time is so fast, I am hurrying to catch the Dover cliffs at 11.15. From your letter I see you organised an atmosphere of literature and intelect, it is very nice, but quel courage mon cher, for breakfast.

I have no time, taxi at the door, I am packing, writing to you, eating water and drinking apples, the last two I do so early for fear I might not get this treat in peoples houses, and health as a means to general state of mind is not a small thing.

Kisses to your state of mind.

L.

(41 Gordon Square), Sunday 16th September, 1923

Deal, that is the spot in Kent,[1] lovely downs on one side, beatiful ships on the other, and France – strech your arms and you are there, except for Goodwin sands. What a place to ride (I had boots but I couldnt pull them on, no strength in my hands, also it was impossible to have a horse in such a short notice), but I looked on the downs and imagined.

Another guest [Gustav] Holst (famous English composer) charming man gave me suggestions how I should diminish the expences with a small orchestra. I promised (I do it so often) to hear his *Planets* at the Queens Hall 13th Oct. With Mrs Johnston we discussed sex, she is studying psychologie, she is much more serious than I, and it is intelect don't you think? I had to go back and be at 4 as I promised in the train. I met a funny old gentelman with a tiny rat dog, who went into conversations with me about his place at Ashford . . . I was placid as a rock, so he left me and went to Ashford, old and lonely, I thought.

Back in London, against my calculations Mrs M. [Martineau], the boys and Basil all came to tea. The boys simply delightful, so is Mrs M., they are going to teach me how to milk a cow, I think I might succeed with my sensitive fingers, I entertained them with male female mosquitoes and harvesters . . . I send *Revision of the Treaty*[2] to-morrow (it is lucky for you that I have two copies so I can spare the other with good humour) for your intelectual ingredients.

I have a letter from Vera, she expects me, she was not well all this time, how should I answer, please I need assistance, I am so negative in action, but with my tender elements to you.

L.

1 Where she had just been staying.
2 Maynard's book of 1922.

Crown Hotel, Exford, Sunday 16th September, 1923

My Dearest L,

Well my first hunt is over – my halves[1] stick to my clothes and I am stiff to death in every limb of my body! It was a terrific affair, so far as I was concerned. 300 or 400 horsemen were out altogether. We started soon after 11 above a deep wooded valley. I saw the stag start running but I never saw it again. It ran for between 4 and 5 hours and at last was caught and killed. Meanwhile the great body of us just rode our horses as fast as we could, occasionally seeing the dogs and the redcoats of the horsemen and hearing the cries, sometimes far behind. The country was very confused – a tangle of steep wooded valleys up and down which we rode until one hadn't the faintest idea in which direction one was going. I went as hard as I could, often in a thick jostle of other horsemen, for about two hours without stopping at all – I had no idea a horse could go on so long. At that time I was up with the hounds and the huntsmen. Then soon after I found myself (the horse being tired and going slowly) almost alone on a tract of open moor with the hunt some way ahead. So I tied up my reins on the horse's neck, let it go as slowly as it liked, and eat my lunch on its back as it jogged along. Sometime later, when I had almost decided to go home, I suddenly found myself near the hunt again, either because it had doubled back or got stopped. Soon after I lost myself in the bottom of a deep valley and then found that my horse had lost one of its shoes and could do little more. Fortunately the last phase of the hunt had not been right away from home and I found myself about 10 miles off. I rode slowly but the horse's foot got more and more tender, until finally, to spare him, I go off and walked. After some miles I came to an inn, stalled my horse and left him there, got a pint of beer from a rascally inn-keeper, and motored home,

getting back a little earlier than those who rode on to the bitter end. It all seemed quite an adventure – but wasn't really! We go out again on Tuesday.
. . .

I am doing quite a lot of work, as there is nothing else to do when one is not hunting or playing rummy – which we do every evening.

I stroke my apple with my lips. The posts are very seldom. I have your letter of Thursday but nothing later.

M.

1 'Halves' – sometimes 'halphes': Lydia's word for buttocks, which Maynard adopted.

(41 Gordon Square), Monday 17th September, 1923

I wanted long time ago to drink coffee without caffeine, so I had a walk with a purpose to Selfridges, and now I have box for 100 cups. The crowd on the street was just as idle as I (both sexes) and 'still another revolution' is taken less seriously than the rate of exchange of a frank [franc], for instance, first quotation 78, second 78.10. My knowledge I derive from Selfridges, but I hate the shop. Partridge [Ralph] came to see me, just from Europe, Carrington, Lytton [Strachey], filled with colds in the country, they all know about our lives in Swanage [the Knoll, Studland] (Virginia's gossip of course), naughty child she has not send me the play yet. I looked in *Devon Somerset* to-day, oh, I say what a good hunt, up to Hawkridge Ridge? Splendid.

Your stag with fleetest of the legs.
L.

Crown Hotel, Exford, Monday 17th September, 1923

Dearest L,

I laughed very much to read your poem,[1] but you have forgotten Lydia's amiability and capability. You say nothing about Sam [Courtauld] – how was he?

I have no news. I rest so as to be strong for hunting to-morrow. The weather is not good and I have spent most of to-day in my room reading and writing.

I enclose a suggestion for you to consider whether you like to write something like the enclosed to Barrie, or would you go to see him. (It is an elaborate imitation of your prose style!)

I don't know what to write for you for the photographers – quite beaten I am, not an idea comes into my head.

105

I wish you were here. I kiss you and re-kiss you and pro-kiss you.

M.

Did you see in the *Times* that Roger has been in Paris with all the other experts (including Captain Douglas) judging if a disputed picture is by Leonardo?

1   Letter of 14th September.

(41 Gordon Square), Tuesday 18th September, 1923

. . .

This afternoon I spent for 4 hours with Sam tête à tête; Vanessa was strolling with Julian in Gordon Square, when I was about to step in Sam's automobile she asked when you come back, I did not know, but she comes back Sunday. Sam and I 50 miles an hour to St. Albans cathedral, rather stupendous a mixture of civilisations including Roman bricks, built by Norsemen (Vikings) and after Gothic. I see from where Russian ballet is influenced from Vikings indeed. Sam and I after the drive, nice fire, tea with blattering bread and butter and conversations flowing naturally, including baths, schools, sport, and Russian ballet reminiscences of course. He does not like to be a bachelor and thanks me for sheltering him, sweet character altogether.

You are in *The Times* (British Association [for the advancement of Science]), I am glad your theory is in discussions, great many peoples minds might develop in the right direction.

You have shown yourself a true friend to your horse . . . your poor halphs will improve very soon, it is only an adventure to them and, being so, not permanent.

L.

(41 Gordon Square), Wednesday 19th September, 1923

5.35 I start to Sharnbrook. I went to 46 to take posession of the railway guide, and then sent a telegramme to Vera. I see from *The Times* that stag was not cornered, then it was me that is why he was not caught. I thank you for the communication to Barrie but I think first I will try to see him when I come back, anyhow I will use all your wise words. I am very lazy these last few days and postpone my exercises till very late.

How are yours? Not the hunting ones but of the mind?

Last night I went to Pavlova's dressing room, but last week I did send her flowers, so I felt in very good mood to go and see her. She was very nice. I decided I was a good 'scaramouche' because [she] said she did not laugh for a long time, but couldn't help doing so with me . . .

I am reading *Crime and Punishment*. More fascinating than ever.

L.

Crown Hotel, Exford, Wednesday 19th September, 1923

My dearest hind,*

Yesterday's hunt was very good. My horse was better and I rode better, so that I could keep up with the hounds most of the time and see what was happening. Indeed I once saw the stag. Also it was mostly across open moor. It's appallingly violent exercise – I was in the saddle 6 hours yesterday and rode about 35 miles; but we had one longish rest while they couldn't get the stag to leave a refuge in the valley. The poor creature got away in the end and we didn't kill him. There were some beautiful sights – most lovely moorland valleys with the dogs and the redcoated huntsman and the great cavalcade of horsemen galloping up them. My halphes were my only trouble, – they came back bleeding and very sore. I am out again to-morrow in another part of the moor.

I shall probably come back on Sunday, but it rather depends on Macaulay. To his immense disappointment he is finding the game rather severe for his old bones and it is not certain that his strength and health is equal to it. I will send you a telegram when my plans are settled. If you go to Vera, will you telegraph her address, as I am not certain of it? Do your best to compose the quarrel with her so far as I am concerned, I don't want to quarrel. Why should one quarrel about racial characteristics? It is no good. (But don't tell her that!)

. . .

With my dear love
M

* female of stag

Colworth, Sharnbrook, Thursday 20th September, 1923

Last night I was a *silly*, going to Sharnbrook I realized myself in the train after 7 o'clock, then I knew I made a mistake, not changing in Bedford; the next station Kettering, very gloomy it looked, so I was off there, made necessary inquirements with my tongue for taking me back first to Welling-borough, then to change and take another train to Sharnbrook, in these last two trains I sat opposite a man, a guardsman I thought (he clicked his heels in military fashion), he wanted to flirt with me. I smiled at him to suppress my laughter, I was so angry with myself, he took it for encouragement, I noticed that and gave my face an expression of a stone, but if I would be in simply good humour I would not have shirked from this crude acquaintance. I arrived 8½ relieved to be in Sharnbrook, a man came towards me said an automobile will be in 5 minutes, I spoke on the telephone with Vera they were very anxious, they telephoned to Mrs Sneddon, she did not know what happened to me but V. did not give up the hope and only regretted why she listened to Garia and did not put her original intention of changing the train in Bedford in the telegramme. All my troubles are known to you now.

Colworth is a very nice place, I see my mulberrough tree and green grass such good carpet for my feet, it is cold that is only a pity so that mulberrough berries very sour, I might catch diarrhoea. V. does not mention the accident[1] yet, will she you think at all?

If you write more about hunting I will have for myself a complete *sportsman sketch* one with the stag dead, and another who never say die.

You are the nice one.

L.

1 Perhaps this is a reference to the row about *Masquerade*.

Exford, Thursday 20th September, 1923

Dearest Lydchka,

Just a line to your new address before I start out (I wrote yesterday to Gordon Square) to give you much love.

I see Lil and I will have to get together to have a serious talk about you and Sam!

. . .

My best regards to Vera,

Your
M

. . .

Colworth, Sharnbrook, Friday 21st September, 1923

I gave your regards to Vera. 'Thank you very much' in perfect English prononciation, the words came out from the depths of a glacial period . . . I had a dreadful night for two reasons: perhaps coffee, perhaps *Crime and Punishment*. V. sais I ought not read it, but what an artistic pshyho-analisis.

I am going to try in a few moments Colworth's Pipsic, my boots give me such trouble. Harland cleaned them very well indeed, so this kind of skin becomes more dry than ever, and I suffer, but use my obstinacy for a 'wild desire to succeed.'

. . . I sprinkle you with a kiss.

L.

Exford, Friday 21st September, 1923

Dearest L.

I have my fourth and last hunt to-morrow and come back on Sunday, reaching 46 about 7.30 in the evening. Yesterday we were out a long time – I was in the saddle 7 hours, but we spent a great deal of time waiting about before we could get the stag to run away in front of us. I saw the slain deer for the first time.

The weather is much better – that is to say it does not rain very much. I wonder how you and Vera are getting on . . .

I see you soon and you are very miele in [my] thoughts. I kiss you.

M.

(41 Gordon Square), Friday 12th October, 1923

My last words to Vera 'you do not mind that I am frank'; that you are frank, *no*, but you are slightly a silly,[1] think it over.' It is a complete surrender to her, that is to appear in the old ballet *Gavotte* only 4 peoples, she would arrange all and pay me a salary. I was not enthusiastic, and said a ballet without corps de ballet does not stand on it's leges, whereas divertissement background was black curtains and nothing else except my execution in dancing, no pretense, and so preferable to my taste. As an old ballet I thought *Coppelia* was the best. We were peaceful in our discussions, but she has a stone in her insides and the doctor sais of good dimensions, great many peoples have it, and only a few feel it.

A message from Sam Lil persuading V. to persude me to join the supper, but I can't face dull guests.

In the Russian magasine in the article 'economics-socialness' you are 'a beatiful professor internationalist, but very simple as a politician.'

With positive sympathy in all your directions.

L.

1 Recently at the Knoll, Studland, Leonard Woolf had spoken of Lydia and Virginia as 'sillies' – a type described by Tolstoy in his autobiography and portrayed by Dostoievsky in *The Idiot*. (V. W. *Diary*, Vol. 2, p. 266.)

(41 Gordon Square), Saturday 13th October, 1923

I have had so many occupations. I remembered Holst's *Planets*, telephone to Mrs Johnstone, take off my dancing pyjamas, fly into a taxi to the Savoy Grill, lunch with oysters, 1 hour later I behold that great Victorian veneration Sir Henry Wood [the conductor]. As for *Planets* I may use the same words of Segonzac [the French artist], when he looked at some pictures, 'Tres puissent'.[1] Now many peoples love music, curious, it is better than eating bananas, probably they do both. Holst was sorry as he could not undertake, and I did not ask about Purcell, it was not the moment. I met his wife a handsome woman with a good country complexion; she is usually chosen as a Madonna in spiritual plays. Proceeded home, Alix and James [Strachey] already in the room,[2] fire also, tea and conversation did not require any waiting, naturally music is the first subject, then men-women in universities, their status and relation to men (Alix is Newnham (did you know it?) she does not look it), after six quite late Vasiline appears, so we turn to the music again, to hear his learned opinion. Couple in physcho-analisis [the Stracheys] departed, we read *Twelfth Night*. Lovely passages! I execute Viola and Olivia (positive and negative), before he goes away we speak about Dadie [Rylands].

I find in my Russian organ an article on Ricardo. Very interesting, he was talented and with temperament of activity. But 'cut your losses and let your profits run' was not an idea of mine, after all.

With a sad kiss.
L.

1 Très puissant – 'very powerful'.
2 They, also, lived in No. 41.

(41 Gordon Square), Sunday 14th October, 1923

You are very well known in Russia, in the other magasine there's writing about the book of Angell[1] that although you both have the same problems, you are very inteligent economist and strengthen all your sutiations with facts and figures and when one wants to know about *victorious imperialism of Entente in Europe* (I smile like a Bolchevic writing this phrase), it becomes a nessesseity to see your work whereas Angell's book is a fiddle faddle.

I have been all day with Vera, she is going to produce at the Coliseum (so she sais) one act opera of Rossini that she discovered and was going to meet the primadonna . . .

V. told me that Lil Sam's party was inadmissible,[2] so very dull (sometimes I strike a right note in my actions – as I did not go there); I feel feverish and Mrs Sneddon is going to give me a warm limonade. *Oh* I feel so sorry for myself.

How are your Cambridge movements? In late autumn there must be a big stimulus, intelectualy speaking.

L.

P.S. As it was after 9 I did not post Saturday's letter.

1   *If Britain is to Live*, by Norman Angell, published in 1923. Angell was a committed pacifist whose ideas were much discussed.
2   The Bowens were generally very critical of the snobbish Courtaulds.

King's College, Cambridge, Sunday 14th October, 1923

My dearest

I don't quite understand V's proposal. Has she got an engagement with a date? and does she make a definite offer of salary? Or does she merely hope to get an engagement? I expect the latter. But if so, how does it help? for your difficulty is how to get an engagement, – not what to put on if you do get one.

Sooner or later I am sure you will get an engagement; so it might be wise to get a few new numbers definitely prepared ready. Couldn't you get Vasiline to find you good music for the Spanish dance and have that definite? Also write a postcard to Holst for his volume of Purcell.

. . .

The pupil who was to have done the index only came back to-day. So I have had to do the index myself.

I kiss your spirit.

M

I have tried to make the handwriting of this letter good! Is it so?

(41 Gordon Square), Monday 15th October, 1923

Yes, my chest is gone wrong, I shall drink more limonade and sit by the fire. I visited Dobson[1] in a lavish way (a taxi) I couldnt otherwise, calculation of time was out of my head, although the taxi driver did not know Mourza-Mirza Road, however I was only a little late. It is much less strain than he painted, you watch his process and move around in your own particular way, almost going to lie down in a basket with a cat and it's kittens; then I took only 3 pences out of my pocket to arrive home.

Vera came in to tea, I entered into curiosity questions about her opera. The truth is that *if* Mr John accepts her scenario, music, decor, [of] her 7 persons 4 must be good singers (she spoke to them if they would like – and of course they would), the other 3 second hand, also her own chef d'orchestre, then she

III

puts forth her best cash and produces it, and then will have a satisfaction in money and glory complete . . .

A complete bancrupt in energy I am, but I will improve in future.

L.

1   Frank Dobson, the sculptor, who was working on a bronze bust of Lydia which he finished in 1924.

(41 Gordon Square), Thursday 18th October, 1923

. . .

On my way home [from visiting Lil] I could not resist that place where they sell glue, by now I have a tube, if I am mad and break furniture it will never be shown to the outside world, I shall mend it.

Oh the destruction of Europe is distressing, in 1931 for one dollar one can acquire 470 english pounds, and all because English steel trust decided to lower the prices of production on 50% (but you will make probably deeper reason). I suppose I speak too much nonsense to you, because I speak every day but I do not eat every day.

I must change the dress and see my prosaical Sappho, she waits for me dinner time. I am still possesed of that lovely ride with you on the bus to-day.

L.

(41 Gordon Square), Friday 19th October, 1923

. . .

I sat for the sculpter, I like myself in the other person's head, when she will be accomplished I am going to kiss her. Mrs Doby [Dobson] has been to lunch with a big stack of hens that she brought to the studio. It was absolutely comic to hear one of them say to him 'Is it not just like Mestrovic',[1] so Dobson 'He probably uses the same stone.' Mrs Doby became a bolshevic and swore she'll never go to such parties again, but Lytton might have acquired material in Victorian sense.[2]

Vera, Hilda and Vasiline come to-morrow to tea, after I am (to be bored if there are other guests) delivering myself to Lil and Sam for dinner.

I have lazy movements but my pulse is strong and I touch kissingly your shoulder.

L.

1   The Yugoslav sculptor.
2   Mrs Dobson's 'hens' were women who struck Lydia as so old-fashioned that they made her think of Lytton Strachey's *Eminent Victorians*.

King's College, Cambridge, Friday 19th October 1923

My dearest

Oh I've worked hard to-day. The American didn't arrive for lunch; so as the lunch was on the table, I made it an excuse to prolong the morning and went on writing my article (the one I began yesterday) until half past two. Since then I have been in meetings and College business etc. After dinner I go to a small at home given by Dennis Robertson.

I have got horses; so to-morrow afternoon I ride with Sebastian and Dennis.

I see that in Lil's family harmony does not descend in the female line! As she is to her daughter, so she is to her mother. But I'm sure she is in her mad period of life.

I kiss your letter; but my mind is too tired to make mine much. So I just sit with you in the bus, not speaking.

M.

(41 Gordon Square), Saturday 20th October, 1923

. . . Present[1] from Miss Holland, my cultured gallery friend, . . . rather nice, they all[2] come to-morrow to tea. Letter from Margaret [Hill], asking me to come to tea on Wednesday, but I go to my sculptor, I suppose I should answer. I have a dosen of handkerchiefs, also a present flowers, a book of masks, I am filled with new objects, and the last very important is Virginia's play;[3] exhilirating comedy, funny, the atmosphere is there, the author cannot do any more, it is for us the actors to begin. Shall we read when you come to London. *Da!*

L.

1   Lydia's birthday was on 19th October – she was 32.
2   The 'gallerites', Lydia's admirers from the theatre gallery.
3   *Freshwater* (it was not, in fact, peformed until 1935).

(41 Gordon Square), Sunday 21st October, 1923

My tea visitors are gone. I gave them muffins and a little bit of myself, that is about 2 hours. We all adored Nellie Wallace [the music hall artiste], and now I know before she goes on the stage she makes funny noises in her dressing room, probably what dancers do with the legs, she makes it with the throat, still Palladium is a *home* of comedy and Coliseum of dancing, that is what I am told by 'connoisseurs'.

. . .

I look into the news about Cambridge, you give a degree of honour to Mr Bruce because he used to be a rowing blue. How jolly!

... I can't write any more because I came in and lost my keyes, how am I to get in when I post this writing. You sympathise with me?

L.

King's College, Cambridge, Sunday 21st October, 1923

My dearest L

The ride yesterday was quite good – terrible hard motor roads getting out of Cambridge but nice in the open country. My horse was very fair, – its name 'Peaceful'. I ride Peacefull (*sic*) again next Saturday.

I have finished an article for the *Nation*[1] but perhaps it will not appear until Saturday week. To-day I have marked for the printer the preface of my new book,[2] – so now it is not possible any more to alter that.

I have just had tea with Dadie; Dennis [Robertson] and Sebastian were there. To-night I give another dinner party.

I feel well and strong. I am going to write one more letter to Smuts, but he will take no notice.

The enclosed tickets were given me by Dudley Ward whom I know very well (his wife is sister of Clothilda Sakharoff – I think I have told you) for the special matinee which the Sakharoffs are giving on Tuesday. I think he gave them because he hoped you would go. I come up on Tuesday, but at the same time as last week – that is too late for the matinee. So I send you the two tickets to use as you like.

I kiss you very much.

M.

1 'How much has Germany paid?' *Nation*, 27th October, 1923.
2 *A Tract on Monetary Reform*.

(41 Gordon Square), Monday 22nd October, 1923

I kiss you for the tickets, after lunch with Florrie, 'the original and pocket Venus' will be off to this dancing enterprise. That your horse is anti-war it is very pleasing to know, but you do not ride often enough. It is very nice that you are full of stimulus, so you might write more for *The Nation* and otherwise.

I acquire more and more comforts in my habitation. I have the bar [*barre*] of beautiful oak and such an alluring miroir, that if only the chair could mount in the air I would not change the situation of my halphes for months (the last word is of too big a measure I admit).

Dobson and I are working, we spoke about war, he was there from the begining in the front line and twice carried in the air by shrapnel. Dreadful, horrid, beastly war is. I asked him about Michelangelo, he never washed himself, when sometimes, perhaps once in 6 months, he took off his trousers he already had another pair that grew out of his skin, so he also had pink legs but did not dance.

. . .

L.

King's College, Cambridge, Monday 22nd October, 1923

Two very gay letters from you to-day. You are in a good part of the cycle – I know it from myself. I feel very strong, and we always move together.

To-night I read a paper to my political economy club.

. . .

Everything you say about what is in the *Nation* is true. How are you so wise? (*No* I don't mock). I kiss you and your big bump of wisdom.

M.

(41 Gordon Square), Thursday 25th October, 1923

I have been reading B. Shaw, it is very good and sensible. Did you know that progress of the world maintains through peoples using their sexual powers continually, while animals only at long intervals, but do not fear it is not B.Shaw. However in life at present it is different, Elinor Glyn [the popular novelist] used to write about 'lluv' for 3 weeks, now it is only for 6 days, I saw it on the streets where cinema is offered. Is it logic to make this comparison? I also look into the 'animals of all countries', charming puffins are there only they do not excel in dropping their surplus eggs into the sea as on the island[1] visited by you, those were wise puffins, do you remember?

Do you like to hear quotations? 'Jew: a man who kills 2 birds with 1 stone and then wants the stone back.' Women: 'Sphinxes without secrets.' . . .

With tenderness to you and your navel pupsie.

L.

1 Holy Island.

(41 Gordon Square), Friday 26th October, 1923

With what eyes do you look at politics after innumerable speeches in the press, a good deal of high polluting or high falluting nonsense. Even I, a non economic person, see that deflation in the extreme just as bad as inflation in the extreme, also no real salvation for the unemployed, no free trade but 'preferences' all over, that will not improve the situation . . .

My passport is in order. I paid 22 shillings to be in such a state for a year. Great deal of money has been smuggled by the taxi. I began in a general but finished in private. Dobby could not work very much as he and Mr Buckingham had to wash the memorial before its separation to Cardiff, it's lovely and white on a pedestal of flat oval form. I bought apples, bisquits and had tea with my spanish maestro diplomeé, as I never prepare lessons I speak with her only, the method seems a workable one.

To-morrow I see V. and the evening to another V. It is for your logic mind to reason out /of/ which 3 V I see the 2, or which is the V that I do not see.

Your blinking
Lidochka

King's College, Cambridge, Friday 26th October, 1923

My dearest pupsik

To-morrow morning we lay the ashes of the O.B.[1] in the vault under the floor of the chapel, – a sad but nice ceremony. It is a suitable place to be put away into.

. . .

It is in the paper to-day that my sister Margaret's husband (A. V. Hill) has been given the Nobel Prize for medicine – it is a big honour. I send you separately four little Shakespeares (in the same edition as your favourite sonnets) which you can take into the bathroom or carry in your bag or on the bus. I saw them on the bookstall in the marketplace and thought of you. I went to the furniture shop to see if there was anything interesting to buy, but there was nothing.

The epigram about the Sphinxes is by Oscar Wilde. Who gave you the quotations? I find your own sentences wiser and more pleasing.

Did you read Baldwin's speech? Goodbye Baldwin – he is finished now. At least the days of praise from all are finished; the old struggle of parties begins again.

I am rather tired and sleepy, but well and strong.

M.

1 Oscar Browning.

(41 Gordon Square), Saturday 27th October, 1923

The little big red objects[1] are such comfort, and their skin is of such well shaved order. I thank you. Oh, before, I forget, each morning when I dress before the flame I imagine you for a moment in a new blue suit. This is done, – another incident is that Vera knows very well Mr Bernard and he told about Holst (also he is her supposed conductor) and me, so she is in the course of affairs. How curious, indeed. . . .

The Nation is very good. 'How much Germany has paid'[2] makes one shiver from wantonly ineptitude of justice on the part of Entente. . . .

. . .

The husband of your sister Margaret is a handsome male man in *The Times*.[3] From now he shall have a big honour and money. It is nice for all who know him.

I touch you with good night.

L.

1   The four little books he had sent her.
2   *The Nation*, 27th October, 1923.
3   As a physiologist, A. V. Hill had just won the Nobel prize.

(41 Gordon Square), Sunday 28th October, 1923

In Vanessa's dining room new decorations to be observed, the wall paper is used in logic proportions, also on the same paper painted spots applied by Vanessa, the general effect is exotic . . .

Roger is back full of vitality, Angelica is to sing in a children's play, Grace [the maid] looks like a 'midinette' in a green silk jumper, and I like to use a toasting fork for tea.

. . . M. Stopes[1] has written a play. I wonder how dramatic critics will demonstrate their opinions. I hear that she is so much intraverted in her subject that even when conversation centres around polo, birth control is applied to it by her.

My dinner with Mrs Martineau and Vaz was pleasant, nice. She is an American, was married to an English man, and always lives here, the climate in America is for negroes and Indians, her statement. Our discussion 'a woman' . . . Mrs M. thought that women were formidable, especially in America, she seems to prefer man's country, you do too. Not a germ of accusation in me, believe me, I see facts.

European sutiation continues in ghastly form, but I will riddle you with a puzzle when you are in London.

L.

1   Marie Stopes, the pioneering exponent of birth control.

King's College, Cambridge, Sunday 28th October, 1923

My dearest, sweet one

We laid O.B. under the ground yesterday morning. It was a nice and proper ceremony. I went down into the hole to look. It is a convenient place.

After that we went into the College Congregation and discussed the New Buildings, – endlessly and much nonsense said. After lunch I was bored with it and left to go for my ride, which I enjoyed much. Peaceful was rather lively, but I could manage her. She had had her coat clipt since last week and looked smart.

. . .

Lunch with my parents; my old aunt[1] was there – the one I always flirt with – 87 years old but not at all changed the last forty years. She said that it had always been a trouble to her to be so short, and that servants would respect her more if she were taller. I asked her if it had given her much unhappiness to be short; she said yes, a good deal, particularly when young – 'I was a wretched looking little thing' she said. I told her about Cleopatra and thought of you. I asked her if she had tried high heels. She said, always but not so high now as formerly. She told how when I was very small, my nurse was careless and let me get wet and I should have had a cold, but she interfered and put things right. I kissed her and said I owed my life to her; and she kissed me and said she was very proud of me now. And then we bowed to one another – very courtly! She is very nice – even though she may be a little short.

. . .

Melchior could not come here for the weekend, but I have asked him to dinner on Tuesday.

1st V Vasiline 2nd V Vera is my solution. Do I blink right?

I feel very comfortable with inside and outside opinion in good and perfect agreement. Shall you and I begin our works on population together and at the same time?

Your
M

1 Fanny Purchase, half-sister of J. N. Keynes.

(41 Gordon Square), Monday 29th October, 1923

Your aunt is very nice, especially because she is so little, probably no more than 2 foot height. Cambridge seems in high fling of scientific and social entertainement. I add a kiss to you. That is also social.

I called Barrie, he said I should see him when [his play] *Little Minister* is delivered to the public. It is very soon the end of this week.

Dobby's Lydia is charming. She has not the hair yet, nor the last cover of the skin, she is such as her mother nursed her in her womb (dictionary also gives uterus but womb is such a beautiful word if I would be a poetess I would use it in great many works). Dobby said if he would be rich he like to buy all Derains, Picasso, Matisse and some English painters; we decided that all the dealers were working for Sam at this moment and that he did not know how to make stimulating fund out of his 50,000. You have much more adventure out of your pictures, in 10 years your Sickert or Duncan should multiply in double geometrical progression.

. . .

I am drowsy with slumber.

L.

(41 Gordon Square), Thursday 1st November, 1923

I have been dishonest! with the busman, but there is logic nowadays for every little thing. I bought ticket for Chelsea Town Hall, actually I stepped out of the bus a little later, so he inquired for a twopence, of course to my eye the distance was not so expencive, then on the strength of my character a declaration poured out of me: 'Every day I pay 3 pence for this same distance.' By that time I got off.

Later in Dobby's studio the psychology about it changed. The couple thought the busman was correct but I hold to my own, perhaps dishonest but logic. Oh, what an imposing affair Buckingham Palace Road, the left side is filled with engeniring articles, a good deal of new London came to my notice.

Back home I jumped from bus to bus experementing new roads like a butterfly from flower to flower, Sam was expecting me already. He did not purchase Gauguin, although the sensuous colours of the above mentioned painter steal a march on Sam. Cézanne makes him tipsy. The 'paganism' of Clive permeates into him. Not bad. He also met Anrep, and perhaps only their bath room will appear in mosaicks (that is the only room worth while to have in mosaicks I exclaimed), then he could read poetry to L. there even without negligée, the words might be very bad, it would not matter, their sexual powers will be at their best, on the strength of being nude.

. . . The carpet is delicious, produces an atmosphere of childhood.

L.

(41 Gordon Square), Friday 2nd November, 1923

Muriel[1] came for the Spanish. We both make progress, Muriel in preparing her lessons, and I on the contrary moving with words in speaking. I had pains in my insides, Oh I did not wish to go to pose for my other self. Sometimes even I do not object to the telephone. Later I pressed and found myself in the studio flirting with Poddle Pins [the dog]. She smiles at me and I touch her cold nose, at the same time she is a hot water bottle for my pains in the day time. . . .

. . .

The telephone was from Fay Henderson, letter this morning to go to dinner, I must use the telephone to refuse it, Hampstead is very far from London. Perhaps you have in Cambridge your obituary on B.L. [Bonar Law] I like to reread it.

I kiss you.

L.

1 Her Spanish teacher has not been identified.

(41 Gordon Square), Friday 2nd November, 1923

Dinner with Vera, Garia, Sam and Lil.[1] Psycho-analisis was the main light of the table talk, of course it was regarded by all of them as a thing of the past, non-existent to-day, Lil thought that if one wanted to make a confession there was a chance as one would do to a priest; V. said that Freud had every chance to make a success, but facts were such that all his patients did not improve their condition one iota, the only man in nerves specialist that interested her was Dr Head.[2] Have you heard of him: she said he was mad but he knew his science. I being ignorant partly silent, partly speaking with G. in Russian, such moments were not allowed by V., quite right too. Poor Sam was bored. We took the same theme into the drawing room and had coffee, then the automobile of grand style took us to Florrie . . .

Then great many of us stayed, we danced fox trot, one step, then the men did charades and one of them was Lop-o-cove-ah. So I thanked them and danced for them a little in return. It was very charming. Florrie and her friends invite me to go to Swiss for 2 weeks in January. I was quite popular, and on account of that I had to accept another party on Monday. It is very late, but I like to tell you all my happenings.

L.

Saturday. I am delighted that your feast solved problem on our poor sex, the only hope how I should know about it, would be your state of tipsiness again, when next we meet.

1 This was at the Bowen's house: 'They [the Courtaulds] seem slightly better here than in their own lair – perhaps it is the absence of cocktails.' (Bowen's diary)
2 The neurologist.

King's College, Cambridge, Friday 2nd November, 1923

My dearest poet,

(I am sure that when you make your contribution to the population, it will be a poet that comes out.)

I had a very good feast last night. Smuts was there (the feast was at his old college) and I spoke with him (nothing more to hope from that quarter). I sat between the Reader in Animal Physiology and the Professor of Zoology, and we talked all dinner about the sexual physiology of women! As we got more and more tipsy, our theories became wiser and wiser. By the end of dinner the whole matter was solved. I now have such wisdom about it as no man ever had before!

To-day I had tea with Sebastian and in a few minutes I go to dinner with Dennis.

I do work, but the cycle is still on me, so that I do not make much progress. How is yours?

I have an amusing letter from Bernard Shaw, refusing to come to our Feast. I have written this evening to Winston Churchill asking him to come.

No signs of Lil in the streets, thank God.

M.

(41 Gordon Square), Sunday 4th November, 1923

Sunday. Vera and Garia like the Angell articles as an interesting subject, so we grew to the conclusion that human beings were still savages, hatred was much more natural than love and papers like *Daily Mail* satisfied those feelings. V. likes the acquisition of G. Wallas, she has heard his lectures, also we spoke about the zionist movement, how unjust it was towards the arabs and that English government should clear out or send a pure English man but not a Jew. I agreed. . . .

As for the pictures, when V. was an expert Mr Lefevre[1] was almost on his knees before Sam and Lil, that although the gallery was filled with 'gens du monde' the required pictures were taken from the walls in front of the public, only to be put in front of Sam. Yes, money talks . . .

I came home had tea with Vasiline. We mentioned Christ, how would [he] be to meet, probably persuasive and frank, not meek but with temper, he said once to St Peter 'get thee behind me, Satan.' . . . Vasiline brought me more music to dance, and sang songs like 'My sweetie went away' and Broadway Blues. He entertained not only me, but Mrs Sneddon who is his passionate admirer; Ruby, the maid, could not keep her feet together, there was an atmosphere of musical tipsiness. . . .

Warm channels.

L.

1   The art gallery owner.

King's College, Cambridge, Sunday 4th November, 1923

Dearest L

. . . I am lunching with Winston Churchill on Tuesday to have a gossip about politics.

Very nice ride yesterday – though a bad storm of rain came on.

I have now complete copies of my book, but they are not bound yet. So I hope it will soon be published.

My cycle begins to pass away. Yours?

M

(41 Gordon Square), Thursday 8th November, 1923

Poor dear Barrie, I called him, the butler said that he was rather worn out, then last night, when the play ended, to the hospital he went, no break down, only rest.

I had a comfortable ride on the bus to Charing Cross, new gloves fitting me to perfection, if to-morrow is just as fogy as to-day I shall put them on my fingers for my exercises, so that I might prospire even there. *Evening Standard* is booming L.G., so did *Daily Mail* with Pavlova, no wonder everyone thinks of theory or relativity. Something in that . . .

$$X = -\frac{P}{2} \pm \frac{\sqrt{P^2}}{4} - 9$$

does it mean then even chicks want to live, I do not see any probability in it, but it looks fundamental.

In writing all this I am trying to acquire Cambridge 'charm'.

L.

King's College, Cambridge, Friday 9th November, 1923

Dearest Pupsik,

Lead had a good rise to-day so that half the amount belonging to you, Vanessa and Duncan got sold at the price I fixed. Your profit in papers is £39

(besides £25 profit on the half not yet sold which may rise or fall hereafter).
V's profit is the same as yours; D's twice as much. . . .

. . .

I kiss you very hard (that is not English – I have translated it from the
Russian).

M

(41 Gordon Square), Saturday 10th November, 1923

Having profits thanks to you, I will use it in the right direction, but I am not
absolutely convinced that I am an investor. I came home late from Hammer-
smith in a Rolls Royce. Dinner was delicious, cold atrocious, and discussion
what human race will be. Dobby's theory disorganised me – no love, no
sexual powers, all abstract – no men, no women – hermaphrodites, children
inoculated somewhere mechanically. I am not ready for that world and it
troubles my mind. I had a bad night, did not do my exercises, instead a sonnet
in a bath.

Sam very much flirted in the room, I ran towards and was caught by the bus
73, 'to the end' I said to the conductor. The traveling lasted hours, however, I
was in the first row with two jumpers in snow boots and I thought sometimes
of apples. Everyone had false blood of 'Flander's poppy'[1] advertised, my own
blood stimulated me more hidden with 2 jumpers. We are going to have a
hard winter, the news from Iceland the ice did not melt there last summer, it is
'en retard' and we shall bear the results, so that your kisses à la Russe shall be
received to the utmost.

L.

Before my teacher diplomée arrived I read Inflation as a Method of taxation;[2]
I understand it and it is still very absorbing, (my own views become now more
pro-inflationistic).

1   They were wearing the poppies sold on Armistice Day, 11th November, to raise
money for the war wounded.
2   This was the first section of Chapter II of his new book.

(41 Gordon Square), Sunday 11th November, 1923

Last night dinner with Florrie, Teddy [Grenfell] was inhaling something in
his bed room, a terrific cold, I dare say it always happens before the general
election.[1] F. is like you she sais anybody is better than L.G. [Lloyd George]
even B. [Baldwin]. (Vanessa repeats this opinion.) I paid a visit to Barrie he
was asleep, getting stronger, I walked on my own feet from 17 Park Lane, very
pleasant, except that everyone looks at my hoofs. Reached 46 saw Vanessa,

we gossiped, she confessing being cattish with M.H. [Mary Hutchinson] . . . Advertising in *The Nation* looks rich and pleasing to the eye. It is good to see Roger again in it.

V. calls me to dinner,[2] as usual I am late.

L.

1 A general election was to be called in December.
2 It was at No. 46, as usual.

King's College, Cambridge, Sunday 11th November, 1923

My dearest L.

Yesterday's ride was the best we have had. We were a cavalcade of six and went about 17 miles at a good pace. I was exhilarated; that and haircut makes me look young to-day, but I fear I shall be old again by to-morrow.

. . .

Last night I dined with Bonds,[1] – a big old fashioned Cambridge dinner party in honour of Graham Wallas. Dennis and Sebastian were there. Afterwards a great meeting of the Society[2] in my rooms; for there has been a new birth and the curse was read.

In a few minutes I have a large luncheon party in honour of Roger who is here. We eat

Oysters	Hock
Salmon Mayonnaise	Grand Marnier
Chicken Chaudfroid	Coffee
Damson Pie, cream	

To-night I dine with Sebastian who has Bunny staying with him.

Your loving
M (argot)

I am much occupied but I do not know with what – many small things. I am strong.

1 Henry Bond (1853–1938) was a contemporary of Maynard's father and an old friend of the Keynes family who was Master of Trinity Hall from 1919 to 1929.
2 This was the Apostles, or the Cambridge Conversazione Society, a select group which had been founded in 1820, and to which Maynard had been elected as Apostle no. 243 in 1903. It met always on a Saturday, and the initiation or 'birth' of a new member was accompanied by the reading of a secret curse.

(41 Gordon Square), Monday 12th November, 1923

I get very excited when you are telephoning from Cambridge, although my mouth is open and I want to speak, in fact everything is ready for words, yet nothing comes out. Do you ever experience such sutuations?

I am so lazy like you to newspapers, sometimes I plunge into a Russian journalistic literature, and no energy for anything else, except perhaps for gossip . . . Did you happen to read about serval cat that damaged a race horse trainer in Café Royal, well I myself took a picture with that creature in Hyde Park, thank God he did not bite me!

Vera has seen 'Our betters',[1] Lady Cunard and Selfridges are unmistakable, he calls her 'girlie' she sais with disdain 'do not call me girlie'. He sais 'I can't help I *must* call you girlie' etc. You are very much occupied, I sympathyse, and so am I in my womanly way.

Your smiling
L (esbia)

1 *Our Betters*, a satirical comedy of English upper-class life by Somerset Maugham.

(41 Gordon Square), Thursday 15th November, 1923

Leaving the station 2 busses had me on the top at their disposal. Reaching Strand (there is a church) I looked up and saw innumerable birds comforting themselves around the tower, never touching the cross. Were they Christians, or there exists a mathematical law about their not climbing up to it? London at 5 o'clock tea time is so engaging to look down from the bus.

After 5 I reached Thérèse. She was so greeting. Sickert was occupied with a business engagement, I took your suggestion and next Thursday we shall go out, where it is of no importance. I feel very lazy after spending 1 hour walking in my new, new dress, I tried so many different coiffures, the best seems an old fashioned one, Alfred de Musset time perhaps, where the knot of hair lies very low on the neck, and well, there is a scent of virginity around such a frame.

Enjoy the feast to the utmost, and have less than 3 memorandums a day if possible.

L.

(41 Gordon Square), Friday 16th November, 1923

Your mother is a nice woman.[1] You have her eyes and searching mind. I like to look at her. I was excited so I spoke too quickly or forgot the words; for instance I did not know for a while how is called a person who catches fish. She kissed me before going away.

At last I have become clever in the atmosphere of busses. From Chelsea to St John's Wood is not a joke, of course the bus men were such pleasant fellows this time; I used their direction.

. . .

I look in this new dress a woman of culture and taste, perhaps a bit of a snubnosed snob. I have no chemise, I touch your bosom without a shirt.

L.

1 She and Lydia had met, evidently for the first time, at the Hills' house in Highgate. Lydia's report on the occasion crossed Maynard's enquiry about it – see next letter.

Kings College, Cambridge, Friday 16th November, 1923

Oh! I'm so sleepy. We had a very good feast yesterday and I stayed up until 3 o'clock. After dinner I was told that if I would stand for Parliament for the University,[1] the Conservatives would support me as well as the Liberals! But I resist the flattery.

To-day I have written the three memoranda.

How was tea to-day at Margaret's?

Good night

M

1 It was not until after the second world war that university seats were abolished.

(41 Gordon Square), Saturday 17th November, 1923

Last night dinner consisted of us 4 . . . Teddy was my partner, Florrie had M. Norman.[1] T. and I immediately plunged into the historical gossip of the moment – Free Trade.

T. by now sides with the government, his idea is that 80 years of Free trade policy did not improve the situation in England although in theory he agrees, and also he thought the young school of economists he mentioned you might have the same idea. . . . M. Norman looks odd, I couldn't make out the shape of his mind, rather quiet, call it curious if you will. As to his age, T. looked a very young man in comparison. About 10½ they went to a political party to meet the Prime Minister again! Before going T. and M.N. advised me to get more dresses at Lafayette, as the tax was soon to be established on imports, I said I thought more of apples than of dresses, and such were not to be taxed at all.

My luxurious attire was exhibited to Vanessa and Duncan, an Austrian artist happened to be there, who holds the same views as yours, that is to look at a new person's hands at once, also teeth establishes the fact if they are false or not. Van. notices the color of the eyes, Duncan notices before he meets someone by description, I had to notice a pair of legs, but I really look in the face altogether. I do not know the cause, but sleep did not come to me for long time, my exercises stood motioneless as consequences this morning.

To-morrow Dobby's birth day that is the meaning of the invitation. I am asked to get tipsy . . . The [Spanish] lesson ended, all departed, except Vaz. who quite ill with poisons in his stomach. He looked so sad and asked why do I never go to his place for a cup of tea after Dobby, so near too. In the end I was frank: 'I do not want to encourage your feelings, you having a complex about your place.' The answer was that he reconciled himself with me, he sees in me a friend of his soul and mind, and if I came in, tea time, it might make him only sleep better at night, he will never insist any more, but he hoped I sometime, from my own free will, will knock at his door, tea time. Poor B. he looked so sad, I promised that I might.

The Nation this week as ever has good qualities . . .

The invitation to you for the Parlament with both parties as a support to get in, is hard to resist and also why? One more thing to do, can it matter to you? It all leads to be amused in the end. Perhaps I am in bad taste, but to-night I vote for Parlament.

L.

1 Montague Norman was Governor of the Bank of England.

(41 Gordon Square), Sunday 18th November, 1923

The day was so refreshing in the early morning, I was repeating 'a man of 68' and not in a bath, there was no time to lose, 10 minutes to 1, Vera asked me to be punctual at 1, so taxi was the expression of my speediness; I had 2 fiancées: the Arab and Peter Murphy of London . . . We went upstairs, the steam heat pipes do impress me in winter time, in that sense I am pro Vera at the moment. With the Arab, his name is Musa, I spoke about the Dead sea, not to be drowned at all in that particular part of the world, and how Jordan stands 400 metres below the sea and how great charm proclaims in the East, while P.M. from the West was singing, and quite well too, 'he may be your man, but he comes to see me sometimes.'

. . .

Why did you take out 'brilliant' and put 'vital', it should be both in the advertising. This is in the *Observer*.[1] When I see it my chest grows hollow, it is an emotion. I go to Dobbies but I would like to contemplate instead.

L.

1 An advertisement for his forthcoming book.

King's College, Cambridge, Sunday 18th November, 1923

My dearest L

While I was in my bath this morning I had such a strong conviction that it was a mistake to publish my book during the General Election, that as soon as I was dry enough I got on to the trunk telephone and put everything off for three weeks, i.e. until Dec. 11. Is it wise?

I agree with you about my *Nation* article this week. It is very bad, – a halting affair. I have no pride in it.

I calm down now and am only a little flustered. The arrears are not so big. But I have not yet begun to write the articles for the next *Nation*.

Friday was the 70th birthday of the Vice Provost. We drank his health with our port and played rummy afterwards. I think that the Provost is very ill – he looks as though he dies.[1]

A nice ride yesterday.

Since I wrote this, I have been home[2] to lunch. Your tea at Margaret's seems to have happened happily.

Lytton is here this week.

This time I don't come to London until Tuesday afternoon.

I feel your warmth

M

1 Provost Durnford survived until 1926.
2 The house where he was born (6 Harvey Road) was still 'home' to him.

(41 Gordon Square), Monday 19th November, 1923

I had a call from Florrie to come to tea because she had a letter from Polunins from Monte Carlo with the announcement from Serge[1] that he is very willing to come to London with a small price; as there is going to happen an Empire Exhibition,[2] he will produce English ballets and altogether he is convinced of big success. He wants again Florrie to be second Lady Cunard! F. lunched with Vera and, as Florrie is not to subsidise the ballet, Vera took the announcement to their favorite agents, as I go to Vera very soon for dinner[3] I shall hear more about it. What Serge needs is a capital, that is clear, but there are possibilities.

Your conviction about the book is not bad at all, although the general elections look very quiet in the newspapers, and so not occupy extra space.

Last night at Dobbies very good dinner . . . Mr Mayer said that you were remarkable in mathematics and helped him to make problems. You probably do not remember, as it is much later than when you were baptised.[4] I returned about 1, and to-day I am so worn out, no blood at all, all the glands seem to be out of relation with one another; I feel even this letter is an anaemic one.

With regrets.
L.

1 Diaghilev.
2 The British Empire Exhibition at Wembley.
3 This was the night on which she kept Vera up until almost midnight discussing whether Maynard was to marry her or not.
4 Which he claimed to remember.

(41 Gordon Square), Thursday 22nd November, 1923

. . . Dobby next week is going to Paris, so Delia and I are going to entertain ourselves with the Turkish baths, the last time I was dissappointed but with another person I might see new possibilities instead of limitations.

'If you hurry you will make people laugh', the word 'reform' frightens a Russian liberal, he prefers a regulation, a reasonableness and solidness. On the whole a small fish better than a big black beetle is the manifesto of these kind of politicks in the Russian literature that happened 30 years ago. I don't approve. Free trade, when you discuss it, is much much more enlightening.

. . .

Your dog.
L.

King's College, Cambridge, Friday 23rd November, 1923

My dearest L,

It has been rather an idle, ruminating day. I had no engagements . . . In the afternoon I walked in the streets – first to the bookstall in the market place where I bought two books, then to the old curiosity shop where I bought some objects which might save you trouble in giving Christmas presents to friends; then to my haberdashers where I got two new ties *and* a jumper equal in brilliance (almost) to yours, – the undergraduates this term outjump themselves.

. . .

I feel I should like to read books quietly and write nothing for some long time.

I ride to-morrow with Dennis.

I am fond of you.

M

(41 Gordon Square), Saturday 24th November, 1923

Free trade is admirable.[1] So decisively clear. Protection as a cure for unemployment! *c'a n'existe pas!* When you speak about our imports as our incomes etc. it seems to me a suicide not to trade free. Life without incomes is deplorable. Moraly Free trade is peace and poetically 'it is better to bless than to curse.' Posessing Free trade in my bones I offered yours to Mrs Sneddon and her disciples. I am glad it is to be distributed so that even those who can't afford to buy *The Nation* will know the truth. James Strachey and Marjorie [Strachey] liked it very much.

. . . Marjorie political gossip about Paisley.[2] Mr Asquith might get into a 3 $\triangle$ fight, will lose, because men with money try to put L.G. [Lloyd George] in bigger power. Dirty games politics.

I thank you for curiosity Christmas ideas, so many yawns are spared! *Oh!* I must tell you the price of myself.[3] I feel uneazy. It is expensive in comparison with pictures. £155 or £160. Why did you order me? *Oh!*

Dobby is going to present me with a lovely small torso, I did not want it, but in the end I chose the one I liked the best and D. is going to make it in bronze.

Monday, Delia and I are undertaking a journey to the Galerie Lafayette, to buy a coat for her, on the strength of yours and Lil's artistic purchases . . .

Dearest Maynarochka good night.

1 'Free Trade' by J. M. Keynes, *The Nation*, 24th November, 1923.
2 Asquith's parliamentary seat, which he was to retain with a small majority.
3 Dobson's sculpture.

(41 Gordon Square), Sunday 25th November, 1923

North Pole is ascending on us. I was not able to part from my chair for a moment, and letting water out seems such an untimely affair. I live with the fire as never before, reading *Monetary Reform*. I arrive to capital levy and ended the chapter on the sitiation in France. I like to read financial literature with taste. Vaz. came later, very nice conversation, music, sang 'Come away death.'

An exciting call from Vera, agents cannot produce any formula with garantie for big Serge (you and I chuckle, we knew it is difficult). Vera being positive wants to attract Lord Rothermere. (When she mentioned his name I uttered unwisely 'you want him to advertise your opera.' She scorned such suggestion, she does not need any help from anyone, but she herself wishes to help Serge.) . . .

Alix and James came in the evening, Karin and Adrian [Stephen] fluctuate in conversation. Karin wants affairs phisically speaking, Adrian is to live in

Brunswick Square, up till now they still spend the day together in phycho analisis. In the evening they go to cinema.

It is well that you acquired new jumpers, wear them in the day time, but in your sleep do not put many covers, Vaz. tells me it is not healthy for men, I myself have innumerable covers, the fact explains itself, I am a woman.

L.

King's College, Cambridge, Sunday 25th November, 1923

My dearest L

Last night I went to a very big feast at St Catharine's College – their 450th commemoration, and got very tipsy on most delicious wine along with Bishops and Masters of College. We sat at the table three hours . . .

Since yesterday morning I have had a rheumatism in my shoulder and want your rubbing for it very much. This afternoon I went to tea with my mother and had a very long rub.

Our ride yesterday was in thick mist but we galloped through it pleasantly – quite a long way.

. . .

Your
M

King's College, Cambridge, Monday 26th November, 1923

My dearest, sweetest L

I always enjoy Monday mornings – to get two letters from you in one envelope. I find them on the table when I come back from the University Council. Oh, what a Jew Vera is with her tirelessness! I see why you and she get on together. You are so very uncircumcised, that the two of you make a good average and are equal when you are added up to two Christians!

Duncan has gone back. I think, now, that he will try not to have too much work to do about the Greek Play.[1] We want to persuade Sheppard to take the big part in the play *himself*. Sheppard is very well again and in quiet nerves.

Wherever one or two of Bloomsbury are gathered together, I find that they gossip about Adrian and Karin – it is the best subject of conversation for a long time.

I am not surprised but rather relieved about Dobbie's price. I thought it would certainly be as much as that and feared that it might be more.

I wear my jumper all the day – sometimes inside and sometimes outside. But not at night – so I am still a man. The colour of the jumper is approved by Duncan.

131

My party last night was quiet but nice.

Unless I telegraph differently, do not expect me to-morrow until after 11 o'clock.

With many vigorous kisses

M

I have a letter from the sister of Leo Myers asking me to a dinner, but I can't go. Also several letters asking me to make General Election speeches about Free Trade – I don't know what to do about these.

1   *The Birds* by Aristophanes.

(41 Gordon Square), Friday 30th November, 1923

The first rate impression of to-day happened gloriously at Dobby's – Lil loved the wise women with hands on their cheeks carved in yellow stone. Lil was penetrated from head to foot. Lil could not concentrate on anything else. Lil loved and paid for it. (250 pounds)

Of course I could not pose, I spoke about 'art' except with Delia and Poddle Pins at intervals. In Lil-Sam's taxi I gave a kiss to Lil in appreciation of her direct communications with art. My 'Lidia' was thought to be the best portrait they ever laid eyes on. The active energy of Dobby swayed them through and through. My tête a tête with Sam was agreable enough, we have always something to say to one another from camels to politics or vice versa. Sam is a protectionist, conservative, likes to give a chance to Baldwin but never to L.G. or Mr Asquith . . .

L.

King's College, Cambridge, Friday 30th November, 1923

Dearest Dog

I went in after a long sitting with La Rees [his secretary] and found Carrington disconsolately waiting. Poor thing! How long did she wait while you bussed round the world? When I got to my tailors, I had to wait a long time to be fitted on. They replied to my complaints that I was in a hurry and had to catch a train, that it was always so and that the customers waited in queues all day long. Did you ever hear of such a thing at a dressmaker's? However I was done in the end; but the suit can't possibly be ready for my electioneering. That may be a good thing; I think it is better to be shabby than smart when one speaks to the electors. I find that my matinée at Barrow is for women only! So will you please write me my speech?

132

I enclose a review of my new book which has come out too soon. Will you keep it for me?

Is Florrie's puppet party on the 11th or 12th? It is dangerous that I haven't got it down yet on my tablet. I have another invitation for one of those days. So will you remind me which day it is?

I have spent to-day on odds and ends, – mostly letters etc. Having no book or article to write, I feel rather pleasantly and as though having leisure although busy.

Who was it said that 'a small fish is better than a big black beetle'?

I come up late on Sunday, after having dinner here, reaching Gordon Square at 10.0. I shall not expect you until much later than that. Will you come into 46 when you get back from Lil's party?

Is this letter written so that I can read the handwriting easily?

M

It freezes too hard for the horses – so there will be no riding to-morrow.

(41 Gordon Square), Monday 3rd December, 1923

By now I know you have all your pains gone from your back and everywhere. First performance [election speech] is over, from now on you will amuse *yourself* in changing your speeches each time. Dobby is well acquainted with Barrow, flappers[1] used to accompany him, but your audiences shall have more inteligence in listening to you, being of all ages.

Sickert and Thérèse took me to the rehearsal of the puppets. Both were charming. I saw again the little fawn I loved so well last time. He is not changed, jumps better than ever and runs on his hoofs as I on my toes. We feel near to each other. The second part of the body is more alert than the cerebral in both of us. I liked the sailor of olden times with a beard and a pig tail, a big black hat, and striped trousers, so quaint!

W.S. [Sickert] was in a good mood saying that it was very important for Dobson to do me well, because already 3 English painters ruined their reputation (Vanessa, Roger, Duncan) and that is why he does not show his work of me, that I was artist's doom and tomb. When we arrived he said he would one day like to do a drawing of me. On the door step we met Roger; Sickert and Roger such darlings when they are together. I have a book on Spain, it looks out with good taste, it must be from you, I thank you very much, you are very nice.

Crosses for each speech and sound sleep in new places.

L.

1 Rather dated slang for girls who were not quite grown up, with implications of flightiness or lack of decorum.

(41 Gordon Square), Tuesday 4th December, 1923

I feel as if you are abroad, and Lancashire became Europe for me. *The Star* announces on its borders 'Free trade victory in sight', 'Woman's majority for Liberalism.' Sometimes impossible becomes possible, it stands some reason for all your efforts in it.

Florrie came to lunch, I gave handkerchiefs instead of napkins. She is pleased and so am I. Teddy speaks to-night in Hackney, must be a hole with rowdy crowds, so Florrie thinks. We went into shops, I agreed, but that I should be allowed to yawn as much as I desire. That is my 'metier' in the shops. After that I walked myself on the streets to choose for Christmas and finished my excursions with buying a Russian book for myself 10 shillings, one of the aforisms 'if you want to be beatiful be a guardsman', also 'better say a little but well' that has a big relation to your economic skill in speeches.

This morning about 12, right in the midst of my labour, Margaret [Keynes] came in, so I stopped and asked her to sit in a big chair. She wanted me to go with her to visit her very sick brother, and I shall do so any afternoon but never in the morning. Friday is arranged for it. Tonight Vaz. comes. I have new numbers of Mozart. I want him to play, so I invited him from the telephone but I am very tired.

Gobbles of peaceful order to you.

L.

Hôtel Métropole, Blackpool, Tuesday 4th December, 1923

My dearest L.

It was not so bad last night. My voice was not good and I was criticised for speaking too fast (which I always do); but they were interested, I think, and there was good applause. It was the biggest audience I've ever spoken to – about 3000. Afterwards I motored to a small meeting in a small town. That was great fun. I was very late and they had already been sitting there about 2½ hours before I came, but they were gay and good tempered. Afterwards I had tea and talked to the lively liberal spirits in a Com room exactly like the scene in '*What Every Woman Knows*'.[1] I feel very democratic. I like the people here.* They are serious and intelligent – quite a different type from London working classes. The interest they take in politics is extraordinary; and the more serious the speech is, the better they seem to like it. The Election is a big education for them; and I feel like a preacher – half enjoying it. If only my voice was different, I'd be in danger of enjoying it too much.

To-night I appear here in the Opera House; – two houses! As soon as I have

* I mean Black*burn*

made the speech, they go away and another audience comes in and I have to make the same speech again! Even that isn't enough and there are two over-flow houses as well.

The candidate has come in to talk – so I must stop.

Plenty of kisses
M

1   The play by J. M. Barrie.

(41 Gordon Square), Wednesday 5th December, 1923

What charming experiences you are having. I have an impression that Liberals, where you stimulate them, are not weak, if they flock by such thousands, *tant mieux* . . .

. . . Back to Dobby sat without clothes almost the last time (to-morrow posing visits end). Florrie and Vera came in. Altogether enchanted, Vera said she did not expect a modern artist could do a portrait with resemblance to the person in question (as bad as Sickert), but for this work she poured all her enthusiasm. Florrie loved also. Both Dobbys were taken with crescendo about Vera's personality and brains, Florrie they thought an English beauty with charm. I sat for 2 solid hours, finished by having tea, when that rascal Holroyd Reece with his wife (not much either) arrived. Gave me an invitation to the party and also *to you*. I became marble and advised him to write his proposal when you are in question. Rascal even in invitations.

Palpitations to you.
L.

Furness Abbey Hotel, Furness Abbey, Lancashire,
Wednesday 5th December, 1923

My dearest L,

I did not like so well the atmosphere of last night's meeting at Blackpool, and I hated the sound of my own ugly voice more than ever. It was much more enthusiastic than Blackburn but not so serious. The interest of the public is remarkable. I have never seen a theatre so packed (the whole of the stage behind me was full of people as well as the auditorium crammed to the roof, and they stood in queues to get in an hour before the doors were opened). However they liked arguments here too, and one speaker who explained very well how exports pay for imports got a round of applause simply for the clearness of the argument.

135

At the railway station this morning I was recognised by the railway officials who had all been at the meeting. The station master and the inspector came to the door of my carriage for a chat, and when the train started the porters jumped on to the steps to wish me good luck and to shout that 'All our fellows are going to vote right'. I think the Liberals will most certainly win this seat[1].

My speeches are reported shortly in the *Manchester Guardian* and at length in the local papers.

I am staying here at a very comfortable Hotel halfway between the two towns I speak in, – it is really a tourist hotel with the ruins of a big abbey in the garden. I like the people in Barrow but they have not much chance. No liberal has ever been elected here. The best they can do is to take enough votes from the Conservative to get the Labour man in.

This afternoon I spoke to about 100 women and babies. One of the smallest babies in the front row thought clapping a very good idea and clapped all the time!

My big meetings are to-night – one in Barrow and one in Dalton. Then, thank God, it is all over and I am back to Cambridge.

I found two miele letters from you waiting for me here.

My digestion improves and I sleep better (even in strange beds) each day. I am very sleepy now! but must think about my speech.

My dear love

M

1   His predictions were correct. Barrow-in-Furness was won by the Conservative and Blackpool by the Liberal Candidate.

(41 Gordon Square), Thursday 6th December, 1923

Oh, dear Lord God!. . . the fog is just as tremendous as one Sunday when I was a 'Sleeping Princess'. I am relieved that the elections are over, and although I dislike politicks I shall look into the newspapers at once to-morrow. To-night I only know that out of 4 places, 1 gain for Liberal and 1 for Labour, not bad! I like your subtlety about the baby who applauds unconsciously 'Free Trade'. You seem to come out of the sitiation with +.

I sat last time for Dobby and Lydia is built and achieved, rather sad.

Roger has been to see it, no one can say more than he when enthousiastic, Dobby is pleased with his opinion.

. . .

Last night I went to 46, Lady Harland [the butler's wife] is back, Vanessa and Duncan prepare the exhibition, my tongue was very loose, when I arrived home I could not sleep till 3 o'clock, no exercises this morning, wicked indeed but fond of you.

L.

(41 Gordon Square), Friday 7th December, 1923

I chucle concervators are not in the lime-light,[1] Labor and Liberals can make a good combination, also Liberals can make a combination with Concervators, at present they, the Liberals, are quite a 'big fish'. Your Lancashire scored except Barrow and if Barrow did combine with Labour, perhaps for the next election, it is not long to await. Poor Cambridge.

I am so very busy, 7.30 dinner at Sangers, although I posess that invisible scratching paper, yet I promised another invitation to Mayers, but I must go to Sangers. I feasted the victory with washing my head and nails, oh, it is late! . . .

Last night when Lib. and Lab. gains were announced I applauded, did not for Conservative, then to excuse my conduct I said I did not care at all for politics, but I do get emotions when in the theatre. Lil's brother, Mr Kelsey, was troubled by my outlook! Oh, I am late, I forget where Chelsea is since I am not posing. With stimulations of the general election results I smile and touch you.

L.

1 The Conservatives won an overall minority (258) of seats; Labour won 191 and Liberals 159 seats.

King's College, Cambridge, Friday 7th December, 1923

My dearest L

Yesterday was a lovely day – I spent eight hours sitting in a nice warm railway carriage reading newspapers. I got back here just in time for our big Feast, – the Founder's Day Feast which was very pleasant. Lytton came as my guest and is still staying here.

Of the five candidates for whom I spoke three have been elected, one of the other two did well and one badly. The results were what I expected from what I saw when I was there. It's an extraordinary political situation now! I can't imagine what sort of a government the next one can be.

. . .

Here is an article by Wells in which I come in, very flattering but absurd!

. . .

You mustn't write [letter of 5th December]: 'I sat for 2 solid hours'. That's common English, but not pure Lydian language! I agree with your treatment of Holroyd Reece. Certainly I shall not accept such an invitation.

Everyone here talks politics, even those who never think of them in the ordinary way.

I am sleepy. I have not had my quiet 9 hours in bed any day this week. But I sleep to-night.

Warm sleepy kisses

M

(41 Gordon Square), Saturday 8th December, 1923

Yesterday I have been visiting the intelectuals of Oakley street [Sangers], with rain over my newly washed head I ran from [bus] 73 to 61 and then 'glory be to the Lord God' to 58[1] . . . Labor's results were estimated with great joy by the host, so I suggested possible alliance between the Lib. and Lab.:[2] the mixture did not work, so we passed to your new book. Hawtrey and I were the stabilisators, Sanger preferred to be in opposition (in conversation it is interesting to disagree). I told them that I reached the 'Quantity Theory of Money' moment and could not continue and yet would not follow your suggestion that all unintelectual readers may close their eyes for this especial chapter. I did not tell them, but I feel that if I escape this chapter I am not an advanced person. How painful would to become such!

. . .

Ask Lytton if it is true that Viola Tree asked him at one of the parties he visits while in London, 'Mr Strachey what do you do with your beard when you go to bed?' Lytton 'Why don't you come and see?' What could he do if she would?

You are described by Wells as one of the few 'imaginative great', it is not 'absurd', but tremendous. I am aware of it! I on the contrary so useless.

L.

1 Many London buses, including the 73, follow the same routes today.
2 Which is what occurred.

(41 Gordon Square), Sunday 9th December, 1923

I have been studying with Vaz. 'J'ai deux amants', although in French yet I do not object, any person can follow the meaning, also suitable for my comedy expressions. Vaz. sang old Irish songs, that was pure matter, still I have a feeling of decay in me for a few days . . .

Is R. MacDonald to be Prime Minister, or Mr Asquith will survive; both are not of an invigorating character . . . Vaz. voted for Lib, but Mrs Martineau for Cons, Vera, Dun, Roger and John Strachey are using their speed for the 11th. Van. said you married Hatrey [R. G. Hawtrey] with one of the Jelly's[1] sisters but Duncan married Mr Fakire with another, but you did more, you almost put to bed Saxon [Sidney-Turner] and Barbara [Bagenal], why are you such an expert in love pranks?

. . .

I posess enormous gossips in my bosom, I cannot stretch it out on the paper, no fluctuations of energy, but double elements of warmth to you.

L.

1   The Hungarian sisters Jelly and Adela d'Aryani, who were the violinist nieces of the great violinist Joachim. Jelly, who was a pupil of his, had a distinguished career. Adela, less well-known, did indeed marry a Mr Fakire.

King's College, Cambridge, Sunday 9th December, 1923

Dearest L

There is a good deal of end-of-term gaiety going on. Last night Lytton and I went to a mock musical comedy (written by Dennis Robertson) given by the undergraduates. To-day I have been to a large luncheon party of Dadie's, and to-night I give a dinner party. Then to-morrow everything is over. I shall arrive in London some time between tea and dinner.

. . .

Politics is a big confusion. I want to get to London and hear the gossip. Liberals must move towards Labour and not in the other direction.

. . .

I have an invitation from Mrs Myers [wife of Leo] to dinner on Decr 18. I am not replying until I see you. Are you going?

M.

King's College, Cambridge, Sunday 9th December, 1923

I have sold all your lead. Your profit is £106.16.4 which you can have in papers when you want.

M

Apart from this you had £96.10 left; so, now you have altogether £203.6.4.

Letters from
13th January 1924 to 14th March 1924

On 24th December Maynard had written to his mother [King's Archives] saying that he and Lydia had been to the Hills' house in Highgate the night before; he also discussed the legal position over the divorce, making it clear that even if Lydia had any doubts he had not. On Christmas Day Maynard and Lydia went on a brief visit to France. Maynard returned to Cambridge in early January where he continued to write articles for the Nation *and to pursue his hobby of Babylonian and Greek weights; on 18th January he even said he was 'feeling rather leisurely', and he was continuing his afternoon rides. Although Lydia was unemployed she was preparing her performances at the Coliseum for a fortnight from 31st March, and her forthcoming Parisian season at la Cigale which, at the invitation of Massine, was under discussion. Lydia's friendship with Maynard's sister deepened; and on 21st February Lydia and Maynard's mother 'unloaded our feelings for you and for each other in relation of your being our entire idol.' Lawyers were at work on Lydia's divorce papers and sent for her trunk. She went to Cambridge for the weekend on 8th March to see* The Duchess of Malfi.

(41 Gordon Square), Sunday 13th January, 1924

Perhaps I take away the time for you but the gossip spins out of me. Roger appeared to be very well indeed, surrounded by 3 sympathetic observers in the world of pictures (his latest creations). I even encourage him for a near future exhibition, but as I can't like every picture of his so it comes as a result to a 'fair', very nice, and next to not so nice 'unfair'. In the drawing room the pleasant anthracite stove added to our complete accord in food and conversation. Food = Christmas pudding, heavenly carrots and that good looking bright red meat which you also had it in your house a few 24 years ago. Conversation = we jumped with devastation on Holroyd Reece, pinched Lady Colefax habits of 'snobism' and laughed without doubt when Mrs McCalum gave the explanation of 'concrete' 'abstract' by a little boy, as example he said: 'concrete' my drawers, 'abstract' yours, miss.

Mrs McCalum[1] is a charming woman, very witty, should be Mme Recamier of to-day. Soon after the Chinese Bloomsbury, Mr Waley and Miss de Zoete, with pictures by a Russian woman for an opinion from Roger (the matter was soon cleared by R. disinteressness in the objects), I and de Zoete became ardent speakers discussing our old friend Vera, although despising Vera's financial dealings with the Stage society. She touched me by being really very fond of her, so I am moving in a direction of a tea party 'en trois'.

Bus 29 drove me to Tottenham Court Road, further 19 drove me to Berkeley Square and to Miss Naylor, Vaz. was there, so we were not intimate.

I cast a 'good night' nod to you.

L.

1   Mrs McCalum has not been identified.

(41 Gordon Square), Monday 14th January, 1924

Massine came in to tell more about his engagement, not in March nor in the opera, but in May in a theatre of a not 'music hall order'. The season [in Paris] is to be 4 weeks, 3 weeks rehearsing. I then confessed my Coliseum,[1] we agreed that 2 weeks would do. By his description 3 new ballets to be given, his friends' associators shall have control over everything, he (Massine) employs his power only as a *maitre de ballet*. One could not think of big salaries as it is not an American venture. He excited me speaking of new channels in choreography (Mrs Sneddon after thought I was ill). All that is best in painting and music shall unite. As intentions they sound well.

Tea with Vera and Garia. My Coliseum engagement explained like this, 'Maynard's last book very good indeed, therefore your engagement from Sir Oswald. A splendid achievement by Maynard.' I also agree in this opinion.

As for Serge and Pat [Dolin], dangerous for Serge to be in sexual relations with a Britt. Shadow of Oscar Wilde. I return to Massine, now it is for me to say yes even *en principe*. I promised to do it in 2–3 days. He especially asked not to mention to Monte Carlo friends, as the influence from there might make difficulties. Big Serge must look enormous to Massine.

Vaz. called me, very depressed with life could he not come for an hour. I said yes, I shall try the new songs you bought, and await your miely return to-morrow.

L.

1   Her engagement was not until 31st March.

(41 Gordon Square), Tuesday 15th January, 1924

N 9 [bus] danced according to my thoughts at eaze, I noticed even noble names of shops like Pitt and Scott, then on Piccadilly I met the intricate 44; in Covent Garden section I looked down at one of my innumerable acquaintances, but he was 'roughing it out' with another man. All the time I hold very tight the 5 pounds in the bag, it is miserable even to lose coppers. We also associate the coppers with conscience, if I want to accuse someone of a bad action my phrase would be 'do you not have conscience even for a copper?' The tradition of a bronze age I suppose.

. . . When you go to the East do you carry a small carpet? if so I like to become such an object for you.

L.

(41 Gordon Square), Thursday 17th January, 1924

Oh what a disgraseful day, all the couples in my house are 'in', I creeped out at 5, sent a registered letter to my brother and asked him if he would like to have now a pair of woolen pyjamas and a sturdy pair of boots in my preservation. Last night [in a dream] my sister was introduced to you. She was very pretty with white ballet skirts. I wore a long stately Greek dress. We loved one another very much, she gave you a kiss on a forehead, with my aproval. I reread Vera's letters to you and Diaghilev about *Masquerade*, it is quite nice and sensible, but at those moments our bloods fluctuated differently, her greatest point seemed to establish Lydia with Coliseum, which was really for herself, but it was well covered. . . .

. . .

This is the picture of Sam's sister. When she holidays with her friend in hotels, the maid announces 'the gentelman's bath is ready.' Mary called me up and left her telephone, another social intercourse with females?

. . .

Duncan came and asked to go 46 to see Dobbies, I have so many duties to fulfill, in tremendous haste your fingus[?].

L.

King's College, Cambridge, Thursday 17th January, 1924

My dearest poet,

You were better occupied on your intricate buses than I was, reading Elizabeth in the train.[1] I read on and on most carefully without being able to discover which of the characters was supposed to be me! Toby reminded me a little of Dadie; and I didn't feel inclined to wear as my dress either Christopher or Cyril. Anyway, I found the dialogue extraordinarily tiresome and empty; and there is more literature in your last night's letter than in that whole concoction.

Here is some science for the poet! I offer her a big prize if she can do it *without help* before next Tuesday.

Finance for the Nursery
This little problem is very artless. Said one boy to another, 'Give me one of your pennies; then I shall have twice as many as you.' But the other declined. 'Give me one of yours,' he countered, 'then we shall each have the same number.' The question, of course, is how many pennies each boy had at the start.

It is snowing this morning and rather miserable; so I sit quietly in my room doing odds and ends.

M

1   A novel by Elizabeth Bibesco, *The Fir and the Palm*, 1924.

(41 Gordon Square), Friday 18th January, 1924

A desillusion from Vladimiroff this evening, otherwise from $1\frac{1}{2}$ I have been on speaking terms to the utmost, first with Berta & Co. then the Dobbies. . . . Berta discussed Elizabeth's book, her praize was not abundant; I adored your criticism. This morning holy oil was in my bosom! After Lunch Berta proceeded to a professor who is to tell her for how many thousands of centuries our bones stay as they are, not developing any more. I do not think he will be able to, but you will let *me* know, please. I am also curious . . . When Berta rode me to Chelsea I found Delia packing Dobbies, taking things wisely more or less, only her heart is not of Dobby's stone, Poor Delia![1] We were true friends to each other and I left her with more peace in myself. Dobby wishes to tell you that in 3 weeks the other Lydia shall reach you through Turner, and also he has ordered another cast that will stay for his exhibition, and I understand that no one can order without your and his accord about it.
. . .
Is my financial concoction correct?

the smaller boy had   5   Pennies
the bigger   3

if it is not so, you should grow indiferent to me as it is not possible 'to put to the same harness a horse and a hind.'

L.

1   She was separating from her husband.

143

King's College, Cambridge, Friday 18th January, 1924

My dearest L

I feel little better than a lunatic this evening. It is just like three years ago – the same thing has happened. Feeling rather leisurely, I returned to my old essay on Babylonian and Greek weights.[1] It is purely absurd and quite useless. But just as before, I became absorbed in it to the point of frenzy. Last night I went on working at it up to 2 o'clock; and to-day I went on continuously from the time I got up until dinner time. Extraordinary! Anyone else would think the subject very dull. Some charm must have been cast on it by a Babylonian magician. The result is I feel quite mad and silly.

. . .

Yes – I think Vladimiroff's telegram reasonable.
To-morrow I ride and hope to get the Babylonians out of my head.

With a lunatic kiss and a wild eye
M

1 See Chapter 2, *Collected Writings*, Vol. XXVIII.

(41 Gordon Square), Saturday 19th January, 1924

I am in full sympathy with your Babilonian madness – it is a treasure of your intelectual spirit, I have such an affection for you in that forme. The *Nation* looks 'steady' this week. La reclame for your book holds the eye with an effect . . .

Vaz. gave his recital – in the church. Oh what dried boned spinsters for an audience, although the organ is the latest craze in Paris I prefer piano. Poor Vaz. his hand was damaged. The window lost control while he was closing it and for 4 minutes he suffered immensely.

Handel's menuet I like to dance, but there is a nessessity for a very good violin.

. . .

L.

(41 Gordon Square), Sunday 20th January, 1924

The most important Massine's declaration of todays happenings: the theatre [in Paris] Mogador or la Cigale, the leading persons the Count and Mme La Comptesse Etienne de Beaumont, who connect themselves with other friends and business peoples into an association, he is not to do any contracts, but I should tell the price through you, now it comes out that *en principe* I do agree. He is terrified of Diaghilev.

. . .

His [Massine's] wife Vera came back. I asked him if they were in a state of partition. He seemed not to be wanting in the explanation of a domestic drama. Very soon he thinks he will go to Paris, so he wants to study the new mimic with me before. He asked who is my partner, I said Gavriloff or Vladimiroff. He advised me to take one of Diaghilev's troupe, with an 'arriere pensee' most certainly. Discussing my two brothers (very difficult for him to get male dancers), would I not write if my little brother and 5 others not too big in height, if they would consent to come over, 1,500 fr. each a month, journey paid. I said I would. Also if the season proves succesful he likes to have an engagement at the Coliseum after, with one of the new ballets. Barrie tells me on telephone that Massine coached Gladys Cooper's 'Peter' [*Peter Pan*] in all her movements, especially on the wires! He is so very occupied with the rehearsals, that I can't ever see him, now it is *Alice sit by the Fire*, but he is well and was expecting Nicholas to-night.

My 2 admiratrices came in yesterday, they thought I should say 'yes' to Massine, but not to build up the illusions.

And you, dearest Babylonian, I speak so much to-day about myself, but in truth you are the stirring element for me.

L.

King's College, Cambridge, Sunday 20th January, 1924

My dearest L

I am so stiff – Dennis, Sebastian and I went for a ride yesterday and, as the horses were fresh we gallopped [*sic*] very fast. I talked about the Babylonians to them, but the rain and the horses brushed the lunacy out of my head. To-day I have been writing the speech for the Annual Meeting of my Insurance Company which comes next week. In a few minutes Dadie, Sebastian, Clutton-Brock and Morland[1] (the imitation Garia) come to dinner.

Your letter yesterday was very nice – but what will you do about Vladimiroff? Your arithmetic is RIGHT!! How did you do it? The horse licks the hind (where do your words about the horse and the hind come from?)

. . .

I have a small cough which needs soothings from your hands.

There was a *very* good article in yesterday's *Spectator* defending my policy;

also (I hear but have not seen it) what sounds rather an absurd article of flatteries by Mr Wells in the *Daily News*.

I come on Tuesday evening before dinner.

M

I found this love poem in my Babylonian researches, – written by a woman more than 2,000 years before Christ; it is the earliest we know:

> Come to me my Ishtavar and show your virile strength
> Push out your member and touch with it my little place

1 O. M. Morland was a King's undergraduate who evidently bore a physical resemblance to Garia.

(41 Gordon Square), Monday 21st January, 1924

I looked into 'the Cambridge term.' How progressive you become to admit even female cooks (except that they might collapse). As for the Council [of the] Senate it is powerful, because you are in it and so it shall remain. The choice of buildings begin and end with your name also. From intelect to the Babylonian poem, what openness of mind, I smiled from head to foot. When I tell to you 'thrillings' she sais 'touch with it my little place', a 'positive' woman no doubt she was. I want to hear and listen more to Babylonia, except this poem I remember nothing from history but the Babylonian smashing.

I have a very good gossip to tell you, I like to preserve till when I see you . . .

In *The Nation* I read about the [coal] strikers, my morale holds out a sympathy for them as I think that the diminuendo in their wages to the relation of commodities in prices is not equal. Do not cough, but I shall have the hands ready whenever you are in the mood to have them applied.

L.

King's College, Cambridge, Monday 21st January, 1924

Nothing but work to-day – No news, except that I heard broadcasting last night for the first time.

Will you help me to buy a new blue suit?

There is no escaping one or other of the V's!

I kiss your letters which arrived to-day

M

To-morrow I come between 7 and 8.

(41 Gordon Square), Thursday 24th January, 1924

To-night's news only that I am thinking for how very long I have not been disposed to yawn; and yet while in South America I used to wake up yawning, work yawning and to bed yawning . . .

. . .

My fire like the burning of Rome without Nero, and I have 3 new pairs of gloves (not very good quality) from an unknown person.

Osbert invites me to dinner. Delia is to be included in the set, and the last but not the least that you, reading all this, do not come to an experience of a yawn.

L.

(41 Gordon Square), Friday 25th January, 1924

It is a degradation to be a foreigner, 'week on Friday' means 2 in English but 1 in Russian, as a result Mortimer never came to lunch. It mattered a little; as it was lovely I flew to the bus (visited Delia her dwelling was empty) walked 1 or 2 streets with dresses on and came home exhasted and sensible. . . . Your speaking in Cambridge U.C.A. [University Conservative Association] is humorous, but intelect has no restrictions, especialy in politicks, yet you might seduce them to become as Liberals, saying that inflation is more of a 'fair play' than deflation. . . .

. . .

My inclination is to make order or write letters; there is also a probability of a middle course in reading a book.

L.

King's College, Cambridge, Friday 25th January, 1924

Dearest L

The trains are awful! I didn't get back here until half past one last night, about five hours after I left you, and the carriage was cold and dark.

This afternoon I went the round of the shops – almost like a woman. I decided that it was no good to wait any longer and bought two new pairs of drawers! Then feeling that I was old enough to wear a silk [university] gown on grand occasions – big feasts, processions and the like, I ordered one. It is a fine garment (12 guineas). Next I saw some exceptional amber beads which I brought away (but only on approval) for you to look at. Also various books were bought. But I managed to go into the old curiosity shop without buying anything.

There are posters all over Cambridge to say that Legat and Nicolaeva are coming here to give a Ballet – Divertissement! Did you know that they had such plans? Unfortunately it is on a Wednesday (only one performance) – so I shan't be able to see them. They have taken the Guildhall, which is quite a big place. I wonder if the undergraduates will go.

. . .

So you see I am rather idle. But I wrote some pages about Theory of Money this morning.

Your ever loving

M

(41 Gordon Square), Saturday 26th January, 1924

I had a big gasp of sympathy when I knew *how* you travelled. I smile at your materialistic purchases, as for the beads it is nice of you to have me in your head. I shall look at it on approval. . . .

The contract[1] from Coliseum arrived this morning, I do wish the 'Stas of my heart' [Idzikovsky] would join my legs then the programme would be such:

1) Pas de deux it last 8 minutes
2) Three pussies   3 minutes
3) then Stas and I in a demi character number, Legat could devise one of that kind very well.

Our own pussy Twinkle is going to disconnect herself from her own puppies very soon, her stomach is ever so fat, I touch it and she likes it.

You are dearly milenky.

L.

1   For the performance beginning 31st March.

(41 Gordon Square), Sunday 27th January, 1924

How gay it was this morning. Gordon Square appeared to me à la Cézanne, that ever green picture Sam bought for himself. Everything seemed ripe, brisk and fine. Lunch with Miss Naylor, a German lady from Berlin interested in pictures was there, I an eager person asked about the League of youth, conditions etc., but reading *Nation* I knew much more than she could ever tell. I walked back with my own feet, ever so crisp they felt and found Vaz at 41 who had less depression than otherwise. I asked him what would he do if he had 2 wives? he said he could not be a polygamist . . .

. . .

148

On your progressive intelect I put a kiss with crossings, but otherwise I am *so* fond of you.

L.

(41 Gordon Square), Monday 28th January, 1924

My full admiration for your *Monetary Reform*;[1] there is such fresh literary style of your own, zest of life in your constructive sentences and although Purchasing Power Parity or Forward Market in Exchanges are pure matters and more difficult to grasp for a usual person, there is always a holding interest. With 'Alternative aims' I read it to the end with stimulus.

. . .

Your telephone disturbed me less than another time, the sound was so faint that I did not realise I was speaking to you. I spoke of draws because I had a sexual interest that moment what contained in them and at other moments I want to know all about apples in shoes.

L.

1 A further reference to his new book *A Tract on Monetary Reform*.

(41 Gordon Square), Thursday 31st January, 1924

Oh legs! pursuing, slow witted, genuine, regulated even Jewish couple of legs here and there, that is how I saw Liverpool [Street] station to-day. In the Strand I stepped to Fullers in the hope of having my water piped out, as an introduction I asked for a box of sweets, but the coppers in my pockets were not enough, and I did my best only in 41.

Delia is well, so is Dobbie, she hears from him, also she is to display her feminine abilities in weaving, very appropriate, and Monday I shall see Barrie with tea.

I feel tired, no fond desire not even apples (perhaps in bed) but my spirits are alive and good humored and fountains of feeling for you.

L.

(41 Gordon Square), Friday 1st February, 1924

I have arrived from the Russian boredom at the Coliseum.[1] Mr Croxton wished it would be less German, I said 'at any rate it is very respectable, that is what you like in your theatre.' The ballet is about one hour, never ends, I do not wonder if big Serge took an *express* back to Paris. Most of the time everybody runs as to the Liverpool [Street] station, I am going to walk next time I dance, Like a peacock so very slow, one gains distinction from such an action . . . Mr Croxton thought your speech on the 'Mutual Assurance life'[2] was excelent. We agreed; like you and Hubert [Henderson] in other subjects. Mortimer came, I even put my best afternoon dress, we made a conversation of cats and dogs. He loves cats, I prefer dogs, to defend my cause I said dogs once were human beings and therefore the relations are near to one another, as to that he proposed monkeys, but they never *were*, they are going to be perhaps to-morrow and then I might change my opinion.

. . .

I expect *The Nation* with mental passion.

L.

1 The Russian Romantic Theatre Ballet Co.: A New Relevation of the Art of the Russian Stage. Petipa's *Harlequinade* was being performed this week.
2 Maynard was chairman of the National Mutual Life Insurance Company and made speeches at its annual meetings.

King's College, Cambridge, Friday 1st February, 1924

My dearest, darling L

I have been rather constructive to-day. First I drew up a plan for a short new book,[1] which would be a sequel to *Monetary Reform*. Then I started my article about Klotz,[2] and, writing it most of the day, I have nearly finished the first draft. I waste a lot of time by writing down a lot of rather amusing stuff which is really nothing but abuse and therefore has to be crossed out again after it has been written. In the afternoon there was an 'Estates Committee' of the College and after that I tottered out into the streets and bought a few books (absurd – because I have no time to read them and they are large and crowd my shelves); and then I took back the big amber to the furniture shop. That is my history. Now I am undecided whether to read or to go to the At Home which Dennis gives on Friday evenings. I think I shall read. My fire is very big and it is tiresome to walk out into the cold. So I suppose we shall each be sitting before our fires at this time – or are you out somewhere?

I kiss you

M

1 It was never written.
2 The French Minister of Finance who was at the Peace Conference; the article appeared in *The Times* of 27th February, 1924.

(41 Gordon Square), Saturday 2nd February, 1924

'Gold in 1923'[1] contains your literary prickings with a 'morale' behind the bank reserves. I like it very much . . .

Puddle pins is getting fat, without promiscuity. Delia is a changed woman. Her mentality becomes more of an independent order, and the weaving uplifting to her. Next week the 3 birds (she, Mrs Mayers and I) go to the British Museum. Women are so progressive to-day. We desire to see remarcable carvings of Buddhas I believe.

Your intelectual constructions are flowing 'en plain'.[2] It is very nice, but when Dennis gives his 'at home' please join. It is a change, and gives better fluctuations mentaly and phisically.

L.

1 *The Nation*, 2nd February, 1924.
2 En plein – 'fully'.

(41 Gordon Square), Sunday 3rd February, 1924

Berta R. [Ruck] just had tea with me and muffins, she is going to teach me a new song the essence of it: 'girls, girls, you take this warning from me, never trust the sailor one inch above your knee.' We discussed Ray Strachey, Berta knew her when she thought of silks and stockings, nowadays she wears only tweeds with social activities. My stockings shall never drop into the well, besides I am brought up with silk tights . . .

Molly knocked at 41. A new dress, new coat, very good effect, so we chattered on Bloomsbury before the war, you in a fancy dress asking permission 'May I take off my matinée hat.' *Oh* I kiss you. . . .

Massine telephones that he shall visit me on the middle of a week, in fact I am so active over the telephones and visitors that I prospire in the places where the hair grows.

L.

King's College, Cambridge, Sunday 3rd February, 1924

My dearest L

Last night I feasted with Dennis in Trinity to celebrate the Purification of the Virgin Mary. We purified her with a great deal of port. Indeed I became very tipsy. Baldwin was there as one of the guests. After dinner when I was at my tipsiest I had a conversation with him. He was very nice, but what I may have said to him – I don't distinctly remember it – I tremble to think! for I said whatever came into my head. However I think he was a little tipsy too. I asked him, amongst other things, what he meant when he said 'exports' in the House of Commons, and told him that I thought he was very eccentric but quite sound. I shall have to find out from Dennis what I really did say. Dennis was completely charmed by him; he didn't know him before; and thought him just what a Prime Minister ought to be!

Earlier in the day I finished my article on Klotz and went for a ride. Unluckily my favourite horse has been kicked and is not able to go out. I didn't think much of the appearance of my article in the *Nation* this week.[1]

Will you begin to think which day you would like to come here to see the Greek Play? I must take the tickets soon. Probably Thursday February 28 (when you could come back with me from London) or Saturday March 1 (when Duncan and Vanessa may be coming) would be the best.

The Coliseum Ballet *does* sound dull; but you don't say how the audience received it, or what Mr Dove, Croxton etc. thought.

To-day I am indolent from too much wine last night and read about the Sumerians.

I love you and kiss you
M

1   'Gold in 1923', *Nation*, 2nd February, 1924.

(41 Gordon Square), Monday 4th February, 1924

Virgin Mary, influenced by Cambridge, became Mother of Parlament nursing Baldwin with the part. Your sayings made me smile all over 'ekcentric but quite sound.' I quite believe he [Baldwin] is charming, if only he did not use 'protection' he would be Premier for many years to come,[1] but as situation is, Ramsay [MacDonald] comes out more of a romantic figure.

Florrie arrived . . . She saw when the scandal of Stas occured, at the general rehearsal of the new Ballet (*Les Biches*),[2] he stopped the action and said: 'This costume is too shabby for me I shall not dance.' Big Serge: 'That is enough. Get out.' Also Big Serge does not need Stas at all for the new repertory, so I might arrive at him yet. Barrie thought if I do not get a partner perhaps a puppet would do instead? He seemed depressed inwardly, so we spoke politicks, ballet, stage, in fact everything impersonal . . .

To-morrow appears to me a day of pleasing dimensions.
L.

1   He had resigned on 8th January.
2   First performed at Theatre de Monte Carlo on 6th January.

King's College, Cambridge, Monday 4th February, 1924

Wilson's[1] death took my thoughts back to when I wrote Chapter III. The *New York World* telegraphed for some words; so I dictated a few down the telephone to Miss Rees – I will send them to the *Nation* as well. But there is really nothing to say.

I come up to-morrow at tea-time and go first to Miss Rees, reaching Gordon Square about 7 o'clock. I feel a little inclined to go to the Palladium pantomime. If (*but only* if) you do too, will you get tickets?

I smile to think of you three birds pecking in the British Museum farmyard.

M

1 Woodrow Wilson (1856–1924), 28th President of the U.S.A. serving from 1912 to 1920, had died on 3rd February 1924. Maynard had criticised him severely in Chapter III of *The Economic Consequences of the Peace*.

(41 Gordon Square), Thursday 7th February, 1924

I am a new person since 'we met'. . . . So being in good spirits, hunger spoke aloud from my stomach and in fact I had dinner before 8 o'clock. I like to translate the lettre, not much difficulty, only a little time, as it is the evening I am only pleased to do so; but present moments I just used to look into the scientific world and do you know (I hope not) how mice were called to supper with the sound of an electric bell, 300 lessons passed, then hearing the sound mice came themselves into the dining room, their children needed only a 100 lessons, next propagation 30, next 10, and the next 5. Remarkable! So it comes into my head how bolsheviks base their theory, forgetting that mice is mice, and human kind is filled to the utmost with discriminations, anyhow I want more beauty in life than to become a mice, and I shall not accept things collectively at all (except in pantalets and chemises it is delightful to have a collection of those), nor could you, being so humanisticaly human.

L.

(41 Gordon Square), Friday 8th February, 1924

Oh, such pulsations, I felt my mouth would be out of order, but it was so nice to listen to your voice [on the telephone] after. I thank you very much. Is it 'the way of the world' that I should ask when Duncan is coming, and Vanessa speaks with you about me?

The farmyard. British Museum was visited by Mrs Mayers, Muriel, Delia and *me*, included in the corporation of females. About ¾ of an hour we lasted there, it is magnificent to improve the mind, but the body is carved in painted wood of a Buddasasta (perhaps I do not spell the end of the name correctly) looks so wise and the unknown becomes known on that face, other Buddhas touched me less, they were not so radiant in inward hues of the soul.

I shall telephone to the French count [Etienne de Beaumont] if he can see me to-morrow, it remains for me to be diplomatic, *oh* (I am not clever that way), also I must go out tonight with Legats, I promised, these days are filled with occupations of social and professional order.

Tenderness.

L.

King's College, Cambridge, Friday 8th February, 1924

My dearest L

I hope you or Nessa understood what I was trying to say on the telephone. It was this: if it is necessary, I would accept the 15,000 francs; but perhaps the immediate reply to the Viscount[1] might be – Yes, I will see you to-morrow and discuss details on the assumption that the financial matter will be fixed up satisfactorily, and then you must see what you can do on my behalf with your Paris Committee.

But I daresay this is too complicated; and if when you see him it appears best to accept his offer outright, I would do so if I were you.

My head has been buzzing with ideas of various kinds all day, but I haven't written anything down. However I have been at work in a sort of way most of the time. In the afternoon I walked to see the place where Peter wants to build a dollshouse[2] for his Topsy; and it seemed to me that it ought to be possible to arrange to let him have it. Now, as usual, the moment has arrived on Friday evening when I wonder whether or not to go to Dennis's Salon. (It was a good thing I didn't go last week, because he was out that evening and there wasn't any party in his rooms).

According to Sebastian, who was there, Legat's entertainment was quite a success; a much larger attendance than one would have expected and very good applause. They gave a *very* long programme (nearly 3 hours) although being so few persons, and the costumes were very smart – no décor but curtains.

All the time in the train yesterday Duncan wrote rapidly in a book with a pencil. At first I thought it was a letter and did not like to be inquisitive. At last I asked him what it was. He was writing an article, he said, which he might offer to *The Nation*! It was a plan to settle the housing problem by pulling down all the East and South of London and building instead an enormous number of Squares all just like Gordonia. I am sure you will approve!

M

I hope you can read the bad handwriting of this letter.

1   Count Étienne de Beaumont.
2   It was on land off West Road owned by King's College.

(41 Gordon Square), Saturday 9th February, 1924

. . .

How nice it was to have your letter 'moral support', the count [Beaumont] came and said that *they* could not give me a bigger price, but he understood my points, and so he would do all his possible with the comitee if he can receive something extra for the expences, (but it is a separate idea from 15000 [francs]). After the polite yet not deeply financial compromise I agreed to 15000. (I expect the 'extra' expences will amount to 1 or 2 pounds). He will send me a contract from France, indeed he was charming, explaining all the difficulties. If the affair develops with success it might be another matter, but at present the expences without bringing in were enormous. . . . We gossiped over Big Serge, he thought Monte Carlo is the only refuge for him. I see that it is a competition to S.[1] as this programme hopes to come to London this summer. *Oh.* I am exhasted, the thyroid glands out of order but thymos tendencies to you.

L.

1   'a competition to S.' = 'a challenge to Diaghilev'.

King's College, Cambridge, Sunday 10th February, 1924

My dearest L

I have your telegram – I think it is best the way you have done it. You have made a dignified protest that what they are offering is not your proper salary; but at the same time it is not worth while to trouble too much about 5,000 francs when the work is attractive.

I begin to think how you will live most comfortably when you are in Paris – for it will be quite a long time. I shall pay you a visit at the end, but the first part is in Cambridge term time. Couldn't you persuade Florrie to take a flat for the Paris season, sharing it with her and dividing the expenses? You could have a spare room and entertain your other friends from London in turn.

Anything more from Stas?

I am writing another article to-day[1] for *The Nation* about 'Gold in 1923' answering the letters in this week's *Nation*. But I am already troubled with the thought of the lecture which I have to give before the University to-morrow afternoon. I have only partly prepared it – I leave the rest until the last moment; but it disturbs my nerves ahead.

Yesterday I did not do much – it is always impossible on Saturdays! In the morning there was the College Meeting, – a big debate on the new College Buildings,[2] I was victorious in the end for the idea of inviting other architects and further designs. Then in the afternoon I rode, which made me more inclined to read than write after tea; after that pupils came. And in hall the exercise made me want to drink claret, which is the enemy of further work. So a day goes by.

Geoffrey is in Cambridge to-day. His wife has been ill in bed with phlebitis. She also has a baby inside her. It might be kind to call to see her if you have time. My mother is in London next week. Perhaps she writes to you to come to tea at 41.

I wish you could come to my lecture to-morrow; – now that I hear that Topsy goes to *every* lecture of Peter's, even when he gives the same one many times!

With very much love
M

1   'The Prospects of Gold'. *Nation*, 16th February, 1924.
2   An architectural competition had been held in 1923–4 for a project to complete Bodley's building and to replace the Library and Provost's Lodge. Maynard's view that the winning designs were unacceptable now prevailed, and he began a campaign on behalf of a new architect, George Kennedy. See *A Century of King's*, by L. P. Wilkinson (1980).

(41 Gordon Square), Monday 11th February, 1924

Was this afternoon your lecture on 'The Inflation', yes or no, but the listeners were inflated with enthousiasm. May I give you temperate strokings, now, after the event.

Florrie last night told me that on Thursday I shall see in the newspapers about Teddy's affairs. I looked virginal with moving dimples inside of me. . . .

I have a letter from your mother. Yes, I like to see her.

Vera lunched with me, was quite in delight over Parisien projects, she knows all about the count, he seems to be very respectable with many advantages, except, although married, is like the 'little elephant.'[1]

We walked to Swami, she wanted a small tapestrie with the expenditure of 10 pounds. I was recognised as a 'lady with Mr Keynes', yet prices did not go down, the one that appeared the nicest was 80 pounds, the establishement is *only* for the rich persons; now I have my dinner and think of you.

L.

1   A homosexual like Diaghilev.

King's College, Cambridge, Monday 11th February, 1924

Dearest Kameradchki Lydia,

The lecture is just over. *How* I suffered beforehand. First an ache in my head, then in my stomach, then in my throat, then a dizziness; – a lecture is just as bad as influenza.

I could go with LilSam to *Way of the World*[1] next week either on Tuesday or Wednesday Feb 19 or 20.

I think that the Viscount, if he is a gentleman, will give you 2,000 francs for expenses.

. . .

I had such fluctuations for you in bed last night, and felt *very* fond of you.

Your
M

1 By Congreve.

(41 Gordon Square), Friday 15th February, 1924

Alice Sit by the Fire[1] is not at all an outlook on life by Lil. It is a story of a flattering mother 'who approaches Indian summer', the daughter (might be Lil's Sydney) saw it before mother felt it. A farcical comedy I enjoyed laughingly. Sam is to have a picture intercourse with Roger, but only for *one* picture.

My exercises did not advance, as I put my legs to bed for a long time, took them out to proceed to Florrie, such conversations about servants, the position of Mrs Apple Jack[2] is the elastic one, in Florrie's house the role is occupied by an 'odd man' from brushing the stairs to puryfying bird's cage. Mrs Harland second rate occupations are frequent.

Margot [Asquith] latest: she is very fond of 'parafin' and hot water bottle, having a good supply I suppose for the immediate present, sense of security for to-morrow pursues her, so her forward exchange adress is Downing Street.[3] Vaz came. I used him. He found the music for 'wooden soldier and Grisette dance.'

May I trouble you with income tax? It is not a cage[4] yet, especially if I give a satisfaction needed . . .

L.

1 A play by J. M. Barrie.
2 Unidentified servant.
3 Asquith had ceased to be prime minister in 1916.
4 'A cage' = 'a prison cell'.

King's College, Cambridge, Friday 15th February, 1924

My dearest L

You are only at the beginning of your difficulties with Stas! I can see that. I enclose a suggested telegram. . . . I calculate that after paying other expenses there will be not more than £120 (perhaps less) to divide between you and him; so that if you pay him £60, he will be getting as much as (perhaps more than) you, which would be very bad for his nose. All the same I think you must get him at some price; so if you think the telegram too dangerous, don't send it. . . .

Oh, your cutting about tooth-brushing had a bad influence on me. I was sitting in my bathroom putting off doing it, when your piece came into my head – so I jumped up thinking – I'll be healthy for once, I'll *not* clean my teeth.

Speaking of health, perhaps the new thing which they advertise everywhere Yah-dil might be good for Luba. It is recommended for her kind of illness, and I hear of wonderful cures. Perhaps you might buy a bottle and send it to her.
. . .

M

(41 Gordon Square), Saturday 16th February, 1924

I thank you for the telegramme, it is a 'modus vivendi' with Stas I think, in a composition and a tone. I like to ask the 'little flea' what his maximum would reach? Vera admires the phrase 'proper billing', saying that this trifle Stas[1] knows more about the theatre than we 2 although inteligent (you were not mentioned).

'Prospects of Gold'[2] is clear with such a charming flavour of sarcasm . . .

Vanessa and Duncan invited me first to dinner. Adrian was there, he looked sad going to his square. I traveled well to-night, still more reason not to travel to Cambridge . . .

Good night, milenki
L.

1 Idzikovsky was very small.
2 *The Nation*, 16th February, 1924.

(41 Gordon Square), Sunday 17th February, 1924

I have not thank you yet for Sheppard's *Birds*,[1] it reads 'freely adapted' and charming . . .

My sympathy *again* for [coal] strikers (except Poplarism)[2] they have a hard life without security; my advice to capitalists to yield 2 shillings, besides we might be left without coal (What is the use of B. Empire then?) and all the apples shall be rotted away in the sea.

Vaz. complex is no more. I was in his studio about 2½ very empty with an introduction to lunch in vermouth, gin alliance that sleeked into my strongest dimensions e.g. head – legs; when I started back home alkohol evaporated, I was pure again and even learned a song 'I'd be a butterfly born in a bower.'

And you, do you proceed with vigour in your mental problems or odds and ends, or conversations of an inventive order?

Crossings for everything you do.

L.

1   J. T. Sheppard's translation of Aristophanes' *Birds*, which was to be performed in Cambridge.
2   In 1922 the Poplar Guardians had been accused of wild and wilful extravagance.

(41 Gordon Square), Monday 18th February, 1924

. . .

This afternoon your sister Margaret, it is very easy to speak with her, she is very nice, she stayed till 7 o'clock, then I conducted her with the help of a police to Euston underworld, and after, I do not know how, I found myself on Mornington Crescent, as I saw the tramways I decided it was almost in the country. I took one large road back strolled on and on, bought a *Evening Standard* to see if there was any humour in 'Londoner's diary' since Sir Oswald 'coat frock.' I am a devoted reader of that page.

. . .

Margaret and I agreed that you must be the Chancelor of Excheker to pull out bad conditions of the country.

. . .

L.

King's College, Cambridge, Monday 18th February, 1924

. . .

Yes – this time I agree with you (I ought to agree always, because you are wiser than me – less intelligent but more wise) I think the Strikes are right. I would give them the 2/–. They will get it in the end. You think of coal and apples in this connection; I of lead.

M.

159

This morning the pupil who has consumption came to see me. Did I think that, if he got well, he had enough brains to write for a Fellowship? I lied a little, only a very little, and said that, if he had his strength back and full powers of concentration, I thought he was capable of writing for a fellowship. So he has gone into his hospital fairly cheerful. I behaved like a Russian in this.

(41 Gordon Square), Thursday 21st February, 1924

We, your mother and I, unloaded our feelings for you and for each other in relation of your being our entire idol.

Marjorie stopped in and wanted to know if it is true that the dancers at the Coliseum were the refugees and organised themselves to become dancers in a month or 2? She is very much interested to be a society entertainer, also she reads books about Imperial Russia. R. MacDonald in her opinion is a big party man keeping extremes (I do not see such) in order.

Stas's nose increases in size and develops in the air demanding 60 pounds, so your financial adoption towards the problem shall promote good will on both sides. I like to sleep inside.

Alice is going to sit by the fire.

Rythimical mental flux for you.

L.

(41 Gordon Square), Friday 22nd February, 1924

A misfortune of a minor character, a chimney fire; the elegant firemen arrived, cleaned the chimney, restored the order, but for me not to light the fire till the inspection comes in, might be 2 or 3 days, I console myself and say it could be worse if I should live only in 1 room.

Milenky Maynard I was touched with the money, that in the turmoil of your activities you thought of the 'troubles I give you.'

Ruby just tells me that every other couple has a fire, and I am drawn out of my habits in life. Damnation.

. . .

Did you walk through the corpses alive for your lecture and by and by they stimulated and stood on their legs mentaly and phisicaly by your achieving lecture.

Anemic and forlorn, but very tender towards you.

L.

King's College, Cambridge, Friday 22nd February, 1924

My dearest L.

. . .

Yesterday's lunch at V. Bonham Carter's was quite amusing. Oswald Mosley M.P. and Lord D'Abernon the Ambassador, etc. were there and we had very brisk conversation. While I was there I telephoned again about the Chancellor's consent to the article; and at last he agrees – so I 'get my ways'. I expect that it will appear in the *Times* on Wednesday.[1] Then I hurried off before the gentlemen had left the table and went to the City for a meeting of the Independent.

After the Greek Play comes the Marlowe,[2] who do *Duchess of Malfi*. Does that tempt you to make the journey? – Saturday March 8. Why don't you and Barrie come down together for that play?

I enclose the contract for Stas to sign; also suggestions for a letter to him to go with it. But you know him and can make a letter as well as I can.

I send you separately a *Daily Graphic* which has an illustration of one or two of the *Birds* costumes.

M

I have pain from a small pile (do you know what it is?). Put crosses on it.

1   'France and the Treasury. M. Klotz's charges refuted. Mr Keynes's reply.' *The Times*, Wednesday 27th February 1924.
2   The Marlowe Dramatic Society had been founded in 1907 by Justin Brooke, Rupert Brooke, Geoffrey Keynes and others in order to revive Elizabethan drama.

(41 Gordon Square), Saturday 23rd February, 1924

Tonight I visit Vera, she shall be operated next week, I will amuse her with a story Vaz. told me last night, but first to you:

A young boy tells his father that at present in school they study sexual intercourse; father slightly alarmed interogates the master, while the master solicitates father with natural explanations. All is well. In the evening father comes home and sees his offspring creeping out of maid's room.

F. Why are you there, my son?

S. Father, I am doing homework.

With this I hope to communicate the emotions of laughter experienced by me to you.

L.

(41 Gordon Square), Sunday 24th February, 1924

What a cold dominion Christabel's house is, I hurried off confessing that I had 'business arrangements' to meet at 41. Peoples of mediocre possibilities: the general impression I made a 'gaff' in the beginning, Christabel said how she remembered Princess Bibesco at a party putting into her bosom a kitten and commited unexpected squeaks, I said I knew a lady who put inside of her a young alligator; after this I saw that Elizabeth's prank was quite innocent in comparison. However, anything is forgiven to a foreigner like me . . .

I am so very pleased about 'yes' from the Chancelor,[1] and await Wednesday with fluctuations . . .

I put vaselinated crossings on your poor cracked communities between your halphs.

L.

1 His consent to *The Times* article.

King's College, Cambridge, Sunday 24th February, 1924

I do sympathise in your chimney fire. Was the whole room also smothered in dirt? That generally happens – smuts come down in a thick veil over everything.

You must sympathise with me too in my small ailment. I couldn't have any ride yesterday because of it. Now I have an ointment; since it is made out of a gland, I have big faith in it.

Yesterday was the first complete rehearsal of the Greek Play. I understand that it all goes pretty well. Dialogue at hall lunch:–
Sheppard You mustn't make *any* criticism on anything. If you do, I shall cry.
Provost (smiling) I don't care how much you cry.
Sheppard cries but in Greek.

Duncan and Vanessa come to-morrow. I shall not see the performance until the end of the week – on Saturday.

Have you read in the paper that the name *Russian* has been abolished? I must now call you an Ussrian. It is not a big change – only an *r* in another place. I enclose a paper for you to look through about the new Ussrian Society I have agreed to join. But a Russian for me is a very near thing, whilst for the Society it is a deserving *objet* a very long way off.

I also send you the income tax paper. I have written on it, and there is nothing for you to do except write your signature in the place shown and then post it. But I fear that they have caught you now! You will have to pay something, I expect.

With tender kisses
M

(41 Gordon Square), Monday 25th February, 1924

I am a little nicer looking just this moment, but an hour ago I might have looked like a monster, so dissatisfied with the existence in the bed room; besides the outside is also without any possible elements of gladness that could enlighten my situation; and your ailings? give it to me.

Last night Vera and I had our last intercourse of friendship, next moment when I see her after the operation I am not allowed to make her smile, as the threads might stick out . . . Osbert Sitwell's latest gossip that Big Serge in such a rage over 'our season' that he engages everyone possible with a contract *forever*.

I like to see Sheppards 'inky hinky lacrimo' in Greek.

Lady Strachey article[1] is absolutely comic, otherwise there is not much news except that Dover's cliff is fallen, and per saltum I like to see you.

L.

1 'Some Recollections of a Long Life: II.' *The Nation*, 23rd February, 1924.

King's College, Cambridge, Monday 25th February, 1924

Vanessa and Duncan have arrived. But D. doesn't seem very well yet; at this moment he has gone to lie down on his bed. V. sits in the next room. They go to the rehearsal at 7.15 after an early dinner. But I have my Political Economy Club to receive; so I shan't go. I have a letter from Lytton that he too has been having a bad influenza; so he can't come to stay with me for the play on Saturday.

. . .

I have a letter from the lawyers to say that they have sent for your trunk. It will be very exciting to look inside it, if it comes.

The communities of my halphs are still cracked, and I suffer a little – but not too much.

Your
M

(41 Gordon Square), Thursday 28th February, 1924

I returned without any beams from nature or persons. The sun disappeared, you might have had part of it in the train, wet snow was in my direction . . . I notice complete chatter is in posession of my mental developement at the moment, as a reaction of a realization that 'life is difficult' on this beloved earth of ours. *Oh*. I am so sleepy, yet there is a dinner for me to

163

swallow at 8 o'clock and what not in the course of conversacioni, indeed a promiscuous rattle of a day.

Your Cerberus
L.

P.S. A domestic warning about the caviare that it should be kept in a cool corner to preserve its fresh appearance in the Palate.

King's College, Cambridge, Thursday 28th February, 1924

I come back to find the Caviare – I will give you an equal quantity of my own.

. . .

M

(41 Gordon Square), Friday 29th February, 1924

No versatility or virility – desorganisation, and 'I can't think why?'
The morning was disturbed by a man and a woman from *Vogue*. Vanessa's bed comes into notoriety, therefore photos were taken.

. . .

Very late I flew to Florrie to give the bottle of Yadil to her cousin, stayed a few moments now here before Mrs Mayers, just a few touches of news about Vera, she had 6 stones in her blader, why is this fertility of dead kind?
I am exhasted, give me your hand otherwise I am 'fading away'.

L.

King's College, Cambridge, Friday 29th February, 1924

I saw an *atom* this afternoon. I was taken to the Cavendish Laboratory where the physicists make their extraordinary experiments, and two companions explained things to me. It was interesting. One of the two was a young Russian called Peter Kapitza. He had made a wonderful instrument[1] and seemed *very* clever, I thought.

What do you think of this stamp [enclosed]? – memorial of Lenin. It came to me with a letter from the 'People's Commissariat of Finance' asking me to write an article for them in their paper.

I have not done much to-day – only potterings with correspondence. Sheppard is calm – thinks the play[2] went badly on the first night (not enough full rehearsals) but is better now. Costumes and scenery *lovely*, according to him. I go to-morrow night. He has made amends to his fellow-producer; but the wife was still rude; so God intervened to-day and gave him a bicycle accident.

M

1   Peter Kapitza (1894–1984) was a Russian physicist of legendary brilliance who came from the Petrograd University to work at the Cavendish Laboratory from 1921 to 1934. He had just built a device for producing an impulsive magnetic field, and was studying the deflection of the tracks of alpha particles. His wonderful instrument was later the subject for involved international negotiations, for after he had attended a congress in Leningrad in 1934, the Soviet authorities refused to allow him to return to Cambridge, and eventually the apparatus that he had built followed him to Moscow.

2   The 1924 Greek Play was *The Birds* by Aristophanes.

(41 Gordon Square), Saturday 1st March, 1924

. . .

Now I know en general how a sculptor conducts himself with his object (Dobby and I are not included) like the Chinese men, you have told me, they begin sexual passion from the feet and then 'ad infinitum'.

I was at the Coliseum to inquire about music, almost everything I want this time luckily is orchestrated; then to Legat, he accepts 10 pounds (for me!) . . .

. . .

Dearest Maynard, how are you everywhere? Please improve every moment.

I did not know that atoms could be seen; of course Lenin's stamp is commanding for filatelists, but I am fond of you.

L.

(41 Gordon Square), Sunday 2nd March, 1924

Pussy willows bought by me for Vera (I was not admitted), the bush does not smell but looks enchanting. Bentinck Street, how overloaded with hospitals, I entered 4 wrong ones with a smile in and out, later a telephone message from Teddy (Florrie is in the week end) that Hilda inherited a daughter, she did not wish another Persian Prince.

. . .

A gossip from Lil's only child Sydney who listened to your lecture with admiration except for the word 'ga-ga', the same used by her own 'mother', you and she being such different poles in intelect. All the textiles and Courtauld's artificials long for a protection, a future for Ramsay.

Do tell me if I could hurry the Ministry of Labour for Stas?

I feel very strong and I gobble you in a new fashion.

L.

King's College, Cambridge, Sunday 2nd March, 1924

My dearest darling

I hope you're not still weak and languishing. It is the spring in your blood I expect, – though there's not much in the air. I send you many strengthening kisses and love touches.

Here, though it snows sometimes, there is bright sun, and yesterday (with my halphs cured) I had the longest and best ride of the year, – a cavalcade of six of us went many miles.

The Greek Play last night was quite a big success. Apparently it has improved very much all through the week. The theatre was full and much excitement. Sheppard made a long speech, thanking everyone by name down to the ladies who sewed on the buttons, pressing the hand and almost kissing his hated fellow producer. He even made compliments in the speech to the yet more hated *wife* of the hated producer! So you see the atmosphere – perhaps just a little too much. Everyone of all tastes agreed that the dresses were most good. The delicate colour scheme at the end had tender, humorous beauty which Duncan knows how to make. Afterwards there was a small party in my room and we eat your caviare. I send you a copy of a University magazine which has some photographs of the costumes, but chiefly because they reprint a photograph and personal sketch of Sheppard which they published 20 years ago. Also in this envelope rather a dull description of *D. [Duchess] of Malfi*. Have you asked Barrie? Dennis enquired because he also had thought of asking him; but D thinks he will refuse partly because he always refuses things, and partly because Cambridge may be rather haunted for him by the one who was drowned.[1]

M

1 The Cambridge man Theodore Llewelyn Davies (1870–1905), one of J. M. Barrie's 'boys', who had been drowned.

King's College, Cambridge, Monday 3 March, 1924

Very glad to get your miele letters to-day and that you are strong again. But what does the word 'ga-ga' mean? – I do not understand that bit. About Stas – the position seems good; he is very anxious to have the engagement with you – but why has he not sent back the contract? I suggest the enclosed telegram. We had better wait a few days before attacking the Ministry of Labour again.

. . .

Much love
M

(41 Gordon Square), Monday 3rd [?] March, 1924

The undergraduate spirits swells *The Granta*.[1] I am diverted, as for Sheppard, *Oh* Jack – very sweet, he looks as if he shall become when grown up a respectable 'pere de famille'[2] with 5 – 6 little Sheppards behind his tails. In fact it is so, but he built up another theory. Intelectually he is no doubt a romantic, and the romanticks intend to marry. He may not like my outlook, but then one seldom faces truth.

I read a little of the *Duchess of Malfi*, there is intensity in characters. Dadie should appear pregnant, in one of the first scenes, may I apply for the part as I had apricocks jam for lunch very near from apricocks of the Duchess.[3]

Last night in bed I read a little of *Pride and Prejudice*, it is divine comedy in literature. I called, Barrie being out, if he refuses what would be my 'bisiness of life' about Cambridge?

I have a letter from my mother, she does not ask for help, but she does. When I go there I shall make peace between them all.

I am immensely content that you are well altogether . . .

L.

1 Students' magazine.
2 He never married.
3 In *The Duchess of Malfi* the villainous Bosola makes a gift of apricots to the Duchess who eats them avidly, thus betraying that she is pregnant.

(41 Gordon Square), Tuesday 4th March, 1924

Slight economic news for you, that no one in Russia knows if Chervonetz,[1] is secured, but Chervonetz is so popular that security postponed for a long while, a distintegration in the world of finances I would say, perhaps that's what English Treasury and Banks would think also. Still I am not pessimistic, in the course of time security will be invented, when they come to ask your opinion.

Another most popular species in Russia is Beam [?] & Bum, 2 Clowns, Bum is in the barrel and will not come out, unless the whole audience will stand on it's feet and plead everyone in the audience, including 'camarades-commisares', when that is performed vociferosly Bum comes out in a costume of an old regime policeman!

Perhaps it is not all comic what I relate to you, but it might be as a probability . . .

Comfortings to you, if you are without intelectual classes.

L.

1 The Chervonetz was a unit of Russian currency which had been introduced in December 1922 after the post-revolutionary inflation.

(41 Gordon Square), Thursday 6th March, 1924

I telephoned to Barrie, first in the bath he was (although clean I never thought he takes one), after he telephoned and I proposed the offer to [go to] Cambridge – a drastic refusal, besides he owns a little neuritus.

I do not know why is it (spring?), but I continue my lust for blood in my palatenate, just a few moments ago I had to use 2 heavy weights chops, this moment the craving is dormant but I contemplate on something of a sweet order.

In the *Evening Standard* there is a flair that in Paris all 'shingling'[1] out of fashion, and my little coifure, otherwise 'bun', is the last word of hair compositions.

. . .

I feel so very occupied, surrounded by intelect, letters and energy of my own. The time flies, especially when you are a 'vis a vis' in my mental workshop.

L.

1 In the early twenties the shingle, a very short hair-cut (though less short than the Eton crop) came into fashion and aroused strong feelings for and against, being considered almost defiantly 'modern'.

(41 Gordon Square), Friday 7th March, 1924

I owed to the gift of life this morning, so powerful and musical felt I, with you, myself and sonnets. A charming 'menage à trois'. Then Florrie came naturally too early for me and brought gossip from fishmongers' dinner where she sat last night next to Mrs McKenna, who wanted to know all about me (of course with correctness not touching you at all). Florrie wondered at such a rapid interest, as to my character she painted it with tripos 1[1] . . .

Vera is very well, I have not seen the stones yet, nor the wound, but she is a new human being, the indomitable will as of old, and we plan again for Paris.

What an exstrordinary climax in the 'artificials'.[2] The greedy shareholder overused his language and was punished! Poor Sam and Lil (she was there listening), especially Sam in active difficulties, his speech is not bad but too conservative, it is wise to speak like that when shares jump up, but when a slight decline in shares is introduced one should become a revolutionary with a thrill and economic truth.

How are you milenky?
L.

1 A first class degree at Cambridge.
2 Artificial silk, such as made by Courtaulds.

King's College, Cambridge, Friday 7th March, 1924

. . .

Did you see the Report of Sam's Annual Meeting. *Sam* makes his speech, ending – 'Well, ladies and gentlemen, I don't think I have anything more to say.'
Shareholder rises and says 'I think the directors are treating the shareholders in a mean, niggardly, ungenerous and miserly manner.' (Cheers)
whereupon the Shareholder drops down dead.
Sam (looking towards the corpse) 'This is a most unfortunate occurrence, which we all very much regret.'
Dennis has just come in. He asks you to dinner on Sunday evening.

I see you [in Cambridge] to-morrow.
M

(41 Gordon Square), Monday 10th March, 1924

A decentralised motor car with puffings of sleep coming out from the mouth and the key to 41 is lost again. Cambridge was nice and elegant to me and sleep will be just as necessary in future as it is now, otherwise peoples will not be able to wag their tongs (personal experience at the moment).

Stas arrived soft as a peach with me, the Count [Beaumont] engaged him also for Paris with Massine; he said (the Count) that Diagilev Big Serge was pleading for a favour and should not engage Stas for Paris season, the Count promised, in the meantime Big Serge tried behind his back to destroy Count's season, so that now Count is furious and engages Stas for spite.

We went to Legat and I introduced Stas, but rehearsall shall not begin till next Monday; Stas wants to rehearse in complete order of his muscles, that he did not use since Monte Carlo. His wife is also here, we must arrange about my and his costume to go well together.

You forgive me if I am waiggin [?] to-much with my pen, but I am so fond of you. Very soon I shall be in bed with Morfius, blankets, and a celestial hot water bottle 'like a slave at my feet'.
L.

(41 Gordon Square), Thursday 13th March, 1924

When Vera arrived home from hospital, put herself into bed, and lo! the bed broke, Garia ill with influenza decided to go to his mother's house so that V. could sleep in his bed, but the man with glasses from Hill told V. that she could sleep on the floor and with such conditions she received me. The matrass is like mine and without bed comes out in it's full form. V. is very weak with a centre of illnesses around her, but a little gossip stood out brightly in the world convulsions. Margot [Asquith] lunched with Mrs Stoop, but Margot entertained with descriptions about Americans; '*these* retrogrades, these "stick in *the mud*" young fellows, whenever after a party I gave them a kiss and patted them on the cheek, they were in *terror* from it! Savages!'

I must confess I wouldn't like to be kissed by Margot that is why I do not go to her parties!

. . .

Your dog

L.

(41 Gordon Square), Friday 14th March, 1924

Activity of a practical order as commanding the tights for Stas at Burnett's, that is how his costume for the soldier will be made instead of trousers; Duncan is more than entertained with Stas, so I asked Vanessa to come and be humored, but to-day his artistic temperament was not so jumping; after Burnett we aspired for a buss, however Stas rather would walk, so he treated us with a taxi, and when D. offered his shilling Stas gave him a peculiar look of disdain, I advising D. to put back into his trousers.

. . . I bought a few numbers of theatrical magazines and introverted completely in it's reading the programmes and finding the names of my family. My sister is complete musical comedy star and plays in a theatre which is called *synthetic* (literature, dance, music) but if I do 'my earnings', that is also poetry, dance, music, so we are really sisters in art. Please, look at the 2nd application [for divorce] and think of my tremblings for the sake of the Old Bailey.

Oh Maynarochka 'life is difficult.'

L.

King's College, Cambridge, Friday 14th March, 1924

. . .

I busy myself clearing up College business. I see that the Fellowship election to-morrow is going to be a difficult business – I expect that, like the Cardinals, we shall sit in our conclave all day. I am busy this evening preparing my case in favour of Richard – comparing his work with what others have done before him etc.

The weather is beautiful.

. . .

Touches

M

170

Letters from
5th April, 1924 to 22nd May 1924

Presumably Maynard had been at Gordon Square on 31st March when Lydia and Idzikovsky (Stas), with a small corps de ballet, first presented three ballets at the Coliseum; these were La Princesse Enchantée, Valse *and* Soldier and Grisette. *On 1st April Harold Bowen recorded in his diary that Lydia was not dancing very well, though there was a becoming photo of her in* The Times. *Lydia travelled to Paris on 25th April to join Comte Étienne de Beaumont's company,* Soirées de Paris, *at La Cigale, where it was to perform from 17th May to 30th June; the choreography was by Massine. Despite her sufferings there, attributed both to the drinking water and to the weather, Lydia was a most punctilious correspondent and Maynard expressed appropriate concern in reply. On 2nd May, Sam and Lil Courtauld arrived in Paris, although the ballet company was still only rehearsing. Supported by the Bowens, Lydia refused to dance in the Count's ballet* Vogue, *and Maynard approved of this. At last the first night came on 17th May and was a 'big success'; Lydia was then eagerly awaiting Maynard's arrival in Paris on 24th May.*

During Lydia's absence Maynard had visited the Asquiths for the weekend (26th April); on 30th April he had found Gordon Square to be 'a poor dead place'. He continued his riding on the hills near Cambridge with Sebastian Sprott; wrote regularly for the Nation; *and was heavily involved in College business. On 16th May he paid a last visit to his old master Alfred Marshall. Before he left for Paris Barocchi's first wife, Mary Hargreaves, had been 'run to earth' and the divorce papers were complete.*

The Wharf[1], Sutton Courtney, Berks, Saturday 5th April, 1924

My dearest, darling sweet

If I don't scribble a word now, I don't know how I can be soon enough to catch the Monday post for you. I made my speech this morning before a

171

crowd. It took a full hour to deliver – so much had I written down in my planetary study – one of the longest I have ever given.

The only other guests here, outside the family, are Christabel and her husband. Elizabeth is in full strength. She made an appalling assault on me yesterday to kiss her, but I saw your face looking down out of your planet, and I decided that I would not even be polite. So there was a slight scene. However it means that I have won peace at least for a time.

We play much bridge.

I am now off to a garden party.

I make another informal speech to a small gathering to-morrow.

M.

1   Asquith's house.

Gordon Square, Sunday 6th April, 1924

A gossip of a physchological couple Stephen v. Stephen; Adrian started his solitary life in another Square spending the day as usual with Karin, but the evenings and nights is such misery for him, that he nearly commited suicide, the fact is that he longs for Karin and Karin looks for other dimensions and prefers Adrian not to be with her most of the time. So it is a 'horse and a stag.' Vanessa had a design for cushion, that I attributed to her, alas! Duncan was the originator. Desmond at a party in Mary's house, slipped and injured seriously his knee. Poor Desmond, Freudians, with Molly at the head, would think that he should not visit Mary's house at all.

Did you see in yesterday's papers House of Lords, nullity of marriage happening, brought on a desertion idea of a 'wife who wilfuly and maliciously refused the carnal intercourse.' It does not follow the Victorian song 'she treated him with kindness, she could not give him pain.'

Yesterday in Lil's house for tea I could not resist my non-admiration for her bath room; she still wants you, do you think it would be wise if I postpone it indefinitely, but the phrase would be 'when your Cambridge activities – terminus.'

I use so many I's in this letter I am sorry to trouble you. Sympathy for your vitriolic intelect.

L.

The Wharf, Sutton Courtney, Berks, Sunday April 6th, 1924

My dearest, darling sweet

I am in bed, with breakfast and paper just finished, and have my morning thoughts of you. It is a nice party here . . .

Mr Asquith is in very sweet mood. I sat next him at dinner last night and talked much politics.

At last Spring has come – I can see friendly airs outside.

I put soft crosses and kisses on your aches and scratchings.

M

It seems that the Reparation Reports may not be out until Wednesday, which is tiresome, giving me very little time to write.

(41 Gordon Square), Thursday 24th April, 1924

The empty activity has begun and lasts forever; in the intervals Mrs Apple Jack, Vaz. and Madame Colby. Mrs Apple Jack thinks 2 months is a long time, Vaz. will try to come to Paris. I advise him to marry, and Mme Colby hopes that I have another 'little season in the autumn.' All 3 had something to say, but I feel so empty, being the last fraction of Gordon Square, all is gone. Crosses on your beginnings in Cambridge and everywhere. I kiss and kiss.

L.

May I use your Voltaire for my readings in French?

King's College, Cambridge, Thursday 24th April, 1924

. . .

I saw Peter and Sheppard in Hall. They are very well. I blamed Sheppard not to have visited you and Stas. He declares he will go over to Paris to see you there. The explanation is that one of his sisters died in the vacation; so he had to take the other sister to Venice to console her. Venice was cold and wet and he went on to Rapallo where he gambled a little; then, getting rid of his sister, he went on to Monte Carlo for a week (same routine – Grand Hotel and Restaurant Ré) where he gambled a great deal and, as usual, lost every penny! However he looks very well.

Now I must prepare my lecture for to-morrow.

My dear love to you. I see you in grey coat and pink hat as you were in the station.

Your very fond
M

. . .

Cayre's Hotel, Boulevard Raspail, Paris, Friday 25th April, 1924

The traveling elastic in every sense. Vera, Florrie on the station. When V. saw the basket she thought perhaps there is a 'cadavre' in it, why should I carry such a big one[1] to Paris, I replied 'shoes and dictionaries', both important elements in human nature. Hurried to the hotel, washed my skin, to a restoran and relished in 'petits pois', in the taxi to the telegramme office and now 10½ o'clock, Paris looks beatiful and unknown. The funniest gossip of news is that big Serge, through an intermediary, sent a message that all his life he was in love with the Count Beaumont, and therefore he is ready to collaborate in bed or otherwise and establish a firm: Étienne de Diagileff presents a ballet by Serge de Beaumont. They would look like 'Roman gooses'.

I shall go tomorrow for a rehearsal, it is too late at the moment.

Your lecture was a fluctuation for your listeners, I imagine I was also one of them.

Spaces in affection.

L.

1 It seems that all her life Lydia tended to travel with much luggage.

(Cayre's Hotel), Paris, Saturday 26th April, 1924

Boulevard de Raspail is hell after Gordon Square especially for sleeping purposes, but probably I soon to be very tired, that no sleeping draught should be in need.

The Count and Countess received me with enthousiasm, asked me for lunch including Stas and Eve, then Cocteau arrived with complaints about his connections with *Romeo and Juliet* especially in poison scene. The house is beatiful and 2 big rooms are given for rehearsing and all the furniture is taken away, I have a complex about my exersises, my room is too small, as for the Count's room Massine gives a lesson in the morning to 30 dancers, and to study with them is of no use.

Massine looks well and seems pleasant to everybody. I have not yet the full impression, but dancers look to be not in bad order . . . Vera thought I was driven by a taxi over, as I left the hotel without a word to her – but peace is between us now, I shall be with her for dinner.

Nervous disturbances all over me, but I continue to drink water. What is the Cambridge atmosphere this term? I am very tired, without intelect, but a kiss on you begins and ends this letter.

L.

(Cayre's Hotel), Paris, Sunday 27th April, 1924

Lydochka has been so ill, in the insides of her stomach (perhaps Parisian water), did not want to trouble Vera, but after 2 hours of waiting called her to come and help. She rushed with brandy, 2 hot water bottles, and casteroil and Florrie, so I used the first 2 items and improved myself by now. To be in room all alone with pains was indeed a suffering, although I looked at you on my table and that was the mental improvement.

Last night we were in the theatre, *Apres l'amour* is the title. I admired for the first time Lucien Guitry, he is like a sphynx in his activity, immouvably moving. The only reproach I make is his being a 'pycknic' with an enormous sises in the stomach, and the play itself was ugly in it's cheap mentality of la Vie Parisienne.

The weather here is of a gloomy report, detached pourings of rain; what is your situation? Do you ride on Saturday as of old, how did *Nation* achieved herself this week? I have not seen yet any newspapers, but probably Poincaré still has a good 'digestion'. Vera remembers to you, and I put all the eloquences of my feelings to you.

L.

Under the influence of Vera and Florrie I hope tomorrow order new coat, dress and perhaps evening dress, also a hat. As they *both* insisted, I felt some wisdom and gave in.

King's College, Cambridge, Sunday 27th April, 1924

My dearest darling L

... Here I find myself plunged into a mass of local business. Yesterday the College Council met for six hours and to-morrow the University Council may do the same. I gave my lecture on Friday – quite a difficult one to a fairly intelligent looking audience. Yesterday my pupils came – including your friend Morland as brown as a berry, and the one who has phthisis returned, half-recovered, to do his examinations. Last night I went to my Society [Apostles] – Richard very pleased to be a Fellow with a motorcar bought out of the proceeds, Dadie pale and piano, Sebastian not quite killed by his walking tour with Peter – his heel got sore before Peter's but Peter's toe got spoilt before Sebastian's.

Dennis came in yesterday looking very well. I told him that you were aching to marry him off and that you were sure there were dozens more equal to the one who chipped his heart in the holidays. He had a very nice letter from Archie Rose who is 'enjoying matrimonial bliss' in Shanghai, his wife having now joined him. I hope he really is. Dennis doesn't like 'M.P.' and thinks that he gives the *Nation* a catty air.

. . .

Hubert says in a letter that he and A.G.G.[1] had lunch at the Reform Club – 'Afterwards we got drawn into a group, containing H. G. Wells who seemed very disposed to be friendly, and rambled on in this kind of way. "I'm thinking of leaving the Labour Party and joining . . ." "What, the Carlton Club?" "No – the party of John Maynard Keynes. He seems the only man in England with real radical ideas . . ." and so forth.'

So you see that you and Wells agree after all!

I expect to get a letter from you to-morrow very full of Vera's gossip.

Your very fond

M

1 A. G. Gardiner wrote a regular column in the *Nation* on 'Life and Politics', while M.P. (see above) wrote one on 'The House of Commons'.

(Cayre's Hotel), Paris, Monday 28th April, 1924

Absolutely without any strength, my legs twich incessantly and even the hands and I can cry every moment.

. . . Tonight as Florrie goes away tomorrow I consented to go to the theatre to see a farce, but what an air of congestion in the theatre, behind us sat the daughter of Baroness D'Erlanger who married the French Marquis, who sat behind Vera with an American lady, who in her turn told him that I was a famous dancer. The Marquis said, looking at my plover egg, 'Impossible, I can't believe it, look what kind of hair pins she wears', he was almost disgusted with my appearance. I was amused.

Tomorrow I lunch in the Beaumont house with Picasso's. Stas begins to make difficulties (not with me this time) and asked me a 100 franks.

I look very sad and give you a sad but tender kiss.

L.

Florrie is posting this letter in London.

King's College, Cambridge, Monday 28th April, 1924.

Dearest miele L

I got your two letters (Friday and Saturday) by the second post this morning. I hope you sleep better. I have just been closing my eyes in my chair and should have liked to have you properly tucked up and in my possession on the sofa (even though it is an intellectual Cambridge sofa!). It sounds uncomfortable for the exercises. Can't Vera, with all her resources, find you a

176

larger room? Or could you study in the other Beaumont room which Massine doesn't use? I smiled very much over the proposal of Serge to Etienne. But I want to hear much more gossip yet.

Here there is much rain, but I shall start to ride again on Saturday at the end of the week. I live very quietly – with work and no excitements. Last night we had a concert to celebrate a new grand piano which we have subscribed to buy. The Provost 'opened' the piano with a pretty little speech; he is very well. I have arranged for the deposit of my old gentleman's ashes in the Chapel.

. . .

I am very well but a little sluggish in my spirit. I soothe your nervousness (can I from so far?) with calm touches and dull words. I think I might come to Paris for a night at the end of this month.

M

(Cayre's Hotel), Paris, Tuesday 29th April, 1924

. . .

I see that Cambridge is filled with 'dash and go', but why Dadie is 'pale and piano' I do not know. Too much *Dutchess of Malfi* perhaps. Florrie just left for 'Europe' and left me a box of ink 'Onoto'. I think I'll keep it for you. Picasso and his wife were at lunch in Beaumont's residence. They are charming. Picasso is making also one ballet called *Mercury*. I appear only in the 3rd tableau that last 2 minutes, and my part probably lasts a second, but I am called 'Proserpine'. . . . From the other side Stas sat next to me so one of the translations to Picasso was 'no one should trouble me then I dance like a God.' Beaumont himself is very nice and absurd, he is very fond of his wife, Volkoff's suggestions wrong . . .

At last I bought French *Times*, one of the editorials screeching loud against depopulation, Being a Malthusian I smiled sadly at the ignorance, but French are French and so the matter stands.

Touchings to you.
L.

King's College, Cambridge, Tuesday 29th April, 1924

My dearest darling Lydochka,

I hate the Boulevard Raspail and fear the Paris water. I hope your pains are better and that it is only the sudden change of life which makes you ill. (Is Florrie at the Raspail as well as Vera?) Here too we have been having pourings, but to-day the sun has come out and Nature is agreeable. After lunch I went down alone into our garden and sat in the sun and read your letter over again and felt very sentimental and fond.

This morning I wrote my bulletin of stocks – dry matter. This afternoon College business – new Statutes discussed with the Vice Provost, dryer matter still. I go to Gordon Square this evening after hall dinner and get there just in time to go to bed.

It seems to me that what you buy will cost more money than you have. So I send another £20. Is that enough? You are wise to be under their influence in buying. But do not be under their influence in *what* you buy. I hope that you go to the shop *alone*, but I fear this will not be so.

I can imagine what a sad face you had with your pains and I kiss it.

M

(Cayre's Hotel), Paris, Wednesday 30th April, 1924

. . . I am much stronger and had my sleep (such a necessity yet), had lunch by myself as Vera was gone (she had to for her child Nicholas) and I happened to have only English money, but of course an English genteleman gave me 10 shillings by 67, he took me for an English one, and so did the taxi man (who also was English). French taxi men are dreadful, so ruff in their manners and never content with 'pourboir' even when I am not frugal . . . Then we went to another place for the ballet, maison Lanvin (where Lil buys her toilettes), they took my measures for the Strauss ballet and Mme Lanvin was very nice, the idea is taken from Constantin Guys; I saw Mary Pickford, V. thought she looked like a daughter of a 'white negro', to me she had more sweetness than I can bear.

When you close your eyes I sit with you on the sofa in such a way that I do not steal an inch of intelect, and yet be a thief.

L.

I have need for money. Hotels are paid every week, in the place where I am established. I like to send money to my mother also.

46, Gordon Square, Bloomsbury, Wednesday April 30th, 1924

I came up last night to find all darkness and desolation, – not a soul here. Vanessa is still away with Angelica. Duncan, I am told, comes back to-morrow. I crept round to No. 41 like a cat to see if there were any letters for you. Darkness and desolation there too. Gordon Square is a poor dead place . . .

. . .

I write with a quick pen because Miss Rees comes and then I have five Board meetings one after another and then back to Cambridge. But I'm *very* fond of you.

M.

(Cayre's Hotel), Paris, Thursday 1st May, 1924

I kiss you vociferously, I have your letters yesterday and Tuesday and money and pictures etc. What a desolation Gordon Square sounds, but now you are in Cambridge and there is an atmosphere. Today is 1 May no taxis, so I walk from one metro to another with my tongue out to every policeman I meet and progress more or less, and yet I trust my legs more than Metro, in such a way I arrive to lunch at 3 o'clock. In the boulevard where I am established, there are no concoctions of revolutionaries, in other places probably such are feared, but would not arrive.

How much Germany shall pay is more *a propos* than anything else I suppose. The impression of Paris is that men and women struggle and work very hard and that is how they survive after war and postpone the difficulties; the people here would themselves annihilate Poplar's Guardians doles or pensions at once. Their conversation is vivid, so much that when they *Bonjour* to each other I tremble to see a scene of savages. Every nation has it's characteristiks.

. . .

My mother received money. Next time if you send me the letters, open them and include in the envelope for me only interesting ones.

I thank you for all the troubles, Maynarochka miely.

L.

King's College, Cambridge, Thursday 1st May, 1924

My darling L

I have from you a very sad letter written on Monday; and then the letter on Tuesday says nothing at all about how you are and feel. It is very naughty. You must tell me even when you are weak – or I threaten to telegraph or *telephone* from here! But I kiss you very much and want to be there to soothe the twitchings. I expect it is sleep that you do not have enough. It does not sound to me as if comfort and rest were provided in your beastly Raspail. But perhaps you are strong again by now – only you don't tell me. Yes, I could 'make arguments' about it; for instance that, when I think you may be a sad Lydochka, I think about you when I might be thinking about dryer matters. Which way does that argument work?

. . .

To-day I have been working very hard – my lecture for to-morrow and much College business – and have more still to do (letters), so I feel a little tired. However in the afternoon we had a little ceremony down under the trees by the river, because an old Fellow,[1] who has married a rich American widow, has presented the College with new gaudy gates. I stood there in my new silk gown and wanted to smile more than was allowed. I enclose the programme.

Last night I read Bunny's new book.[2] It is very sweet, I think. Its flavour very like *Lady into Fox*. It will amuse you anyhow. I am sending it to you in a separate package.

M.

1 Sir Charles Walston had presented the College with new gates opening on to the Backs of the Colleges.
2 *A Man in the Zoo.*

(Cayre's Hotel), Paris, Friday 2nd May, 1924

I am much stronger; I have today a big room at last . . . From 1 till 7 o'clock in the morning I sleep without disturbances, so twichings have dissapered. As for the 'argument' that I do not tell you how I am and in that fashion I interupt your subjects of intelect, *Oh* that gives me mental twichings! I am no more ill, on the contrary! I feel easier now. My appetite grows more astounding every day, I swallow cream cheeses with cream into direction of my mouth (I do not care to weigh myself) . . .

We rehearsed in the theatre today. I looked with attention into the colors of theatre inside, so that Picasso's curtain will be more than in place to look at. Strauss ballet is for 'the grand public', while the other *Salade* (I am not in it as it was supposed) is interesting only for a little while, there is too much 'futuristic' movements, but Massine is admirable in it . . . I like to read Bunny's book, so I thank you very much . . .

Lil and Sam arrived. We lunched with them at the Meurice, but the lunch was ordered as if we were Berkeley Square, you see the atmosphere. Lil flirted with Sam, and he as ever with her rose to the occassion.

What a talkative person I am, but crossings to your lecture.

L.

King's College, Cambridge, Friday 2nd May, 1924

. . .

To-day I made my second lecture. The audience was much bigger than for the first one, which pleases the vanity of the lecturer. In making up my lectures, the shape of my new book[1] begins to form in my mind, and I contemplate about it a good deal. This afternoon I was lazy and went to the University Library to take out more books about early civilisation; and after that I read them with satisfaction and they inspired me for my own book – I don't know why.

I have big feelings for you and kiss you very hard. You and the new book too are a little mixed up in my dozing imagination. I stand over you and touch you with fertilising drops and water you like a plant. He is big as I write and smells of incense and holds his moisture like a cloud.

But I must go away and have a dinner at 6.45 (which is an impossible hour) with the French Ambassador – to prove how pro-French I am when I am not. It doesn't suit my mood at all.

M.

1 His next book was *A Treatise on Money*, which was not published until 1930.

(Cayre's Hotel), Paris, Saturday 3rd May, 1924

As I lead such an 'iron life' at present and see nothing but the demolished ball rooms of Beaumont, where we rehearse, so my constitution revolted and instead of going to a rehearsal at 10 o'clock I called up Vera and we went off to order hats; I *myself* chose almost *what* to wear, 1 hat for all occasions black, another for my tailleur suit red, to match the little bag of the same colour, each 150 francs, in pounds it is not very much, then arrived at 11 o'clock and lied that I was too ill to come earlier, excuse was that yesterday was very hard work.

Muriel Gore arrived from Italy. One of the survival of fascism is a revived hatred for the Germany in a big degree, but order was there and also true that most money is spent by rich Germans, who seem to be richer than almost Americans. What an out of place conduct and millions of struggling Germans who suffer for these few 'illegitimate profeeters' . . .

I go back again to slave in pink legs, my costume of *Gigue* (a series of dances by Bach) by Derain, is more than lovely, a costume of a princess, short skirts, colors grey green and blue, adorable and with touchings of adoration for you.

L.

King's College, Cambridge, Saturday 3rd May, 1924

. . .

Dinner with the French Ambassador last night wasn't so bad after all, – but only because it was in the most beautiful room in Cambridge, the Combination Room of St John's College, and the food and wine were very good; the

Ambassador was a commonplace man and his breath was not sweet. Oh! also because I sat next Cecil Taylor[1] (Sheppard had been asked to the party and insisted on bringing Cecil with him) who is just back from Greece and had stories to tell of his travels. Afterwards I refused to go to the French play and sat gossipping with the Master of St John's who is an old gentleman and the head of the Conservative Party in the University.

This afternoon I have been riding on the hills with Sebastian and am just back with my riding breeches still on. He went to the party given by Carrington and Bunny (to which we were asked) and gave me an account of it. Jorby MacVorly[2] gave her entertainment and was a big success, – only there were again some who were shocked and said it was morally wrong that so much ugliness should be displayed (especially E. M. Forster thought this – I agree with you that his *Nation* article about Wembley[3] was most amusing). Other entertainments were French Songs by Cyril Carr[4] in his over-good French – indecent but noone could understand them; also recitations by Dobbie! Lytton was there and seems to be better.

I kiss you

M

I send you the *New Republic* for rather an interesting article about Picasso.

1   C. F. Taylor (1886–1955), a schoolmaster at Clifton College, Bristol.
2   Not identified.
3   This was 'The Birth of an Empire', written after his visit to the British Empire Exhibition at Wembley. *Nation*, 26th April.
4   Not identified.

(Cayre's Hotel), Paris, Sunday 4th May, 1924

I have been to the Longchamps races and with Sam's Lil's consientous advice have been able to establish 5 more franks to my pocket. The horses with jockeys looked attractive mixed with nature surroundings, but humanity crowd was rather ugly . . . For lunch I was again in Berkeley Square with lamb chops, green peas and filet of sole. I had so much to tell them about *The Man in the Zoo*. You called sweet, I call 'touching'. There is no more doubt Bunny is talented when he writes . . .

I see how a composition creeps out into a forme out of your lectures; in a different and lesser degree it is when I make exercises and then compose dance, of course your head is infinitely more elastic than my legs. As for this lecture, having more audience is a very recordation of your last one, but then you too belong to progress and I catch it from your eyes.

L.

How are politicks? If McKenna duties are not in 'duty' I might send for a box of Bath Oliver crackers.

My hotel is about 500 franks room, coffee and water. I pay every week; it is comfortable now but expensive.

King's College, Cambridge, Sunday 4th May, 1924

. . .

I don't think you will find anything in this week's *Nation* into which to look closely. Rather dull. I have to write two articles for it this month; but after that once more I make a good resolution to write less. Journalism eats one up; leaves no energy for bigger matters. I have a letter from Frank Ramsey from Vienna about the mad philosopher genius Wittgenstein. It seems that *three* of his brothers have committed suicide; so perhaps it is better not to be so wise and to be unphilosophical.

I expect by now you settle down completely in your new life and have steady impressions. What are they like?

M

An old pupil has just come in for advice. He doesn't get on in the world and "can't think why". How can I tell him that the reason is a certain ingredient in his soul which causes him, quite discordantly from the rest of his character, to leave his finger nails dirty? So I make a few feeble suggestions on other lines.

(Cayre's Hotel), Paris, Monday 5th May, 1924

A new choregraph the Count himself? The ballet called *Vogue*, our tableau about three minutes, with a young man and young girl who is like a boy, and I the woman of smart set. We lie on the beach in Lido, the man and the boy are 'getting on' so that I must produce a vexed face and stand in the middle, showing a costume made up of miroirs (*dernier cri* naturally). I do all I am asked except that I cannot look jealous, not in my nature of such circumstances. Massine does not interfere, it is not worth while either. A good *reclame* for *Vogue*, but perhaps I sound too sarcastic . . . I am pleased as ever that you write for *The Nation* again, it is an easy task for you, and does not diminish your intelectual energy for the book, and also it is not a question of finance, and also that is why I am a subscriber to *The Nation* with a 'favorite'.

When you come to Paris, do you go to your old place, or I prepare one you like to choose, it is better to know ahead long time. Paris is overfilled. I feel very small and tired and like to sit on your couch without motion.

L.

King's College, Cambridge, Monday 5th May, 1924

I got two letters from you this morning – Friday's and Saturday's. But I'm not *quite* convinced how well you are. It doesn't sound like enough sleep. And next Friday, poor creature, you start the cycle, I calculate. Anyhow I put crosses and kisses on you, and as soon as you write convincingly I shall be convinced. How do you like the parts Massine has made for you? How many are they? Are they heavy work?

I see that by the time I come to Paris you will be completely dressed up as Vera's Lydochka and I shall have to look through the wrappings for Maynard's L.! But I'll hope for the best.

My dinner yesterday was quite nice – two new ones – a red-haired freshman who is a genius at mathematics and a young Oxford Fellow who studies philosophy. So it was all about Einstein and Wittgenstein and Freud and light gossip of that kind!

This afternoon we began again to discuss the new buildings. I think that Kennedy will be given his chance to make designs but I doubt if they mean to accept him.[1] We will see.

To-night my Political Economy Club meets and I read yet once again my old paper on Malthus which most of them have not yet heard.

Will you be able to get a room for me in your hotel when I come to Paris?

Yes, I saw that Elizabeth had written a poem in the *New Statesman* but I did not read it. I also saw her portrait by John in *The Times* (Royal Academy); he makes her long and slim, but she is short and fat.

M.

1 George Kennedy was an architect introduced to King's College by Maynard when a new building was being planned. Kennedy's design was eventually accepted, but it was never executed because it would have involved demolishing some fine old buildings.

(Cayre's Hotel), Paris, Tuesday 6th May, 1924

. . .

My red hat arrived I look saucy, in the black I have an air of 'Mlle Nitouche'. The suit will be ready tomorrow, I am yet to acquire a coat and that will be about 1500 franks, quite expencive but [not] so expencive for Paris. I do like to know how much capital I posess, the Count does not offer my 'voyage' yet, and I do not like to ask, or should I?

Massine this morning asked me an advice to give 3 ballets or 2 and a one act play. I thought with the play is better, because his *Salade* and *Mercury* are all the same in movement, and also better to make it different from big Serge, but of course they try to imitate him, although denying it. They also should aim at the 'grand public' and not for little groups, Big Serge always knew that, I wonder if they realize it.

Older I am more critical I become, and older I become more prudent (with men) I am.

Tender kissing.

L.

King's College, Cambridge, Tuesday 6th May, 1924

My dearest, darling L

I have been to Longchamps too a few times, but I don't think I ever came back with a profit; but then I never went with anyone so prudent as Sam – last time I went it was, I think, with Falk.

I have been in a bad temper all to-day, because early in the morning when I was in my bed I heard someone prowling round my rooms, and then later it came again and it knocked hard at the door of my W.C. while I was in it, and I hated it and locked my bedroom door and knew it must be some terrible bore, and at last after 2 hours I had to come out of my bedroom to do my morning's writing and there it was, sitting on the sofa, – a dear old friend back from abroad whom I hadn't seen for many years and had been very kind to me in the past and *was* a paralysing bore; so my passions rose and I glared at him and just pushed him out, which was very bad behaviour and therefore left me still in a bad temper.

. . .

M.

Cayre's Hotel, Paris, Wednesday 7th May, 1924

'I hope he shall not hate me' Vera said, when I was completely Vera's Lydochka in a new suit and hat, but she smiled very much on your comment on 2 Lydochkas. One evening I promised to go with Allegri to a club to see 'La vie Parisienne', however V. put it this way: 'in the interests of Maynard I shall be your chaperone.'

Sam and Lil lunched with us before going to London: pictures excite so much Sam that he spends sleepless nights, he visited (with Garia) Degas, Braque and Constantin Guys' exhibitions. At lunch, in Russian, I mentioned a false tooth. V. asked me to be careful in English, because she detects very easely false teeth so that Lil-Sam had it; I told that you agreed with her on that matter, you also could see at once and recognise even a pimple on the gum! Garia thought false teeth were like Chinese to him, he never did know when one begins and another ends . . .

Your filosophical dinner sounds good to happen once a week, but then I am not a philosopher, I know nothing, but apply myself to you sentimentally.

L.

P.S. I do not order for you the room here yet, as we might go to a better destination.

46 Gordon Square, Bloomsbury, Wednesday 7th May, 1924

My dearest, darling L

I shall come to Paris on Saturday May 24 for the weekend. I should like to stay in your hotel if it is possible. Will you try to engage a room for me? Any sort of room will do. I should also like a ticket for the ballet that evening.

When I arrived last night I went first of all to No. 41 for your letters. All your carpets and curtains have been taken away – I suppose to be cleaned; so again the desolation was complete. Then I came to my study here – curtains also away and no smell of human life. But upstairs I found Vanessa and Duncan with a hot gas fire painting tiles – at least D had an air of painting them and V was actually painting them; so at last the house seemed to live again. And gossip warmed the walls.

It seems that Vanessa only got back yesterday, having stayed all this time with Angelica who has been quite bad, but is now better. Angelica is still away because it is thought that the country is good for her. Duncan was pleased with himself having just received a cheque from Falk for five guineas for advising him about the Ingres picture. We decided to have a dinner party here next Tuesday asking Virginia without Leonard, Mary without Clive, Desmond without Molly, and Osbert without – well, I don't know, but at any rate without.

. . .

The Income Tax people have taken no notice of the return you sent in, but have sent you a demand to pay the £2375! But do not be alarmed. I am taking the necessary steps. If you see Sam again, will you ask his advice whether he knows an expert for dealing with such matters?

Goodnight. I want your warmth for my spirits.

M

I enclose further £5. I sent letters from your mother, the general etc in another envelope.

M

Cayre's Hotel, Paris, Thursday 8th May, 1924

Milenky Maynard you put me [in] such a laughing temper in relation to your 'bad temper' with a friend belonging to one of those 'bores', you think he knew he was a bore? . . . I thank you for the money and the Lloyd's bank for my mother . . . My mother sais that she was ill 2 weeks, but she thanks me for papers [money], and also she made peace with my sister, after my counsil; but the lettre is just as short as when I write to the others. Heredity works sometimes.

The lettre from general,[1] he thanks me also for papers and hopes to depart to America not to be so lonely, and he needs capital but he does not ask me, the lettre is quite nice in spirit and a little mad. . . .

I wish I could hear again your 'Malthus', when you come to Paris bring it with you.

My fermentive impulses for your mind, body and soul.

L.

1   There is no way of ascertaining whether this general, to whom Lydia has clearly sent money ('papers'), was the officer with whom she was rumoured to have eloped in 1921.

King's College, Cambridge, Thursday 8th May, 1924

I am just back in Cambridge after my usual buzz in London. Last night I gave dinner at my new Club[1] to Lord Weir, who is rather a genius in his way, I think, and E. D. Simon M.P. (one of the directors of the *Nation*) and we talked about how to make 1,000,000 houses. To-day I gave lunch there to an old banker who is the Treasurer of the Royal Economic Society. I'm still terrified of the waiters, but less so than before!

At No. 46 Harland (who must have been making a lot of money lately to judge by his clothes) produced what he bought at the Monckton auction – a lot of old glasses, an old mat for which altogether I had to pay him £4, but when it came to a terrible old tablecloth and some broken crockery I couldn't humour him any more! . . . The stick, which I thought of for Kyril, went for £10, and so wasn't bought for you, you'll be glad to hear!

Vanessa says that, as we thought, Mrs H. and Grace were absolutely charmed by our chauffeur at Charleston. Apparently each evening he got himself up as George Robey[2] and danced Salome dances in the kitchen.

. . .

I found waiting for me here your letters of Tuesday and Wednesday. Your capital is still £91, and you will get about £250 from the Count. I will send some more money when I have been to the bank. I think that perhaps you might ask the Count for the 200 francs for 'voyage' saying that you don't want to have to change more English money than is necessary. But don't ask, if it seems difficult.

I thank V for chaperoning you. (Tell her that the word chaperon is Italian for 'old castrated hen'). But you don't speak truth, I hope, when you speak of mentioning pimple on gum?

I feel jealous of those who speak to you and read your letters twice to see how fond of me you are, and it is difficult to tell. But I find some miele sentences.

M.

1   The United University Club.
2   George Robey was a celebrated music hall comedian.

Cayre's Hotel, Paris, Friday 9th May, 1924

Oh such activity from 2½ till 7 in the theatre, first time with the orchestra the Strauss ballet, and my bleeding effects as well. My costume was very atractive I thought, but the direction decided to change and also instead of having a black wig (that does not suit me) my own hair, perhaps it is the plover egg form of the head that is lost in the wig.

Much compliments from the all concerned in the direction, my vanity is roused, I put my nose high and say to everyone *'Merci bien, mais il ya beaucoup à travailler encore.'* Stas is so discontent that he makes even a sour face at me, but the other dancer took me home in a taxi, I felt uncomfortable not to pay for it, although I insisted as much as I could.

About your room, Vera sais if it lies in her charge then you absolutely will have a room, but if I begin to think of it now, the menageresse will make me pay from the day you conceived the idea of your coming.

. . .

So many I's in this letter again, but I kiss violently, abundantly and quietely. I thank you for money, crackers, shoes and the troubles I give you about everything including the taxes! Nothing but 'damnation' for me to exclaim!

. . .

How is your book moulding, did you have a lecture also today, and do you prepare for the *Nation.* I feel so 'touching' towards you in all senses.

L.

King's College, Cambridge, Friday 9th May, 1924

Miele Lydochka,

I sit under the sun in the garden by myself, and so write in pencil. I am rather depressed and a little tired (I expect it is the cycle – I always have one at the same time as yours) and want to be comforted. However I've just got a very nice letter from you and that comforts me a good deal.

I consider how all your circle follows you and cannot be content without you – Veras, Sams, Florries all in Paris. If you had an engagement in Pekin, they would all be in Pekin. You are their elixir, and without you they are not fully alive. I should like some elixir too.

This morning I gave my third lecture. There are now only two more to give. This afternoon we decided to elect Frank Ramsey to a fellowship, which satisfies me.

This evening I go to a Feast at Trinity. Lord Balfour, who is Chancellor of the University, is opening a big new laboratory to study the chemistry of living bodies,[1] and the Feast is to celebrate this.

. . .

Warm kisses
M

1   The Department of Biochemistry, of which Sir Frederick Gowland Hopkins was the first head.

King's College, Cambridge, Saturday 10th May, 1924

I've just come up from playing rummy in the Combination Room and there are not many minutes before the post.

It was a big feast last night to celebrate the new laboratory, but Lord Balfour has gone soft in the head through old age. The one who wrote the article about salt in the *Nation* (he works in the new laboratory) was there, and I told him about your experiences, – so you see you promote science. But I think you put *too much* salt in. It ought to be only 1 part in 100.

This afternoon I went for a ride; but the ground is already getting too hard and I think it is the last time I shall go out this term.

I enclose a prospectus of the new Society I have joined for getting into intellectual touches with Russians!

I also enclose another paper for £5.

The lawyer writes that Bar [Barocchi] has not sent any letter, – so I suppose he changed his mind. They are still searching for Mary Hargreaves.

The man comes for the post.

Good night
M

Cayre's Hotel, Paris, Sunday 11th May, 1924

I sleep from 11½ last night till 8 this morning, then your letter written in the garden Friday served with coffee. I am comforted. You flatter me saying

189

that I am an 'elixir' to my circle, in fact I am every day plain water not even bubling.

. . .

I have a complaint to make against *The Nation*, they are quite a few misprints this week, so *the Bowens* might not buy any more although the copy they complain of is given to them from me. That and alcoholic questions were discussed in the restoran, Garia and I are for wine as a stimulus without danger . . . When I said I had a letter from you V. used Russian humour, 'I see he has not dropped you', but I like to have dropping instead.

A circulation of comfortings for you.

L.

P.S. I thank you for the papers. I give them all to V., she pays for everything. I buy apples.

King's College, Cambridge, Sunday 11th May, 1924

I am contemplative this morning and can't get dressed – it is half past twelve and I still sit in my pyjamas. I hope you are in similar mood at this moment and rest. It took me nearly an hour to gain resolution to clean my teeth. Perhaps the cycle is passing, or the sun and better weather is the cause. When I have finished my lectures and other odds and ends I have on hand, I think that I shall not begin the new book immediately but will first write a lecture which I have to give before the University of Oxford next autumn (an honourable occasion).

. . .

I am fond of you.

M

I enclose a paper for £5. Tell me when you have enough.

Cayre's Hotel, Paris, Monday 12th May, 1924

Oh I have been through fire and water with my nerves, as last night I came to a decision that I could not do *Vogue* ballet for so many reasons, and with Vera and Garia help[1] a letter was composed and dispatched. This afternoon when I saw him 'Did you receive my letter, forgive me.' The Count, 'Je vous deteste.' So I received his answer with a smile and now I am a free woman again. When the letter was composed V. asked 'would Maynard approve of it?' I said 'a thousand times so' and now when you read it you do approve of it?

. . .

. . . Only theatrical news for you to-day . . . The news are that the Russian ballet comes to Covent Garden in July for 6 weeks (I perceive Lady Cunard's influence). V. chaffed him [Diaghilev's friend Nouvel] for the 'favorites' and mentioned me, but he said, 'she is too fat for us.' V. said that Stas and I had big success in London, so Nouvel wanted to know who really had the success. Massine will be furious, because he hoped to be in London also . . . I saw a lovely 'toilette' for the afternoon appearance, aspired to it, but V. thought if I walk in this costume you should have a top hat, when we walk together, therefore that was not practical.

I cling to you with an administration from the heart.

L.

1   In his diary Harold Bowen explained that the ballet dealt with various forms of sexual perversion, and that Lydia was to have performed with Rupert Dome at that time 'the rage of Paris'. Lydia excused herself partly because the ballet was 'foolish in itself', but also because it was to be a curtain raiser for the first performance, unsuitable for a prima ballerina. However, Lydia did not disabuse those who thought she objected on moral grounds – 'such prudery is very piquant', commented Bowen.

King's College, Cambridge, Monday 12th May, 1924

. . .

It seems from the Evening paper that Poincaré is *beaten*.[1] It is wonderful – no such good news for a long time. The world seems a new place. I was very noisy in hall about it. How does Paris receive the news?

. . .

M.

. . .

1   In the French General Election that took place that day, Prime Minister Poincaré and the Bloc National were unexpectedly defeated.

(Cayre's Hotel), Paris, Tuesday 13th May, 1924

By now I am like theatrical rat, always in the theatre and without end we wait, there is not one controling voice in the situation, except the Count's polite but weak falsetto . . .

Last night after dinner we walked into Elysée, the trees and chimneys were envelopped in such soft pink grey skyes, I was loving nature very much: so did the others; the woman whom we paid for the chairs looked as a witch, taking the money and taking a few steps from us near a bush, but so that everyone could see, she picked a skirt and probably watered Elysée, strange French habits. Then we walked and spoke about you. Vera and Garia also love like me when you 'write purple'. So please, do not forget us in future. I thank you for paper but I did not ask the Count for money, I feel perhaps it is better not, anyhow the next Saturday I probably acquire what I derseve with my legs for a week.

. . .

Warming dispositions to you.

L.

King's College, Cambridge, Tuesday 13th May, 1924

I deposited my old gentleman's ashes[1] in the vaults of Chapel this morning, – quietly and without any ceremony.

At lunch a German Professor came – not very attractive. He travels with me in the train to London in a few minutes, since I am going up to Gordon Square for to-night's party. The Germans are so silly – they are not pleased with the fall of Poincaré because they think he will be more dangerous in opposition! It is not good for a people which is not subtle to think of subtleties.

I don't send any 'papers' in this letter, so Vera will be able to say that at last I have 'dropped' you! I send you something instead which you can't hand to V and is only for you and won't buy anything and is no good to anyone else.

M.

1   The ashes were those of W. H. Harris, a Fellow in law.

(Cayre's Hotel), Paris, Wednesday 14th May, 1924

This moment I am without clothes soothing my sick leg, although nothing can help but time and rest. Vera sits on the chair, I ask her to find news for you in the French *Times*, all in vain . . . I spend a great deal of money, but life is so expensive here. Garia makes my countings, till yesterday I spend 13 pounds each week for life, I do not think it will be less in future. Do not send me more papers, it is enough at present. With all my spending time in the theatre and heat, just like a woman I tried on my new coat, I need it. To-day you are in a buzzing atmosphere, and I contradict you with a still affection.

L.

46, Gordon Square, Bloomsbury, Wednesday 14th May, 1924

Yes, I'm sure you did right to refuse the unsuitable dance. I saw doubt in your words when you first mentioned it, and I suppose it got worse and worse.

19   *Vanessa Bell by Duncan Grant*

20 *Lydia with Virginia Woolf, 1923*

21 *Lydia with Dadie Rylands,
Raymond Mortimer (standing) and
Leonard and Virginia Woolf*

22 *Maynard by Roger Fry*

23   *Lydia and Duncan Grant at Studland, 1923*

24   *Clive Bell and Duncan Grant*   25   *F. L. Lucas*

26   *Sebastian Sprott, Gerald Heard, E. M. Forster and*
Lytton Strachey at Ham Spray House

27 *Maynard with Piero Sraffa and Dennis Robertson*

28 *Alfred Marshall, 1920*

29 *Lydia with Jack Sheppard on her right and Cecil Taylor on her left, 1923*

30 *H. H. and Margot Asquith*

31   Frank Dobson with his
portrait bust of Lydia, and the
original

32   Walter Sickert and Thérèse
Lessore

33   Outside the Alhambra: Lydia with Florrie
Grenfell on her right and Stravinsky on her left.
Nijinska and Trefilova are respectively at her
extreme right and her extreme left.

34   *Diaghilev, Polunin and Picasso in Polunin's studio at Covent Garden,*
1919

35 *Lydia practising, probably at Gordon Square, in 1925*

I want to hear the details when I see you next week. How many dances does that leave for you? I have no clear idea of the programme. Is it to-morrow you have the first night? Crosses on you. But I have no doubt about your doing your part, if they do theirs. It sounds a little confused. But probably all will clear up on the night. Loie Fuller's lights terrify me.[1]

Last night's party here was quite different from anticipations – Guests:– Mary, Bunnie, Marjorie Strachey; afterwards Virginia, Leonard, Lytton and Oliver came in. Sickert was to have come but sent a message that Thérèse was not well and he must stay with her. Mary had a scarf of the same material as yours from Paris which I gave you, but not pretty. Virginia was rather cold to her. Mary made up to Vanessa who was dignified and beautiful in her scarlet brocade. Later in the evening Jack came to fetch Mary and stayed some time, which enraged Mary because he hadn't been asked and she didn't expect him. Jack has been in Paris and told me about Lady Cunard's entertainings, – she seems to be full of money again. Jack also said that most of the money behind Beaumont's enterprise is said to come from a rich American called Berry who lives in Paris. Is this true? Have you seen him?

The conversation after dinner was about pornography – whether Virginia ought to write indecent stories and Vanessa paint indecent pictures. Then the discussion of vices came up and Marjorie became shameless and made terrible revelations about her own favourite vices. The conversation was bold and the outside world would have said, if overhearing, – Bloomsbury is worse than we thought; but all the same this might not really be true. Virginia and I came out as the only ones who were quite free from any tendency to bad vices. Bunnie tried to flirt with Virgina, – as indeed he did with everyone; *you* know his ways.

I haven't finished this letter yet but I must go on with it to-morrow. Meanwhile I kiss you hard and will consent to wear a top hat if you want the toilette *very* much.

M.

1 Loie Fuller (1862–1928) was an American dancer who specialised in lighting effects, at first for her own performances, later for ballets. After he had been smuggled into the theatre for a rehearsal, Harold Bowen recorded in his diary that on this occasion her lights were most inefficient.

(Cayre's Hotel), Paris, Thursday 15th May, 1924

Vera and Garia gone to London for 1 night, all of a sudden they had a chance to let their house for 3 months to a one of the favorites of Prince of Wales with a husband and children, V. thinks her house is not romantic enough for such a dame, but 'les affairs sont les affaires'.

We spend from 2 till 7 in the theatre, and I can't see or write to Quentin (he wrote to me). I plead [with] Massine to have clear lights in the scene where the phsyxological moment develops, but he is difficult. My costume is good, but my rehearsal skirts are much better as a costume with the decor. The ballet *Salade*,[1] now I like it is with singing, music is stirring and the decor of Braque very atractive, and the ballet is of a structure that develops like a building . . .

. . .

I bought cherries, beautiful in the mouth and as a color, but apples dear Lord God are of no good value to the present daughter of Eve. Can I exchange that *something* you sent to me on Tuesday, something I 'can't buy anything with' or 'hand it to V.' I feel it is very subtle, therefore I have the same waves for you.

L.

1   Harold Bowen recorded in his diary that although Lydia danced excellently in this ballet, she came off very badly, 'her part being extremely meagre and so arranged that it is impossible for the audience to applaud her if they would.' Massine, the choreographer, was 'determined that it was to be his triumph.' 'The result has come dangerously near not being a triumph at all.'

King's College, Cambridge, Thursday 15th May, 1924

. . .

Last night Sebastian and Lytton dined with me and putting on our full dress clothes we went to the Conversazione of the Royal Society. It was rather amusing – though perhaps the human exhibits in the shape of the old scientists were more interesting than the scientific experiments and explanations. I had never been to one of these occasions before. Wells was there and we spoke together for some time, – he was very flattering but I thought him rather full of gas.

This morning I began an article for the *Nation* of May 24 and felt interested in it[1] (You mustn't read my Insurance article in this week's *Nation*.[2] It is not meant to be read. I intended it to be empty and banale and I succeeded). But I shan't be able to finish it until to-morrow's lecture is out of the way.

I wonder very much about your first night. You have given me no positive assurances about it at all, – nothing has been praised so far except Derain's costume for you. So I wonder.

This is a letter of prose but I give you a kiss.

M.

1   'Does unemployment need a drastic remedy?'
2   'The meaning of bonus'.

(Cayre's Hotel), Paris, Friday 16th May, 1924

Scenes and scenes, the direction now decided for me to have a wig but it is made of black [illegible], and I looked ugly, so I made an unsympathetic face, they gave me another, but it is out of style with the others, too modern. I eat a little now and then taxi back, it is enormous distance, and next week we change the hotel. You are very touching when you consent to wear a top hat, it is a sacrifice. I cannot bear it, but I kiss and outkiss you.

Your party is the dear old Bloomsbury, I would not be suitable, but I like to hear from you, especially this time you come out with +, as you did not register vices that evening. Is flirting a vice? I flirt a little. Very often with taxi men, when they are English and sometimes with other nations.

When you come I shall flirt with you and prepare my vices for you [illeg.]
L.

. . .

King's College, Cambridge, Friday 16th May, 1924

My dearest, darling L

I have been touched this afternoon. I had news that my old master[1] who made me into an economist (the one who had an 80th birthday two years ago – you will remember his photograph) could not live much longer; so I went to pay him a last visit. Lying in bed in his night cap he looked like an old sage, which is what he is, – very Chinese. His voice was weak but he told me how he first came to study economics, and how such study was a sort of religious work for the sake of the human race. He was still able to laugh, but he has no memory for what happens now and has probably forgotten my visit already. I held his hand hard, and then went to speak to his old wife who has given all her life to helping him to do his work. She is calm and wise. He is now rather like a child and is often troublesome. He will do what the doctor tells him but not what she or the nurse says, and he calls out that, though he may be weak, he 'won't be bossed by women'. When I write to you about him, I can't help thinking a little of Cecchetti.

. . .

Much love from your *very fond*
M

1   Alfred Marshall.

(Cayre's Hotel), Paris, Saturday 17th May, 1924

. . .

My fibres are in a state of perpetum mobile, as tonight is the [first] night.[1] Last night general rehearsal did go well, but Strauss ballet is too long; I watched *La Salade* it is one of the best of Massine's. I returned home very late after 1 o'clock, Allegri and I were in the taxi, we were both over drawn with fatigue, not much even conversation.

Today Vera arrived. I am so glad, makes me feel more comfortable, more *chez soi*, it is so difficult to order even a dinner without her; she brought just now *The Nation*, I shall read it later, but it pleases me to see your name[2] in this particular organ.

> I can't write nor think
> a kiss and a cross from you only.

> L.

1 When she created the role of the street dancer in the first version of *Le Beau Danube*.

2 'Investment Policy for Insurance Companies', *The Nation*, 17th May, 1924.

King's College, Cambridge, Saturday 17th May, 1924

Oah, I've been sitting in a College Meeting from 11 to 5 to-day, making speeches most of the time, and feel bored and tired. However it is a very fine day and since then I have been walking in the garden with Leonard and Virginia and Dadie. Virginia has come up for the weekend to read a paper to a Society of Undergraduates,[1] and I am giving a dinner party in her honour this evening.

It seems from your letter that Thursday was not your first night, as I thought it was. Perhaps it is to-night. I re-cross my crosses. I see you soon now and I wish it was sooner – already it seems as if you had been away for months, yet not have [half] the time has passed.

> M.

1 She read a paper to the Society of Heretics on 'Character in Fiction'.

(Cayre's Hotel), Paris, Sunday 18th May, 1924

Your letter yesterday about your master [Marshall] was very nice indeed, and how we all bear relation to each other in this small wide world . . .

Last night everything was a big success, and to-day we gave a matinée already to not more than 100 peoples, why I do not know, but as I dance only one ballet which is last on the programme there is not much difficulty. Vera and my friends find as ever that Massine does everything to shadow me and not make me his equal, but also V. and G. think that I never looked better or danced better, and that my costume is *chef d'oeuvre* and big Serge can't say I am too fat. However we can't change nature of Massine, it is always twisted in the wrong direction.

The society world was very dull last night, all the princesses were there, but I was not sorry to leave them, Mortimer arrived very enthousiast, he knows Allegri so we spoke English a good deal, whenever I am tired English enters first into my head. Picassos took me home.

. . .

Touches to you of a very pure character.

L.

Late, after the performance and the party, I am here alone with your face and your letter, that gives me strength, and my feelings for you grow immesurably, passionately, I had a glass of champangne, but I feel very sad and want to run fast outstretchedly towards you.

(Cayre's Hotel), Paris, Monday 19th May, 1924

The place when you arrive is not Boulevard Raspail but: 12 Rue Jean-Gougan, Hotel St Regis. Vera and Garia moved to-day and I shall do so in a day or 2; there is a peaceful quarter, no milk men with pots at 6–7 in the morning, and the distribution of milk makes my eyes flicker untimely.

As Massine was tired, we luckily had no rehearsal and I asked Picasso's to come for lunch,[1] but in the end he snatched my bill so that I was struggling with him, however quick minded V. saved 'my honor' and while we convinced each other in the corner, she paid bill without bill. They were as ever charming, and of the opinion of V. and G. how Massine is 'mesquin' and that he will never achieve much with his meanness. He is also discontent how they treat his ideas and although they run 'Picasso, Picasso' they do not do what he tells them about his things, but he is wise and smiles and so do I. . . .

. . .

I taken your 'crosses with recrosses' and want more of those.

L.

[1] The Bowens were also there and Harold reported in his diary that Picasso seemed as pleasant at close quarters as at a distance.

King's College, Cambridge, Monday 19th May, 1924

I have your letter of Saturday I began to think that your first night would never come. I wonder how it was. You don't say how many dances you have or what they are like. I get an impression from your letters of a tired Lydochka. Is it so? I wish I was by you. (And I wish you were by me – I have been badly conducted and pinched myself where you forbid it – I could not restrain myself and am very sore! needing a calm hand). Let me see cuttings of what the French papers say about the ballet.

I forgot to tell you in yesterday's letter that a short story came for the *Nation* from Elizabeth just before my dinner party – so I gave it to Virginia to read aloud to us. The sour comments would have satisfied you! – but I expect Leonard will accept it.[1] It is called *Puju*. Elizabeth's letter with it was more reserved than usual, I think – I fancy I am given up, dropt. To satisfy you I enclose her letter. Quite cool – isn't it?

. . .

This afternoon I went to the furniture shop and bought a few things – two small light tables to hold a coffee cup or a glass of water, and a very nice armchair in the style of your chair of which the bottom is falling out but with arms. I have bought this without covering for the seat – and it is for you to cover it for me with stitches after a D and V design.

After that I had my haircut – so as to look young when I come to Paris. But there were many grey hairs amongst them. For once it was not Fitch who cut and I trusted myself to a cutter here. To-night Sir Josiah Stamp – who was the Reparation Expert – comes to stay with me and to speak to my Political Economy Club.

I seem to have work and engagements without end. I would like more moments to contemplate.

M

Next week I am asked by Lady Astor to put on my decorations and dine with the Queen of Roumania.[2]

1 'Puju' by Elizabeth Bibesco appeared in the *Nation* on 19 July 1924.
2 King Ferdinand of Roumania and his English born Queen had arrived in England for a state visit on 12 May.

(Cayre's Hotel), Paris, Tuesday 20th May, 1924

The room in a new hotel is ordered for you on the 24 till the afternoon 26, otherwise you shall sleep with Florrie, she enters the same day your room only in the evening. Parisian hotels are famous for 1 bed 2 people . . . Today in the *Comedia* is a criticism not at all stupid, but I receive hard knocks. 'Lopokova conserve la candeur touchante et *l'incertitude technique d'une debutante de*

17 ans. Tant Mieux pour la femme, *tant pis pour la danseuse*.' You see how badly I am established in Paris, but Vera and Garia insist calling me Mlle Poupsie de l'Opera.

Our season is not well organised, our costumes, except for Strauss ballet, ordered in cheap places, not as good as Mrs Colby and I cannot see any competition with big Serge, I hear he is in good humour already, yet our season could be a good success, that is annoying . . .

V. is already in the new place, but I am still with milk men, now I am told the sound of milk pots is really a liquidation of garbage!

I am inclined tonight to be of irritating character but fixed and constant tenderness to you.

L.

King's College, Cambridge, Tuesday 20th May, 1924

Dearest, darling Lydochka

I have your miele letter written after your first performance. Massine is a rascal. But I do not mind your dancing only a few pieces, for that makes you less tired, provided what you dance is good. And that seems to be so . . .

Last night Stamp stayed with me and was very nice – we gossipped until half past one at night. His address to my undergraduates was *very* good. He told them all the secret history of the negotiations which led to the Experts' Report, and they were much thrilled feeling that they tasted – as indeed they did – a slice of the big world.[1]

Stamp says that Ramsay MacDonald's vanity is now so great that it is almost impossible to speak to him. Also it makes him rude even to the other members of his Cabinet. Apparently he tells people that the Experts' Report is really his plan!

This afternoon I made a speech in the Senate House on the subject of pensions for old professors. Why I trouble myself on such matters I cannot imagine.

. . .

I see you soon.
M

. . .

1 Sir Josiah Stamp (1880–1941) was an eminent economist and statistician of London University. The report on which he spoke was the Dawes Plan, which provided for an international loan and an initial moratorium, with a later resumption of payments by Germany.

Letters between Lydia Lopokova and John Maynard Keynes

(Cayre's Hotel, Paris), Wednesday 21st May, 1924

Last night big Serge came to the theatre, but reports are that he did not express any admiration, he sat with Nijinska and 'favorite' and when Nijinska applauded he seemed disatisfied. To-day in the restoran Grigorieff – Tchernicheva at the other table thought I had an unsuitable part, and also irritated by the idea that Massine might have engagements in other countries, of course their life is not a light burden, and they are terrified of any competition, it is not what they said, it is only the impression of my impulses.

Today we rehearsed *Gigue* and I made a face of complaint to Derain that his superb design should be ignored, he said he shall not allow to have it badly made. I think this is one of best Massine's because no misanscene but only a dance for 4 couples, 2 diplomats and Massine, Stas and I, accompanied by piano with an 'etoile' pianist. Rather nice for a change instead of an orchestra . . . I see that my influence does not reach Cambridge from here, and the best is to give you a 'calm hand' when you piligrimage to Paris, it is to happen in 3 days so it will be very nice.

L.

King's College, Cambridge, Wednesday 21st May, 1924

Mary Hargreaves has been captured, – run to earth! So the [divorce] case is now complete.[1] But you won't be able to have your tea party with her. She lives in Philadelphia U.S.A. and sings with a touring opera company. More than a hundred enquiries were made before she was found. We have a signed statement by an uncle of hers that he saw her alive in 1919 – which is all that it is necessary to prove.

. . .

This evening I walked down to the garden after dinner – it is now very warm, and sat there as it got dark; but heavy rain came down (it has thundered here every few hours for many days past) and I had to hurry back with my gown wrapt round me.

. . .

. . .

I hope you get enough sleep. I invent this Coué-ism for you to repeat

I cannot peep
So soon asleep

M

1 Although to the layman it might be thought that bigamy was bigamy, whatever happened subsequently, in order to establish a nullity suit cautious lawyers found it necessary to prove that Barocchi's legal wife, Mary Hargreaves, was still alive.

(Cayre's Hotel Paris), Thursday 22nd May, 1924

... I am still in my hotel Boulevard Raspail and I shall send you a telegramme if I change, otherwise would you like to come to my place if the other room is not ready in Hotel St Regis for me ... My state of health is rather weak, I am tired everywhere and all the time, the heat contributes without doubt ...

I shall come on the station [on 24th May] if I am free, otherwise later.

Compound sympathy to you.
L.

Letters from
26th May 1924 to 19th June 1924

Following his two-day visit to Paris during the Cambridge term, Maynard wrote a boastful letter (28th May) to Lydia, which she unfortunately read to the Bowens, suffering one of Maynard's rare rebukes as a result. On 30th May Lydia reports more trouble over Massine's jealousy of her. On 2nd June she refused to dance in Mercury, *the Satie-Picasso-Massine ballet; the Dancing Times reported (July, 1924) that 'all the artistic world of Paris and a considerable proportion of that of London' could be seen making their way towards the première of that ballet. On 4th June Maynard said that, since returning from Paris, he felt 'extraordinarily well in the head'. On 7th June, Lydia, Vera and Florrie all lay together in Lydia's bed. On 8th June Lydia reflects on her desire to become, 'by my legs or comedy powers', an independent rich woman again. She was working really hard at last, as was Maynard; and – not for the first or last time – she did not wash herself for a week. She vividly reports (16th June) the riots over the ballet* Mercury. *She was buoyed up by Maynard's plan to return to Paris on 21st June, where he presumably remained until the season ended on 30th June.*

(Hotel San Regis, Paris), Monday 26th May, 1924

I myself a strange figure just now, when you are gone, as a temperature it is probably 3 5 or 3 6°, but looking back when we were together the temperature of our life had been productive, and we did promote something – outstanding, vivid and conquering.

I told Massine about my refusal,[1] Stas was displeased, he read the names in the newspaper who were coming to this ball and grew up a nose, so Massine is going to stage a new number, probably not his best effort, and I even asked the Count to give me a free evening and allow me to come into the stalls. He and Massine speak of nothing else but 'nos enemies' and although to-night there is a premiere of big Serge[2] a certain *princess* will arrive to Cigale instead, and satisfies our set.

. . . I wish you had come sooner than 4 weeks, I am a rich woman I received from the Count 4,000 franks so you could be my *entretien* at once.

L.

1 To perform at a charity ball – although she did so in the end.
2 Diaghilev had a season of twelve performances at the *Champs-Elysées*.

(Hotel San Regis, Paris), Tuesday 27th May, 1924

Vera and Garia and Florrie impressions of last night's big Serge's ballet are not at all tremendous: a good organisation it remains, and what we thought in Monte Carlo is the essence of their outlook. Lady Colebox spoke with Florrie in such a district: 'Diagilev's ballet is no more, Beaumont's ballet is the art of to-day, so I will use all my influence in England to let the others see what I see.' I see the dangers for big Serge but another Lady C. will stiffen his reputation for spite to Lady C . . .

Massine is very pleased over Serge's ordinary success and is planning to go to Spain.

After lunch we visited Constantin Guys[1] exhibition, it is not any more, but a good number was on the walls yet; he caught the scenes of life well, as illustrations it is charming, otherwise the noise about him is rather of a grandiose character and does not coincide with his pictures.

V. an G. went to see what we did see yesterday. Utrillos and Valadons, and of course in complete disapproval.

Do not spend your flirtations with Queen of Roumania she is only 'remains of the past', you being revolutionary will find a more comfortable seat in the 'burgeois society'.

L.

1 The decor of *Le Beau Danube*, by the Polunins, was 'après Constantin Guys'.

46, Gordon Square, Bloomsbury, Tuesday 27th May, 1924

Oah what a day! It is extraordinary what a big arrear even a short holiday makes. I have not paused for a second. Now I am just back from the Queen of Roumania party exhausted too exhausted to write you a proper letter. It was a terrific party – very amusing. I spoke chiefly with Austen Chamberlain, Lloyd George, Baldwin and Don Alfonso of Spain. The party looked very well with the Archibishop of Canterbury in his purple clothes etc. etc. After dinner all the world came in – perhaps you will see a list if you look in the *Times*. But I will write more interesting matters to-morrow.

I am happier to have seen you in Paris and to know your surroundings. We had a happy two days. I kiss you and have not yet become dry.

M

(Hotel San Regis, Paris), Wednesday 28th May, 1924

V. would like very much to have her name[1] as Vera Bowen, she does not like the idea of V.B. as it might suggest Vanessa Bell, nor V.D. [Donnet] which is out of date. If this result in writing will produce something monetary in her pocket, she shall be 'economically independent' hence, thence or since.

. . .

Count is discontent with me; I do not wear blue socks, but I give very substantial reasons. I acquired a pair of dancing slippers, as mine have not reached Paris yet, in the shop was a man whom I took for a Minautaur, he was of monsterously big dimensions (a singer for Wagner's operas) so I moaned of humanity with it's extra disproportions, later in the shop with cherries (1 pound is already stomached by me) I substituted my gloom with good humour; (the woman who sold was full of proportions) I think I always fall under an atmosphere.

Why do I speak so much, there is nothing original or surprising, yet miely inclinations to you.

L.

1   An article of hers on the Soirées de Paris was to appear in the *Nation* of 7th June. According to Harold Bowen's diary, Maynard had 'demanded' this article, which he, Harold, had largely written.

(64, Cornhill, EC3), Wednesday 28th May, 1924

I am in Falk's office attending several meetings . . .

When I sat down in the train and opened my *Times*, I found that they had about half a column criticising (but not unfriendly) my *Nation* article.[1] I have written them a letter of reply to-day which might be in to-morrow's *Times*. I find that the article has attracted notice (the *Financial News* had two columns of stupid abuse). The sea-crossing was quite calm for once and I got to No. 46 to find V. and D. sitting in their little dining room drinking water and so gave them the news of you and your affairs. (They may call to see you on Saturday about teatime at your hotel and would like to have a coupon with which to get cheap tickets for Sunday.) Then I posted the letter to Mr Dove asking him to send you the music – though I suppose that you won't want it if Massine stages a special number; also the rest of my proofs, which I had finished in the train, to Franck.

. . .

At the party Austen Chamberlain told me that Klotz and Colonel House are now both in London – so that little quarrel[2] will soon be settled. I asked that I might be his second, if it comes to a duel. As usual Baldwin was very sweet – I asked him about the interview – he said he would never open his mouth again, that never until his recent experiences had he fully understood the depths of human depravity,* that he had been rolled in mud for a week, that he sought sympathy from Mr Asquith, and that Mr A. said that he was no longer shocked or surprised by anything. After dinner was over he came up and put his hands on my shoulders and said (I was wearing my order of the Bath) – 'You look such a good dog with that collar round your neck'. At dinner I sat next but one to Lloyd George[3] and talked to him a good deal. He praised my *Nation* article and approved it very much. Then he made indirect flatteries to me, saying to the lady between us – 'I approve Keynes, because, whether he is right or wrong, he is always dealing with realities.' Very dangerous! When the ladies left the table and we stopt to drink port, I was called to the top of the table to sit next the Infante Alfonso of Spain (I suppose he is the brother of the King). He was very surprising for a Spaniard – indeed almost incredible; he spoke English like an Englishman, said that of everyone I was the person in London he wanted most to speak with, that he read my books with greatest care (more flatteries), and then went on to discuss Dawes Report and European situation with full knowledge. He said that no Latins could do finance because they were not honest enough and that Spain must be a decadent country until she changes her moral outlook. Anything less like one's idea of a Spanish Infante I have never set eyes on. He introduced me to his wife, who seemed suitable to him.

. . .

I kiss you and put crosses on the part of the body which had pains; it is a precious part and you must take full care of it.

M.

. . .

* Adding (to me) – 'I daresay you know all about it, you're such a wise old serpent.'

1 'Does Unemployment Need a Drastic Remedy', *The Nation*, 24th May.
2 The British Treasury had been accused of manipulating the French franc.
3 Lloyd George had written in *The Nation* on 12th April calling for a large-scale programme of public works.

Letters between Lydia Lopokova and John Maynard Keynes

Hotel San Regis, Paris, Thursday 29th May, 1924

What an attractive stimulant *your* party has been, it is very interesting when you describe it: the remarks of a 'such a darling' as Baldwin and the mental output of the Infante produces a thrilling of life. L.G. saying is also very inteligent; the result is that you were the *international* approval of this ingenious assembly.

Now you see that I had to read it to Vera and Garia. They were enthousiastic hearing it. I shall buy *The Times* to see your reply: it is exciting. Everything is closed here, Jesus raised himself to the skyes, but I hope the big poste will be opened as I need stamps and such necessities, I think, are left without Jesuse's influence.

Massine is more than polite and admires my cristalls, so does every one who seems them. I sleep in them and as it is summer I do not expect the heat of amber from them.

Good critisism of me in the French *Times* but it is probably bought, it praises the Count and ignores big Serge so I draw the conclusions.

. . . I am pleased to be utterly inactive, and re-read your letters.

L.

King's College, Cambridge, Thursday 29th May, 1924

I have been sitting in the garden reading a book about Ancient Weights, – the laziest possible occupation. But yesterday and Tuesday I did not rest for a moment and so need a little peacefulness.

My letter appeared in to-day's *Times* – on the City page – in fine large type. I shall also have to write a short article for next week's *Nation* on the same matter.

There is a slightly troublesome piece of business which I am afraid you must do in Paris; because there is another paper to be sworn for the lawyers. You will have to go to the Paris office of the lawyers – Messrs Kenneth Brown, Baker, Baker, 5 Rue Scribe, Paris – to sign a paper, of which the enclosed is a copy, before the British Vice-Consul. They will have the necessary instructions,[1] but it might be well to ring them up first on the telephone to fix an appointment. Take Vera or Florrie with you to hold your hand and sustain courage. This business ought to be done as soon as possible.

I am sending the £10 to your mother to-day.

. . .

Do you know why Utrillo and Valladon are exhibited together? She is his mother!

M.

1 This refers to Lydia's divorce proceedings. (The lawyer Kenneth Brown was Maynard's uncle.)

Hotel San Regis, Paris, Friday 30th May, 1924

I am a determination itself, and that is how I arrived to such a decision, I went to a rehearsal for that damnation ball to-morrow, Stas came into the dressing room with a newspaper of announce and it said how this charity ball includes all the amateurs society and L. Massine. As it is a thing of *charity* I absolutely want my professional name, and as Count is very busy I left the dirty theatre and here I am confessing it to Vera and Garia who of course approve it.[1] Besides my costume is the same as corps de ballet and they do not take least trouble to make it better. I long to have one evening free and that is such an occasion. The Count must not overlook these matters and, if he does, there is penalty for him; the announcement certainly comes out of his organisation. To-night I shall tell him so.

. . .

I sigh, but cherish for your intelectual embryos with positive advantages over such hideous mental corruptions.

L.

1 The Bowens shared Lydia's indignation; however, on the night Lydia and Idzikovsky had a great success with their *pas de deux* and had to repeat it. (Harold Bowen's diary.)

King's College, Cambridge, Friday 30th May, 1924

. . .

It was naughty of you to read out my letter about the banquet to Vera and Garia! To *you* I can make boastings and not fear to be misunderstood – it is an internal boasting. But to others it is not so well.

I am glad at last to get a letter from you in which you seem no longer tired – I expect you sleep better?

. . .

My *Nation* article attracted attention. There are articles about it to-day in the *Spectator* and in the *Manchester Guardian Commercial*; so I must make a reply to my critics in next week's *Nation*.

Perhaps V.B. will alter V.B. in the proof, – anyhow I will tell Leonard. Yes, she will of course have the usual payment. (I had forgotten that both the V.'s were also both V.B.'s – very confusing!)

. . .

I also am content to be inactive just now. I think of you in bed with your crystals on.

M.

. . .

Letters between Lydia Lopokova and John Maynard Keynes

(Hotel San Regis, Paris), Saturday 31st May, 1924

Last night I had my 'conversationi' with the Count, he of course pleaded not guilty that he never edited this advertising etc. and he asks a *favour* to do it for him, so you see Lydochka agreeing towards it, but very independent telling him that director should be a director and not overlook mishaps.

Duncan and Vanessa arrived after the performance, I stayed with them in the dancing, Segonzac, Clive and some other unknown types. V. was tipsy and very nice. Segonzac danced a Russian dance rather with gusto, D. followed him a little, but S. was almost professional . . . Vera said that she had a letter from you with kind words to my womb, *Oh* Maynarochka!

. . .

I thank you all the troubles I give you.

L.

King's College, Cambridge, Saturday 31st May, 1924

I hope I didn't terrify you by sending you a telegram this morning! But the lawyer telegraphed to me – it seems that there is a risk of our being too late[1] for the July sitting of the High Court, which would mean a good deal of delay.

To-day again I have been bored and tired by one of these College meetings which last all day and prevent one from doing any serious work. . . .

You see that Mrs Russell has won her case.[2] A wrong decision, I think. I thought the two judges who were against her made better arguments than the three who were in her favour.

Will you send me a copy of the *Temps* which had the criticism of you?

Miely inclinations (I plagiarise*)

M

* Do you know that word?

1 Although it was not too late, the divorce case was not taken in July owing to the illness of one of the judges.

2 The Hon. John Russell had brought a divorce case against his wife Christabel because she had given birth to a son although she had never allowed him to consummate their marriage. She insisted that she had never had sexual relations with any other man, fought it through to the House of Lords, and won. Since her defence rested on intimate details about what went on in the Russell marital bed ('Hunnish practices' on the husband's part, according to the wife), the case had attracted much attention.

Hotel San Regis, Paris, Sunday 1st June, 1924

Yesterday's ball seemed very prosperous, the Count's perfect 'metier'. Stas and I were prosperous also in success, although we danced with a net in front of us, and Massine in another scene danced without it. I register facts that do not encourage me with devotion to M.

. . .

I had not my sleep well, towards lunch time Florrie invited us to a charming spot in the Bois for lunch with Grigorievs and an attractive list of dishes, saumom, pilaff and fraises de bois, all of which was pure delight, yet too small in portions, however in ½ hour we go with other rich friends to Prunier (the restoran I wanted but could not mention to you for loss of memory when you were here) so by now we contemplate to order a bigger course.

My room is the only room where Vera and Florrie come lie down and do not fall out as from their own, you also thought it was one of those comforting beds, so I shall preserve it, by the majority opinion.

Tremendous shots of guns were going to 10 minutes, such fear entered into me, another war, I ran to Vera, Florrie assembled already and Garia, Vera thought the Germans or English were invading the spot, the supposed reason is the change of Governement, F. perfectly English in this sense, said 'how rude of them.' G. wanders from room to room and asks for 'gossip' and I touch you with a miely quality of a kiss.

L.

. . .

King's College, Cambridge, Sunday 1st June, 1924

I have been wonderfully well and strong to-day, and accomplished what I don't do above one day in the year – I wrote for five hours with full concentration and without flagging. The result is that I have almost finished a long article (replying to my critics) for next Saturday's *Nation*.[1] If only one was always at the top point of one's cycle!

I went out to lunch with my mother and father whom I found very well, and I've just had dinner with Sebastian and Peter and two others. In the afternoon I walked out to see the pupil who has phthisis. He is very bad but was full of the charm and sweetness which very ill people often have. They will take him away soon to a sanatorium and it is just possible that he may recover.

I wonder what your programme will be this week. And how is your stomach? Have you made Massine do away with some of the liftings? As a punishment for getting two letters from you on Friday, I have now had nothing from you for two days.

I feel strong and courageous and very fond of you, and kiss you correspondingly.

M.

1   'A Drastic Remedy for Unemployment: reply to critics' *Nation* 7 June 1924.

Hotel San Regis, Paris, Monday 2nd June, 1924

What an intelectual achievement, so that I wait longingly for the next week *Nation*. I also worked for 5 hours to-day, but the product of it is not of much importance, it is the new little ballet *Les Roses*, only dancing, no play; Stas, Polish girl and I. I refused politely to dance in *Mercury*[1] and have an air of a primadonna with Massine. Last night I had a wonderful dinner with rich friends (Sam and Lil), my latest food passion big and little lobsters, this fishy taste eventually shall lead me to try an octopus one day . . . I told Sam how I despised the protectionist country as I have to pay 78 franks on 3 pounds of dancing shoes from Italy. What indecency of culture . . .

Tonight Hilda (the Persian subject) arrived. I shall see her in Beauvau in a few moments with a new coat on. It is very nice 'you feel strong and courageous' as I am an antidote of such elixirs and like a leech I suck a *little* from you not without your permission.

L.

1   This was a series of 'poses plastiques', devised as much by Picasso as by Massine.

King's College, Cambridge, Monday 2nd June, 1924

My dearest darling

A quiet day and the prospect of another quiet day tomorrow. I have finished up and posted my *Nation* article; otherwise meetings and odds and ends.

Two letters from you this morning – one the beginning and the other the end of your onslaught on the Count. Evidently you're in a galère where you must look after yourself. I am sorry for the poor damned soul of Massine.

I shall come back to Paris, so far as I can foresee, either on Saturday June 21 or Sunday June 22. I think it might be prudent for you to speak to the hotel manager at once about a room for me.

. . .

M

What a big political crisis in Paris! However I don't *at all* mind the fall of the franc.

210

Hotel San Regis, Paris, Tuesday 3rd June, 1924

I am again with rich friends (Sam and Lil) we speak about known and unknown, I prefer the known, but Sam thinks differently. Lunch I had with Vanessa and Duncan at Beauvau. They liked food and me also, it was quiet without Clive; V. and D. go out and stimulate themselves till 3–4 o'clock every night, I belong to the set of people who wake early, so many strange mixtures in me, at present I am tipsy and have feelings of irresponsibility to you, and if I do not declare it now you would not get my very wet kisses that buble out in such good forme only for you.

L.

King's College, Cambridge, Tuesday 3rd June, 1924

A most remarkable day! I haven't had a single engagement of any kind. 'Happy is the country which has no history' – I repeat of myself. The result is that I have quite finished the Memorandum of Stocks of Commodities, which has been hanging over me for months. Thank God!

I have had an answer to-day from the owner of Tilton[1] (the house near Charleston) offering to let it to me in the summer. I think that I shall accept it. You don't disagree, do you? Will you tell Vanessa?

I have a letter from *Vogue* asking me for a portrait of myself. As it is a paper which *you* read, I am going to make an exception to my rule and send them one!

I am told by the scientists that the Death-Ray is a complete hoax.

Have you had any good dreams lately? –

> She had dreams all yesternight
> Of her own betrothed knight
> And she in the midnight wood will pray
> For the weal of her lover that's far away.

M.

. . .

1   The house in Sussex that he was soon to rent for the rest of his life.

Hotel San Regis, Paris, Wednesday 4th June, 1924

Now it is 3 days since any washing was done on my body; we rehearse in the morning, afternoon come home, in the evening without any strength, but to-night I cannot resist ticket bought 60 franks to see big Serge's ballet . . .

Last night Sam mentioned his complete faith in you and awaits with patience the frank of 120, I do not see the papers but I know that the President trembles in his chair all day long. I do not know if it is important enough to deposit him off.

. . .

. . . I run to a rehearsal with my extencive fondness for you.

L.

(King's College, Cambridge), Wednesday 4th June, 1924

This has been one of my rush days in London – a great contrast from yesterday. I came up by the 10 train and am now sitting in the train again on my way back for dinner with my father and mother to meet a distant cousin called Conyers Keynes who is interested in the family pedigree and wants to pick my learning on that matter!

My last meeting with Falk to-day for some time – he is taking a month's holiday in his castle in the north. We succeeded in getting our way to-day (as usual) about some big changes of investments in the Insurance Company – it looked last week as though there would be a storm, but we quelled it.

I handed Hubert the corrected proof of my *Nation* article. He liked it very much and I had to admit that I myself thought it a good one.

Ever since I came back from Paris I have been feeling extraordinarily well in the head and able to get through a great deal of work without feeling tired or fussed. I hope you're the same!

This is a very dull letter and I must bring it to an end. I am in healthy and prosaic mood, but very much inclined for tender touches towards you.

M.

. . .

Hotel San Regis, Paris, Thursday 5th June, 1924

Oh! Maynarochka, do not have your portrait in *Vogue*! perhaps I am jealous to see it printed there; I kiss you touchingly now.

Last night at big Serge's performance, he gave me a very cool welcome and considered a few moments (that is how I felt) to embrace or not. Silly Serge, rather small headed this time.

The performance was smooth and proffessional that I always admire, but nothing or no one stirred me, besides I long now for very old fashioned ballets without abstract ideas, I want simplicity and *Poetry*. Massine or Nijinska choreography, clever as it is, have too much intelect, I rather be without in *this* direction. Picasso's curtain is more moving and alive in Serge's posession. The theatre was beatifully dressed and I had my cristalls, who sinse deserted me and dropped themselves on the floor, the string has been broken!

My face has been looking very sad towards the Count, so much that he decided to make a new costume for *Les Roses*, it is this Saturday.

. . .

Lil and Sam are going to London to-morrow, I have had so many dinners with them lately (Sam likes to feed me with lobsters and other preciositys, but I like poetry).

L.

. . .

King's College, Cambridge, Thursday 5th June, 1924

My dearest, darling L

This is my birthday (41 years of age) and I have had a miele birthday present from you in getting *three* letters on the one day. The weather is fine after many days of rain and I am in contemplative mood. The work in hand is finished, and I have to tune my mind for the next. This takes a little time and I have begun nothing fresh to-day. I am reading a good many books, chosen, anyone who looked over my shoulder might think, haphazard – but it is not so really, they make an atmosphere for me.

It is *very* wrong of you to say that you are an antidote of the elixir. I drew it from you in Paris. It is since then that I am strong. But I'm afraid that it can't last much longer. The moon in its courses will turn my cycle round. My water will become thick, my head fluid, and all small troubles will grow into big ones, courage disappearing.

When do they do *Roses*? Does that or *Mercure* come first? (I suspect that *R et J* [*Romeo and Juliet*] is a flat jeu d'esprit).

I also like lobsters. I eat half a large one at lunch several times a week at this time of the year, and the Provost (who shares the passion) eats the other half. When we come together again you shall be my Provost and we shall suit one another very well in the lobster matter.

What is the reply to this letter from *Vogue*? (Are we to appear together, do you think?) There is the drawing in my bedroom or the oil painting in my study at 46.

. . .

I put crosses on your sleep and on your bleedings and kiss you fondly.

M.

Hotel San Regis, Paris, Friday 6th June, 1924

Oh the joy of living, I bought a real apple, it is the same in Paris as to find a rarity in British Museum. Last night *last* dinner with Sam and Lil . . . Lil asked

213

Vera if I would not mind to take as a present Lil's new dress that is cut too small for her, price 30 pounds; I certainly shall, more than pleased to accept, would you do the same on my place?

Your lines written in the train on Wednesday bubble with gay spirits, and my mental womb is already in the atmospere to receive your *Nation* 5 hours intelectual production.

. . .

Florrie gave a ride in the Bois for me, we spoke about men, women, society, disqueting but interesting to indulge into words about it. To-night I am going to see *Les Biches* that made more stir than other [Diaghilev] ballets; I am free to-day as nothing is ready for our new ballet *Les Roses* but in a philosophical sense I profit by it, so as to say restingly contemplating, and increasing my dimension of tenderness to you.

L.

King's College, Cambridge, Friday 6th June, 1924

This afternoon I walked round the shops and ordered for myself a pair of fawn coloured trousers which are beginning to be the fashion – I don't know if I shall dare to wear them! Then, as usual with fear and trembling, I bought you a pair of earrings – eighteenth century paste; but with strict understanding with the shop that I could send them back – for perhaps you have a prejudice against paste, or they don't suit you, and I don't even feel sure that I like them myself.

I go to a party at Dennis's to-night.

I would like to embrace you hard to-night.

M.

Hotel San Regis, Paris, Saturday 7th June, 1924

I was lying in bed, Vera on one side, Florrie on another, my bed is suitable for more than one, then telephone rang, a Russian well known writer Kooprin (whom I never met) who asks me rather insolently to help another Russian young writer, I said I shall see what I can do and gave telephone to V. where he continued to be like leech with her. It is an unbearable conduct . . . Being a genuine case I cannot refuse and will give 50 franks.

Vera's *Nation* arrived.[1] She is dissatisfied with cuts[2] [in her article] not because they exist, but because it is done without meaning, especially about Picasso's curtain. Enough of complaints, I loved your letter on your birthday, and I shall give you the long promised Eau de Gurlain when I receive more money from the Count (that I hope will happen Monday), otherwise I kiss you with birthday as without in such variety forme that you shall not notice the monotony of it.

Last night I saw *Les Biches*, I thought it pretty. Serge was even colder than before. The Queen of Roumania arrived, she seemed not to take revolution of her nation seriously, I would stay 'at home' in her place . . .

I think Duncan's drawing of me would be serviceable for *Vogue*. Please if you have a few moments to compose an answer [to *Vogue*], I have so many engagements, and also it is difficult matter for me to write in English, except to you.

L.

1   In her article on Massine's Paris season she criticised the corps de ballet as 'inexperienced', and was generally scornful of the production. Her praise of Lydia, especially as a mime, was fulsome. As for the ballet *Gigue*: 'Massine is stately, Idzikowski marvellously agile, Lopokova utterly exquisite both in dancing and appearance.'

2   In his diary Harold Bowen reported that almost one-third had been cut out and that Maynard was unconcerned.

(King's College, Cambridge), Saturday 7th June, 1924

I am sitting in the Summer House in the garden with the rain pouring down a foot from my toes – very much by myself. A pleasant smell rises from the wet ground.

I make *very* slow progress with my new paper, but when I have my ideas clear, it may run quicker.

What do you think of the enclosed letter? You must frame it and hang it in your dressing room! Lydochka is now 'an eminent leader of world thought and opinion'!

Speculations have taken a turn for the better just lately.

Here is a subject for an intellectual conversation: 'A taste for chastity is as arbitrary as a taste for big buttons.'

And here is a poem for you:

> J'ai calculé mon age,
> J'ai presque trente ans.
> Ne suis-je pas dans l'âge
> D'y avoir un amant?

I sigh to hear that your beads are broken. Can you get a new string in Paris? Crosses on your new ballet to-night.

M.

My cycle begins to turn.

Letters between Lydia Lopokova and John Maynard Keynes

Hotel San Regis, Paris, Sunday 8th June, 1924

. . .

Last night Derain came into my dressing room, to express his feelings of admiration. He was charming and touching, and I had a reflection that I could give him nothing back, I thought perhaps I was a stingy nature.

. . .

Oh I had a desire yesterday and to-day to become a rich woman again independently by my legs or comedy power; I saw so many old dancers, they are most poor or mad, 'Life is difficult', I sigh all over and lean on you.

L.

King's College, Cambridge, Sunday 8th June, 1924

. . .

In my bath to-day I considered your virtues – how great they were. As usual I wondered how you could be so wise. You must have spent much time eating apples and talking to the serpent! But I also thought that you combined all ages, – a very old woman, a matron, a debutante, a girl, a child, an infant; so that you are universal. What defence can you make against such praises?

I have written quite a lot of words to-day – my pen runs faster.

I *do* agree with you about the new ballet;[1] it must escape from these ugly abstractions just as painting has from cubism; it is *no good* really, I'm sure – just dernier cri.

My *Nation* article[2] has no purple for you at all, I fear, or even humanity.

M.

1 He is referring to her letter of 5th June.
2 'A Drastic Remedy for Unemployment: reply to critics' *Nation* 7th June 1924.

Hotel San Regis, Paris, Monday 9th June, 1924

After the performance last night Florrie gave her last party in a 'Caucasian Cave' (to-day she is in London), we were Vera-Garia, Leon-Hilda, J. H. Smith, Florrie and I, champagnes, 1 step, roasted nuts, good band with a leader that we excepted [accepted?] as Clive. I tried to seduce Smith and make him a marriage proposal, but soon I gave him up, he was too much of a 'snob' although he told Florrie that I was a 'perfect duck'. Garia was the ladies man, Florrie danced with all her might and we even told her that she should not open her legs so widely, she took the hint and improved the position, she is a sweet duck herself . . . My Russian American friend has established herself in Florrie's room, she saw your face, also she asked 'does he love you, does he respect you?' To fortify my 'yes' I showed my precious bundle of your letters.

That did stir a serious impression and no more explanations, but she is very nice and loves me well.

As for [Lydia as] the 'leader of world thought and opinion', I say after reading it 'Dear Lord God!' and I almost vomit . . .

What does your poeme imply? Do you advise me to become naughty in Paris? The intelectual phrase about 'charity' [chastity] I think is very inteligent, but I do not believe you will have a cycle this month even if you write 'purple'.

L.

King's College, Cambridge, Monday 9th June, 1924

This has been one of my dreadful wasted days, – I have spent more than eight hours in College and University Meetings and am much too tired to do anything sensible.

Also it is Bank Holiday – so I have had no letter from you, and yesterday being Sunday I didn't have one then either.

So one way and another I'm quite dried up and must just ask you to kiss me and moisten me out again.

M.

Hotel San Regis, Paris, Tuesday 10th June, 1924

Oh Maynard what you thought of me in a bath room on Sunday is something like wooing in absence. I am flattered and shy, and flattered again, I am not all what you say, but I shall improve with time and eat more apples.

Last night we had to dance, after our representation once more to an empty theatre, *Gigue* and *Divertissement*, because in the middle sat the Queen of Roumania coming after the Opera, so when the dance was over Massine, Stas (who is not in speaking terms with me lately) and I shook the hand of the Queen(she is well preserved!) and I asked her to contribute something in the world of dancing . . .

. . . Mondays always seem to be your dry days so I put my dispositions of licking you kissingly.

L.

King's College, Cambridge, Tuesday 10th June, 1924

Two nice letters from you to-day – but I have not had any letter of last Friday: did you send one? Three women in one bed! I felt a little shocked. How much longer does Florrie stay? I am sure that it is, as I said before, about the elixir. Sam and Lil have taken away with them enough true life to last them a short time. But they will have to come to the spring (or the well) again before long.

. . .

I live a very quiet life, still without many engagements, and sit in my room a great deal reading and writing. A visit from Desmond [MacCarthy] to-night. I do not go to London this week until Wednesday evening.

It seems a long time since I kissed you, but in 11 days I will be in Paris. I am fond of you. I am fond of you. I am fond of you.

Your dried up,
M.

Hotel San Regis, Paris, Wednesday 11th June, 1924

Again we work very much all day long, 3 rehearsals a day, this Saturday a complete new programme is established, *Mercury*, *Les Roses* and a sketch about a girl who dreams of dolls, I am one of the dolls, it lasts 7 minutes, but we are just developing and therefore almost dead . . .

. . . After lunch I ran to buy a new hat with little holes in it, and a pair of shoes made in such a fashion that the air penetrates the foot (complete blessing from the heat), altogether a ventilated person I am to be.

I have an impression from *The Times* that Cambridge is filled with 'dash and go', it seems you do not notice the 'season' because your head has so many compositions of thoughts, including humoristic phrases in your letters and flirting with me at a distance.

L.

King's College, Cambridge, Wednesday 11th June, 1924

My dearest, darling Lydochka

I have no news or even gossip for you because I sit all the time quietly in my room reading, copying prices out, and sometimes writing a page of my own. In the paper I am writing I want to make some short remarks about the history of opinion on certain matters for the last 200 years, and for this I have to turn over endless books; but the historical part is nearly finished now – it's probably waste of time.

. . .

On June 21 I come to you.

M.

Hotel San Regis, Paris, Thursday 12th June, 1924

The head waiter in Place Beauvau thought until lately that I was an unmarried miss and Vera – Mme Lopokova, so he told that V. dances at Cigale to all his clientele, so she is the 'smart woman' of our little group; he thought that Florrie was long and gay, but to me any day I expect a mariage proposition, as all the waiters have a soft spot for me. I still work like an elephant, I do not know why? I told Massine that he must give us one free night before Saturday to come into a normal condition, and also I have not washed myself for a week, because a hot bath wears me completely out, so I wait for the night of liberty.

. . .

I also want to know about the 'history of opinion', but 200 years does not seem formidable of an opinion. When you come to Paris I will ask you explanation on matters about 200000 years ago, and if now you have not many engagements you will have to spend your time in research for enlightening your 'precieuse ridicule'.

L.

King's College, Cambridge, Thursday 12th June, 1924

. . .

I sent the drawing of you by Duncan, which lives in my bedroom, to *Vogue* this morning. (I have not yet sent them one of myself!) Shall I be able to have the room of your American mother when I come next week?

. . .

The word in the intellectual saying was not charity but *chastity* – which makes much more piquant sense.

The Queen of Roumania occupies too much of your and my time! (Why aren't you on speaking terms with Stas?)

Not dry to-night – but very tired; so I kiss you.

M.

Hotel San Regis, Paris, Friday 13th June, 1924

In the theatre from 2 till 8½ for ever waiting, trying on costumes, and not been able to dance with the orchestra except for 7–8 minutes. I told Massine that except himself he considered the other dances as mud (in *The Roses* he does not dance), but the ballet with him he rehearsed for hours, so that musiciens when tired were logic to stand up and depart . . .

. . .

To-night is the night of liberty, I shall put my worn out legs into the embrace of hot water and recite ('Not from the stars do I my jugement pluck') and become irrational in my jugement of you, do you see my deep thoughts? That is that hot water inflames not only legs but consecuterely a head.

L.

King's Colllege, Cambridge, Friday 13th June, 1924

Yes – I take no notice of the 'Cambridge Season'. I see the poor things out of my window, but, as it rains all the time and is very cold, they can show nothing but the latest fashions in raincoats. However I take a part next Wednesday, when King's gives a big luncheon banquet in honour of the opening of an addition to the University Art-Galleries (Fitzwilliam Museum) by Lord Balfour. All the art bosses are asked, and amongst the names of those who have accepted the invitation I find Sam and Captain Douglas! I daresay I shall arrange to sit next Sam and so hear some news of you. Poor old milking-cows! I had a visit to-day from the President of the Three Arts Club – it doesn't exist yet but is an idea for the establishment of a Centre of Art, Drama and Music for the undergraduates. He had the original idea that perhaps Sam might be the benefactor for whom they have been looking in vain for a few years! But he was wily; he found out that Sam had had a daughter at Newnham; so he asked the daughter to lunch, expounded the scheme to her, and made her promise to use her influence with Sam! She suggested that I might be brought to beg too – hence his visit to me. But I replied – better not; if Sam consults me of his own accord, I will give him good advice. Sam will soon be the most famous milking-cow in England! and will be made a Lord;[1] but I think that his udders must be sore with so much pulling by strange hands.

To-day I have been reading a German book – short, fortunately, but one of true learning. But I also looked over a few English pages and found the following for you:

> But if the First Eve
> Hard Doom did receive,
> When only *One Apple* had She,
> What a Punishment New,
> Shall be found out for You.
> Who, to get wise, eat up the *Whole Tree*.

That was written two hundred years ago and has waited all this time for an application!

What a good thing you don't dance in *Mercury*, with so much other work.

. . .

M.

1 A mistaken prophecy, though it is possible that he declined such an honour.

King's College, Cambridge, Saturday 14th June, 1924

Lytton has arrived this evening and I am taking him to the performance at the ADC [Amateur Dramatic Club], so my 'season' has begun at last. In fact it began at lunch when I entertained a very nice middle-aged Burman who came to visit Cambridge with an introduction from Luce[1] (Luce sent you his love).

At last the sun has come out and the poor visitors are warm. I hope it isn't too hot with you. M's mania for rehearsals sounds crushing. My blessings are with you for this evening's première.

I have a vague idea that on July 1, when your season is over, we might go to a mountain somewhere (Switzerland or Pyrenees) for a few days before coming back to England. But I daresay not, – we can speak about it. Only I know you like a thing to be mentioned a long time in advance! Very likely you'll want to get back to Gordon Square as soon as you can, and I don't yet know for certain the date of your case.

. . .

I have a good complexion to-day and am fit to kiss, so I put my cheek against the mouth of my 'precieuse ridicule'.

M.

1 G. H. Luce (1889–1979) was a lifelong friend of Maynard's who had become Professor of English at the University of Rangoon and married a Burmese girl.

Hotel San Regis, Paris, Sunday 15th June, 1924

I boasted of your letter about Sam and his milking gifts, it was truly so funny, including the 'udder'. While you tell me about Sam, Vera reads to me Sam's letter to her about the same famous lunch; the only Sam's sorrow that he is not entitled to a red gown, but his face would do instead. What a swift carriere he has made for himself!

. . .

Last night the 'furore' of the evening was Stas, he had to repeat his variation, in it he does the same turns in the air as in the *Lac des Cygnes*, I looked very well, but there is no chance for me to develop any dance as all the pieces all too short. *Mercury* to me seems a decadence, Picasso perhaps wanted to pull the noses of the public, the colours are very good but the way they brought on, or executed, or what they represented is beyond my measure of comprehension. It is no ballet, no parody, but somehow a stupid fake. Smart audience and success, as always on the first night. I nearly came to blows with the Count; I refused to put ugly cheap (in taste) flowers, and he stamped his foot at me, I did not answer 1 word (I thought he was mad) but did not put the flowers just the same.

To-night I think he shall be enough composed to hear my opinion about his conduct.

Volkoff arrived, he asked me to go out with him, I shall for a little while at 5 o'clock. He lives in a house of titled English friends with an automobile in his disposition, he also inquired if you were in Paris . . .

How is your 'essay' with my favorite purple, I am just like a woman and want to penetrate in all your processes.

L.

P.S. I hope that my [divorce] 'case' is mentioned without a photo.

King's College, Cambridge, Sunday 15th June, 1924

Tom Eliot has just been to tea – it is the first time I have seen him since the fiasco about his being literary editor of *The Nation*.[1] I thought him very nice, and – apparently – steady in the nerves. Sheppard is more cheerful too – but I think you must hurry up in finding a nice wife for him, before he is too fat and grey.

. . .

The play last night[2] – Pirandello's *Henry IV* – was extraordinarily good as a play, and also very well done. Frank Birch, who produced *Troilus and Cressida*, was the producer – and I am getting convinced that he is the best of the rival local producers. Even Sheppard, in writing a notice of the play, had to admit that he couldn't find much fault.

. . .

This letter is dull; but it is my 'season' and I live trivially.

I enclose an article for you to glance at from the *Sunday Times* about the father of Vanessa and Virginia.

M.

1 Leonard Woolf having been appointed instead.
2 At the A.D.C.

Hotel San Regis, Paris, Monday 16th June, 1924

Oh what a demonstration last night. *Mercury* being the last on the programme, I went into the 'promenoir' to look steadily at the ballet and have a firm opinion about it. First tableau began with cries 'Vive Picasso', the other party replied 'Vive Eric Sati' (who wrote the music). 'En bas E. Sati et vive Picasso.' After the 2 tableaux pro-Picassoists became enormous and shouted 'Vive Picasso *seul*. En bas E. de Beaumont, les garcons, et toutes *Soirées de Paris*,' I was only a few steps afar from the young man who proclaimed this. Then the policeman rushed to him and arrested, anti-Picasso group ran to his box and shouted 'En bas Picasso' (to-day I hear that his wife stood up and screened him in the way of protection), yesterday I trembled, felt myself so very small and frightened, I ran back to my dressing room and so was relieved, humanity is very ugly when loses control of the mind.

To-day Volkoff came instead of yesterday, as we have no drawing room establishment, I offered to sit in Champs Elysées, however he had a splendid automobile to invite me in so we rode into the Bois and gossiped faster than we rode. He was asked to lunch at Count's house, the Count and Massine both pressed him to undertake a message to Cochran for an engagement in London as Volkoff knows Cochran, he will say 'why do you not go to Paris, and see a season at La Cigale that might interest you?' Such are his responsibilities and no more.

I received the newspaper and *Vogue* and *The Nation* and I kiss you backwards and forwards.

L.

P.S. My [divorce] case is with 2 earl's daughters, no so bad . . .

King's College, Cambridge, Monday 16th June, 1924

. . .

My visitors have gone away, and I am quiet again. Perhaps I am not very sorry to be so. Too much conversation, too much disturbance, all to too little purpose. I prefer to be quiet with you and read and write. However my 'petite saison' is not quite finished. We have the College Concert to-night and I put on a dress coat after dinner.

I still wait to hear about your first night. Is it too hot now in Paris? Here the weather has changed, and there is a warm sun. I am lazy to-day and do nothing but odds and ends.

I have an invitation to address the American Economic Association in Chicago in December about my monetary ideas. It would be a very suitable occasion, but it is too far. The International Labour Office in Geneva also takes up my ideas. I have written a little letter for next week's *Nation* in reply to Brand's. It is a busy life to be a propagandist.

. . .

M.

Hotel San Regis, Paris, Tuesday 17th June, 1924

. . .

I like to mount Pyrenées, yet at present I am in a state of no desire for an activity to perform, I want to read Pirandello's plays, they must be so imaginative. Package from 'service de colis postaux' arrived, Lil's dress for

223

me, 300 franks to pay, damnation; Vera advises to send it back to Gordon Square, 'she is such a free trader' and so am I, only to glance at a new dress is rather of a happy incident, so I am without an opinion, but with tender touchings to you.

L.

King's College, Cambridge, Tuesday 17th June, 1924

I hate Massine for his hateful ways – for apparently he has again tried to dull your light. If I had seen your sad face, I would have left no room for the others to kiss it.

This has been a quiet day with no engagements, but I have been very busy – for to-morrow I leave Cambridge for four months, so I have to finish up all my little affairs here.

M.

No photos and nothing else about your case except the mention in the list of cases in the paper I sent.

Hotel San Regis, Paris, Wednesday 18th June, 1924

It seems that on Saturday, if you come, there is no dancing performance, *Romeo and Juliet* instead, would you not like to see it, if it is too long and boring we might come out of the theatre before death survives the lovers.

How very nice that you are wanted everywhere and your intelectual seeds become plants in so swift a time. We are still rehearsing to perfect ourselves or to give something to do to the Count or Massine.

. . .

It is long time that I am spending in Paris, I have enough, and yet I did not see anything worth seeing; Louvre, Luxembourg, when my legs work professionally I cannot use them in other directions.

I come after the theatre later, but I see glorious moon, and the world from the window appears such a *magnetiser*. This word is learned from dictionary, but it's application is more favorable than magic.

I am filled with a forward outlook for your arrival.

L.

46, Gordon Square, Bloomsbury, Wednesday 18th June, 1924

The famous lunch [at King's College] is over. I enclose the full programme of the proceedings for you. I sat next to Sam and afterwards he motored me back to No. 46. I like him very much – by himself. Will you learn from him in

July how to drive a motor car? – so that you can be my chauffeur in the summer. You didn't tell me that he bought another Cézanne in Paris. I think that he might buy the big Seurat with persuasion. While we were motoring back, he asked my opinion about the Three Arts Club for Cambridge (the project I wrote to you about before).

I have an article in the *New Leader* this week – in simple words for the working man. It is not new but really extracts from the lecture which you heard me give at the London School of Economics.

. . .

On Friday the exhibition of modern French pictures opens in aid of the Contemporary Art Society (chiefly Derain, Picasso, Matisse etc. – my Matisse is there). The Prime Minister is to open it, and his speech has been written for him by Roger [Fry]!

Two miele letters from you to-day. What a to-do about *Mercure*! But you don't say what your firm opinion was in the end.

. . .

Warm and tender kisses. I see you soon.

M.

Hotel San Regis, Paris, Thursday 19th June, 1924

. . .

Will Sam offer his Cézannes to the gallery, his face is not printed at the moment in *The Times*, yet Sam has 'a happy disposition and a wild desire to succeed.'

My latest passion is cherries, I eat it by tons, my stomach becomes very puffy, I also learned why: all the cherries contain inside little worms who blow themselves with ease and grace before my requirements draw them out of life.

I sleep better and last night moon did not visit me, instead I listened to a thunder-storm.

The finance page [of *The Times*] follows your direction in a loan at home (it is terrified only of inflation), as for home investments it is not in complete accord with you yet but it looks inquiringly as wanting to help such matters.

At lunch we arrived (I do not remember at first how) to the temperance conversation, it is a good idea and would make peoples happier (and public house in Goodge Street would be of a better character on Saturday); I relate my own experiences.

How talkative I am, now it comes to an end, I coo you with my cheeks.

L.

Treasury Chambers, Whitehall [deleted by M.K.], Thursday 19th June, 1924

This has been a day of meetings – I put off my usual Wednesday meetings until to-day. Rather a waste, because in my bath I felt what you call 'inspirational' and could have written something.

Vogue has written that the drawing of you by Duncan will not reproduce well and that they will use a photograph of Dobson's bust instead.

. . .

I arrive at the Gare du Nord on Saturday at 6.15, – so this is my last letter. I keep my kisses for then.

M.

Letters from
20th July, 1924 to 23rd September, 1924

On 6th July Maynard wrote to his mother, 'L. and I got back early last week. Paris was hot and tiring . . . Now they want to do the same programme at Drury Lane, but we are discouraging it. We very nearly went on to the Pyrenées for a week, where I see you are, but my work quickly accumulates and I thought I had better get back.' (King's Archives.) There was also the hope that the divorce case might be taken in July: news of its postponement did not come until the end of the month. Maynard's old master, Alfred Marshall, died on 13th July. In July Maynard and Lydia went to Tilton (which was very close to Charleston) for the first time, renting the house for over two months. This charming farmhouse, nestling beneath Firle Beacon in the south downs, was due to be rented by them from Lord Gage for over fifty years. Lydia spent most of her widowhood there until 1977. Maynard and Lydia never felt happier than when they were there together.

Maynard spent the weekend of 2nd August with the Asquiths, and Vanessa and Duncan were rather double-faced when they visited Lydia at Tilton then, for on 15th June Duncan had written to Vanessa: 'Its I see rather serious the Keynes taking Tilton but I daresay we shant see too much of them – I trust not. Maynard's marriage is a grim fact to face. It will be more grim still if Maynard sees it to be grim before embarking on it.' (King's Archives.)

On 20th August Maynard and Lydia went up to London to consult the lawyer about the divorce case, which it was then hoped would come up in October. Maynard completed his memoir of Alfred Marshall.

King's College, Cambridge, Sunday 20th July, 1924

My dearest darling,

After a long sleep I am a living man again and have worked hard all day. I am just back in my rooms after speaking for three hours and a half with my old master's[1] wife and gathering from her materials for my memoir. I must see her again to-morrow afternoon, – so I don't expect to be back in Gordon Square before 6.30 to-morrow evening, if so soon. I shall then have much to do – Must I, do you think, go to Lil's? Beg me off if you can. But – I am cruel – you must go yourself to protect Vanessa and Duncan.

It is quiet and empty here.

I enclose a letter for Florrie. Read it and – if you approve – address the envelope and post it.

your fond
M

1   Alfred Marshall had died on 13th July.

(41 Gordon Square), Wednesday 26th July, 1924

I have no paper to write, nor spicy news to tell, except that all the streets on the bus looked like 'summer madness' and I forgot that London was a city of civilisation. Many passing bys creaked on my feet, while I longed to reach the establishment where I could become 'winged'. I did so in fact for 6 shillings. Vera came to see me, but luckily or unluckily I was not in, she promised to the maid to telephone. I posess discomfort in relation to her and your party. At 9 o'clock the ancient friend of Vera comes, gossip will be spread all over us, she did not see me for months, therefore it will act as a balsam and we might both derive benefit from it. I reread your policy of the Bank of England. It is so compact and the quality of writing please my eyes and ears completely.

L.

P.S. I am fond of you!

Tilton, Thursday 31st July, 1924

. . . My 'constitutionals' consisted in exercises and lunch produced with 'moderato', owing to my tongue being coated with white fog I may say. The opening of the box was witnessed by me, the soaps are very lovely, towards the end of summer there is no escapade from being clean . . . After lunch I rolled with the grass and hangings. I also wondered if I was losing time.

A miely kiss to you from my Tilton planet.
L.

46, Gordon Square, Bloomsbury, Thursday 31st July, 1924

My dearest, darling

I spoke on the telephone with Florrie. She will motor down [to Tilton] on Saturday morning. I told her that we could put up her chauffeur and also her car. So get the nymphs to prepare the bedroom on the way to the bathroom for him and to ask the young man to open up the garage. . . .

It says in the *Evening Standard* to-night that 200 divorce cases have been left over unheard! rather a scandal!

Much kisses and fondness
M.

Tilton, Friday 1st August, 1924

. . . How did London appear after the Eternal Downs, did Piccadilly fill you with an ecstasy? My London book states that on that particular spot one can get any amount of different newspapers day or night. So be it . . .

As for yourself and your speech [in Cambridge] the result should be conquering one, so that the Downs and I could welcome you back.
L.

P.S. Just received your letter, I post a kiss immediately in return.

46, Gordon Square, Bloomsbury, Friday 1st August, 1924

My dearest darling,

I have been round to No. 41 and found the enclosed. Poor Vera seems to have been writing to you a good deal without result! I also found the woollen dress which I will bring back with me. But nowhere could I see the earrings, – I looked into every conceivable box in vain. Are you *sure* you haven't got them with you on your planet [Tilton]? Is it possible that the wicked little maid has stolen them?

. . .

Thanks for sending on the telegram. I've had so much to do here, what with selling King's College land, speculations, the *Nation*, copies of my Oxford lecture, and letters for Miss Rees (I have now bought Miss Rees a typewriter and she taps out my letters in the dining room). I am not going to the Wharf until after tea.

. . .

I wish you a pink tongue again. I shall be back on Monday between tea and dinner I expect. I send pulsations to your planet.
M.

Tilton, Saturday 2nd August, 1924

Florrie arrived with the full glory of an automobile and brought me apples and caviar. We gossip so much that there is only a few minutes to complete these lines to you and explain that I received all you send me, and I was in stimulus over so many letters in Tilton. Yesterday Vanessa and Duncan came to me[1] and stroll me over to their tea, first examining our house and even deciding to paint the back of the house with chickens as pets I suppose. At tea we spoke about fishes, I did not mention the fish with blood passing through her every month, but the one that feeds her child in *The Times* swam on the surface of the conversation . . .

At this moment I put swelling crosses on you for the speech.

L.

1   From neighbouring Charleston.

Tilton, Tuesday 23rd September, 1924

I am thoroughly reconstructed at this moment, that means after lunch, and also after lunch Ruby advised me to have a fire, and I couldn't, could I, very well say *No!* But my exercises were left undone, at the time when they should be commencing my desorganisation still clung to me, so naturally by now guilty conscience arises in me.

Beans in the garden are not 'fading away', and each family begins with not less than a quadruple. I plucked a few turnips and forgot the sitiation of a Brussel sprout designed by you. The postman pointed out that by law Tilton was the *last* stand [delivery], but Ruby and Mrs H. [Harland] explained as you coresponded with the governement (income tax!) Tilton should be approached first. I listen, smile and grow fat.

I hope the Russian will be nice and inteligent . . .

Fresh and miely touch from your harvester
L.

46, Gordon Square, Bloomsbury, Tuesday 23rd September, 1924

My dearest, darling L

My spirits are revived a bit, – I hope yours are. But the taxi was falling to pieces so that I had to hold it together to prevent wet coming in, the rain at Berwick station [near Tilton] was crushing, and I had to wait a long time for the train. So my spirits started by falling even lower than you saw them.

The Russian came to lunch – nice, boring, clever and absurd. He knew English badly.

. . .

I am very fond of and kiss you.

M

Some amusing episodes in speculations this afternoon.

Letters from
10th October, 1924 to 12th December 1924

After their long holiday at Tilton, Lydia resumed her 'bachelor's quarters' in Gordon Square and Maynard was often in Cambridge, where Vanessa and Duncan visited him on 17th October. On 24th October Lydia refused to go to Cambridge to hear Maynard's electioneering speech at a mass meeting, as this would 'disturb too much my way of life.' Her only dancing engagement was a brief appearance in November in a 'cocktail ballet' at the Coliseum, for Diaghilev had refused to engage her for his subsequent season; it was no wonder that she had become temporarily despondent about her divorce prospects. On 29th November Lydia wrote a remarkable account of a cultural relations meeting she had attended at the Chelsea Town Hall. After uncharacteristic hesitations, Maynard finally launched himself on A Treatise on Money (1930) on 30th November. On 11th December he went to Edinburgh to deliver a speech on foreign investment.

On 24th December Maynard and Lydia dined with the Woolfs. Reporting on the occasion, in a letter to Jacques Raverat, Virginia wrote – '. . . the poor sparrow [Lydia] is already turning into a discreet, silent, serious, motherly, respectable, fowl, with eggs, feather, cluck cluck clucking all complete. A melancholy sight indeed, and I foresee the day when she dislikes any reference to dancing.' (Nicolson, ed., 1977, p. 149).

(41 Gordon Square), Friday 10th October, 1924

I do not know how, but I proved myself able to reach Guilford Street and Theobalds Rd from the station? Then I called assistance first from the policeman, then Southampton Row bus N 68; my feet were tinkling with perspiration when I reached my bachelors quarters N 41. . . . I write now because Florrie might entertain me to cabaret restoran, so I have a chance not to be in time for the postman.

Crossings for all your tasks from your amorous harvester.

L.

King's College, Cambridge, Friday 10th October, 1924

Everything much as usual, except that my rooms have new electric light all through so that I am bathed in brilliance, and also new matting which looks very nice.

Sheppard lost all at Monte Carlo and went on to Lucca. As soon as I got here, he took me aside to tell me that I mustn't mention that he had been to Monte Carlo, because, when asked on the first night, he had lied about it! We gossipped College politics – the vacancy which is coming in the Vice Provostship etc.

The Vice Provost Macaulay is very well and has been hunting the stags furiously. Sheppard says that the Provost looks bad – I haven't seen him yet.

I go to see Mrs Marshall to-morrow.

I kiss the bacheloress, as though she were something *quite the opposite*.

M

(41 Gordon Square), Saturday 11th October, 1924

Vera looked all radiance embracing me, with her black dress and white collar, I suggested to wear this style of a dress all her life, seeing her like this, one has no doubts that she is actually a contribution to society, be it intelect, science or sex. I was only Galerie Lafayette. After a few moments of gossip, entered a friend of V., Mrs Coltrap, a worker in the Labour party. She was charming, I thought how important was for men to meet quite a number of our best lot, but by perplexity of life how often both sexes mix with unapropriate kind. V. inquired especially to her about the Russian Loan,[1] she admitted that the treaty was bad and should be revised, but it is better to go into the connexions with Russia than no step at all. Still V. questioned her with medivial cruelty and said no matter how much sentiments were rushing in the heart of people, loan was a loan and therefore should have security which was out of sight in Russia for present . . .

Why do I say all this to you? I do not show you any new way of thinking, I wish I would know Chinese or Sumerian, then I would be on a better level with you and be 'big bellied' in my brain.

I have your letter to-night, I am glad of your electrico-matting and otherwise comforts, but I frown if you 'kiss the bacheloress, as though she were something quite the opposite', one of the meanings might be a bachelor (Cambridge influence), but I am *not* serious, and with so many *Oh's* I am fond of you.

---

1 The British Government's proposal to guarantee a Russian loan became bound up with the Zinoviev letter – see Lydia's letter of 25th October.

(41 Gordon Square), Sunday 12 October, 1924

I had my Russians for tea, 1 extra man who is with them, and Legat (his wife could not come): they were sweet and simple, and how much they would like to cling to any possibility to stay here or anywhere without communism: the work they said was better there, but hunger and miserable salaries especially since the N.E.P. [New Economic Policy] had it's end and also since Lenin's death. They praised my brother, but he is so poor what can I do for him? I feel so ashamed to have all these comforts, my sister earns very well, with bobbed hair and works only in theatre and hopes to come here sometimes. Tea lasted 4 hours, I had thousands of muffins that they made an aproved comment on, and it was very nice to gossip. Since the flood the State theatre is closed; the water reached stalls; the same terrible episode happened in Petrograd 100 years ago . . .

Returning to my brother, he is going to stage a ballet called *Bolsheviks*, one of the scenes is described 'The blossoming of socialism.' Well, if socialism there reaches on points all I declare is, 'why what a very cultivated kind of socialism, this kind of socialism must be.'

I saw Vanessa, Duncan and Angelica, but more gossip will due to-morrow, now only warm and quiet touches.

L.

King's College, Cambridge, Sunday 12th October, 1924

My dearest darling sweet

I have missed the post, – so you won't get this until Monday evening. It's because I've been talking ever since lunch. For lunch I went to see my mother and father. I have been asked to stand for Parliament for the University of Cambridge, and my mother for the town of Cambridge! We have both refused. I gossiped there for some time and then went on to tea with Mrs Marshall. (She sent you her love and called you a dear.) I stayed two or three hours with her looking through papers and things.

On my way home I met Dennis and took him back to my rooms. I told him the contents of my egg and he told me the contents of his.[1] By that time it was the hour for dinner, so I asked him to dine with me in hall. After hall in the Combination [Room] with him and other fellows my tongue wagged for three or four hours more. And now after the poor thing has wagged for eleven hours, I take up my pen to write to you, and the post is missed. So you see I am practically a Russian to-day and must be forgiven accordingly.

Last night I dined with Lord Chalmers, my old chief at the Treasury, who is now the Master of Peterhouse.

234

I am too tired to write any more sense or nonsense and am just your very fond

beardni[2]

M

---

1 Dennis Robertson's 'egg' was effectively his book *Banking Policy and the Price Level* (1926).

2 *Beardni*, properly *biedny* (see Lydia's next letter): Russian for *poor* in an affectionate sense, as 'poor darling'.

(41 Gordon Square), Monday 13th October, 1924

I aprove very much all the 'conversationi' for 11 hours, it only shows that you do not look for a word into your pocket, and have your stimulations in any circumstances. *Oh* I feel so red, I just have been speaking to Vera on the telephone, she met Clive and Mary, and Clive told her that one day we all spoke about her, but did not say what, yet might tell her sometimes. V. asked what that was, and I said we discussed if you were a Jewess or not and if you married Garia for money or not? I feel so uncomfortable now, perhaps I shouldnt. . . Now I shall go to Vanessa and tell her about my conversation on the telephone.

I feel better at present, but my last night was disturbed by coming bleedings.

The last moral degradation of Bloomsbury – Carrington is in love with Henrietta [Bingham]! She always wanted to be a man! I do not want anything to be, it is what I *am*.

Your biednia
Lydochka

King's College, Cambridge, Monday 13th October, 1924

My dearest darling,

Oh! I feel so tired – too many meetings and uplifting of the voice. But now the pressure is less and I can look forward to being quieter. I boasted yesterday about wagging my tongue like a Russian; but I read in your miele letter that all the time the real Russians were outdoing me!

At last, this morning, the Marshall Memoir came: I am sending you a copy of it.

To-day I have two unexpected announcements. I have been elected Vice-President of the King's College *Musical* Society!! Most peculiar. They must have heard about 'Fading Away', I should think.

The other one is that I have been elected a Foreign Member of the Royal

Swedish Academy of Science. This is to fill the place made vacant by the death of Marshall. It is a nice distinction.

. . .

Your

M

(41 Gordon Square), Friday 17th October, 1924

The sphere of occupation was destined to my dentist, and although pains were irresistible, he bullied me so much that I did not dare to produce an outcry . . .

In the morning I still feel very weak after 20 minutes of practice and although I sweat, it is not my costumary warm liquid, but cold – so I hurry to take a warm bath to reverse it, then that time Margaret (Geoffrey's) came with her sister [Gwen Raverat], they only saw me for 2–3 minutes, and I put my restricted remark about limitation in children, but she is determined to have more, a daughter next time . . .

Having spent hours with the dentist and feeling like a mouth full of false teeth, in some places only the bridge is saved and all the rest is false matter, I became exceedingly hungry; knowing how much I receive for a 1 shilling, I bought bread and cheese, the value of which was almost 2 shillings, and having other matters served as decorations for my hungry insides I can proceed now with good thoughts and a peaceful kiss to you.

L.

. . .

King's College, Cambridge, Friday 17th October, 1924

I have been giving a dinner party to Duncan, Vanessa, Bunny, Sheppard and Braithwaite. They are chattering in the next room and I have come out in time to write this for the post. It seems that the house which they think of buying in Norfolk is very cheap and beautiful and suitable; also it stands in a pretty village. But the general country in the neighbourhood is more doubtful. So they haven't made up their minds. Vanessa thinks it a difficult problem.

. . .

I am flattered by this letter – from Sir J. C. Stamp, the one who invented the Dawes Report. Excuse my showing you. But it is not like showing anyone else.

The conversation in the next room is about *Vogue*. There was a man here all the morning making photographs of my room for it.

M

(41 Gordon Square), Saturday 18th October, 1924

I joyed in reading Stamp's letter, and everyone who reads your [Marshall] 'memoir' cannot apreciate less than he. In consequence I felt very young and active (but not for exercises), I took a bus and went to Sloane street, all the wools are gathered to confirm my cross stiching. Going back I met Sacheverell Sitwell also on the bus . . . They are going away soon for 5 months to Italy; for tea I had Vasiline, he likes to give me rides, but I am not clear in my answers and say 'perhaps, sometime, but I cannot promise.'

. . .

Now I shall try to produce order in my dormatory, but Oh, time is flying, and you are a dear creature Maynarochka.

L.

(41 Gordon Square), Sunday 19th October, 1924

Increased gossipings my day's work, with Florrie and Teddy, (*both* this time are having autrocious colds), all 3 running down Ramsay,[1] and then concluding our wishes in the name of Baldwin as Prime Minister, but Florrie likes to see Birkenhead; I simply couldnt be ready to go towards Vera, as I had my skirts lifted and warmed my halphes constantly, yet I tore myself away from this pleasing feature and strolled by and by to the opposite of Wallace Collection.[2] Vera was a dutiful mother, while nurse and Garia had their vacations. She is profoundly touched by your 'Marshall' . . .

In her [Vera's] bedroom blankets were taken, perhaps to wrap up Prince of Wales, whose favourite sport is to sit on a tea tray and descend from one floor to another on a staircase, sometimes the neighbours are so annoyed, that they call police to stop this extra clatter. Life is difficult, even for Prince of Wales! Please look into the first passage of Alpha and Omega, 'elderly and infirm to boot' (perhaps my knee) gigled. I suppose to-day you also were gifted with your tongue, but in speaking or writing you always bring fresh vision of thought.

L.

1 James Ramsay MacDonald, who formed the first British Labour government which lasted from January 22nd to November 4th, 1924.
2 The Wallace Collection is in Manchester Square. Vera's house was on the square's other side.

King's College, Cambridge, Sunday 19th October, 1924

My dearest, darling L

Vanessa and Co. went off yesterday afternoon, after pottering about in the morning in the beautiful weather. When Duncan came back from a visit to one little place, he was seen to have a roll of paper in his hand, which he had absently mindedly brought back with him . . .

. . .

My dearest biednia – I hope your cheek and teeth are living matter again, and that you are in good spirit. I have touching feelings to go and kiss you and am fond of you. I would like to hear your voice and see you on the sofa. I am beside you in my feelings.

M

. . .

(41 Gordon Square), Monday 20th October, 1924

Utmost exhasations, but the pictures of Mond's[1] collections are impressive, when one looks at Raphael 'joie de vivre' is his essence . . . Beatiful Titian and lovely Botticellis. Then being there[2] I gave a friendly look to the 'Nativity', Piero della Francesca, it is eternaly touching and to the charming one 'Death of Procris', Piero di Cosimo, the 2 last ones one knows and loves more and more. With decision to go home, yet I decided to look into Eric Kennington's phantasies in Leicester galleries. He has certain means, but I felt looking at it as if someone put a red hot poker instead of a cushion on a chair, for me his sculpture is better, influenced by Dobby . . . Yet his pictures are sold quite a few;[3] but I hear from Florrie that as people of to-day have no money to pay, they are bought in instalments, say 5 pounds a year for a picture of 75 pounds, money is made so slow in so many occasions.

. . .

I see you soon.

L.

1 Sir Alfred Moritz Mond, Bt., who was to become 1st Viscount Melchett in 1928: an industrialist who had made a magnificent collection of works of art.
2 At the National Gallery.
3 Eric Kennington (1888–1960) was best known for his portraits of men of the armed forces.

King's College, Cambridge, Monday 20th October, 1924

My dearest darling,

I had a good many giggles over your letters this morning, – especially 'elderly and infirm to boot'. *To boot* is an old English expression which has nothing to do with boots (or legs) but simply means 'as well' 'also' 'besides'
. . .
Last night as Vice-President I felt it my duty to go to the College Concert; but I did enjoy it. I have also had a little political activity – I have written the Liberal Candidate here a letter for circulation to the electors, and next Saturday I am to make a speech for him at the big Meeting in the Corn Exchange before the Election.
. . .

M.

(41 Gordon Square), Wednesday 22nd October, 1924

Do you think judge will give me a divorce, after all he might not, and I am a pessimist at present in 'decree nisi'. Please be very fond of me, otherwise I'll pour oceans of tears in the night and instead of bed I'll have a flood.

With a direct kiss into you.

L.

P.S. On re-reading it I find the sense of this letter is just like a woman. *Oh* I suffer from my own mentality.

(41 Gordon Square), Thursday 23rd October, 1924

Although I advocated histericks to you only yesterday, my sleep was healthier than many a night, and this morning I read a letter from my mother, very short; she will write me a longer one *soon*, perhaps the flood was the reason, but I was glad to receive it.

Vera called me on the telephone and told me that big Serge's first ballet is *Train Bleu* and his intention is to give a gala season in summer; I thanked her from your donor, we turned to politicks, I teased her conservatism, so she will abstain and wait when you arrange your own political party . . . I went on the streets to buy tickets for to-night . . . Then again I 'bussed' around and now soon expect Margaret [Hill].

Up and down and reverse crossing from me, by this method and having no relations with drafts, the cold will be bound to leave you, and perhaps will enter into the bodies of Mrs Clapham or Milner White.

L.

. . .

King's College, Cambridge, Thursday 23rd October, 1924

My dearest sweet,

You must have *no* doubts. The [divorce] case is good. And even if there was a difficulty, which I don't expect, there are still other possibilities for us to use. We *will* get the decree nisi. I am writing to the lawyer to see if a date is yet fixed; – I expect week after next.

And I am so fond of you – *to the utmost*. Please do not be sad; though it is impossible not to be nervous until all is settled.

. . .

Won't you come to stay here (at the hotel) for Saturday night? Then you can hear my speech at the Mass Meeting, and I can console you with kisses. Come by the five o'clock train from King's Cross. I will meet you at the station.

M.

(41 Gordon Square), Friday 24th October, 1924

I thank you for your consoling counsels, I feel much better and wiser; your sister Margaret and I amused ourselves . . .

Margaret's next desire is to go to the Savoy to see dancing, and her husband never saw a danse in his all life, and in spite of that on the steamer he was asked every night to perform socially. I led her to the tube station, she was in very nice spirits, and I took the right figure on the bus for myself.

Florrie came to lunch and Lo! Behold! with a shingle! Not to disturb Teddy she introduced her new head by paying a visit into his bed (room). All peace with him, but I was shocked, of course she has nice little chicken-neck, after all. I told her that men go often bald because they cut their hair constantly and that would be less suitable to a female class.

. . .

I can't come to Cambridge, it would disturb too much my mode of life, but if you post kisses that would do very well for me.

L.

King's College, Cambridge, Friday 24th October, 1924

. . .

In the afternoon I walked a little in the streets, got you some paste buckles on approval for you to look at, and tried in the best possible shop for a scrap-book for you, but what I want does not seem to exist, and I shall have to have one made to order. Also I bought one more Shetland wool waistcoat to wear inside my ordinary waistcoat, and a new stock of socks.

I now come from Pigou's Memorial Lecture on Marshall. Mrs M was there with the two old ladies, of whom she spoke to us, who were the very first to attend his lectures about 54 years ago. They looked very nice and the one who used to be the gay and lively beauty is the gay and lively beauty still. The lecture went down very well with the audience; but I didn't like it much. Being too much like a sermon itself, it brought out all the feeblest side of old M. and then said that was what we ought to admire.

. . .

M.

(41 Gordon Square), Saturday 25th October, 1924

. . .

For tea I had Mordkin, his wife, his child, her dancing partner and his classical dancing partner. *Oh* Life is difficult, and what I understood they go to America without positive engagement, of course they have good material in dances and costumes and music and Mordkin is a name and a person, but all is tinged with melancholy.

It seems from their experiences that in Russia one must burn onself with work to please the masses, and at any moment camarade Mordkin should be ready to dance at a political meeting, and yet nothing in return; the religious Jews are also prosecuted [persecuted], but then they are 'survival of the fittest' in my opinion.

The 'Red' plot mystery[1] will make all the conservatives or otherwise very eager to vote pink or white. In the meantime I am glad you bought more Shetland wool for your insides, so that you prevent your darling C.B. [?] from cold dangers.

L.

1 A letter inciting rebellion, purporting to be written by Grigori Evseevich Zinoviev, at that time chairman of the executive committee of the Communist International, had been published in the London press. It was almost certainly a forgery, but damaged Labour's chances in the forthcoming general election.

(41 Gordon Square), Sunday 26th October, 1924

My gallerites also are laborites, in spite of Ramsay's undoings; and Harry is going to bring 'Red flag' on Wednesday night at the Coliseum. They are young and charming, can't bear protection and refusal of the alien artists on these shores, besides they want education with Mr Asquith as a master of Balliol College at Oxford; and they thought me a Conservative Liberal, but I myself really beyond politicks.

Stas has not yet any engagement, but he speaks of going to Paris, Massine is to dance at the Empire, so probably the State dancers will last no more than a week longer. My friends stayed almost for 3 hours, for lunch I visited V. . . . [who] wanted to know your thinking about Zinoviev's communication, she believes it authentic, but she was more interested in faith healing process, so we might go together if they let us into church, but we look so healthy, she is interested in physhology of masses, and when I interfered with Coué,[1] she found no comparison between the two. . . .

My further utterings contain no words but a widespread kissing on your attractive eyes.

  1 French psychologist, famous for his slogan 'Every day and in every way, I am getting better and better.'

King's College, Cambridge, Sunday 26th October, 1924

As usual I got through my [election] speech respectably but without éclat. It will be reported in the local paper on Monday, and I will send you a copy. It was in a huge building with 1500–2000 audience and, so, very bad for the voice. I hate political meetings. They are always *exactly* the same – the same vamped-up atmosphere and the same underlying boredom. It makes one feel a fool and a liar. No – I'm not cut out for politics. I don't *enjoy* it enough. However the situation for Liberals seemed better than one would expect. The local experts say that it was the best Liberal meeting in Cambridge for years.
. . .

I am much shocked at Florrie's wickedness – to do such a thing [as shingle her hair] without a permission – Yes – seriously! But I am glad to read in the letter that you are shocked too.

I will arrive on Tuesday in time for dinner – but don't know the exact train yet.

Yes I send you kisses by post, – but they are poor dry things sent that way.

M

(41 Gordon Square), Monday 27th October, 1924

It is almost 6 o'clock, most of the time is spent on the chair, and yet I am not bored at all, and have good spirits and learning *Midsummer Nights Dream*, but without sticking. Your speech even if it was slightly uncomfortable for you, was advantageous for Liberals, still biedny Maynarochka I understand.

I looked over quite a few speeches in *The Times*, very poor material, I am intrigued about Ramsay, did the Foreign Office publish the red bambuzzle[1] without his permission, and he does not want to acknowledge it? It is the best 'star attraction' in the election yet and ¾ of the population are delighted.

. . . I forgot to let you know that I visited yesterday Wallace collection with Vera and Garia to look at glass . . . Vaz. comes for a few minutes, he goes away to Norwich; in the meanwhile I shall run for the *Evening Standart* and be very fond of you.

L.

1 The Zinoviev letter.

King's College, Cambridge, Monday 27th October, 1924

My dearest darling,

Two miele letters from you this morning. I see that the life of dancers *is* a difficult one. The *Criterion* announces as a fact that you and Massine are both going to dance with Serge at the Coliseum! You see that the star whom the Coliseum has got at the last moment for this week in your place is Fay Compton.[1]

. . .

I have asked Gwen Raverat to come to tea with me to-morrow, and I shall reach Gordon Square between 8.15 and 8.30 just in time for dinner. Oughtn't we to take steps to amuse ourselves on General Election night (Wednesday)? What shall we do? If you feel inclined, will you take tickets for the Coliseum. Would Dun and Van like to come with us, do you think? Act on your desires – I enclose a paper.

I am shocked about your lunches at 41. You must buy chickens for yourself and get Mrs K to cook them.

. . .

M.

1 The British actress, who had made her adult debut in 1911, for whom Barrie wrote his *Mary Rose* (1920).

(41 Gordon Square), Thursday 30th October, 1924

Leaving you I thought of seeing Virginia for a moment or 2; Leonard said on one side 'Maynard must become Labour' and on the other how much he despised Ramsay, by that time Ramsay was in for an M.P. by 2000 extra against my wishes[1]. Virginia asked me to tell you how much she admired your 'Marshall' and she will write besides. She looks splendid and gossiped how much Elizabeth wants to meet Leonard, ignoring Virginia, so Leonard will write a note that he had a pleasure once in his life to know Empress Eugenia, and therefore princesses are of no value; my gossip was about Mrs Asquith

... how the best hair dressing shingler in London refused to shingle her, saying that already her nose was prominent, therefore the shingle and the nose would both suffer from it. She agreed to abstain from it. 'Londoner's diary'[2] passes kind obituary notes on lost Liberal seats, I regret especially E. D. Simon, Jowett and Masterman.

... Alas! Your 'stick in the mud' is in! and also in an American dancing magasine there published a song by Duncan sisters, those that sang about the Jews and the Greeks at the Coliseum.

> 'Stick in the mud, stick in the mud
> It's meaning I just really can't explain,
> But one thing I know
> Where ever I go
> Stick in the mud's my name.'

Now I must prepare my appearance, although my mind is limp. Did your meetings work beneficently?

Tender inclinations to you.

L.

---

1   The Liberals were reduced to a rump of 40 seats, compared to 159 seats at the previous election.
2   In *The Evening Standard*.

(41 Gordon Square), Friday 31st October, 1924

From 3 till almost 7 I embroidered with my tongue constantly, Mim [Marie Rambert], past friend of Vera was my debater. We both agreed that Vera had complex about money, especially since she became rich; she also heard Bernard Shaw on Socialism, he was so well dressed, his suit was of a good cut, that she wants her husband to go to the same tailor. Besides this, she called him Zeus or Jupiter so magnificent he was; from intelect we descended to Stas and his legs. He told Mim that I was an impossible woman have last year [been] offered one week more to appear to the Coliseum, in April I threw it off and went to the country with you. It is not first time that I have a disreputable reputation.

... Last night Osbert, Sasha, Muriel, Dobby, Delia, were other chief occupants in the Mayers gathering ... Osbert gossiped a good hour to me after dinner, how Mortimer imitates you, how he plunges himself into a seat like you and speaks like you and Bloomsbury (what insolence to sit like you, my strong objections are rising), how Ottoline speaks exactly like a cow – you will see yourself if you pronounce a word 'Derain' with sounds 'à la vache'.

At dinner I said I liked everything red and that was succesful, why I do not

244

know. Osbert voted Liberal this time, the others did not elect anybody and I arrived home about 1 o'clock,

miely swallow

L.

King's College, Cambridge, Friday 31st October, 1924

My dearest darling

I am still rather depressed about the Election. The poor Liberals are simply cut to pieces. But I console myself that it makes a clearer situation and probably gives time to think matters out better than they have been thought out lately. I have begun this morning a short article for next week's *Nation*[1] on the question of the balance of power as shown by this Election. (Hubert has taken to his bed with a cold, I hear.)

I hope that Duncan and Vanessa are not counting up their losses on the [election] bet! because they are gigantic, probably over £70 each. Please tell them that I let them all off (including Angus) – because I had not imagined that I was letting them in for the possibility of so much loss. As for me I am compensated otherwise; for the Stock Exchange is so pleased with the Conservative Victory that they have raised the prices of everything, so that I get more profit in other directions than I lose in this.

To-day Piero Sraffa, the Italian who has been translating my book, came to lunch. We talked for nearly three hours and I told him the Credit Cycle Theory. He was enthusiastic; so I was satisfied. As usual, I thought him very talented – no!, not because he agreed, but because of the sort of questions he asked.

I have bought a copy of the new edition[2] of the [Shakespeare] *Sonnets*. I have not read the general introduction yet; but it seems to me to be very good in explaining the meaning of difficult passages. I have found several places where I have made mistakes hitherto.

No! I was not taken in by the new handwriting – particularly on a Hotel San Regis envelope! I see that you and Virginia agree in your instinctive feelings to Elizabeth!

. . .

The conversation with Sraffa about Credit Cycle has made me very eager to begin writing my book. But I must put it off until I come back from Oxford at the end of next week.

With calm and warm touches

M.

1 'The Balance of Political Power at the Elections', *Nation*, 8th November, 1924.
2 This was presumably the edition of the sonnets edited from the Quarto of 1609 with an introduction and commentary by T. G. Tucker (Cambridge, 1924).

245

(41 Gordon Square), Saturday 1st November, 1924

Terrible the only word to be used for [betting] losses of Vanessa, Duncan, you do not mention mine, did I not declare to be a reckless woman on that night? Still I have a feeling that they are probably smiling over the matter, and when I tell them your charitable conclusions . . . they will burst into a hare's lip.

It is well that you write for *The Nation*, I and the great wide public welcome it. It is also very nice how you discuss the 'Credit Cycle Theory' with the Italian camarade and prepare your intelectual vitamins ready to spread with inspiration in the book. I myself very sleepy, although I did my exercises with perspirations of a few degrees, but I couldn't, could I, stroll out, so many pourings, even the feminine Spaniard did not come to teach me, so unapropriate are the streets to-day.

. . .

I like to hear your voice in the new edition of Sonnets.

L.

(41 Gordon Square), Sunday 2nd November, 1924

I told Vanessa and Duncan about your graciousness [over the bet], they stopped counting already, as they could never repay you such a figure of pounds.

. . .

Just now Sickert came in he is so delitful, we must gather one day when you are free. We spoke about many subjects and I said women were like men nowadays because of shingling, and he said 'but they cant shingle anything else.' He is very well and Thérèse cooks for him joints from Smithfield market. I gave him a kiss in the entrance and exit, as I always like to be his daughter, but I smell you with all my warm instinkts like ever your true dog.

L.

King's College, Cambridge, Sunday 2nd November, 1924

Last night I dined with Dennis at the Trinity All Saints Feast and saw several old gentlemen shortening their lives by eating and drinking too much. Dadie was there as someone else's guest and he came in to Dennis's rooms afterwards. Much as usual he seemed, and rubbing along all right with the Woolfs.

To-night I have a dinner party in honour of Lytton who is here for the weekend and afterwards I shall be at home to all the young cultured. Why does one give parties? so much nicer to go to other people's!

To-day at lunch with my mother (who got elected to the Town Council in the elections yesterday!) Margaret (Hill) and children were there.

I have just finished my article 'The Balance of Power at the Elections' for next week's *Nation* and have sent off copies to my various continental papers. What do you think of 'An Examination of Capitalism' as a title for my next book but one?

This time the new handwriting took me in! [cf. letter of 31st October] When my letters come to me in bed, I always look through them to see if there is one from you (or whether I must wait for the second post) before reading the paper. I looked through as usual on Saturday morning and found nothing! (Ottoline is much more like a Cow than Mortimer is like me.) [See Lydia's letter, 31st October.]
. . .

I kiss your patience and good spirits
M

. . .

(41 Gordon Square), Monday 3rd November, 1924

. . .
I was there [at Vera's] last night for supper and soup (without hares) (I could not disagree with V. about it) and it was tasty. . . . I also went into the domestic questions that dead Daddy[1] is selling even wines from Colworth, but in fact Garia and V. will posess them and a Russian maxim comes into my mind 'cannot deceive cannot sell.' V. and G. want to get rid of all the nasty objects like Chippendales etc. and give a little stimulus on the paper for the outsiders. Such is the law of human nature. . . .

It was so benevolent to-day, good spirits surrounded me, so I stepped into a shop; now Florrie comes, as Teddy has a man's dinner in the house, so Florrie flies to me . . .

Your gossipuss
L.

1 Garia's father, Sir Albert Bowen, who had recently died.

King's College, Cambridge, Monday 3rd November, 1924

My usual day of meetings, and to-night I read my paper on *laissez-faire*[1] to my Pol. Econ. Club[2] here – a sort of dress rehearsal for Oxford.

My party last night was a success, I suppose – I gave them most delicious sandwiches made of breasts of chickens. But myself I was slightly bored in my heart. When one talks to the young intellectuals one has to say so many things that one has said more than once before in one's life.

. . .

I have bought a book of short stories from the Russian in English. You must get all the same stories in Russian. Then I will read them in my chair in English and you on your sofa in Russian.

Kissings to my very dear dog until to-morrow.

M.

1   Finally published as *The End of Laissez-Faire* (1926).
2   His Political Economy Club, which met in his rooms on Mondays during the Cambridge term.

(41 Gordon Square), Thursday 6th November, 1924

At 5 o'clock I was sitting in Dobby's studio, opposite their window there is another that looks like a factory window with something mechanical working up and down, but at 5 o'clock all stopped. I had intense crossings for you and comforted myself. Now when you gave so much out of your spiritual and intelectual insides I hope your host will give you the best chair [professorship] in Oxford so that you can rest and receive the fruits of thanksgivings. I heard once that in Oxford there is a guitar preserved that Shelley played and sang to his love, and also portraits of Shelley,[1] otherwise Oxford and Cambridge in a way probably like 41–46 Gordon Square.

Delia told me a good deal of her life, her work is great contentement for her, so that she does not concentrate as much as she used to on Dobby, later Dobby came and I brought statue of the abstract body with me.

Vaz comes to-night, I forgot about, but he telephoned to remind me, I shall ask him in a general conversation about the musicians social possibilities, values.

My palpitations for you.

L.

1   The guitar is at University College.

(41 Gordon Square), Friday 7th November, 1924

. . . Yesterday I also met Virginia, so when I strolled a few steps with her, I introduced Mirsky[1] while speaking, but L. and V. know him already, he goes to their house . . . Virginia . . . puts great beliefs in *Memoirs* of Jane Harrison[2] I think myself that would be very suitable acquisition to the *Nation*, this cultured lady who in her old age broke away from Cambridge to try the Parisian breath of life. I, in my old age, will never be revolutionary;[3] I even will not learn new songs but repeat the old ones, or I might smoke a cigarette after change of life.

I tried to squeeze out a few tears founded on your new Ethicks, but is no pleasure to have them without handkerchiefs and [? illeg.] while I have the rag [a handkerchief] I cant squese the water from my double holes [her eyes] another time, it is difficult like everything else, so I need your sympathy and tenderness.

L.

P.S. I write this expressly that you should see yourself reacted in me already; I can't help it if I smile at it, will you also?

1   Prince Dmitri Mirsky, a Russian lecturer at King's College, London, who was later to write *The Intelligentsia of Great Britain*.
2   *Reminiscences of a Student's Life* by the Newnham archaeologist.
3   A correct forecast.

King's College, Cambridge, Friday 7th November, 1924

My dearest darling biednia

I have spent the evening reading my letters and am not yet quite finished. But I am tired and sleepy and so write to say good night to you and give you a tender touch.

You will see in to-morrow's *Times* that I have been reelected to-day to the Council of the Senate. The Liberal Party in the University (of which I am the Treasurer) has carried every single seat in the Council in this Election – a thing we have never done before! Is the pendulum swinging already?

M

(41 Gordon Square), Saturday 8th November, 1924

Interesting comments on Birth Control by Lord Dawson [of Penn] . . . *The Times* wants not at all to give a good 'puffing' for birth control, so it is more enlightening in the *D. Miroir*.

The Noble Lord said that young people took to exersise it, and the Roman church failed from spreading it.

Vaz. called me up, he seems to have a spring fever for me, so I said I was 'engaged everywhere', he said it was a year since I gave him my daily visitation and he grew sentimental, he should have a reaction by now . . . My Spanish maestrina came . . . she was very nice and said how much she liked

Valentino,[1] but when she saw him in the *Vogue* without clothes (you remember that silly picture of a fawn), dissapointement beamed out of her, the best she can do is to go to the cinema and see him dressed, but I gobble you skins and all.

L.

1   Rudolf Valentino, the famous film actor, b. 1895.

(41 Gordon Square), Sunday 9th November, 1924

'My bleedings, my bleedings', what an imperfection in woman's life! I was in need of poison, so after lunch I went to Vanessa and begged her for coffee, and she gave me 2 cups at once, I mean one after another. Anrep's wife Helen was there and a guest of Duncan, Polish artist married to a French artist, shingled, painted, hideous and French. D. kept up the conversation with her, and probably prospiring from effort, whilst Van, Helen and I (nice little trio) could chirp without reserve.

. . .

Then we were both interested in Trefilova-Massine affair at the Empire next week, I am glad I do not have to appear to-morrow, my pains reappearing again and I am looking grim and sallow. In these hard moments of life I seal my lips with yours, otherwise life is too difficult.

L.

King's College, Cambridge, Sunday 9th November, 1924

Yesterday I woke up very tired and sleepy, read a long time in bed, had a hot bath and dressed slowly, and did nothing difficult all day. To-day I am strong again and clear up odds and ends. By next Friday all odds and ends should be ended and I ready to (at this moment Faith and Hubert came in unexpectedly – here for the week-end, and six hours have passed since then before I can take up my pen again) begin the new book. One always begins with a mixed feeling of pain and pleasure – pain at the thought of so much hard work to come.

Last night I went to my Society [the Apostles] for the first time this term. To-day discussions with Hubert on The Future of the Liberal Party – I think he agrees with you more than with me. While I was giving Hubert tea, a very nice, very rich old gentleman (brother of the Vice Provost) came in, so I gave him tea too, thinking as I did so – now why shouldn't he leave his money to the College? When Hubert went, he stayed on in rather a shamefaced way to tell me (very privately) that he was leaving his money to the College and was making me one of his executors!

I have had the enclosed letter [about Lydia's divorce] from the lawyer –

which means, I suppose, that nothing will happen in Court for two or three weeks. It will be time enough if we can complete our evidence any time before Christmas. What a relief it will be when it is over. But I expect the lawyer is right not to take any risks about the evidence.

I expect you have courage again by now, but, if not, I send you a share of mine; for I have *full* courage at this moment and send you a strong kiss filled with it. Are we not fortunate in life, you and I, if one really looks at it carefully?

M

I send five papers.

Also a cheque for Vanessa which I forgot to give her when I was in London. Will you give it to her?

(41 Gordon Square), Monday 10th November, 1924

If I could get money as eazily as you do without even asking, for instance ('the very nice, very rich gentleman'), perhaps you coué'd him? I only know how to distribute the papers and ordered a pair of boots at Gamba 5 guineas, but double soles and best soft leather and almost no heels, I thank you for the papers, how many do I owe you? I shall take to Vanessa the check to-night, what will she do with this fortune, an endowment for Angelica trousseau? What a soft pale day it was, even fog was lovely; I gave one of my clocks to be restored at the Stores, and on the street I met Mara (Massine's love) so we exchanged friendly queries, she also dances besides Trefilova to-night. Delia came to tea . . .

Why do I blab so much, I think I ought to be like Lytton when he is in society, but then there is no beard attached to me, I do not posess such 'virtious property', also that when your book is ready I will read it and be *very fond* of it.

L.

King's College, Cambridge, Monday 10th November, 1924

Two *very* miele letters from you this morning, even though you do bleed. This has been my day of meetings. But I went to lunch with Peter and Topsy [Lucas] to meet Peter's young brother who has just come up to King's as a scholar; he didn't say much but seemed very nice – absurdly like Peter, a regular Peterkin. After lunch we went to look at the new house – Topsy's doll's house – which is now nearly finished. Topsy's study bears the same relation to Peter's as Vera's to Garia's. Then to the New Buildings Committee to consider Kennedy's designs.[1] Some are very much against them, but others not; so he is to be kept in the competition.

...

My economists' society meets in my rooms to-night – I wish they didn't. I should like to read and close my eyes and see Lydochka on the sofa.

M.

1   See page 184 footnote.

(41 Gordon Square), Wednesday 12th November, 1924

The crossing of parallel lines if one looks from Euclid's geometrical point of vue is absurd, but if it is not Euclid it is truth, this is the idea of a revolutionary Russian writer, who breaks Euclids to pieces and strives towards Einstein. I see very little in it, because of ignorance, but you might see new forms in it.

Otherwise I embroider and learn 'my gentle Puck' and look at the books you left me, but as it does not rain I like to have my stroll on the bus, this time again I'll take 73, because it is not as old as Euclid and I want to be a revolutionary also,

including kisses for you.

L.

P.S. I do write sometimes absurdity.

(41 Gordon Square), Thursday 13th November, 1924

It was a gloomy morning so I wore my Pyrenese appearance till very late, it is so big that while in it I become like one of those unfortunates in 'Save the Children Fund', a sceleton in fact. I do not see how the wool draws out my flesh, but such are my experiences. A visit to my dentist there must be trouble in it, therefore he took Ex-rays for that blatant tooth. No energy for bus riding to-day. Vera came in and told me all she has heard about Boshevik's evening party: all bolsheviks came in 'plus Fours'[1] to demonstrate A Russian peasant (as the peasants have their trousers rather large with the boots), and they thought the English shops make this trousers also for the glorification of Russians! Some of them complained about the evening, one said 'I am discontent, what I want is a bottle of brandy for myself and then a comfortable seat to fall into sleep.' He asked too little, after a *bottle* of brandy one needs a bed . . .

. . . Helen comes in. I hear her hoofs, your mare

L.

1   Baggy breeches ending just below the knee, worn with golfstockings, which were in vogue at that time.

King's College, Cambridge, Thursday 13th November, 1924

My dearest darling

. . .

We met at a meeting this afternoon, which may lead to our building a small theatre[1] for the University which is just what we want

. . .

from
M
(who is *fond* of you)

1   It was to be the Arts Theatre, but was not built until a decade later.

(41 Gordon Square), Friday 14th November, 1924

Oh Maynarochka, do have more leisure and no overwork; when you come to London I shall be your jester and even inquire into 'Bank rate' or 'Credit Cycle', as for cotton I see that it stands up with 'vital tempo'.

What are the exceptional circumstances that promote M. [Montague] Norman to succeed himself [as Governor of the Bank of England] in the 6th term; low bank rate no doubt is favorable to the many of that Banking Set?

. . .

. . . My desire was to know out of what consists Faith and her relations with Hubert, how much love. Love only came from Hubert, who sees in her beauty, she even refused him in the begining but he said 'I shall wait till you become more sensible.' I see that all women are not catchers.

. . .

Touchings of calmness.
L.

King's College, Cambridge, Friday 14th November, 1924

. . . This afternoon I went to my tailor here and ordered a new suit – very nervous without your approval; I have now forgotten what it was like, but I think greyish. I hope it will be all right. In another shop I bought a new kind of vest and drawers; and also a grey cashmere scarf for you – again very nervous (it is meant for a man, yet adapted to your magnitude, I think). In still another shop I got you a scrapbook – which may prove very good for the purpose. The pages are covered with gum – so that all you have to do to the cuttings is to put a little water on to them!

253

The Architects' plans are still talked about. Tell Vanessa that opinion is moving slightly in Kennedy's direction, in my opinion.

I haven't after all begun the new book yet, partly because there was still College work to do, partly because all the things which go inside one during a Feast do not favour it (we go on feasting to-day at lunch time which aggravates matters). I had strange dreams last night. I was in a garden where there was a tiger; also there were many glass houses and whenever one saw the tiger coming down the path one hurried into a glass house. But there was one man who took no notice of the tiger. When I asked him, how this was, he replied 'oh! I am not at all tasty – look at my hands', and then I saw that he was a Jew. After that I was compelled to wash a baby on my knee and at the same time carve a chicken, and from inside the chicken there came out a series of white cauliflowers shaped like the plaster casts of the heads of Greek goddesses. Interpret this dream for me, o wise mare!

M.

(41 Gordon Square), Saturday 15th November, 1924

What an extraordinary dream, I am amazed. The first part is probably a relation to a speculation, they are bears and bulls, why not tigers?

I do not see any point in your washing the baby, after that everything is solved: chicken is your mental fertility, cauliflowers – your books, which turn to be classiks . . . I aprove all your purchases with a scarf suitable for my 'magnitude.'

I have read Roger's essay, he sais first rate artists never dream in the day time, while for bad ones (like for instance Berta Ruck), to produce what they write it is necessary to hypnotise themselves. No new discovery but said with such style and clearness and tact, so that if I would be a pshycho-analist and listening to this lecture a blowing kiss would be my acknowlegement towards his literary recipée.

Give Dennis my sympathy that he is not well, and if ever your and his idea about a theatre succeeds, in *Midsummer Night's Dream* you must engage me as Oberon, the 'fairy lord' who would not be satisfied unless his Puck is Dennis. My Espanolita comes late to-night. I was wise and prepared my lesson, I even entertain ambitions for reading *Don Quichote* in Spanish.

I thank you for the [scrap] book, I'll use very little water indeed. After my lesson I promised Lil and Sam to demonstrate my face (they are tired after the boat), and my Cashmere kisses to you.

L.

(41 Gordon Square), Sunday 16th November, 1924

Gossipus enters: Lil and Sam have not changed, nor fat nor thin, just in their middle course of build in their middle ages; they spend their time in a progressive set parallel to Bloomsbury, and their kindness more than out-streched, Sam goes back in the spring, Lil remains, *vice-versa* wouldn't be a bad thing at all. Naturally, they wanted all the news about my knee, and I replied that London knew how to stimulate this article in my body towards restoration. The night was pure and I journeyed with N 73.

Today feeling rather buxome after lunch used coffee in 46, not without pleasure. Clive came back from Paris, no news, only Americans are very populacious over there. For tea Vaz. and Mrs Martineau were expected, but poor widow has troubles with her other son[1] (enormously with rhematism). She is to go with him away for 6 months to Switzerland and Vaz, uncomfortable about it.

. . .

Now I hurry to Florrie, what a busy bee, tender buzz around you.
L.

1   Basil Maine was Mrs Martineau's metaphorical son.

King's College, Cambridge, Sunday 16th November, 1924

Last night I dined with Petica [Robertson] – Topsy's sister. Steven Runciman was there and after dinner I walked back with him – so took the opportunity of getting out of him for you what gossip I could about Vera. She taught him Russian in 1915 – at that date she didn't know any English at all! He never discovered her maiden surname; but her patronymic was Arkadievna. Her father owned mines[1] – which he called by the names of his children; he was well off; Vera had quarrelled with her family. Have you ever heard her sing? That used to be her leading accomplishment. Steven thought it an example of her remarkable talent that although she had no voice at all and was not musical, she could keep up appearances with her singing. In 1915 she was 26; so that she is now 35. There! in return I shall want to hear more of your cat's prattle with Anrepevna.

Still I have not begun my book. There are so many odds and ends to finish first, and I tidy my room, putting books into shelves and throwing away papers.

I did not tell you one confession of Falk's when he was here. Last Wednesday when I was at the company meetings with him, a message was brought in by his Secretary Miss George. He did not say at the time what it was. Afterwards he confessed. La Bibesco had sent him to the office a Chinese bronze pot filled with blood-red carnations. Miss George, the Secretary, is so much shocked that he hardly knows how to look at her!

I am a little sad at the death of Edwin Montagu[2]. I owed – rather surprisingly – nearly all my steps up in life to him. When I was a freshman at Cambridge in 1902, he was President of the Union (the chief undergraduate society) and picked me out in my first term to give me what is called 'a place on the paper'. The first electioneering I ever did (in 1906) was for him. In 1913 when he was at the India Office, it was he who got me put on the Royal Commission on Indian Currency, which was my first step into publicity (my name was known to noone outside Cambridge before then). It was he who got me called to the Treasury in 1915 during the War. It was he who got me taken to Paris in February of that year for the first inter-Ally Financial Conference and so established me in my war work. It was he who introduced me to the great ones (I first met Lloyd George in a famous dinner party of 4 at his house; I first met McKenna through him; I first met Margot sitting next to her at dinner in his house.) It was he who got me invited to the dinners of the inner-secretaries during the early part of the war (private gatherings of the secretaries of the Cabinet and of the chief ministers who exchanged the secret news and discussed after dinner the big problems of the war). He was the Minister to whom I was responsible during the first part of the Peace Conference. It was he who appointed me Vice-Chairman of the Indian Fiscal Commission in 1921. It was he who invited me to join the Mission to Brazil last year.[3] Thus for more than 20 years I had reason to be grateful to him; and there was a certain affectionate relation between us. He was so moody and temperamental and unhealthy and ugly to look at, that I daresay he wasn't very sorry to die. But he had a big talent in his way; one of the Jews of divided nature – half artist and lover, and half consumed with extravagant desires and ambitions. He was an Emperor, a tout and a child; also a wit, an actor and a gambler; he eat and drank too much and always had indigestion afterwards. Although he was extraordinarily hideous, I (unlike many) never found him physically repulsive.

I write too much! It is the result of a little leisure and wanting not to begin the next job.

Your horse,

M.

1   All this information about Vera must be suspect, since her father was a big landowner not a mine owner – see p. 342 below.

2   Edwin Samuel Montagu (1879–1924) was a Liberal politician and administrator.

3   Maynard did not go with the mission.

(41 Gordon Square), Monday 17th November, 1924

I do not think I ever received such literary supply from you as this morning. The portrait of E. Montagu and your relations with him is remarcable listening from your pen, and the gossip is charming. Vera as a primadonna, how unimaginable of her kind and the princess, what a vulgar occupation to send flowers to business men. As for myself, I did not sleep last night so in the morning I felt and looked 'pathetic', 'big brown bags' and eyes as small as buttons couldnt start my *chauffage* with the legs, but ran on the bus to have my head washed, out of 10 women 1 is not shingled to-day, that helped a little but there is still something wrong on the left side of my insides, but it will pass one way or another.

When I finished your letter last night Virginia came with Leonard to offer a seat for 300 club, and besides to borrow my wig that looks shingled to go to Mary's party to-night, she wants to be à la mode, Leonard hates all parties. Mortimer told Virginia that now he prefers *Nation* to N.S.,[1] while Nancy Cunard sat on Leonard's knee and he did not like it, it bores him, sensible man in Bloomsbury.

. . .

I see that you do with the book, what I do with my lessons, it is human nature.

With my weak organs I am very fond of you.

L.

1 *New Statesman.*

King's College, Cambridge, Monday 17th November, 1924

After writing to you yesterday about Edwin Montagu, I had a sudden feeling that I had written it to you all before on some occasion, perhaps when he asked me to go to Brazil. Did I? Or is it one of my usual delusions?

Yesterday my aged aunt [Fanny Purchase] (87) was here. She was in gay spirits. I see that it is a great advantage to be short.[1]

. . .

A warm kiss to my dog, my jester, my mare and my buzzing bee.

M.

1 See Maynard's description of his aunt on page 118.

King's College, Cambridge, Monday 17th November, 1924

Dearest, darling Lydochka

A terrible day of meetings. In 12 hours I have less than an hour to myself – which is at this moment as I write. To-morrow we have our great College Meeting – the Annual Congregation which lasts all day. However I expect that it will be over in time for me to catch my usual train. If not, I will send a telegram.

Last night there was such a high-class Bach concert! But I enjoyed one number very much. To-day I had tea with Richard to meet his mother – a white-haired old character, very nice, and very like him.

I expect you feel rather nervous and excited for the performance to-night.[1] I wonder how it will be. If I was Serge I should not have full confidence. I see that Doline's [Dolin's] name is put modestly, not at the top of the list.

I am very tired and lean my head on you.

M.

1 Diaghilev's company was giving one ballet every afternoon and one every evening in the music hall programme at the Coliseum – the so-called 'cocktail ballets'.

(41 Gordon Square), Thursday 20th November, 1924

Touching life incident. Sickert entered with a picture of me[1] to give it to you. As a new R.A. [Royal Academician] he is very content and later will drag (with his influence) all the other painters in except Roger. A few days ago late in the evening 3 (perhaps masked) men arrived to speak out the honour in Italian (such is a tradition) to Fitzroy square. Sickert only could say one phrase over and over to them, 'Well, I am buggered.' Being an R.A., new possibilities will descend upon him, as hanging his own pictures on the right kind of walls (no dealers), and besides it is the most honorable institution, a pleasant connexion in atmosphere with the great past English masters . . . I spoke of your intention when you are in London, to feast him 'without slinking doubt.' He is pleased also with the picture you bought at the Goupil[2] . . . [After] seeing you last, I walked on the streets about 2 hours, so lovely it was, acquired a book on the life of Beaumont suggested by Clive, and a Spanish weekly, so that now I can only exclaim Oh, Dear Lord God, life is no folly at all, and I must attend to all these occupations; your book, Londoner's diary, *Midsummer Night's Dream*, Dean Swift, there is no time even for me to eat apples, except perhaps as a bed matter.

Recurent dismal of sympathy.

L.

1 *Portrait of Lydia* – inscribed *verso* 'To J.M.K. from a hereditary mathematician.'
2 It was *Théâtre de Montmartre*.

(41 Gordon Square), Friday 21st November, 1924

Punch and Judy were on Tottenham Court Road, why Judy has such a hooked nose, but both moved so well that I did not mind if words were not to be understood. I was charmed with this primitive performance and gave 2 top-pences [twopences] when asked for financial support. Then all in that near neighbourhood, thinking how nice Sickert was, I wanted to become nice myself and visited Thérèse. She had yards of plate and saucers painted in her own style, all for a new coming exhibition, and from a practical point of vue this stock of commodity is less expencive and more necessary than pictures, one should always supply the markets with desirable objects, and naturally we turned on to Sickert as it was the desirable conversation . . .
. . .

Your messanger.
L.

King's College, Cambridge, Friday 21st November, 1924

My dearest, only love

Mrs Marshall has just sent me, to look at, her husband's only poem. It isn't as good as mine! – which is something (but you mustn't ever show mine to anybody).

An American Professor has just been in to see me. He only stayed for half an hour – so I give him very good marks.

I like your account of Sickert very much. Have you actually got the picture ready waiting for me? When shall we give him his dinner? It must be after I get back to London . . . I suggest we might ask to dinner Sickert and Thérèse, Duncan and Vanessa, Vera and Garia, Dobbie and Delia, and others in to dessert (to drink wine and eat raisins). There must be speeches – by Sickert, you, Duncan and me. Full dress will be worn by the guests, with decorations.

M.

(41 Gordon Square), Saturday 22nd November, 1924

Oh Maynarochka, I became excited thinking out your suggested party à la Sickert with decorations; it is flattering for you to posess them, as for myself there is nothing but little warts around my neck, and that is never sufficient. Sam telephoned, Lil is not well, would I first visit Tate gallery with him and then comfort Lil. I did both. Anrep's [mosaic] floor is a magnificient realisitation, but of course very few notice it, because so many walk on it. It is full of meaning and talent; in the same room a big picture of Seurat bought with influence of Roger, 'bathers'[1] must be the name, masterly and calm and different process from yours in 46.[2]

French pictures were the best, Cézanne that intoxicates Sam with it's serenity and subtlety, most of the Courtauld fund you and I have seen already.

Sickert's man and a woman and a miroir, Degas influence very good.	Duncans where Vanessa looks like me is his best there.	Vanessa still life a pitcher also very good.

So much thrash is there also, Lamb's picture of Lytton[3] is not to my acceptance either, and the old masters I did not see and they are probably good. Sam wishes me to tell you that he is jealous over your Cézanne,[4] he used to admire even the photograph. I always feel a pact of friendship to Sam (without going to bed, and that is why it is so nice). Lil in bed, looked handsome, but I promised to be a 'grave' and keep the fact silent, no Londoner should know that Lil suffers ill health in the day time! . . .

Perhaps it bores you, then turn away your eyes from this. I will look into them.

L.

1   *Une Baignade*, transferred to the National Gallery in 1961.
2   A study for Seurat's *La Grande Jatte*.
3   Lamb did many portraits of Lytton; presumably, this is the large one of 1924.
4   Possibly *Oncle Dominique*, purchased by Maynard in 1924.

(41 Gordon Square), Sunday 23rd November, 1924

This morning with great interest I entered into House of Lords gossip on 'birth control', the old foggies mastered the case in accordance to their standart of Victorian morals, they are probably so old, never go to bed with anybody, and so they grow such conclusions. However, there was one good Lord who differed.

Big Serge gives 'clever' interviews, I see, at present he does not need me,[1] I wish he would just the same.

I brought Vanessa chocolate to interchange with coffee. Duncan and Clive with Angelica were there; (official unofficial fathers)[2] both were going to Tate gallery, both praized Sam for his 'enlightening purposes' in the same gallery . . .

. . .

To-night I am in Florrie's, but in this moment I rub my head against your shoulder.

L.

1 Although she had already appeared at the *Coliseum* on 17th November – see Maynard's letter of that date – she was rejected from 25th November when Diaghilev took charge.
2 Angelica's true father was not known to her.

King's College, Cambridge, Sunday 23rd November, 1924

Yesterday I decided not to be shabby any more. So I not only tried on my new suit (which is all right), but bought 6 new shirts at a cost of £9 (which seems to me terrible) and a new hat (which is rather nice, I think) and two ties (which I hope you'll like).

Very tiring – but not so tiring as the real clean up of my rooms which I carried through on Saturday. Everything is now in such order that by next Friday (perhaps) I shall have no excuse at all for not starting my new book. Why does tidying up need so much strength? I suppose because it requires so *many* decisions. I have framed the *Times* photograph of you on your point which looks very nice.

Last night and Friday night I dined with old dons and their wives. Yesterday I lunched with Frank Ramsey to meet his young brother,[1] who is not so interesting as Frank. To-day Dadie and Sebastian lunched with me. After they had gone I closed my eyes and now I open them to write this to you.

Yes – I also begin to be a little interested in the Mr A case;[2] but not so much as others. When I came back in the train on Thursday everyone in a full carriage was reading it. Here all the dons speak of it at dinner. But it is not so *very* interesting. I agree with you in hating Sir John Simon. I thought at first that it might be Aga Khan – but he is more than 24! The Provost says that it is the Maharajah of Cooch Behar.

I send you a little present which I found when tidying up. Also 5 papers.

Since I wrote this Spring Rice came in – he is connected with the Birth Control centre in Kensington. He says that on the first night it was open no 'patients' came in, on the second night 8, and on the third night 17.

Warm touches
M

1 Michael Ramsey, the future Archbishop of Canterbury.
2 A bookmaker called Robinson was suing the Midland Bank in connexion with a cheque for £125,000 allegedly paid for sleeping with his wife by an 'Eastern Potentate' referred to as 'Mr A', about whose identity there was intense speculation.

(41 Gordon Square), Monday 24th November, 1924

I thank you for the present and the papers. I pulled the trigger only after lunch and discovered . . . but such a nice pussy, would be atractive to play a character in that costume, while Mrs Apple Jack and Sam both advise me to shingle.

I have a letter from my mother, she thanks me very very much for money, but except that and kisses, there are very few other words because she sais I owe her a letter therefore she is not able to write very much out of proportion? But I see it thrills her to receive money, and also I think she feels that I am not sailing in swamps . . .

I speak like an old woman sometimes, and yet I know so little.

Your Maharadja[1] of Gordon Square.

L.

1 Reference to the Maharajah of Baroda who, like Lydia, was involved in a law suit.

(41 Gordon Square), Thursday 27th November, 1924

. . .

In my Russian monthly I see the description of communism as a peak crowning our epoch with everything that is best in the minds and hearts of only best peoples, and Lenin and Leninism is the example of a very emotional nature; if some peoples think that it is a somme of mechanical knoweledge, or old fashioned dogmas, where life is eaten up with formulas, such are called 'burgeois' and should be exterminated. 'Ah! mi!'

On reconsideration 'our betters'[1] probably will be our choice, after all it is much more interesting than Communism, of course I look on everything from 'human point of vue', so that 'Quantity theory of money' gives purchasing power, and thence acquisition of papers that I spend so often and that is very human.

Current of fondness.

L.

1 *Our Betters*, a satirical comedy about upper-class English life by W. Somerset Maugham.

(41 Gordon Square), Friday 28th November, 1924

. . .

At dinner we chatted and then M. [Margaret Hill] stood up and said that there was nothing in the world better than to chat with persons she liked, I chuckled and said there was relations semblance with you, it is in your character also, when you like the persons, to interchange your tongue.

To-day I have a sleeping sickness, no matter on what chair I sit, I depart to the world of dreams, I saw that my sister did not have as nice teeth as she used to, although they were hers . . .

How are your creative powers, perhaps they are still visialising in your head, but that is something, whilst I a parasite; it gave me a mental knock yesterday when I bought [theatre] seats for M. an me, that it was your money, but *I* invited her. Do you see any social adjustement in such a 'mode of life'?

L.

King's College, Cambridge, Friday 28th November, 1924

To-day I have bought a blue greatcoat and a second Folio of Shakespeare. Both are extravagances. I am not at all sure that the first is nice, but I got bored looking at patterns and plunged.

Margot is still excited. Even when I am in my bath, here in Cambridge, telegrams come, for which I have to get out . . . Her telegrams ends – 'You have forgotten me.'

. . .

. . . To-night I give dinner to 5 Liberal undergraduates, none of whom I know, and make my speech afterwards to the members of their Liberal Club – perhaps less enjoyable. I feel tired – which probably only means that inside opinion is aware that a speech has to be delivered in two hours' time.

. . .

Yes – you must be very tactful in law courts and must not call Barocchi a baboon, Mary Hargreaves a cat, or yourself a horse, dog or bee; and *me* you mustn't mention at all!

Your
M

(41 Gordon Square), Saturday 29th November, 1924

Imagine, my stupid head imagined that the 'intelectual intercourse' meeting took place in Chelsea Town Hall, seeing only dancing there, we were told to go around, and so we 2 poor chickens ran into public baths! Then we looked ferociously at the ticket, and there it was 3 Victoria Rd. The moment we arrived we were asked to drink coffee, being negligent to that kind of drink, we mounted on the other floor and were met by rather good looking lady with silver head, red scarf and a good deal of zeal on her face, I showed the card and we both were taken, Mrs Martineau and I, for 2 Miss Keynes.

We both protested and then I became famous. By some people I have been congradulated being married (again seeing it in Russian papers). The crowd looked 'bizarre', of course East and West were meeting each other, I advanced myself to Clare Sheridan, a handsome calculating vagabond, who was pleased to see any one who knew her, I waited till she saw somebody else and tried to get into a sitiation with a chair near the pedestal, from where Susan Lawrence would be first to speak. She was an idealist, nice and mad, all for an idea, but life itself was dead in her. All the Russian children were wonderful (you remember that remarkable boy in the *Nation*), but still Susan is honest and smokes cigarettes as she really enjoys it. Then Clare was much more atractive as a speaker and as a woman, she was asked not to mention politicks but who could resist not to drag in such an important item, especially coming from Russia. She and her brother, by some circumstances in some places, had to travel in bycycles, and all the Russians thought it was Churchill on a bycycle with her, having the letter of introduction from Rakovsky, they were comforted in a big degree. Of course personal expereiences like diaries are always charming, because of self expression on easier terms with oneself. She was the success of the evening, of course she is a rascal. Then the third member was advertised, he had good intentions, but a face with features one did not notice ('muy palido' in Spanish) and a hot potato in his mouth when he spoke, a quaker besides, no outer or inner force, but very good intentions. When we survived his speech, we ran, it was so hot, perhaps 100 people all breathing at once; when we descended, 3 women adressed each other as 'camarades', so that element was searching for a taxi, like us, poor burgeois.

It was really diverting, and Mrs M. was very nice company. We kicked our shoulder knuckles many times in the course of speeches, as I dared not open my speaking palette.

I have desires to see your new coat, blue color is so smooth, it goes with London climate. I see how active you are, but it is very nice, except that you can't read *The Times all over*, but then you never read it in Cambridge. I had grinning affairs on my face how I should behave in Law Courts you gave such suitable names to B.[1] ('baboon') and M.H.[2] ('cat').

Your poupsic

L.

1   Barocchi.
2   Mary Hargreaves.

(41 Gordon Square), Sunday 30th November, 1924

. . . This morning spring was in the air, I felt healthy, did my study[1] with good will for about 2 hours. Then rubbed myself with alchogolic glove (the same one that performs after your poet's work in the garden). After lunch Vanessa, Duncan, Clive and Miss Bell welcomed me with coffee. Clive is going to take 'dancing lessons' and Vanessa backs this idea, so that they will be in musclurar conditions. To all the parties Clive goes, dancing is the principal and he gets bored . . .

Tea with Florrie who comes from lunch of Mrs Mathias with Serge as the central figure: he has been to a Westminster Cathedral to hear Byrd's music and liked it so much, that he plans a ballet for a future season, very content with the success, and the 4 Russians from the State theatre are in his troupe. I am glad for them. Vera Savina being through the humiliation of the last row in cordebalet [corps de ballet] is to be given better parts. Stas is to dance at the Empire after Massine.

Now turning to one of your walks of life, Teddy [Grenfell] is enchanted with your memoir of E.M. [Edwin Montagu] and asked me (if he may) to include it in my conversation with you, so I protocolise about it.

L.

1   Whether she was currently dancing or not, Lydia took her exercises very seriously.

King's College, Cambridge, Sunday 30th November, 1924

I have begun the new book! – to-day, and have written one page. This is the first sentence:– 'I begin this book, not in the logical order, but so as to bring before the reader's mind, as soon as possible, what is most significant in that which I have to say.'[1] But I don't expect that it will survive into print. However it is very well to have broken the ice which was beginning to freeze me in.

Last night I went to my Society.[2] We discussed the question whether – for example when one is in love – one can ever know the mind of another person directly and not merely by arguing from their movements and from the sounds they utter. What do you think?

. . .

My meeting at the Liberal Club on Friday went off quite nicely. They were all very much to the left – almost Labour if not quite, I thought. The best speech in the discussion was made by an undergraduate called Hardman,[3] who is the President of the Labour Club. I thought that he might have real talent.

I do not feel satisfied with Hubert and the Nation this week. For two weeks now neither he nor Wright have written an article between them.

I enclose some purchasing power (5).
And am *very* fond of you

M

1   *A Treatise on Money*, 1930. 'The best way to expound a subject of this kind can only be discovered gradually as the result of the experience of successive authors.' (*Ibid*, p. vii).
2   The Apostles.
3   David Rennie Hardman, who was to be active in Cambridge local politics during the '30s and '40s. He became M.P. (Labour) for Darlington, and Parliamentary Secretary, Ministry of Education, from 1945–51.

(41 Gordon Square), Monday 1st December, 1924

. . .

I like your begining of the book, it is so intense; last night speaking of Garia's book[1] as it is finished, I asked if he started the 'Index' and Vera called herself and me 'literary wives', asking such detailed questions.

First excitment is that I invited to-day for tea Russian poet Minsky, whom I always invited without an apointement and at that meeting of intercourse he caught me, and to-day he came with his wife and a lovely girl of 16, who wanted an advice in the life of dancing. I gossiped very freely said that I was not a bolshevic, and then discovered that the young creature was a daughter of Rakovsky. I did blow red baloons inside of me, prospired in the little place where raizor is used sometimes, but altogether it was nice and now we are all friends and I will go and see a small Russian exhibition at Chesham house to meet Mrs Rakovsky! What saved me I think that I had on the other table the Red Russian monthly!

Vera and Garia acquired Colworth affirmatively, and I call them the Squires; in their house in London they brought from Colworth very nice Caneletto, and when I was on my top of the bus, I thought of a perfectly English Canaletto vew on Tottenham Court Road today. The last excitement is that V. lunched with Hilda [Sokolova] and Leon [Woizikovsky] and they said that in the troupe there are noises that I will be probably asked for *Boutique*,[2] but there was no positive statement about it; what a crooked mind of Serge's, he is a born wicked prima-donna with intrigues . . .

Touching utterings for you without words.
L.

1   This cannot be identified.
2   She was not.

King's College, Cambridge, Monday 1st December, 1924

My dearest darling poupsik

I liked your account of the Cultural Relations Meeting! I am sure that the characters you give are quite true. But it seems to have been amusing. Were they mostly English or Russians there?

I had meetings this morning, but this afternoon I have been at my new book again. It's *terribly* difficult; my brain creaks with the difficulty. But I expect it will get easier when I have wound my way in.

My Shakespeare has arrived. It seems a very good copy; but I cannot be quite satisfied how much is in facsimile. (You remember the other one which I bought and sent back to the shop?)

Yes – I liked Jane Harrison's Memoirs [Lydia's letter of 7th November]. I wonder if she will tell the story how she went across France, riding a bicycle in black knicker-bockers, and the peasants crossed themselves when she passed by, thinking it was the devil.

. . .

M.

I have a letter from the lawyer that the [divorce] case will probably be fixed in the week beginning Dec 15 – that is, after a fortnight from now.

(41 Gordon Square), Thursday 4th December, 1924

. . . Paul Nash was my neighbor in the stalls, and in the dark it was not so bad as for the ballet, considering of course how young the producer was it was certainly refreshing and coherent. All Mim's [Rambert's] pupils danced it, and some of them promising, but the one who produced was my favorite, she looked exquisite, nice legs, arms, bust, head and in her dressing room my picture as a mascot. I was indeed touched. After praizing them all, Mim asked me to praize all the 'mothers' also who undressed or dressed their daughters, I was at first a little mocking but she said it would do them good, so I promoted that feeling into them.

. . .

. . . I am most *ocular* with the dictionary you gave me. There is a word 'puceron'[1] that means a 'louse made of grass', or 'probost'[2] is the man who takes care of prisoners. I see that my to-nights evening will be dedicated to *disembowelements* of this book, and with a fluffy kiss to you I shall run to the post.

L.

1 A plant-louse or aphis.
2 Presumably 'provost'.

(41 Gordon Square), Friday 5th December, 1924

. . . Florrie told me about the lunch she arranged for Serge, but he came after 2 o'clock and did not have any, and asked Florrie to invite him again kissing her hands 500 times; Margot and Colebox [Sybil Colefax] were also invited, and Margot told Serge that there was too much movement in his ballet and posed herself as it should be, Serge laughed and asked about Puffin [Anthony Asquith] and that way changed conversation; as to Florrie, Margot promised to send her a letter from Mr Asquith with the description of political events in Egypt. Last night she went to the patriotic demonstration with Baldwins. She held a little flag and was doomed to boredom.

. . . I trembled to be late for Mrs Grant [Duncan's mother], and so I proved, she went out and luckily came back, but I treated her with pastries of a very fresh order, and she told me that mixture of white peoples with Indians is out of question, lately 3 parsee educated ladies told her; although English acomplished useful good things in India they cannot bear English superiority and rather be governed by other blood, any color but not white.

A financial close for you, that Serge receives 1500 a week and first week he was given a 1000 only; Vera thought the troupe is worth 500, I [thought] 600, and Florrie 800, I like to hear your educated figure about the matter.

Oa Maynardochka I am fond of you.

L.

King's College, Cambridge, Friday 5th December, 1924

. . .

For tea I have been to Mrs Marshall who has given me various manuscript scraps of A.M., which I am glad to have, – she has a passion to get rid of everything she possibly can, – like you 'making order' at your frenziliest. (Since this word doesn't exist, I expect you will find it in your dictionary, – I deeply suspect that book; only one of the words in your letter existed and all the rest were wild inventions of the disordered brain of M. Alexandrov!)

To-night I go to the Peckard Feast at Magdalene; very bad for my insides with our Founder's Feast coming to-morrow – but I feel greedy for it all the same.

In a few minutes pupils come for the last time this term.

I wonder if you have any news – only from your own poor female body, I expect, if my calendar is right. I give you very tender touching of consolation.

M.

(41 Gordon Square), Saturday 6th December, 1924

... Dinner at 41 went with an eclat equal only to your Feasting Founders. Caviar, bottle of Pommard, pastryes from Rumpelmayer and a chicken of a quality indeed. They did enjoy it, and what a gratitude to a host ... Languages only English and German spoken, Grigorievs spoke French explaining they did not know any other being Russians, and consequently were pardoned. The biggest ballet success *The three cornered hat*; *Femmes de bonne humor* an ice of a reception. By now I give up hopes of dancing *La boutique*, but I mentioned to Grigoriev if Serge engages me now, me I forgive his debt. The 'conversationi' began from Germany, although their success was astounding they lost 400 pounds, as the contract was signed before the stabilisation of the mark it produced a deficite in Serge's budget, and the traveling expences were enormous, Germany on the whole seems to be well, merchandise in output as big as in England and prices more or less on the same level. Of course I always said Germany was an iron nation. Stoll pays him 1100, and takes off every week something like 5 pounds for the past, the biggest money is paid to Zenon who returned the costumes already, the new influence in the ballet is towards acrobatism, and *Sylphides*, *Carnaval*, *Cleopatra*, *Sheherazade* are not given any more, poor Luba all her good parts. The 'Princess Enchantée' is going to be danced by 5 different executants, one of them is Vera Savina, Serge's idea is to make the ballet absolutely impersonal. I think he should go back to the 'masses' it would be nice anyhow for 'grannies' to dance with their grandchildren in the same row, everybody would be then a 'young boy and a young girl'.

You are *right* I received my bleedings, I thank you for much needed consolation, as for yourself I wish you feast 'till break of day', to-morrow is Sunday.

L.

(41 Gordon Square), Sunday 7th December, 1924

... In *The Observer* your colleague J. Stamp that if America continues to hoard her gold she will emerge herself into a great trouble, while Europe will save herself with a new monetary reform, and crown gold with a 'taboo' when offered. On re-reading my letter of last night I did not mention that I even took Luba [Tchernicheva] to the Empire, she wanted to see Massine-Trefilova, they danced very good numbers almost all new, the engagement was offered to Trefilova and probably Massine's salary is not big, all the expences are Trefilova's. Then we visited stage door, and I told Trefilova how I liked her but not her numbers 1st week, we did not ask for Massine, he is such a brat, he wants join Serge, telephones him, but Serge does not answer yet.

My few remaining hours before the night sets in I intend to spend on the bus, all day long my nose has been smelling fire, I shall inhale Hyde Park, and think of the little holes in your vest[1] that I could also penetrate with my 'inside opinion' of a nose.

L.

1 Maynard's underwear with 'little holes', to which Lydia often refers, was probably an early example of cotton cellular material (he refers in his letter of to 'a new kind of vest'), which was a health fad in the 20s and 30s.

King's College, Cambridge, Sunday 7th December, 1924

In spite of Feasts two days running, I feel very well – but lazy; they have come at a good point of the cycle. Anyhow it was no good trying to write the book to-day. There are too many visitors here, who come in and out of my rooms . . .

. . .

Last night at the Feast I sat between Duncan and Sir Josiah Stamp, and next to Duncan was Roger. I enjoyed the dinner. The Provost made a very charming speech, full of artistic fitness. Afterwards the undergraduates entertained us and there were Vive-las. I made up several[1].

. . .

If I am told that Serge gets £1500 a week – I just don't believe it. Not, if Sir Ozzy [Stoll] told me himself! But there might be some sham arrangement about old debts, by which he gets a high nominal figure of which part goes to old debts and only part in cash. My 'educated figure' lies between you and Florrie – £700. I wonder if your letters to-morrow will have any *Boutique* gossip. I only hold very moderate hopes.

. . .

M.

1 *Vive-las*: impromptu stanzas on the lines of 'Vive la compagnie', a traditional feature of Founders' Day celebrations on December 6, old Christmas Day. They were ribald, and eventually became so indecent that they are no longer allowed.

(41 Gordon Square), Thursday 11th December, 1924

Hilda [Sokolova] telephoned and the lunch took place to-day instead. We tore the breasts and legs with our hands, as the chicken was rather tough, Leon [Woizikovsky], Hilda and I in succession could not do anything with a knife, because the chicken died with her own death. Hilda thought my letter was too late to Diaghilev, because they rehearsed since Monday and would be more difficult to take the part from Nemchinova now, otherwise Leon and

Hilda receive good money but only in London. Leon 53 pounds, Hilda 40, I am glad for them; in Germany they were almost in debts, as 5000 franks makes a 1000 marks or shillings. Nijinska wants to leave the troupe[1] at the moment, but then she has 2 children, mother and husband to support. What a life! They all hope for a season in the spring separate from the Coliseum, and the biggest success of the ballets till now was *Children's tales*.

It is very cold and yet foggy, do you breathe Eidingbourogh's [Edinburgh's] purity on the outskirts by now? I cannot say anything atmospheric about this [?illegible] city, but I dare say some Scotch poets were born there, Walter Scott comes to my head, but is he apropriate? It is much nicer that you are there and you will give the Edinboriens the treasures from your head and heart.

L.

1   She did so.

London to Edinburgh, Thursday 11th December, 1924

It *is* nice to spend a day in the train. For three hours I read the papers. Then I finished preparing my speech. Then lunch (not much appetite – I shall be an invalid until I have delivered my efforts). Then the eyes closed – not for long. Then I read Eliot's 'Homage to John Dryden' – *very* good, I have never read better criticism. Now I write to you.

> But hark! My Pulse, like a soft Drum,
> Beats my approach, tells *Thee* I come;
> And slow however my marches be,
> I shall at last sit down by *Thee*.[1]

M.

1   From *The Exequy* by Bishop Henry King.

(41 Gordon Square), Friday 12th December, 1924

Double purpose dwells in me for writing you before 1 p.m.; to conffess that your 'Pulse like a soft drum' is touching, this done I escape my exercises, the energy of last week comes to a stand still.

. . .

Fog is no more, it was dreadfull for the throat, it is a chance for you to be in Edinborough so that the atmosphere of the soil is in relation with your voice, which in turn will give your intelectual dynamite to the listeners. I am hurrying to go to Florrie, washing is needed to perform on myself, but I am with your efforts and crossings from myself.

L.

Edinburgh, Friday 12th December, 1924

My dearest darling poupsik

Your letter arrived with my breakfast this morning. When, last night, the time of breakfast came to be discussed, I had the courage to say that I wanted mine in bed. Now I am spending a quiet morning before making my speech.[1] The air is warm and beautiful – one scarcely needs a fire. When I have looked through my speech again, I shall walk in the streets and see if there are any warm shoes for you.

. . .

I feel a little weak and need at half past one all your crossings.

M.

1 He was to lecture to the Edinburgh Chamber of Commerce on foreign investment.

Letters from
10th January 1925 to 13th March 1925

At last, on 15th January, Lydia was awarded a decree nisi of nullity of her marriage to Barocchi; her consequent elation is evidenced by the changed style of her letters which become more happy-go-lucky. 'I feel weak and ride in taxis without reserve, my legs are so very shaky.' To compensate for her lack of a university education, her 'decree' becomes a 'degree'. She receives many letters of congratulation. Maynard was happy and indulged himself by buying oddments of furniture in Cambridge. On 1st February, after exceptionally devoting the whole day to his book, he wonders whether he usually has too many distractions. He was writing on Inter-Allied Debts for the Nation and undertaking, as ever, much college business. On 9th March Lydia objects to Maynard's proposal to make a formal announcement of their engagement. While practising for the Postman ballet, she keeps on falling off her bicycle in Gordon Square; with its decor and costumes by Duncan Grant, this ballet was first performed by Lydia and Idzikovsky at the end of March.

(41 Gordon Square), Saturday 10th January, 1925

. . . Pat [Dolin] stopped me for explanations as to his behaviour towards me in the past, and gave me a good old English name of 'sport'. I felt uncomfortable but forgiving. Hilda [Sokolova] was filled with 'hinky, inky lacrimi' as *Aurora's wedding* is more like funeral to her. Florrie, Vera, Muriel and I did our very best in sympathy and understanding, there was 'every rhyme and reason' for such. At last I saw Ninette, of course she is sweet, we are to have our tea in May! . . .

Teddy presented me with 4–3–2–1 Maundy money, with good luck to the divorce. No more accounts to state just now . . .

L.

(41 Gordon Square), Sunday 11th January, 1925

To-day *Oh* what a life! The fog is very domineering, and head, throat and lungs are the first victims. So embarrassing it is that I lost my own self in Gordon Square; a feeling of 'deluge' greets one, and what a desire to 'survive.' To enter the room with electric lights, warm fire, is to become at once very kind to everybody, and depressing mood vanishes quicker than 'vanishing cream.'

Vaz. played music in the afternoon, but soon he will play Jesus Christ in Masefield's play, I advised him not to wear a beard. Then I had to see Florrie for the last time this January, she had a little pimple in her mouth so I looked in, while she did same to me, to examine my teeth. The amount of cavities appears the same, only she has more gold and I silver . . . Florrie sais I am still the topic of conversations [apropos the divorce] at lunch, dinner and tea partys, you are implied as P. = R. I shall work now on your literature, there is nothing I like to do better at the moment.

L.

(41 Gordon Square), Thursday 15th January, 1925

How fortunate I am, after these swift dramatic developments,[1] my mental state no more bedraggling, 'Gods divine' have been benevolent to me. I hope for their future kindness transposing a part of their wisdom on me when needed.

I bow into your knees and kiss your feet.

L.

P.S. [On a photograph relating to her marriage to Barocchi.] I forgot but once I was bobbed also.[2]

1 She had received her decree *nisi* on the day of writing.
2 'Bobbed' means having a short hair-cut.

(41 Gordon Square), Friday 16th January, 1925, second day of *degree* [*decree*] *nisi*

. . . Geoffrey's Margaret came in my absence, with warm words of gladness and Florrie answers with many words of affections. I feel weak and ride in taxis without reserve, my legs are so very shaky. Vera gave me a counsil that no matter how interesting a woman is, when she has a house the man will like her still more if she is a good housekeeper, I told her about 46 and Regent Park house for her. Garia is in love with his new gardener Mr Henry (Skotch extraction like me)[1] and writes to him every day.

The day before my divorse Sam thought I'll never obtain one, but Lil said to-day what a 'good reading it was!' . . .

Now to my Russian compatriate the legal advisers to the Russian Trade Delegation, what an industry, and what laughter, and what an innocent magistrate.

L.

1 Lydia's mother was partly Scottish.

King's College, Cambridge, Friday 16th January, 1925

My dearest darling,

The *Times* report[1] is really much the best account of what happened, but – characteristically – the bit about B's [Barocchi's] taking your salary is left out! I am sure your guardian spirits will always give you wisdom as well as protection, – for perhaps the two are the same thing. I kiss you for your letter.

The fog stretched all the way to Cambridge and my train was very late. Sickert's picture[2] is here – very fine – but not yet hung. . . .

. . .

M.

1 According to the report in *the Times* (16th January, 1925), in this undefended nullity suit, before Mr Justice Horridge, Lydia was granted a decree nullity with costs on the grounds that the ceremony of marriage she had gone through with Barocchi in October 1916, in the United States, was bigamous, as he had not then received the decree absolute regarding the dissolution of his first marriage with Mary E. Hargeaves – who had still been alive in 1919.
2 'Venetian Model', 1903, pencil, pen and ink.

(41 Gordon Square), Saturday 17th January, 1925

Stas's shares of pride are lower than last year, my jaundices subdue inside of me yet, (Monday morning is his answer), they will flow to me again, not because of my desire to dance so much, but of the idiocy of that little worm. I cannot relate all the rubbish he was carrying through conversatiation, a waste of even this particular paper [i.e. Hotel San Regis paper].

I visited Beaumont's 'Boutique', he showed some more styles of the costumes you designed for me in the past. Peoples of to-day do not know how great many things were lovely yesterday . . .

I thank you for the papers, they are untouched yet.

L.

(41 Gordon Square), Sunday 18th January, 1925

The 3 Bloomsbyrites Vanessa, Duncan and Clive sang in chorus how I disgraced Bloomsbury going on the point of degree nisi, and how much more moral they were than I:

> 'All said and done
> It's little I
>   against a throng.
> I'm only one
>   and possibly
> I may be wrong.'

. . .

Returning to my divorse, am I with King's Proctor?[1] Vera thinks I might [be], so that you never can come to 41 or I to 46? (the only place for us is Hyde Park), 'what a lif.' As for my engagement at the Coliseum, Vera thought the idea of post man very amusing, but that the piano part should be orchestrated by Bernard, (there is an idea we should give attention to).

I dreamt that my little brother had two sets of teeth from nature, I must write to my mother, but the embroidery pattern looks at me with a caressing eye and gallerites are coming to greet the 'virgin'.

By now Cambridge atmosphere is opening it's gates very wide and you look pure and wise. It is lovely to-day. I behold that strange couple of Karin and Adrian like Siamese twins in the square. My worshippers arrived so that I can worship you more.

L.

the last phrase contains mathematical inspiration but I cannot explain.

---

1 In the period before a decree nisi was made absolute, a petitioner for divorce could risk losing the case if it came to the knowledge of the King's Proctor that he or she was having sexual relations with a third party (the implication being that they had petitioned for divorce because they wished to have such relations rather than on one of the few then-legitimate grounds). Lydia having petitioned for nullity rather than divorce, did not in fact have to worry about this.

King's College, Cambridge, Sunday 18th January, 1925

Yesterday afternoon I went to my favourite small furniture shop to see what he had got during the vacation; and bought so many things!
(1) a full-length eighteenth century mirror on hinges for you
(2) a small mirror for the hall
(3) a complete dessert service of plates etc. (which turned out to have belonged to Vanessa's first cousin who was Mistress [Principal] of Newnham)

(4) a small Dutch picture (for £1)
(5) a nice box for your stationery
(6) a fine wooden chest on legs with brass handles for you to keep your decree nisi in
(7) a small table like the one you make coffee on

I was in the shop for more than an hour. It sounds like an auctioneer's Catalogue. I hope they will look as nice when they get to Gordon Square as they seemed to in the shop.

Your decree absolute

M

. . .

(41 Gordon Square), Monday 19th January, 1925

Jaundices again: rage, fury, despondency, 'the dancer of the age' [Stas] insists with 75 pounds for his legs, so wistfully I said 'good by', and sat in my chair like a tomb stone ever after; but your letter and the book subdue my ugly passions and I am much more human at present. The miroirs and other objects divert my mind not a little and the wooden chest for my degree; I hope there is place enough for other honors also. I had a post almost as big as you in proportion, from your mother, Mrs Marshall, Margaret, Florrie, and no one belives that I am a 'virgin' except you; and I kiss you for it . . .

I understand that speculations were in a bad cycle, because my matrimonials realised so much above water, therefore the metals began to melt out of their own accord, but it will not take long for them to raize as high as Christ has risen. *Oh*, what a talker I am!

. . .

My gallerites thought Mrs Snedden [the cook, recently dismissed] was an awful woman and Winston a dangerous man. They were very nice and we had muffins. In the evening Vera was so pleased with my degree nisi that I thought she was myself, ready to enter into your substance, Oh I am still talking, in a way it is bad for you to listen to this chatter boxing, but from a different angle it is good – because there is no one's tongue like that in Cambridge.

L.

King's College, Cambridge, Monday 19th January, 1925

My dearest darling,

This has been one of my usual Mondays of meetings, so I am rather tired and bored. One of them was about the New Buildings, since the other architect (the one who is not Kennedy) has sent his designs. I think them horrible. But I see that feeling is going to run high, and that it will be a terrible fight to get Kennedy taken (and easier to defeat the other man than to win for K.)

. . .

Yes – you are with King's Proctor. But *I don't think* it matters with a nullity (as it would with a divorce) how you behave now! The K.P. must only concern himself whether your evidence, as given, was true.

I expect Vera is right (I am always saying that now!) about the orchestration of the Beethoven piece.

I am more fond of you, so that you can be more fond of me, so that I can be more fond of you, so that you can be more fond of me, and so on to infinity

M

[postcard]   King's College, Cambridge, Tuesday 20th January, 1925

I have had a very good French Press on my debts article; so I send these by post to amuse you in bed to-morrow morning.

M

(41 Gordon Square), Thursday 22nd January, 1925, (degree nisi week off)

. . . I bussed to Legat's couple, meeting them on the threshold of their studio, and invitingly proceeding to the Lyonses. Sat there till 7½ o'clock uttering complaints about the trickery of the theatrical world, citing Basil Dean who last year made promises to Legat, but still engaging Fokine for 2000 pounds, while Legat would take definitely less. Naturally, now Legat sais 'what a fool I was not to ask 400 pounds instead of a 100 last year' (and morally he is right, and even practically), of course I poured my hatred to the 'anti dreams' producer. However, next week they appear at the Coliseum (that same Stoll tour only I did not know). I shall go on Monday and send flowers across the stage. Mentioning my divertissement,[1] Legat suggested very charming idea worth snatching that the first number should be with 3 girls and when I finish they still continue, so that I change . . .

My intra vetred sympathy of delicate touches, because you have a stomach-coff.

L.

1 Maynard was again endeavouring to promote her career – see his letter of 26th January.

(41 Gordon Square), Friday 23rd January, 1925

I look into *The Times* all over, nothing seems to be worth noticing except St Pauls, but not as a newspaper reading so I wait for *The Nation*. What an early spring happened this morning. After lunch I threw myself on the streets. Beaumont was very occupied, the couple achieves one way or another to do many things of life in the shop when I entered, the cooking was streaming all over the place, I just had time enough to look for a Russian costume, and one by Bakst, but not used, was extremely suitable for my pesantic purpose; I'll establish myself tomorrow there again.

Was it 4 York Terrace that splashing house we looked over, if so Vera and Garia have been there, liked it in every way except for the pocket.

. . .

Oah I am so sleepy, I shall run to the box with this and then my first course of sleep on the chair; I have not written to anyone yet, I am a bad woman but there is some good in confessing it to you.

L.

King's College, Cambridge, Friday 23rd January, 1925

I need your delicate touches, – because I don't feel very well to-day. The 'stomach cough' has become more stomach and also more cough. It might almost be a slight influenza; however I shall see to-morrow how I am.

Sheppard is back, – seems moderately well and cheerful. He was very sorry that Florrie didn't find him, – he didn't see her either. He lost *every penny* he possessed (including his expenses £200 in a fortnight) and now he hasn't enough money to pay his income tax! He is disgusted; but I expect he will go again. He says he was not well and therefore played without skill!

. . .

I wrote my book this morning but have done nothing else interesting. I enclose a copy of my article for your scrap book. Also a Cultural Relations Card (though it doesn't look interesting). And just kiss you.

M.

(41 Gordon Square), Saturday 24th January, 1925

'More stomach and more cough'? *Oah* biedny Maynarochka, how unsympathetic; for I know your stomach soon will reassert himself, and the throat will be in 'the pink of conditions'.

What a monetary debauch on the part of Sheppard, 200 pounds, with that somme he could lay a fundament for a Grecian library in honour of Aeschylus, or visit the remains of Queen of Atassa.

. . .

I visited Beaumont again, he lent me the magnificent edition of Bakst, it is rather enormous and I worked it's way into a taxi. The particular design I like was only prepared in 1922 and never used.

If you came Tuesday we should look into the whole inside of the book, Diaghilev is described as a 'fat chubby chap from provinces.'

My Espanolita read to me a Spanish story, it was quite silly, and I understood it with the thinking capacity of a caveman.

Please, take good comfort around you, dont stand on the drafts, and continue to wear your little holes garments, it is the only warm ones you posess while the early spring is false.

L.

(41 Gordon Square), Sunday 25th January, 1925

I told Vanessa and Duncan about ... how the crisis about housing problems arose. Van. said she would like to know more about 41 if there is a definite answer to her desired composition of the rooms from James; however she suggested a house in Bedford Square for you, it would be awful next to the Princess [Elizabeth Bibesco] and Margot Oxford, so although I carry this message it's with the inside opinion of discontent[1] ...

. . .

What is your temperature today, intelectually and physically? I put crossings on both.

Sam and Lil came and I dared [to say] 'bring sometime Sydney to tea.' I did not hear a promise to it, but the seed is thrown ...

Lately there is again a boom for Einstein, so I am not out of date.

> 'There was a young lady called Bright
> Who travelled much faster than light
> She went out one day
> In a relative way
> And returned the previous night.'

Einstein in a nut shell, but heart-splits for you.

L.

---

1 Vanessa was trying to get them away from Gordon Square.

King's College, Cambridge, Sunday 25th January, 1925

The cough is better, but I am still a little pitiful; – it marches its course. Going home to lunch to-day, I found my mother in bed with a bad sick head-ache, – however a little gossip cheered her up a bit. What medicine it is to the female constitutions!

. . .

This week my book has made quite good progress, considering that it is Cambridge term.

Our splashing house in Regent's Park was another Terrace, – not York.

I am leading a dry life and time passes. You must moisten me again with your springs.

M

I enclose five papers

(41 Gordon Square), Monday 26th January, 1925

I spent money lavishly thanks to your papers, with each purchase I blew a racket out of me, and my existence became not null, but a plausibility. Last night the stomach did not demand a dinner, so to-day one lunch was a small fragment of my apetising desires, so I had hot chocolate and sandwiches at Fullers, good place, and the girls do not wear Lyons uniforms of vulgar demure smartness, then to the Russian rascal's shop, pullers [sic] were stale, cigarettes were taken instead, as a Russian politeness, you can dispose of it in Cambridge, then to the French shop, with their standart articles in a confectionary way, and then to *my* Russian shop, where I chattered contentedly with the nice woman, and bought a diary of Dostoevsky's second wife and music. The only thing I noticed in the diary is that when Dostoevskya walked hand in hand with Dostoevsky she had to make 3 steps for his 2, the reason lies in his height of course . . .

I am so fond of you that I am sad.

L.

King's College, Cambridge, Monday 26th January, 1925

My dearest darling,

I have a letter from the Coliseum. They want you to make another try with Stas, rather than have the other programme, and they want to know what money he asked for. This means that I must go to see them personally, I think. I shall tell them that the only way is for *them* to put pressure on Stas; for I don't suppose for a minute that they will pay him £75. It is still possible that they may prefer the programme without Stas when they hear the difference in price. Meanwhile you must carry the idea of *both* programmes in your mind! I am still rather a biedny – though there's really nothing the matter with me. I have sat in my room by myself most of the day, – thinking very much that I

281

should like some touches from you. As I said before, I feel very *dry* without you.

Until to-morrow —

M.

King's College, Cambridge, Tuesday 27th January, 1925

I can only do one word in this Cross Word; and I expect that is wrong?

JMK

[newspaper cutting of crossword attached: clue, King of Lydia; answer, Maynard]

King's College, Cambridge, Friday 30th January, 1925

I have taken a very quiet day as a reaction from the perturbations of London, — sat in my rooms most of the day, walked in the streets a little, got shaved in a shop, read a *very* miele letter from you, and closed my eyes a little at tea time. In the morning I put the last touches on the first section of my book, of which the first draft is now finished.

[newspaper cutting] What do you think of this house in Regent's Park? — no, not for yourself, for Sam. Three tennis courts for Lil and plenty of room for a gallery for Sam. There may be disadvantages, but it really looks rather a bargain.

. . .

I send five papers, because you may have expenses with your vast Coliseum party to-morrow.

With very tender touches
M

(41 Gordon Square), Saturday 31st January, 1925

. . .

Your Margaret's family arrived 'so sproost', I thought them very nice especially the smallest Maurice who was indignant when I addressed him 'David', most of them have Keynes blood I noticed this time: they loved Harry Tate [the comedian] and a juggler whose legs did everything instead of hands, German no doubt so consientous catching 3 big balls with the palms of his 2 feet in fact no 'haggle over trifles.'

. . . At 41 the children had 3 plates of bread and butter, it was wonderful they eat everything from the table, but with good manners, each time *asking* for a continuity of thier feeding apparatuses: the Christmas cake (at last!), chocolate, apples, jams, pastry 'out of date Fullers', went inside with a 'joie de vivre'. It was so sincere.

Margaret said 'that is why I look poor', she does not yet, but sociologically it is more than possible. After tea they all danced on their toes, and as a hostess I put the ballet shoes and stood on mine, then we walked on heels and finished our excitements on the floor. They were very happy and I excited.

. . .

I am exhausted, subtle touches where the soft hair grows.

L.

(41 Gordon Square), Sunday 1st February, 1925

This afternoon I heard a loud voice inquiring after me, could that be K.P., not this time, only a Russian Jew (or a German?) of an agent (who met me at Legats) with a proposition if I am ready to jump for an engagement via Berlin or Dresden or Baden? I refused and did not invite him inside of my dwelling, do not like agents in principle, perhaps this one might be better than others, but it was nice to feel free from, they are 'vampires.'

Saw Vanessa and Duncan, they still live in an inn, although the servants occupy the house where they paint with central heating, how absurd, even if they are terror stricken after their untidiness, it is only for a week or 2. Next week they go to see the house that was *sold* last time, but it is not sold after all, it does seem that people do not say the truth most of the time . . .

. . .

I am very glad how you progress with *your book*, and I kiss you with it and without.

L.

P.S. I thank you for the papers.

King's College, Cambridge, Sunday 1st February, 1925

My dearest darling,

. . .

Late in the evening I got on to a train of thought, – to apply my theories (of my new book) to the twenty five years before the war to see if they fit. I have pursued the same matter all to-day, sitting at a table among many big books copying out long tables of figures and then gazing at them with would-be wise eyes. You would say that I looked 'intellectual'; – perhaps a little, the figures fit the theory as well as one could expect.

. . .

When I sit, as to-day, at the matters of my book all day long, I feel it would be better if I had *nothing else* to think about. But I daresay it is not truly so. The mind becomes quickly stale and infertile (at least mine does) if it thinks only about one matter; so the distractions do not lose so much time as it seems.

. . .

I don't care a sixpence (except in the way of kindness) for anyone but you.

M

I enclose a handkerchief for you to put your face against when you sleep in the chair or on the sofa.

(41 Gordon Square), Thursday 5th February, 1925

I walked back to 41 from your taxi, swallowed in well measured bitings a Cox orange pipin apple, gradually sinking into a big chair and thought what a 'miely human being' you were above all else i.e. besides your quantity of other qualities . . .

With you and me that would be different,[1] up to 35 years of age I could have an engagement by my professional legs and earn at least so much that you could make a few 'grand coup' and regain the lost sitiation. I am very glad to think I am able to do such things.

L.

. . .

1 She has been relating, at some length, details of the poverty of Dostoevsky's wife.

(41 Gordon Square), Friday 6th February, 1925

The air to-day was like a 'mild apirient', the wind blew everywhere but ever so softly, I was on feet and on the bus, took the beads of amber from the place where they correct the strings, and not only the strings, they improved the lustre, and it is ever so wistful on the neck; however before that I went to Gamba with a new pair of shoes from last summer that are not particularly right and told them I'll never order anything else, as my patience was exhausted. To minimise my discontent they offered to make me a new pair of shoes without money, but I said 'I do not want something for nothing, but that shoes in question should befit my feet.'

. . .

. . . I am sad that Piccadilly fountain is not to sprinkle any more, not withstanding it ever does, one of the places I observe with the soul of a poet almost every day, and those beatiful laundry baskets with flowers, no more? And the fat ladies with such aimable excelent shawls . . .[1]

I am fond of you.

L.

1   The flower-sellers of Piccadilly.

(41 Gordon Square), Sunday 8th February, 1925

My jaundices are still influencing, and my color is sleepy yellow. Vanessa, Duncan are laboring now in Mortimer's flat, so that after coffee everybody deserted Angelica. I have read the 2 articles on Liberalism and Laytons is a fresher one, still I came to the conclusion they have no wise leaders (Liberals). You are very good brains but you wouldn't give all your head to Liberals, you like to have other dreamings of thought in other directions, and should. . . .

I have started 'Sunday friendship' with Mim, she wanted to see me, therefore she comes and I shall learn more knowledge about 'our lot' in general and particular.

Clive is invited to stay with Peter in the 'Doll's house' but Topsy is not enough of a seducement and recompense. How capricious men are. Sam called me to say that he likes the idea very much of the Artists cooperative society but he wants to speak with you to understand completely the scheme, and being Sam he doubts the practicability of the idea, but he means well and desires to contribute. I gave 'King's College' as your present embassy. At the party they had a Russian pianist Orloff and Adilla Fakiri[1], Mortimer was the only 'intelectual'. As to my not coming to the party, I said 'I never forse myself to go to parties when out of "season"'.

I communicate my fondness.

L.

1   See footnote on page 139.

King's College, Cambridge, Sunday 8th February, 1925

My dearest darling,

I find myself pretty well, but still rather feeble and not good for full work. My first duty on getting back was to deal with the guardian of one of my pupils, who turned out to be a formidable county lady; however I did my best to satisfy her! . . .

This morning I began an article for the *Nation* on the Bank Chairmen and the Gold Standard[1] but am not yet beyond the beginning. I mock them too much, which is not wise; so I must alter it. You would like what I have written so far much better than the bank Chairmen would!

Kisses and courage. I am still only three-quarters of myself.

M.

1   'The Bank Rate', *Nation*, 7th March, 1925.

(41 Gordon Square), Monday 9th February, 1925

Being a versatile business woman I went to the Alhambra, watched Nicolaeva – Legat programme, their last dance is a Jewish one, Legat was magnificent dressed in everyday clothes with a long coat and a nose of a Jewish dimension, the hooky one, almost aquiline and isn't, I did my best with hands and voice, but it is uninspiring to be in an empty theatre; I think it is one of wooden stubborn opinions of Ossy Wossy [Stoll] that it brings profits, how can it?

Then to the familiar stage door – stayed there for about 2 hours, to-morrow I shall bring the music to him, we drank tea and Legat was exersising in Jewish make up . . . They thought I looked bad, in fact I have ear-aches and a slight enfluensa, I shall drink hot limonade and go to bed at the earliest and to-morrow will be my progress.

As for yourself, although you describe as ¾ you *are* producing satisfactions for the 'country lady' and the Provost, it is wiser for you to meet them, than they should meet each other. The last ½ of a phrase suggests non-sense as I feel brainless and without enterprise.

Your ¼ L

. . .

(41 Gordon Square), Thursday 12th February, 1925

My calendar is fascinating, without any reason on the 23rd of March (the day of my Angel), on the back side of the page, there is an explanation about the lightest tree in the world called 'balsam tree' and ferrys are built out of it. I see that I am a born slave, and I am to carry you through my back, other news you probably know already, but I have not any others to tell, that eels the moment they are born in the sea, strive to get into rivers and live there comfortably till late of life, when insistent call is upon them, they rush back to the sea, flood thousands of millions semences of little eels and die for ever.

Not all mysteries of nature solved yet. I am fond of you with a kiss and without [illegible] it.

L.

[postcard] King's College, Cambridge, Thursday 12th February, 1925

My dearest darling poupsik

Do keep yourself indoors for 2 or 3 days and don't go out to Stas, or the post, or anywhere. That is the only cure.

I send you the *Vogue*

M

(41 Gordon Square), Friday 13th February, 1925

I accepted your counsel and *The Vogue* with gratitude, therefore my phisical side develops progressively; a telegramme was invented for Stas with regrets and sorrows, yet I had a morning visit from 'Berta Ruck' with red tulips for me and Russian boots perhaps also worn for me. We aproached each other not less than 10 feet of a distanse . . .

Since her departure I live with the 'chair' and also books, calendars, dictionaries, and all that is of a 'printing order' comes under my eye, thanks to Henry Pestalozzi or was it Hutenberg? Some 'mathematicks' of a small degree comes from a banker Parvus, who died it seems not long ago; the workers, as ever, naturally wanted the augmentation of their salaries, then in answer Parvus sent a letter such:

a year has	365 days	every year	31 days
you work only 8 hours		2 weeks holiday	
that means ⅓ of a		every year	−14 days
year	−122		17
Sundays taken away	− 52	holidays made by	
	70	the law	−12
on Saturdays after			5
lunch no		and at least 5 days	
work that makes	26	of the year one is ill or	
	44	any other reason of	
one hour for lunch	− 13	absence	− 5
	31		0

That is how 'bourgeosie' treats the workers!

Your affectionate dog
L.

King's College, Cambridge, Friday 13th February, 1925

My Balsam,

. . .

I seized the *Evening News* in the Combination Room to-night. But again there was nothing. I think that perhaps we have checked them.[1]

. . .

Healings on your cold

Your eel

M

1   This must refer to gossip about the divorce.

(41 Gordon Square), Sunday 15th February, 1925

. . .

. . . Yesterday Duncan said he would like to be called Lord of St Ives, and I would not mind to be called Lady Turquay. Vanessa made the offer for the house,[1] the real cause of disturbance, that husband-wife on the road to separation, but Van. will give the tenants a chance – her opinion about the house is still 'radiant'. Cambridge gets better degrees than I in London, more honorable but like me not absolute, it is your atom scientist Russian friend Kapitza, a Don for 3 years I understand in the magnetic research; the tea drinkers are coming, Mim, Francis [?] and her friend the ballet slippers are on the table instead of pastries.

I kiss your warm nest of a mouth.

L.

1   There were to be changes as Lydia was to remove to No. 46 on marriage.

King's College, Cambridge, Sunday 15th February, 1925

By yesterday I had got so very 'liberal' that there was nothing for it; and though I don't like having hands on me which are not Fitch's, I went and got myself shingled. So now I look (what you call) young, and (I suppose) conservative! But I will tell you one thing about shingling – it makes the back of the head feel *very cold*, at any rate at first. N.B. Shingling would have just the opposite effect on you – it would make you look MIDDLE-AGED AND COMMUNIST, with 'high ideals and burning zeal' (see the enclosed cutting).

This morning I have at last finished my *Nation* article on the bankers. It is a long one, but why I have taken so long about it I don't know, – relics of

36　*Vera Bowen with her son Nicholas*

37 Harold Bowen   38 Florrie Grenfell

39 Lydia with Florrie Grenfell and her husband

40   *Samuel Courtauld*

41 *Lydia by Walter Sickert*

42 *Lydia in* Les Sylphides, *1924*
('An instantaneous photograph . . .
taken with a Taylor-Hobson
Cooke lens' – The Times)

43 *Lydia and Maynard with the Melchiors*

44   *A studio portrait of Lydia and Maynard, probably 1925*

45   *Their wedding made news*

46　*Outside the Registry Office, 4th August, 1925*

47   *At Studland, in 1923*

influenza perhaps. So now I can go back again to the book and start the next section . . . I decided this morning that there was no pleasure in the world so great as thinking and writing.

I think it must be Valentine Day. So I send you a crossword Valentine.

. . .

M.

L	Y	D	I	A		
O						
P	U	P	S	I	K	
O	H		A	L	E	C
K			M	A	Y	N
O		A			N	O
V	E	R	A		E	
A		T			S	

Across
1. My dearest darling sweet
4. Another name for (1.)
3. What (1) ought to say
5. What (1) does say
6. Deborah
14. A pure woman
8. Dances in cabaret
10. (1) says (12) to what (10) is 4/5 of, and (2) to what (10) is 4/7 of
12. What (1) says to what (10) is 4/5 of

Down
1. What the world calls my dearest darling sweet
2. What (1) says to what (10) is 4/7 of
9. Makes one think of Lil
11. Wed to the supernormal
7. Me
13. Common in No. 46

(41 Gordon Square), Monday 16th February, 1925

I have been troubled with your sweet Valentine, I did not achieve my exercises because of it, and I am late everywhere on account of it, 4/5 and 4/7 are still in my dislocated mind without solution – or was it composed with an idea that I could not divulge it?

After lunch I ran to the Haymarket theatre with Nicolaeva Legat to see an Indian ballet composed by him [Legat] rendered by amateurs – Russian officers and English ball room dancers; some dancing was charming, but I hear Mr Johns after having been treated with a splashing dinner remarked 'I do not see why I should have it at the Coliseum.' Then with steps 'a la presto' to 41, where Sam was expecting me with 'white lilacks'. So we drank tea and spoke about marriage in general, prohibition, artificial silk in America, how Ford stood firmly for prohibition because he visualised the 'eclat' of his own car-production, and women wore artificial silk stockings and jumpers in the automobiles, yes everything depended on relation to one another. Lil came snatchingly for Sam . . .

Your crossword tempered
Lydochka

(41 Gordon Square), Thursday 19th February, 1925

Forgive my nervous centres of irritation, was I a burden to you? I am very tired and hope to jump into bed when the hour strikes 10.

I read all the adresses on your writing and smiled pleasantly at 'Londoner's Diary'; otherwise I am such a consistent dog of yours.

L.

P.S. Russian University was established 100 years ago in Petrograd.

(41 Gordon Square), Friday 20th February, 1925

To-day I proved myself a person of movement, at 10 o'clock I started my sweatings with good results, and at 12 I was at Stas's studio in Gloucester Rd as I promised to see his class. He had 10 pupils . . . and Stas himself incredibly small, at first with golden hair, no glasses, woolen jumper, the first part of the body so very tiny, after the 'navel' luxirious muscular legs, that looked like 'plus fours', although he wore your trousers, with a stick à la maestro, method of dancing à la maestro, his French à la negre, and his English à la Cockney, but altogether magnificent. Maestro himself would be proud of such 'dancing survivals.' We chatted with good manners and he even paid my busses ticket on N 59, at Oxford Circus; I jumped off, so did they somewhere for macaroni, while I to Fullers, with 2 cups of stimulating liquid chocolates and sandwiches, then to Legat, finishing my titbits, my muscles became so very elastick that I could dance much more and so I did, remembering old assortements with Nicolaeva, with great deal of delight, at present I am only good for chair and soon after bed. Vera asked me to go with her to a cheap but excelent Jewish tailor she discovered, yes I like to have a double brested English tweed or home spun coat; this is the 'dernier cri' in cuttings for us 'female lambs'.

Frank is still dripping off, perhaps it will drop to 20 [?] until Caillaux[1] comes back, or is he old fashioned by now?

I look with sympathy into your eyes.
L.

1 The erstwhile Minister of Finance who had just been amnestied.

King's College, Cambridge, Friday 20th February, 1925

My dearest darling,

Influenza is a strange thing – I still feel collapsed most days between 5 and 7; for instance to-day – not fully myself. However I suppose one recovers in the end. I daresay you had influenza nerves yesterday. But I kiss you and console you for them all the more.

. . .

To-day Kennedy is here. We go to Pirandello's *Henry IV* this evening. He was very good with the New Buildings Committee this afternoon, and I think that the project makes slow progress – perhaps.

College business and a Memorandum about Tithe (also College business) have occupied me to-day, and I feel discontented that I can get so little time for my book. For three weeks I have made no progress, – though of course there are reasons. I considered in my bath this morning how much there was still to write about one thing or another, and whether I oughtn't to give up some of my other activities to make more time.

I am *very, very* fond of you.

M.

I have written Madame on the envelope from weakmindedness, but it will make too much mess to alter.

(41 Gordon Square), Saturday 21st February, 1925

Like a trembling poplar I opened 'Londoner's Diary': saw how famous you were, how you 'boom' *The Nation*, what a 'harmony' co-operates between you and the 'other Londoner' in the matter of 'gold standard', though for different reasons I believe. All that made me change my plant existanse into a 'domesticated rabbit', but I do not know why.

291

The invitation for your speech on Inter Allied debts was very agreable to read, and the refusal from you does not sanctify other times. (Of course it must be in English.) As for Universities, they are indeed 'outstanding mental comforts' for better mankind, but do not go to Jerusalem yet, rather a puzzling journey.

To-day my muscles have a reaction and my 'bleeding purposes' are on the eve, so I had my Spanish lesson (while Lil has her German). . . .

L.

I thank you for the 'breezy papers.'

King's College, Cambridge, Saturday 21st February, 1925

. . . Lord Gage[1] . . . spoke of the picture of Duncan's which he has bought; wanted to know if D. had painted other pictures of his territory – I replied 'Hundreds'; wanted to know if D. would paint a picture of his house; he is a complete snob and now feels a little reflected glory from his Charleston tenants; said he would make arrangements to let Tilton to me.

Maud Cunard is coming up to-day to see *Henry IV*, with all her retinue – Ivor Churchill etc. etc. She might come into this room at any moment and my hand shakes, as I write this letter – so you must excuse bad writing. Such people oughtn't to be allowed in Cambridge – not suitable, I'm sure you will agree. She may come stumping in, whilst my pupils are with me – and then what shall I do?

. . .

I went to the furniture shop to tell the man that you don't like the looking glass. So I have sold it back to him and bought instead a stupendous chest of drawers either for you or for me and another small round table (for £2) just like the one you have.

I was very much amused by your account of Stas. Also I look forward to your double English breasts.

. . .

1 Owner of Charleston and Tilton.

Sunday

Oah – I'm so cold. Hubert and I have been standing outside, our paths going in different directions, unable to part because our tongues were wagging à la Russe; – we went through a lot of old assortments with great deal of delight.

This morning I have begun the next section of my book. So the ice is broken and now I shall be able to make progress again.

Did you see Sam's results for the year in yesterday's paper? *Far* more successful than anyone expected, and there will be a sensational rise tomorrow in the price of the shares. Sly old fellow! Many speculators, arguing from the pessimistic things which he said in his speech, thought the shares would fall and sold shares they hadn't got, – now they will make very big losses.

. . .

Lady C. has *not* been in; but I was still nervous this morning while I was writing my book and wanted to lock my door – but then thought that Dennis or Hubert might come in.

I touch you with cheerful spirits

M

(41 Gordon Square), Sunday 22nd February, 1925

Oah Maynarochka, nothing prevents the pain of my 'bleedings', I am so suffering. Celandinie Kennington came to lunch with me, as I wanted to reach Polunin through her, she asked me to go there, but I offered *vice-versa*. She is to have a child in a month, I touched the stomach, enormous, every night she pours sweet oil on it, the skin cracks out of effort in dimension. Cel. cant do anything for herself, life has become double in every sense. She is going to be a reader of *The Nation*, I feel like a boy Scout. I asked how do Polunins live: his wife *has* a very small income, their house is 70 pounds a year, and Russians never employ food when there is not any, but drink tea instead.

I have read again 'the return towards gold', before I painted in the book, and again was impressed with it's truthful mastery . . . Lately I have looked into *Hamlet*, very difficult and I would think much better to read than as a play, then I came back to my Oberon and Troilus. I catch their poetry quicker than *Hamlet*. Also touch my head with your nice hand, the 'flower egg' from phisical discontent sways too much one way or another.

L.

Polunins came, we had all the explanations about the teknicalities of the decor [for *Postman*]. We agreed on the price of 25 guineas, they charge 5 shillings for a square yard (proffesional price), they make it less for me, he can use the other side of the decor very well, the next best thing for Duncan is to speak with Polunin before macquet is made and how to use the canvass. I feel very satisfied about. My stomach is recovering also. Your painful pupsie.

L.

King's College, Cambridge, Monday 23rd February, 1925

My dearest darling pupsik

My kissing sympathies – but I expect you are better now. The worst of you is that you have gained two days again, and put all my calculations out! It now seems, unless you can lose a day or two, that the bleedings will come on the last night of the Coliseum Engagement – or perhaps earlier. So pre-punctual in this to balance post-punctuality in all other things!

It seems that Lady Colebox was in Cambridge (entertained by Sebastian!) as well as the other Lady C! What perils there are even in this innocent intellectual town!

M.

(41 Gordon Square), Monday 23rd February, 1925

. . .

Miely Maynard, I am glad you progress with your book, and I hope no one unsuitable will come in in the moments of your serious conceiving. I did see Courtaulds profits were in geometrical progression, but his accumulations in discord with Lord Overstone principles on brokers (Sam is morbid about finances). . .

L.

(41 Gordon Square), Tuesday 24th February, 1925

I think Stas dances as ever admirably, so I melt and forget his caprises, also Legat is really interested in his work, we all labour like dogs, no difficult steps and yet it is difficult, after my first entrance that continues about 2½ minutes my bosoms swell indeed from breathing, and Stases aproach saves me from collapse, that when eventually I meet him it is with fresh forces but not for long, of course we get very tired because of repeating so many times; I am afraid to praize before time, but it is so charmingly humourous. 'What a lif' you have on Mondays from 11 a.m. to 11 p.m. but it is better than to be visited by the 'undesirable element' from London.

. . .

Have joyful feastings to-night and that all your friends you are contacting with will give you nice stimuluses of recreation.

L.

P.S. I rehearse to-morrow at 5 o'clock.

King's College, Cambridge, Tuesday 24th February, 1925

Florrie's writing is really impossible. I can hardly make out a word, and I'm sure you can't! However her 'unplatonic friendship' with Pat caught my eye. Do you think she means by the word the same as we do?

I have been to tea with Mrs Marshall this afternoon. She is now beginning to get afraid of being bored and (age 75) wants me to get her appointed as one of the librarians of the new Marshall Library![1]

Sebastian came to lunch. I have hardly seen him all the term; so I had to get all the gossip I could out of him – he's the best Jewish post[2] in this town.

. . .

I smile at 'geometrical progression' and 'sui generis' (*both* used correctly) and kiss my learned miele Lydochka.

M

1   She thenceforth worked at a table in the library until 1941, when she was 91 years old.
2   'Jewish post' appears to have been a slang expression for 'gossip': see Maynard's letter of 26th April 1925.

(41 Gordon Square), Thursday 26th February, 1925

. . .

Maynarochka, forgive my opinionated opinion, but if Stas enters on a female bycicle,[1] an atmosphere of burlesque might creep in, which is undesirable to the comedy, or perhaps I only talk too much now, but I shall prove myself better on the bycicle, when next we meet.

Your fond and low graded bicyclist.
L.

1   In *The Postman* ballet (see 12th March).

(41 Gordon Square), Friday 27th February, 1925

I did write to my mother to verify the fact I registered and hold the ticket. All day long I felt there was so much 'soul in me' that it was even troublesome, but after the rehearsal I gobble dates one after another, it is true that Shearns[1] offers this stock of commodities with abundance.

Sam wants me (Vera told me the other day Sam went to her straight from the train unexpectedly), we are the real tissues of silk to him, and it is warmer than artificial . . .

Do you progress with a credit cycle dialogue, what a blessing that nature gifted you with mind 'human and divine', and that you never spoil the paper when you write (millions do).

I saw Mr Tyzie at the Coliseum, and they have black velvet from all sides, my bicycle is not in Gordon Square yet, and what shall I do when it arrives?

Thank you for the *Vogue*, Maynarochka, even this female outburst is organised by you for me.

L.

1   A vegetarian shop and restaurant in Tottenham Court Road.

King's College, Cambridge, Friday 27th February, 1925

My dearest, darling Pupsikochka

No meetings, no engagements to-day; so I can write my book and feel at leisure. This afternoon I went to the suitable shop for the purpose to see if I could get some really nice notepaper for you. I ordered some to try and you shall see it next week. I also got you this pen, the wrong end of which is also a paper knife. . . .

Yesterday a Fellow of the College, a younger colleague of Sheppard (the one he used to complain about last summer) was rather unexpectedly elected Professor of Ancient History;[1] so in Hall last night, when we were in the middle of our dinner, all the undergraduates suddenly stood up in their seats and gave three cheers in a very loud voice. Sheppard is a little upset, partly jealousy, I think, poor Jack, and partly that he doesn't know how he will arrange his work.

I had the enclosed letter to-day from Tom Marshall. I think his suggestion for the title *The Pillar Box* is very good. As for the bicycle, I tell him that all the music is now arranged for that and ask if he could come to a rehearsal. His other title *A Pillar-box Ballet* is also not bad, because it suggests the double meaning 'a pill-box Ballet' – that is, a very small ballet. What do you think?

I have only one fear about the opinionated bicycle – that it is too difficult to get on and too easy to fall off. But we will see.

Would Thursday about 5 o'clock do for the rehearsal [of *the Postman*] which I come to see?

I hear to-day the important news that the Governor is going to put up the bank-rate. So that part of my *Nation* article has turned out a good forecast.

I have strong desires to come up to-morrow to spend the evening with you.[2] But I suppose it would be wrong?

Your very fond, desiring
M

1   F. E. Adcock.
2   He sent a telegram to say he was coming.

(41 Gordon Square), Sunday 1st March, 1925

Beatiful paper, beatiful pen, one could go far with such ingredients and build nests of intelectual order introducing combinations, yet it's difficult for me to write, and perhaps for you to read it.

In Florrie's house I read the lines of a newspaper 'First queen to shingle her hair; Mr Baldwin opposes it in the house.' . . .

. . .

I come back to the bycicle, Muriel does not like the idea, and Florrie does not like the name as 'Pillar box.'

I am very glad you wrote about 'the bank rate' as it is the most appropriate sphere to have your reflexions on it at the moment, while I had such nice heart head functions as ever to be with you.

L.

(41 Gordon Square), Monday 2nd March, 1925

Duncan came this morning to alter Stas costume, especially his bag; he does not like the name of *Pillar box*, as for the bycicle, yes, he likes everything 'shocking'.

My head is not what it ought to be, it all comes from jaundices and I wrap my stomach with woolly effects.

I paid my visit to Gallerie [Lafayette], bought a pair of stockings that is called 'Tigre' [because] of it's strength and a pair of gloves with elegant flounces over the ankles of the hand, these small items are the preparations for the new spring appearance.

. . .

Sam did not telephone to me, but asked if he could lunch with Vera in her house one day this week, will he consult her about Bradford Dyers or about separation?

. . .

Your pale chaffinch
L.

(41 Gordon Square), Thursday 5th March, 1925

No other news except 'rat-catchers' existing in all parts of America, that is to struggle against all rats that bring baciluses of plague, when the rat is caught they send her to a hospital to be inspected, if there is an infection then the sanitary authorities would at once take a necessary measure, otherwise I am led to believe the rat gets free and becomes a fellow-citizen, as it is statisticated that every city holds the same number of rats as of citizens . . . London holds then 20,000 'survival of the fittest'. *Oh* 'what a lif'.

I dip myself into Chechoff's [Chekhov's] letters, he gave 10000 roubles for the Moscow Art Theatre as one of the shareholders, when they were seeking to form a stronger footing in their own theatre, otherwise he signs as 'your husband in woolen underwear', of course at once it makes me ponder over your little holes, I am so fond of them and like to put my nose in any of them, not out of mood, but of real feeling.

L.

News for the University:—
The visible planets are Venus and Saturn in the month of March and same in April, as for May I will think over the planets, and let you know before the term is ended.

(41 Gordon Square), Friday 6th March, 1925

The novelty of the day: Vera gave me so called 'wedding present', that Italian box for clothes was always in my admiration, so that now when V. realises her mahogany furniture, I realise it at 41. It is in my bed room (probably mathematical) because it is composed in pieces, too difficult for me to build the combination, you will give me counsil when you are in London please.

I was 'startled' gazing at the beatiful photos[1] – you are so famous, that it gives me a slight curviture of a spine (mentally) but your names looks very nice printed with 2 feet hight. '*The exact scholarship* with an interest in contemporary art and a restorer of a tradition for Universities that has been lost since Renaissance.' I smile a little with you, and after a kiss.

. . .

To-night my bed is willing to receive me, as I used my body in many yards of action.

Your pupsicoler [illegible]
L.

1 In *Vogue.*

King's College, Cambridge, Friday 6th March, 1925

My dearest Ledusa,

I sent you a big package of reading matter last night, – but specially Londoner (with whom I know you always agree) on shingling. I think that what he says is certainly true and is the explanation of Nicolaeva's moustache! I never read anything so wild as the *Daily Chronicle* on you, but it was quite nice and gentlemanly. The pictures of my room in *Vogue* come out remarkably, but as usual far grander than the truth. I've bought another copy as a present for my bedmaker,[1] so as to make her feel more important (and therefore more happy) while she dusts it. To-day I send you Sam's article. It is very good, I think, and extraordinarily *characteristic*. As it is long, I have marked in pencil some of the most Sammish things for you to read.

When I got back here I found an invitation to me to address the Commercial Committee of the House of Commons on the Gold Standard. I am very pleased about it and have accepted. Also the letter of invitation was a model of flattering politeness. I send it for you to see and would like it back.

This afternoon I looked into the question of envelopes and send some samples. The only ones of the right *size* were the one in which I enclose this letter and the white one enclosed. Of course you could *paint* these any colour you like. But I also saw in the shop some of the *real article*, – that is the envelopes in which maids actually write love letters. I enclose some of these. Are they too small? perhaps we could get plain coloured paper and fold it ourselves. *N.B.* These are samples which I must *return clean* and *uncreased*; for it is impossible to buy less than a box of them at a time. So use your care.

Your Saturn in little holes
M

1   Women servants in Cambridge colleges are known as 'bedmakers'.

(41 Gordon Square), Saturday 7th March, 1925

I thank you for Sam's article and with your paincilings the value of the article improves. Honesty, sincerity, competent inteligence, modesty, are Sam's feathers, but he can't soar, his 2 little feet follow him, and it is better to be Sam than pretend.

It took me long time to inquire about acetate, viscose, cupra ammonium and nitro cellulose, now I know they are all chemicals with a different tint, perhaps I wasted my time, as I knew they were chemicals before, and difference lies in degrees of a sphere in artificial silk. Well, is it not too much of a 'Lady Talky'? I run to Florrie's to listen to 'get thee to nunnery'. As an interval a sympathetic look at you, if you are not too intelectual. *Hamlet*[1] was very interesting, respectably performed, and some of the scenes by the way of speech very beatiful, but the play is too long. Hamlet is inteligent, not an ideal Hamlet, but then was he? I loved the end what a right dimension for all of them to die. I was so glad. Ophelia [as] Fay Compton charming, the Queen mother good, but yet undetachable from 'our betters' and the ghost father made one think of spiritualism and Sir Oliver Lodge. I applauded for the noble exposition of the play.

How very nice that you accept for the Commercial Committee, and now I deliver my substanse into bed, with a good night warbling to you first.

L.

1   At the Haymarket, with John Barrymore in the title role.

King's College, Cambridge, Sunday 8th March, 1925

My dearest pupsikochka,

Yesterday I went to a political luncheon where Runciman was the speaker-guest; I too was asked at the end to speak, and made a little one. . . Also Mrs Runciman, who having her mind on such matters, asked me afterwards if she could congratulate me on my approaching marriage. I am not sure whether it wouldn't really be better for us to put an announcement in the papers ourselves (if it is not unlawful), and I'll take an opportunity of speaking with the lawyer to consult him about it. It is nice of Vera to give you the wedding present.

Jacques Raverat has died at last, poor thing.[1] He had lived about 9 weeks without taking any food.

I told my mother this afternoon about the plot of your ballet. She was very much amused, because apparently the exactly same thing happened to my grandmother Keynes when she was young; and if she hadn't managed to get the letter back from the postman, I shouldn't exist! – or at least, not the *same* me.

I have wasted two more whole mornings over that same mathematical rubbish which I was doing on Thursday. Now at last this morning, after wasting the best part of a week I have satisfied myself that there is nothing whatever in it and have cheerfully torn it up.

To-night I have the dinner party to which Mary H. comes. Afterwards we all go on to Sebastian's farewell party, – for he leaves Cambridge for good at the end of this term.

To-morrow – Cambridge is so political – I dine with the Earl of Oxford and the Countess of Asquith before he speaks at the meeting here.

. . .

This is a dull letter, but I am fond of you.

M.

. . .

1   He had suffered for some years from disseminated sclerosis.

(41 Gordon Square), Monday 9th March, 1925

. . .

No, for the dear Lord God do not ever put announcements in the papers. It is well for 'virtious, very young, and innocent', but we two with our more or less scandalous reputations (especially mine) were never engaged to one another. Think of the invitation to the country, with sheets. What we plan in 46 is only a practical solution of a *inteligent* arrangement of life, and Mrs Runciman should not have poked her nose into your intimacy. I am prosaic with the society and romantic with you tête a tête.

. . .

. . . The day audacious, ferocious and splendid. I was on the top[1] [of the bus] with a 1000 jumpers. Keep all my warmth for you.

L.

The invitation to America is not interesting for you yet to accept. When you will be 60 you might.

1   All double-decker London buses had open tops at that time.

King's College, Cambridge, Monday 9th March, 1925

. . .

Last night's parties went off pleasantly. Mary behaved herself quite well, but Sheppard after dinner developed a slight flirtation with her and held her hand on the sofa.

Tom Marshall is engaged to be married – to Margery Joad, the one who used to work for the Hogarth Press down in the basement.

I will order some of the red and blue envelopes for you, and then we can see how they do.

The review of Mrs Thrale is by Frankie Birrell – who isn't always one of your favourite authors.

M

(41 Gordon Square), Thursday 12th March, 1925

I tried to make my bronxituses very loose, so I executed *Postman* twice, but 3rd time just walked. After the first my womb raged a little, I gave her a suitable rest in the distance of 7–8 minutes, and since then all is well in that part of the body.

Duncan was enthousiastic to a very high degree, and wanted to take a part in the ballet[1] to shift the pillar box from one place to another. Stas was much to laugh at, he boasted that he never prospires and Duncan questioned, 'What do you do for it?' Stas: 'I get married often.' I cannot explain why, but we all laughed.

. . .

My oval and direct crosses, when going in the automobile, entrust yourself with 10 or 101 jumpers, with the little holes as a permanent base.

L.

1   The very pleasing costumes and scenery of this 'ballet-comedy', which were by Duncan Grant, included a peculiar pillar box in a deserted street. Idzikovsky was a postman on a bicycle and Lydia a maid servant. Legat had devised the work, which was to music adapted from a Beethoven Sonata. *The Dancing Times* (May, 1925) critic thought that the very broad demi-caractère style fitted Lydia like a glove, making her 'the popular idol she is with the London public today.'

(41 Gordon Square), Friday 13th March, 1925

My latest splach of gossip: Vera and Florrie met Sydney at Berta's party, V. sais it is a mixture of Lil and Sam and threw herself like a mad dog on her; after invited her to tea and asked her adress, Sydney said she was in the telephone book on her own name. Florrie thought she was better than Lil, without pretentions. I admire Berta's bravery, while Lil and Sam are away.

My chest is complicated with bronchitic coughings. I live on hot milk with a fraction of whisky, food is free from any appeal to me, but I'll do all I can the moment I extravert the bacillus.

. . .

I have letters from my mother and sister (pangs of remorse, I forgot my mother's angel day but I never knew it since I left Russia). My sister might come to London to dance at the Coliseum, she does not say when. She writes me a 'business letter' à la Russe. If she comes [which she did not] that would be extra exciting for me.

The ice age settled on us: keep yourself with many degrees of heat so as to protect you from the 'undesirable aliens.'

This is a dirty letter – but I am very fond of you.

L.

King's College, Cambridge, Friday 13th March, 1925

My dearest darling pupsik,

I am very much under the influence of the cold – a miserable night under its influence, and to-day College business *all* day so that I haven't been able to sit for one minute by my own warm fire, and outside the weather is awful. I

302

complain almost as much as if I were a Russian! I don't look forward to my trip to-morrow and am looking for excuses to put it off. I shall have no time to make my speech for the House of Commons and my cold will get worse. . . .

To-morrow we have the Fellowship Election. As usual it will be difficult. I don't think any of them good enough and I shall probably vote against *all* of them.

I have no news except that I have a cold

Your warm
M

Letters from
11th April, 1925 to 14th June, 1925

Lydia was still in Postman *at the* Coliseum *when Maynard went on holiday to the Lake District on 11th April – some of her letters to him there seem to be missing. The last night of* Postman *was on 21st April; Duncan in a letter to Vanessa (King's Archives) reported that it was 'a very good farewell with bouquets and even caricatures handed onto the stage – which Sickert said he had never seen done before.' On 26th April, Maynard declares he is much fonder of Lydia than of Cambridge. Greatly opposed to Britain's return to the gold standard at too high an exchange rate, Maynard realises with dismay that he has misinterpreted Churchill's new Bill. On 9th May, Lydia goes with Virginia Woolf and Berta Ruck to see Sheppard's Greek plays at Chiswick. On 14th June, Maynard was appointed as Cambridge University's representative at the Bicentenary Celebrations of the Soviet Academy of Sciences in Leningrad in September, when he and Lydia would be visiting the Soviet Union. Maynard's pamphlet* The Economic Consequences of Peace *was published in July.*

(41 Gordon Square), Saturday 11th April, 1925

Visits in the dressing room from Hendersons with their child 'Toby', Hubert wore I suppose what all Englishmen wear Easter (except you) a coat whose sides meet at the back, and dissolve in the front – conversation peaceful and friendly about nothing . . .

My mother writes how happy she is and everybody that my life is acquiring a better shape, and asks me to 'pray to God' in future. Also she is going to send me a photo of herself in a new coat, so I shall thank God for the coat and you for money and other things.

Rain the prognostication for to-morrow, but you have the advantages to reach the 'Keswick waters'[1] dry footingly to-day . . . I imagine you 'Lord Gossip' about P = M/? + C and Dennis 'Lady Talky' in curency credit section of life.

Notwithstanding my gay style in writing to you, I have melancholy tinges for your absence.

L.

1 His last such expedition as a bachelor, Maynard was on his way to a 'reading party' at Derwent Water, organised by D. H. Robertson and E. A. G. Robinson.

Cumberland (in the train), Saturday 11th April, 1925

My dearest, darling sweet

I still see you not only in pyjamas but also with a slightly sad face – but I hope that has gone by now. I have a lazy face, as always on one of my delicious train-days. What could be nicer than to have no duties and no responsibilities, but 25 newspapers, and to be conveyed, reading them, in a travelling arm-chair through blue skies, fields of skipping lambs, and elegant tall chimneys?

When I got to Euston, I remembered that I had given you no money and wondered if you would have to go without taxis and oranges until this evening, or if you would borrow half-a crown from Harland; also that the Legats might be away from their studio on the second-day of Easter, and it might be better to telegraph to them. Too late! – all these wise thoughts.

Your Ivanushka

(41 Gordon Square), Sunday 12th April, 1925

What a day! The sun is filled with 'the milk of human kindness.' I wear my 'garconne' outfit, and no pantalettes. Nicolaeva-Legat lost themselves in Russell Square and arrived after 2. Lunch passed spiritedly in the sense of food and gossip. Nicolaeva had a few helpings from the sweet dish, but Legat couldnt swallow 'ambers', so called burned sugar. You were not at all English and your face is full of expression à la Russe, that is their opinion about you; . . . We spoke about God and nature, they said God organised nature, I didn't say so, they said mankind was the lowest kind of creature, and that other planets possessed superiors (I have not noticed) and the power of moon was to inflict on women their monthleys. *Oah* wicked moon! if one could stop moon's actions by wireless through aeroplane, yet with all their naive belief in planets higher up, there was beauty in their spirits. So much for them.

I received their photo with touching words and a box of chocolates, as for you I looked for a 'microscopic egg' [for Easter] but they were just as big as last year, and too big to post it in this letter. Stas accused me that last year I took off 9 pounds instead of 8–6–8, I offered to repay, but the motion was not carried, otherwise between him and me lately exists a 'League of good will.' I wanted so much to give *you* all my papers even if I take so much back after. I kiss you with 'Christ has risen' decorosly and respectfully, sort of an adagio, that ends with spring-leap-gobbles.

L.

Hawse End, Keswick, Easter Sunday [12th April] 1925

A line of handwriting before we start out on a long walk. This morning I have written a short article for the *Nation*.[1] Now we go an expedition into the hills.

This is a fine house. My bedroom is half window looking out over the lake and the hills beyond. In the brilliant sunshine of this morning, the outlook was almost Swiss–Italian. Such weather is very uncommon here – generally it rains.

Dennis is a sweet host – the young men mild and pleasant; but D and I, though so bald, have more dash and go than the young ones – at least I think so.

I am reading Aldous's [Huxley's] *Those Barren Leaves* – one of the worst books I've ever read. I don't recommend it to you.

Your *ever* loving
Iv. [Ivanochka]

1 'Is Sterling Overvalued?' *Nation*, 18th April.

(41 Gordon Square), Monday 13th April, 1925

I absolutely live in your house; with the fire in the drawing room, I strech my legs on the sofa and read the *Daily Miroir*. Mrs Harland brought tea, in fact all the things of practical importance are performed to my heart's desire.

At the Coliseum they put us last N before the interval, and Birmingham Band instead of the *Postman*, which is silly, but more convinient for us. The theatre packed to the utmost degree; the rain helped not in the least, the ballet passed well, yet it was not our public.[1]

. . .

Sam, Vera and I entered into a political era [at Vera's house], V. having spent the afternoon with the German *Berliner Tageblatt* who said that Hindenburg had big chances[2] because he was a sweet lad of 78 with peaceful intentions? Apart from it, Hindenburg is brought up so much in the old regime, that he asks formal permission from Kaiser to stand for a President, in fact he asks permission from the Kaiser to go to one little place, 'Germans are sweet sometimes.' Vera saw a general reaction, but Sam saw progress in Austen Chamberlain, but not in Hindenburg, of all that I give my support to Baldwin, he is so good and without any tricks. Do I talk too much, it is better for you to see it in the paper, than to listen to. Your letter from Cumberland is very nice, I call it 'lyricks of the train.'

Your pupsie
L.

1 *Postman* was the only ballet in this variety show.
2 Of being elected president of Germany.

Hawse End, Keswick, Easter Monday [13th April], 1925

Yesterday's walk was pretty severe, but I survived. We scaled a hill about twice as high as Firle Beacon,[1] but it seemed four times as high. I puffed and blew, and lost my breath and my heart beat hard; but slowly I reached the top.

To-day, too, has been strenuous. This morning I wrote a long article for the *Nation*, different from yesterday's article – for the Insurance Supplement which comes out early next month. In the afternoon another longish walk. After tea I explained and discussed and argued my new views about Theory of Money (Yes!–$P = M/wT + C$) with Dennis and the other economists for about two and a half hours. And after dinner we have read out loud Shakespeare's *Coriolanus* taking the parts in turn.

. . .

I have finished Aldous's *Barren Leaves*. It is an exceptionally bad book in my opinion, and would bore you to death. Now I have begun the *Constant Nymph*.[2] That seems much better, a hundred times better, and I think you would like it.

I have your sweet letter to-day and kiss you for it and am ever fond of you.

M.

. . .

1 Near Tilton.
2 By Margaret Kennedy.

(41 Gordon Square), Tuesday 14th April, 1925

I kiss you good morning with the brilliant sunshine; while you have Swiss Italian perspectives from the window, we in London are taught to read *The Economic Consequences of the Peace* and Dennis's *Money* under your editorship . . . What an age of scientific thought, but I have nothing to say as a 'producer or consumer' and only be 'sympatic' towards you. My impression from your letter that your room must be very big and you stand naked in the morning having a contemplative sunshine bath, and little holes are out of question for your body. Poor little holes, as I said before, everything is in relation.

We are still the last number before the interval and last night it did go very well, the sister of Nicolaeva, who sells the pantalettes, came in and in the course of conversation I asked for two pantalettes more (the worth should not excel 3 pounds as a condition from me.) She liked very much the ballet and forgot the troubling life of today.

Stas told me that I was lazy, and should never practice in the room but in the studio, (if I ever go to the studio it shall not be his).

The tyres [for *Postman*] were pompted by Mr Hyde, as the bycicle was tired for her exercises . . .

I am fond of you, Ivanochka, Maynarochka.

L.

(41 Gordon Square), Wednesday 22nd April, 1925

You went, I returned, gave my love to the apples, found one more quality unnoticed in the past: they clean teeth, and my every toothing in a very neat condition. Another thought sentence –, (and no *more* lady 'Talky') Cambridge wants you, I understand, am glad yet my bosoms are sad to-night.

L.

P.S. I must make myself good looking for going out to meet Pinero's *Iris*.[1]

1 A revival of his play of 1901.

(41 Gordon Square), Thursday 23rd April, 1925

I feel that Cambridge orientation is settling on you, as it should within those nice rooms of yours.

. . .

Tonight I go to Vera, I asked her permission not to be dressed, 'come in a night gown if you like'. I shall not go to Colworth this week, too much of an ice age yet. Last night was very pleasant, the play [*Iris*] old fashioned, but the last act saved the monotony, Gladys Cooper should never speak but be a manekin and wear clothes. One of Pinero's wits is that a 'financier' is a 'pawn broker with imagination.' The audience chuckled, I a little. Edna May[1] was in the first row, beatiful bones and nice little feet.

My mother received money, a very short letter but I feel content. I put my warm crosses on you to the overture-lecture to-morrow and otherwise.

L.

I saw this morning that tin had 'sympathy' in all markets, how touching!

1   The musical comedy artiste (1878–1948) who had retired in 1907.

King's College, Cambridge, Thursday 23rd April, 1925

My dearest darling L

I dozed pleasantly in the train last night. When I got here my room was full of smoke which was beastly. *Why* do chimneys smoke? In hall, the Provost fairly well, Sheppard, who lost all he had at Monte Carlo in less than a week, and the rest of them. No work has accumulated here, and I feel rather free to go plodding on with the book.

This morning the Vice-Provost (the new one – not Macaulay)[1] asked if he could congratulate me; so I told him all about you. That old gossip Miss Blanche Smith is at the bottom of it. She is going about Cambridge saying that our engagement was publicly announced at Tom Marshall's wedding tea party! In this afternoon Gerald Shove came in with the same news; so it is clearly all over Cambridge. It is really a very good thing, I think – this gradual rippling flow of gossip, so that in the end noone has any chance of being surprised. I kiss you and promise them all that next term they shall touch and see you, and that you are very nice!

. . .

I send some papers to pay for the hat.

I feel without much spirit or stimulus and would like to touch you and to hear Lady T. [Talky] for hours and hours.

M

1   Arthur Berry, who had succeeded Macaulay in 1924.

(41 Gordon Square), Friday 24th April, 1925

I pushed Stas out, as it is more than 9 o'clock, and I want to enter into speaking terms with you. Stas starts to-morrow for Barcelona to join big Serge (Pat [Dolin] is absolutely fallen into abyss by the way of a favorite) so that probably Stas will re-acquire all his parts . . .

What a life. I mixed this afternoon Vera and de Zoete for tea, the effect was pleasing, the Princess – sister of Nicolaeva – came with pantalettes and I sucked the silk into my eyes, marvelled and purchased, so exquisite it was and is. They will live at least for a year, and perhaps longer if it is not washed too often. The price is 8 pounds for 3 couples, I am ashamed for the extravagance, but it was so immeasurably seducing . . . I prepare a shock to you. V. influenced by Garia wears *combinations* but covers it up with pantalettes; I think the same friendship cannot exist between us; but her present bed room of utmost severity in dark wood, pleases me more than her Italian 18 century arabesques. Absolutely a shelter for a intelectual man, so austere and serious is the atmosphere.

Now to your activities, I give my sympathy after the lecture, I feel it had the unity of purpose. As for the 'wedding gossip' I understand *their* point of vue, it seems piquant and therefore irresistible to taste in conversation with you about it.

. . .

My tenderness to you.
L.

King's College, Cambridge, Friday 24th April, 1925

My dearest sweet

I spoke the first chapter of my new book as this morning's lecture – rather short, three-quarters of an hour. It was a good class, about a hundred. It is very easy to lecture when one has the written material of a book in front of one; but all the same it spoilt my morning!

. . .

Have you read what Virginia writes about you in the *Nation*? – I like it. But it *proves* that Virginia is *colour-blind*. She thinks that Stas was dressed in green! I am v. glad (to quote Florrie) that Serge does the G.H. [Good Humoured] Ladies – but what about *Petrouchka*. Isn't that mentioned? If he does not engage you to dance, I shall shoot him; so he must be careful.

Your so very fond
Ivanushka

(41 Gordon Square), Saturday 25th April, 1925

Opened my eyes, read your nice 'Ivanuskha', leapt into the streets, wanted to deliver some 'tit wilting' to the air that was filled with such reserved freshness. Then long after, but yet before 1 o'clock, I searched for ties for the Spaniard (my last choice as gratitude). I bought 2 for him, and 2 for you, and of course now I tremble as you sometimes for me. When I returned the air intoxicated me [so] that after lunch I embraced Morphius till one of our cooks Mrs Betts asked me to lend her a lemon, as I have quite a few that co-habit with apples and oranges lately, adds so much color, I in return asked her for tea, then my faithful paper bag and to the Coliseum.

. . .

The Nation looks well, I did not read anything yet, except where I am praized with Stas, I cannot raize objections because it is very nicely written, and the front page is full of promises.

. . .

Now I do want to wash myself, have not exercised that right since you went away.

Your white nigger L.
with red red
lips that turn
into kisses
for you.

(41 Gordon Square), Sunday 26th April, 1925

I met your oncle the doctor,[1] what a nice wooly creature! I understood the children that climbed on him all over. 2 Margarets, Geoffrey (the [baby] boom is slower at present) (always happens with the doctors), your Margaret's husband and your oncle's wife were the company. She[2] has 'moustaches'? I thought I smelt whisky near, otherwise she is bright, ugly and nervous, dressed in artificial silk. But he is sweet nature and warm. Another excitement was dictaphone,[3] I heard my own voice, much pleasanter than would be wireless, and I know I have a 'foreign accent'. Your Margaret rivals you in singing, she has a deep dyed contralto and performs the 'lost chord'. Her mouth does not open as funnily as yours, that is *a priori* distinction.

. . .

. . . I also re-read your letter to *The Times*, and satisfied my mind and literary appetites, and now if you are not writing your book I climb a little around your neck and become also very wooly.

L.

1 Sir Walter Langdon-Brown.
2 Frances Langdon-Brown.
3 Owned by A. V. Hill.

King's College, Cambridge, Sunday 26th April, 1925

Rather a blow – we can't have Tilton this year. The Lynn Thomases refuse to budge. What shall we do? I am quite confused in my plans by it (how lucky you are not to have plans at all!). Perhaps we might take the Marshall house in the Lakes where I stayed with Dennis – what do you think?

I have begun a new chapter of the book; but I am also engaged on material to be ready for next Saturday's *Nation*[1] as my final effort about Gold, if – as seems likely – Winston announces the return to Gold in the Budget speech. I am not yet sure whether to print this or not.

Rolf Gardiner ('Troilus') has just been in to bring a young German to see me. He only talked German and that not clearly – so it was rather tiring. However the chief thing that came out was that they think Hindenburg will be elected (so Vera's Jew post on this matter may be right after all!), and the young German would have voted for him if he had been in Germany, because he is the Father of the people and a symbol of German recandescence. If he is elected, it may make a little shock in the rest of the world.

I have ordered three tickets for you for Sheppard's matinee[2] (he will lecture for a little before the curtain goes up and by that they will escape the entertainments tax) on May 9.

The lawyer's bill [for the divorce] came in yesterday – a wonderful document of many pages. Costs – about what I expected. I will bring it to you to cast a satisfied eye upon.

I feel a little nervous to-day and would like to be touched by my Lady T.; also a slight ear-ache. But at any rate I can remember with pleasant feelings that she does *not* wear combinations. No, never by my influence shall she bow the knee inside them. But then, you see, I am not really English, but – if looked at close to – a sympathetic Russian. So, I send with enthusiasm some papers (£10) to pay for those silk matters.

And kiss you very hard and am much fonder of you than Cambridge
M.

1 'The Gold Standard' *Nation* 2nd May.
2 The Greek plays, *Helen* and *Cyclops* by Euripides.

(41 Gordon Square), Monday 27th April, 1925

Maynarochka, Ivanushka, do cast off your ear-ache. With this cruelty of climate yesterday and to-day, drafts in Cambridge are probably abnormal, and that is how the root of the trouble crawled into your ear. Advise cotton wool, $\frac{1}{100}$ of a centimetre. In spite of the ailing, you produce programmes for your book, for *The Nation* and for me, so that I chucle at least 12 times a day from your lettre . . .

. . .

I received this morning a touching book with the pictures of French cats and English horses, international rats, and perhaps Russian rabbits. It is you. I kiss you gobblingly for this for that and for what not, including papers, tickets etc.

L.

King's College, Cambridge, Monday 27th April, 1925

Dearest darling Lydochka

. . .

I expect to arrive to-morrow about 5.30 (I dine with Lloyd George as you will remember) . . . How did you meet that family party? Did you go to tea with my Margaret? I am glad you have seen my woolly uncle – but did you see how fat he was and how I might be?

. . .

I have had no history to-day.
M.

(41 Gordon Square), Friday 1st May, 1925

. . .

. . . I took a bath at 46, as someone ever occupies 41, then I saw Vanessa, who *wanted* to gossip with me, and thought that it was ridiculous for Jack H. [Hutchinson] to have a divorce, and if so she might be stepping into courts also, but altogether she was smiling and very nice, and said that she had a special sympathy for me and you when I shall come to 46, as it was 'natural', but not so for J.H.

I had my lesson and lunch; it was pleasing to be in a class of 'communal feeling', we were 6 and studied 1½, now I had tea and oranges, rather exhausted but the tapping at the door revived my nervous activity, the 'midget' came with my skirts, and told me how she hated sewing, and dream of her life was to be interpreter in French, English and Chesho-Slovakian, but she was not atractive for men to be engaged, I said 'Life is difficult' and with my own dancing legs I obtain no more than 3 weeks engagement in a year, perhaps that will take acid out of her 'attraction complex'.

Your
Lydochka

. . .

313

King's College, Cambridge, Friday 1st May, 1925

Oh! the weather has been so beastly to-day. Not fit for the human race, the Provost and I agree – no better indoors than out, since the wind blows the smoke down the chimneys. So I cough a little, as a protest.

To-day I lectured on the Gold Standard and spoke scornfully towards the Report of the Currency Committee. But I am now very much upset to find that my interpretation of the new bill, as given in my article in the *Nation*,[1] may be a mistake. If so, I shall have to agitate myself on the chance of getting the necessary change made, when the Bill comes before the House of Commons next Monday – writing beseeching letters[2] to the Chancellor,[3] to Snowden, and to Mond. I have telegraphed to the Treasury to find whether or not I have made a mistake; but have no answer yet. If I am wrong and if it can't be altered, I shall be *terribly disappointed*.

The best news is that Kennedy's model makes very big progress with opinion; many people seem to be coming round in his favour; and some say that the chances are now in favour of the College accepting him!

The Cyclops' mask[4] I have delivered safely to Sheppard; but it looks too gigantic. How the poor Cyclops will wear it on the tiny stage here without hitting the scenery, I don't know.

. . .

Eat dinner *and* lunch *every* day

Your loving
Ivanushka

. . .

1 'The Gold Standard' *Nation* 2nd May, 1925.
2 Not to return to the gold standard as was, indeed, proposed.
3 Winston Churchill.
4 For the Greek plays about to be performed by the Cambridge Amateur Dramatic Society.

(41 Gordon Square), Saturday 2nd May, 1925

I have read again your 'Gold Standard',[1] it is interesting and am glad it is not changed, so that next week I hope to see other ideas about Currency C's [Committee's][2] report, and I shall faint with pleasure after into my literature volume.

. . .

. . . I thank you for the papers. I ordered a hat to-day 3½, expencive but so

314

modest in appearance, and the woman who sold it was very nice did not press me, so I tried all the hats in the shop without disturbance.

Tin is flat – but I am so puffy for you with the intrinsic value of my bosom.

L.

1 In *The Nation* Maynard was very concerned about the impending return to the gold standard.
2 A Treasury Committee which advised the Chancellor of the Exchequer.

(41 Gordon Square), Sunday 3rd May, 1925

. . .

Outside dreary with rain in the afternoon, taxi necessary, 2 gallerites came to tea, discussed Budget as all 3 parties seem discontent it might not pass the 'legislation' then Winston might be left 'on the beans'. I said because he tried to please everybody, no one is satisfied. They thought it is W. last chance as a carriere. Then we spoke about Karsavina they were bored to the utmost, but she will dance probably 3 weeks and change the programme. Mim is back from Monte Carlo, had lessons with Maestro from whom she learned Italian, 2½ hours lasted her lesson from which 2 hours maestro talked like Lady T.[1] Once he nearly died in Torino, had a priest for the benefaction, and then somehow pulled through (change of life no doubt) and since enjoys in full degree.

I . . . have already my noble instincts of a spaniel to you.

L.

1 Herself – Lady Talky.

King's College, Cambridge, Sunday 3rd May, 1925

My dearest, darling sweet,

I *had* made a mistake in my article.[1] There is a Section in another Act, which I had forgotten. So I praised the Treasury too soon – they are not doing the wise thing I thought. I am very much disappointed and upset by the whole thing. I have had to send out telegrams cancelling much of the article in foreign countries; and in next week's *Nation* I must print a recantation. I must also recant in my next lecture here; for I had also spoken to my class about it. I have written to Snowden, Pethick-Lawrence, and Sir Alfred Mond pressing them to move amendments in the House of Commons to-morrow; but it will be no good, I expect, even if they do.

I shouldn't have been so much upset by this, if I wasn't still rather ill. Very bad sleeping on Friday and yesterday I was quite broken. Last night I slept very well, and am *much* better to-day. All the same I need very much consolations from Lydochka, and have missed you so very much. I think of you very much – (Why should that happen much more when one is in bad spirits than when one is in good?).

Our first wedding present is coming! – from the Master of Trinity Hall, the one we used to see at Studland. Here is his letter.

I have had an answer about the house near Lewes.[2] They want to let it for June and July as well as August and Sept; so I have replied offering them a higher rent, if they let me have it for August and Sept only.

. . .

I am *greatly* recovered to-day, but still not full strength – so kiss me.

I am free both Tuesday and Wednesday evenings this week. So shall we see a play? *Caesar and Cleopatra?*[3] If you agree, will you get tickets (or ask Harland to get them!).

M.

1 In his *Nation* article 'The Gold Standard', 2nd May. He published a long correction in the next issue of the *Nation*.
2 Presumably this was the house at Iford, which they were to rent.
3 By G. B. Shaw.

(41 Gordon Square), Monday 4th May, 1925

Miely, miely Maynarochka I am so glad you are on the recovery towards strength, I offer you anywhere calm but stimulating touches. I looked into *The Times* [for] 'Gold Standard', my instincts knew you would be quoted, and so you were, but do not be discontent.

. . . I riggled with laughter for the 'wedding present', I do not want to be unkind, but probably to the end of the year there shall be a good idea of trash accumulated, people's ever want to get rid of such things.

. . .

Your telegramme[1] – I swell with good spirits

your griffin
L.

P.S. University news: Griffins are guardians with wings and lions legs, and so am I.

1 Saying simply 'much better.'

King's College, Cambridge, Monday 4th May, 1925

My dearest darling,

My spirits are much better to-day, but my physical condition is still very weak and queer – a bad head and strange feelings. I must have had influenza at the beginning of last week, and am now suffering for not having noticed it at the time. I sit in my chair sometimes doing little or nothing – which is very uncommon for me. I have quite given up trying to write my book – though that doesn't make much difference on a day like this, when I have continual meetings. (This evening at my Political Economy Club a Labour undergraduate is going to read a paper on Russia.)

The meeting this afternoon, however, was splendid. The Building Committee by 5 votes to 1 has decided to recommend the College to accept Kennedy!!!!! I couldn't have believed it possible. Three of the four chief opponents have been converted I now think it *almost certain* that K. will be chosen.[1]

Sheppard's *Helen*[2] has been a good success; I have seldom seen him so happy and well satisfied after a first night. I expect that you rea[d] the account in the *Times*.

Dennis came to see me last night – he also in good spirits. (He made the same mistake as I did about the gold law, and also spoke about it wrongly in his lecture).

Don't be too sorry for me. I am not as bad as I make out – which you will see when I appear to-morrow at about a quarter to six.

M

One of my troubles is that my room is always full of smoke! Whether it is the weather or my chimney, I don't know.

Here are some more papers (5) for the hat. I hope you ordered it *by yourself*; such are worth *double* those ordered with Combinochka[3].

1 Only part of Kennedy's scheme was actually built.
2 This was Sheppard's English verse translation of Euripides's *Helen*.
3 I.e. Vera.

(41 Gordon Square), Thursday 7th May, 1925

What a day of *centres*: political with L.G., economical with 'gagas' of the Lordly kind, and theatrical with *Cyclops* and Sheppard. My centre was mostly dancing, after the lesson I took a taxi to the Coliseum and watched Karsavina, she danced Polka (difficult on points) very prettily and technicaly strong. I aplauded and went to her dressing room, the others soon departed, Wolheim [an agent] and a woman painter, and we went on speaking about dancing, who was the best to study with, she thought, Legat better than maestro, as less gymnastic, but the ideal for her was woman maestro, daughter of a famous maitre de ballet [illegible], she said she understood her ideas so well, that she could study by herself. We gossiped over Fokine, she wanted to dance *Spectre de la rose* and he asked her to pay 100 pounds to perform 3 times. She refused, then he was angry that she did not perform. He sounded rather horrid. The dancing conversationi drew to an end and I ran to Piccadilly, I longed for pastries of Rumpelmayer degree, it was so lucky to have money, as there were times in my life when I had less of a chance. I payed 4 shillings for my beastly apettite and they were devoured before and after dinner . . .

. . .

Your Lady T. or tender Lydochka

(41 Gordon Square), Friday 8th May, 1925

We are starting to-morrow 1½ but shall not take the route indicated by you as Virginia and Leonard have planned their own, that is to take from Charing Cross R. a train. I met there [at Virginia Woolf's] Mr Brace your publisher;[1] not much to say, he looked pale and decent, my visit was no more than 3 minutes as I have to hurry so *much* to live.

My hat being paid and good looking, how precious it is to a woman one wonders *Why?* it seems more important than a good chair, but yilds as to a good bed.

. . .

Last night de Zoete came in, I gave her an orange and chocolate, we delivered great many words about Vera justly and unjustly as to her 'money complex.' After we walked into beatiful night to post your letter. Perhaps you notice how well I write this letter in a new bottle ink, since no 'inky hinky lacrimose' . . .

With a kiss and a touch to you I run into another square,

L.

I hope you are comfortable, also without smoke.

1 He was from the American publisher Harcourt, Brace.

King's College, Cambridge, Friday 8th May, 1925

My dearest tender Lydochka

I had a terrible flirtation with Ll.G. [Lloyd George] yesterday, and have been feeling ashamed of myself ever since! It ended in my promising to ask him to dinner at No. 46 to meet H. G. Wells, and now I don't want to at all; – because it isn't really any good. However we had a tête-à-tête lunch party, in which (amongst other things) he declared himself to be inclined to be against gold and in favour of birth control; that the Liberal Party was in a quite hopeless position; and that of the Labour Party the Clyde men and Lansbury etc. were the best and Snowden and Ramsay the worst. He was slightly pathetic and forlorn, without a friend or an intimate in the world – or so it seemed – and that helped to melt my heart. But one's heart should *never* melt. Don't you agree?

Gugga Haldane of Cloan was quite sweet and helped us through our business and sat heavily on stupid members of the Society when they made tiresome suggestions.[1] He pretended that he had been reading my book on Probability. The Ass[t.] Sec[y] (my clerk) was greatly impressed by him and thought him in every way beautiful! I made a speech in the discussion – but a very short one.

At the station (about 7 o'clock) I rang you on the telephone to hear your voice, but you weren't returned from Rumpelmayers. I got to Sheppard's play almost in time. It is certainly amusing, but what percent is Sheppard and what percent Euripides I leave you ladies to decide to-morrow (Start in good time – you'll find that it takes very long to get to Chiswick). Menelaus, Helen's husband, is a scream. I send you a *Cambridge Review* which has a criticism.

My usual lecture to-day to a very good class, and I was satisfied with it.

My health nearly normal, but I have felt very sleepy all to-day.

M

1 Lord Haldane of Cloan (1856–1928) was President of The Royal Economic Society at this time.

(41 Gordon Square), Saturday 9th May, 1925

Shall I start my day to you like algebra principles?

It is almost 12.30 hour ago I returned from Boulestin with Florrie, Teddy and J. H. Smith (whose copper and tin less puffs than expected) thence my head of Dobby remains with Dobby. Dinner was elegant with caviar and asparagas, but we all were draggy tired, especially I coming from Greece [Greek plays].

How exhaused we were by the second play *Helen* I can not tell you, out of sympathy for Jack [Sheppard] I applied pullingly Virginia back to her seat in the middle of *Helen*.[1] *Cyclops*, on the contrary, so fresh, Dennis speaking and skipping par excelence, satyrs very nice, lambkins so beautiful, music and lyricks so simple and gay and costumes in good taste. After, Sheppard's speech[2] was so welcome, with a new suit a new stick on him, he ran with such vivacity from one side to the other and told us what a treasure we had in Sir

Oss Stoll for his kindness and more that Sir O. Stoll gave a son to Cambridge, where all the dons could treasure him, 'Why, what a most particularly pure young man this pure young man must be.' The other halph of the speech devoted to Euripedes, his pacifism and his writing romantic comedy as a relief to tragedy. The speech was full of Sheppard's cocles! But the play was bad, and the costumes deplorable. Probably there was beauty in poetry, as I remember, when he read at Tilton, as a play it did not act. The end was the best of *Helen*.

We ran into a tram, and reaching a station I plunged into a taxi. Virginia and Berta offered their contributions, but I was the invitator . . .

I shall write more to-morrow, I must go to bed being full with sleep. Your 'correction' is very good, and I understand how necessary it was. Before I close my buttons (eyes) I kiss you and your photo.

L.

P.S. I thank for the papers. *Les biches* [the ballet] in English translated as *House Party*. When I told Vera that I should sweep away my debt to big Serge if he pays by performances, she said 'Keynes school.'

---

1   Her visit to the Chiswick Empire to see the Cambridge Amateur Dramatic Society perform Euripedes's *Helen* and *Cyclops* in versions by J. T. Sheppard, was made with Lydia and Berta Ruck, and is recorded in Virginia's Diary, 9th May. At last Virginia praised Lydia, though there is a sting in the tail: 'Little Lydia I liked: how does her mind work? Like a lark soaring, a sort of glorified instinct inspires her: I suppose a very nice nature, and direction at Maynard's hands.'
2   On 'Euripedes and Comedy'.

(41 Gordon Square), Sunday 10th May, 1925

Early this morning, without being washed properly, I was carried in new automobile into the country called Colworth, somewhere near that spot an airrial intercourse is to be established between Bedfordshire and India, and Hendon or other airodroms are to be of no importance. Mr Henry the gardener, to whom Garia writes so often, was a man of character as he instructs 8 other gardeners (his corps de ballet) and in time, in connection with soil and men, trunks of cucumbers, tomatoes, grapes etc. will compete with, shall I say, Cape town markets. The country was beautiful, that unripined green that happens only once in a year, the birds shrilling with exuberance, the wild flowers independent where they grow and the grass, that has so much good in itself, made one feel philosophic and content. Vera and Garia are going to live this summer on the top floor that was once a nursery, the proportions of rooms were to my delight and the rest of the house closed to be rebuilt in future and made smaller . . . At 2½ we started back and here I am at 5½ exhausted but with peace inside of me . . .

Your kissing unit

L.

King's College, Cambridge, Sunday 10th May, 1925

My dearest pupsik

I am leading a quiet life, with calm nerves but rather sleepy and content to close my eyes for half an hour in the afternoon. I have put on my grey flannel suit, so as to encourage the summer. That makes me need one of your new ties, – but you still have them. Yesterday morning – after quite a long while – I got back to my book and wrote a few pages; but it is very difficult to make progress in termtime.

I have been to the furniture shop and bought you the dressing table, – I think you will like it; also a little box for you, which is nice; also a small washstand, which may be useless but is pretty – I have liberty to return it.

Last night I dined with Petica [Robertson] – Topsy's sister; afterwards there was a pleasant party, many people coming in, and amongst them Dennis on his way back from Chiswick. He said that he heard you were in the audience and went round to the front to speak with you, but couldn't find you. How did the three literary ladies like it? I have come to the conclusion that Menelaus, though a scream, was a mistake, and really spoilt, by too much burlesque, Sheppard's conception of the play.

Your creeper

M

(41 Gordon Square), Monday 11th May, 1925

I went to my dentist (did you?) but mismanaged my rendez vous, as I should have been there last monday: yet I wanted some scientific reasons performed at me and I chose in washing my hair, for a moment with ondulations I look very 'womanly woman', but to-morrow I shall resume my manly sleeky substanse of the head.

. . .

Sam is arriving to-morrow and Vera called Lil! I told her she was 'a snob'. She denied, and said in her illness Lil was very kind and on reflecting she decided to ring the telephone. *Oah*, my bones are very painful, yes with a sad smile I am gouty . . . In *The Observer* you are famous, I saw it late last night, after playing my castanets. I like to see very much the relicks you purchased

321

and the wash stand excites me most, I am so keen on washing lately, as much as V. on gardening.

It is very nice that you are progressing, and do not forget to be comfortable, and go the *dentist*.

Your lively vitamin
L.

King's College, Cambridge, Monday 11th May, 1925

My dearest darling

The weather to-day is such as to make it possible to live again. My meetings were over by 4, so I walked into the garden for the first time this term, closed my eyes for a little (one of them wants some assuagings again from your cotton wool), and then read your letters through again – which were very nice ones.

. . .

I liked your poetry about spring at Colworth and am *very* fond of you

Ivanushka

King's College, Cambridge, Friday 15th May, 1925

My dearest darling pupsik

. . .

It's almost too hot – though lovely – and I sit writing with my coat and waistcoat off – hoping you feel in good mood in spite of what Nature does to you. Take the Square Key for 46 (perhaps it is still in my bedroom) and sit looking at the pale greens.

To-night I dine with the Wine Committee (the supposed connoisseurs of the College) to taste many kinds of claret and decide what to buy.

I have received another wedding present to-day! – a pair of opal sleeve links, very suitable to Stas, in which direction perhaps they will find their way in time.

Many kisses to your mood

Your
M

3 papers enclosed – more to follow.

(41 Gordon Square), Saturday 16th May, 1925

Today: no exercises, no intelect, no buss riding, no castanets, in fact laziness 'à la supreme'. Everything is traced to my stomach being fluffy with pains and blood, and my back is not totally recovered; it is beautifully warm in the Square. I took your key, read ¾ of *Mrs Dalloway*,[1] it is very rapid, interesting, and yet I feel in that book all the human beings only puppets. Virginia's brain is so quick that sometimes her pen cannot catch it, or it is I who is slow. However I shall pursue the book to the end in a short time, and be established in the critisism. . . .

I thank you for the papers, I shall buy 'Eau d'Atkinson' and sprinkle myself everywhere except the hairy spots.

Be comfortable and I am so very fond of you.

L.

P.S. I have been on the bycicle since, but my skirts make my pantalettes flick before the passers-by. I could not do for long.

1 Virginia Woolf's novel, which had just been published.

(41 Gordon Square), Sunday 17th May, 1925

Sunday gossip: Sam back from America and Lil with olive branch towards Vera, Garia and me. Past was never mentioned. Sam is not pleased with the Chancelor [of the Exchequer], why he asks should they offer him [Churchill] that unsuitable post . . . V. asked him if he is to become a ruined man. Yes, or no, would be a suitable answer, but Sam said *No*.

2 more pictures, with valuable names on the canvas of Cézanne and Renoir. Both big beauties.

Lil was at a party where she met Mrs Lamont, who raized me above the mountains to sink you below the ocean. The American 'biche' spoke not to Lil, but to Mr and Mrs Lynd of the *New Statesman*, Lil only listened: 'How charming what a radiant person was Mme Lopokova, but she could not say the same about her friend M. Keynes.' I was her tool to diminish you, *Oah* Maynarochka, is it not a wicked combination between you and me, at other parties it will be on the opposite; how interesting and charming M. Keynes is and how unsignificant is his friend Loppy.

Have you noticed that Big Serge announces *Carnaval* instead of *Three Cornered Hat*,[1] is it possible that Leon has mumps,[2] that is how I explain the change, or perhaps big Serge wants to please Stas(almost impossible). Shall I ask Serge about my future to-morrow night?

323

I suppose you contemplate on your book a great deal, nature is so helpful this last few days to live and I imagine also for your intelectual structures.

Your pupsie
kissing yours.
L.

1 The Diaghilev ballet was returning to the *Coliseum* on 18th May.
2 According to Beaumont, Woizikovsky had strained his ankle – but see 18th May.

King's College, Cambridge, Sunday 17th May, 1925

My dearest darling

I have been rather sociable the last two days – perhaps it is the weather. On Friday night we had our Wine Committee Dinner, trying 11 bottles of wine, and, being a little tipsy, played bridge afterwards. Yesterday evening I went to three parties – first dining with Lord Chalmers for old sake's sake, then on to a party at Robot Runciman's, where were Dennis and Dadie and many others, and after that to a party at Richard Braithwaite's (mixed sexes – lots of young women – modern up-to-date but I don't know who they were).

To-day I have been to a large family luncheon party – one father, one mother, one brother, one sister-in-law, one sister-in-law's-brother, one uncle, one aunt, two cousins – but not quite so fearful as it sounds. Geoffrey and his Margaret were two of the list. . . Margaret says you spoke of taking her to the ballet – if so, it must be before June when she goes away for three weeks. She seemed very well. Her brother Charles [Darwin] (who would like to marry, I think) had a long conversation with me how English women have made a terrible mistake with their equality movement and have taken away from themselves all their charms and that it is a desperate situation. In fact he agrees with Molly. You must find a nice Russian for him.

Now in a few minutes I give a supper party to Frankie Birrell and to Peter and Topsy.

James Strachey[1] is here for the week-end; also Marjorie Strachey, who spent all the time at Richard's party last night proving to a very serious Christian undergraduate that Christ never happened. I read out the book of Jonah to show what a funny old fellow God was, and we all laughed a good deal.

All the same I have done some work the last two days and have finished an article for the *Economic Journal*.

Your pupsik
M.

1 In a letter of 19th May to his wife, James Strachey wrote that he was having a row with Maynard over the rent and rates on 41 Gordon Square which, he reported, was in chaos.

King's College, Cambridge, Monday 18th May, 1925

Oh it is almost too hot to-day and I feel sticky. This afternoon I sat in the garden, reading the proof sheets of Dennis's egg which is now in print. But I still don't like it – I can't help it – so I went round to tea in his room and criticised and bullied him; and I thought he seemed very sad. It would be better, I think, to let him print it as it is and say no more.

. . .

I have fetched more papers from the Bank and send five.

M

My crossings on your meeting to-night with big S[erge].

(41 Gordon Square), Monday 18th May, 1925

The only place I had courage to leave my comfortable 41 was to galerie Lafayette. I bought 2 pairs of 'Tigre' [silk stockings] that hails from Lyons, and at present I try them on and thank . . . silk God.

When I left [bus] 73, near Francis street, ahead of me walked Harland, and as I thought much about stockings naturally I pondered into his, and curious enough it was the same shade you wear, that deep, deep green, it suits male feet so well.

Very sad accident with Leon, no mumps but he broke a muscle in his knee in *Petrouchka* and could not finish the performance, and there is no one to replace him. Florrie will do all she can with sound advices for good doctors . . . We all must help Leon somehow, he is a nice creature.

I like very much your description of the family party with 'one father and one mother' etc. I am convinced now that you have had birth out of married parents, and so have I, besides I was 3rd child (my parents had time to cover the law) . . . You speak about Robot Runciman's party, but do you go next Tuesday to his 'one father' party? Vera is going to be there and hopes to sit next to you at table, (perhaps she is arranging it invisibly). Last night we discussed Christianity, and the outlook for 'free thinkers' is very dark, also if

Mrs Eddy did not call her 'science' Christian she would never be able to amass such fortunes, and her science would be putrid by now.

Tonight Florrie gives dinner before the ballet (Karsavina and I of the 'Old Gards' to be there). Please, do not write to me if it is too warm, but 'go to the dentist'.

Nice touches.

L.

(41 Gordon Square), Thursday 21st May, 1925

. . . I had tea with peaches from your stock of jam commodities. Well, the jam was used in it's entirety and I am ready to have 40 winks in my chair. Innocent existence comes into one's life after visiting shops. *What a life.* I bought 2 pairs of rope shoes beautifully comfortable, one is blue, and the other white with blue trimmings. Telephoned to Domenick Spring Rice, and next Tuesday from 5½ till 7½ the [birth control] clinic is open . . .

Your firm tin with cash this week end.

L.

. . .

King's College, Cambridge, Thursday 21st May, 1925

Quite a lot of shareholders came to the meeting[1] this afternoon – including Falk's father, a nice little old gentleman (rather like mine) whom I'd not seen before.

Here is the wedding present – and the nice letter which came with it.

I kiss my dearest one

M

1 The Annual General Meeting of the Independent Investment Company.

(41 Gordon Square), Friday 22nd May, 1925

Florrie had a very big dinner party with Teddy's cousins thrown here and there, on one side I sat next to Garia, so that was very pleasant, . . . Then we witnessed *Narcisse*. What a bad ballet, oah those Greeks, I wish they would wear tights instead of bare legs. I suppose what looks nice on the vases somehow losses the beauty in the same movements. Music well conducted but disturbing in quality. Just before the curtain descended in full stillness an X cried in Russian 'how awful'. Pat used to cry the same for me in *Masquerade*.

326

Big Serge does himself into the wrong, as the audience including myself felt cheated at the end of the performance.

Lytton was in the audience with Angus, he did not see me, I am so unlike a Greek, everywhere.

After the theatre Florrie drove us to 'Café de Paris', very good dancing place, better than Savoy or Embassys, less hellish, Teddy and Vera did not dance, but Florrie very happy opening her legs in all directions . . . I spoke a few words more than 15 secondes, but nobody else did, they only said what a pet I was . . . I drank champange, impossible not to in such a place. There was an entertainer with plates, top hats and apples, I had a new longing, suppose we have a dinner party and after I could perform something with 3 plates without breaking them! I wish I could.

. . .

Mrs [H.G.] Wells had tea, very nice woman, I asked her about literary couples. The happiest is B. Shaw, and when he does not come to parties if she is not asked, because he feels he is only asked for his famousness, therefore she plays an important part phychologically and he is discontent when she is not asked. Otherwise they are friends, and she does not spoil his work, as I think shows in fact. Mrs [Arnold] Bennett impossible tedious, boring woman who would like to go back to him, but *alas*! he is full of good sense.

Mrs Barrie is not a great character either.

. . .

Now I turn to your personal person, how is neuralgia, was the lecture satisfactory, and how your intelectual streams progressing?

I like the letter with the [cuff] links, they would make such nice buttons for a dress,

in meanwhile I kiss your own lively pink 2 sucks.

L.

King's College, Cambridge, Friday 22nd May, 1925

My dearest pupsik

This afternoon I pretended I was you and bought a new hat; then I became myself again and went to a discussion in the Senate House about whether undergraduates should be allowed to have motor cars;[1] then to my desk in the College Office; then to the garden to read more of Dennis's egg. It won't do *at all* – I'm *sure* it's wrong; so afterwards I went round to bully him again and almost to say he ought to tear it up and withdraw it from publication. It's dreadful. When I've finished this letter, I shall write to him about it.

I have now heard from the agent that the Lewes lady won't let the house furnished – which is very tiresome. So I have written offering a higher price. If that fails, we shall have to start house hunting all over again.

I lectured to-day – and next Friday is my last lecture; but I'm not nearly at the end of my argument yet.

. . .

The weather to-day has been just what weather ought to be.

Your pupsik
M

1   They are not allowed cars today.

(41 Gordon Square), Sunday 24th May, 1925

I returned to 46, drank coffee and critised Virginia's book: Adrian agreed with me that somehow she had no psykology of life and did not create characters. Duncan did not finish the book, not because he fell asleep 3 times like me, but because he was very busy, otherwise he thought it was very clever, there was so much vividness in it, that it made him cry, and also that it was not an old fashioned novel and Angus thought there should be chapters. After I said how much I liked her essays, that it was influenced by Lytton, and how good was the influence, then Duncan said that I should never mention that to Virginia, and laughed very much.

Adrian spoke about Ray [Strachey], she was one of the dangerous femi-nistes that should be destroyed, that she always wears trousers in the country, and no doubt much too many combinations.

I talked a great deal and said you called me rightly 'Lady Talky' (Big laugh).

D. thought Big Serge was injuring his ballet by giving such awful old 'gagas' like *Narcisse*,[1] the old brute went to Paris not to witness the performance himself.

It was more than nice to see you. Your rubbing chemical (without practice to-day alas!).

L.

1   The 'Greek' ballet by Fokine (see 22nd May).

(41 Gordon Square), Monday 25th May, 1925

Strange! all day long I am filled with hunger, and with lunch and dinner delivered I was twice at Fullers; perhaps some kind of subconscious excite-ment, that made me leap into the feeding quarters.

Oah, it was difficult to study to-day, the atmosphere was cloudy; but as the earth moves around it's axle or arbor so I spindled with my legs around my pupsic.

Visited my dentist, my tooth is dead, it did not pain, but the hole was so big that the dentist worked for hours and hours. After dental acrobaticks I asked him if he was rich, he thought it would be possible if the clientele paid, but the English public ravished on their credit system and the richest were utmost creditous. Of course I sympathised with him and advised not to work very hard with the credit system.

I thank you, Maynarochka, Ivanouchka, Johnnoushka for *Kipps* [by H. G. Wells], the first page is so engaging, besides I bought *Tongy-Bongy* [*Tono-Bungay*] for 9 pences. When most peoples do not read H.G. I, on the contrary, show no solidarity with the others. For instance, just now, 3 men are yelling at my window with their songs (is it wooing?), but I cannot introduce any *sotto volce* in response. Again no solidarity except for your bright intelect.

L.

P.S. At 6½ I probably will be gone to Birth Control.

King's College, Cambridge, Monday 25th May, 1925

My dearest darling talky,

My stomach is quite recovered to-day – so it must have been the motor car which shook me more than the food. It has been a quiet day to-day – not so many meetings as to exclude life, but all the same nothing to relate.

When I got back I found a long letter from Dennis pleading for his egg. I think I shall tell him that, before he decides to publish he ought (1) to allow a little time to pass for reflection, and (2) to get another opinion besides mine.

Mr Bicknell thinks he has found a suitable room for the new artists' company[1] in George Str, Hanover Square. It certainly sounds very suitable and is not expensive.

. . .

M.

1 The London Artists Association was set up in 1925 to provide financial support for painters of merit and to organise exhibitions of their work. Maynard and Sam Courtauld were among its guarantors.

(41 Gordon Square), Thursday 28th May, 1925

. . .

I met Sacheverell at the door of Waley's, a little title tatle of no importance passed between us.

329

I read (with my tea) about the old lady 104 who just died that remembered Victoria sliding on a tea tray with her halphes; one is simply astonished by the chances of heredity, if one thinks of Prince of Wales performing the same trier. (His reputation for that is established.)

Oah how I wish my father was a juggler. Yours would be 'box of tricks'
L.

Universities News: When *we were* reptiles.[1] Tails were most important in those days, now we have better brains, especially I not having any sign of a tail, one way or another.

1   A Russian newspaper cutting, showing an upright dinosaur balanced on its tail, provided the occasion for this item.

(41 Gordon Square), Friday 29th May, 1925

What a musical night, last night, but I was not bored in the least: the artists very nice Germans, made one think of the Imperial theatre, the same taste, good manners and traditional understanding of the theatre. The woman who sang Rosenkavalier had lovely couples of legs and inteligent face, the music series of valses and Mozartian airs beautifully orchestrated and the chef d'orchestre stole my musical (for that evening) heart away.

Yet I thought of you, that of all the theatrical schemes you would stand out so well as the 'chef d'orchestre'. It is the right imagination about you.

Lil is very important,[1] Dame Nelly calls her 'our fairy God-mother', big Serge kisses her hands (3 times in one evening) and hints on the conbination of opera and ballet. Lil knows that beauty of her sex does not stimulate big Serge, but is pleased 'above her knee' for the admiration. Sam is gleaming. Theatre is filled with splendor (men women dressed) . . .

. . .

My lesson and tea with Nicolaeva (my offer at Lyons). Speaking about dancing she told me how Cecchetti spoiled my 'heroic line' and gave me a 'grotesque' instead. I understand her point of vue.

. . .

As for myself I changed my big Bob and bought shoes without heels, (nice loose feelings in my toes since). You might be resting on the proceeds of your argument lecture to-day and look thinkingly ahead.

I am very fond of you.
L.

1   As an opera impresario.

King's College, Cambridge, Friday 29th May, 1925

My dearest Pupsiko

I had a beautiful night and feel quite recovered to-day from Christabel's [Aberconway] party. I gave my last lecture – quite a good one. After it an undergraduate came up to ask if I could give him sympathy and encouragement in his studies, because he was lonely and couldn't stop thinking about philosophical questions until he became hysterical and then had to take a rest by going sailing on the sea! He was touched by my lectures, he said, because they were delivered in good English – the English of the other lecturers gave him pain – he thought good English very important, and had himself started to keep a diary every day to improve his own style. A trifle mad you see, but intelligent and nice – so I gave him some sympathy and advice. Also my pupils came to me for the last time. Their tripos begins on Monday.

Did you see that Sheppard has got into 'Londoner's Diary' this evening?

I have actually fixed with my dentist for next Tuesday morning – beastly. To-day I did something pleasanter – went to my barber, the one whose cutting you admired last time; so I am rejuvenated.

We withdrew from the tin market to-day – so the price fell a bit, but not seriously, which was very satisfactory.

Your tail
M

(41 Gordon Square), Sunday 31st May, 1925

The wind last night blew into my spine again, and I so to speak out of sorts sitting for hours in the bath; went to your house, absence of human beings there, visited your rooms and read on your table a letter from Pethick-Lawrence[1] asking your opinion to 'annual taxes' and the treating of your answer in 3 possibilities, 1) to keep it as a mystery, 2) ½ mystery 3) and no mystery. I do not see how annual taxes could be mysteryrious.

. . .

Spoke with our new servant Charles,[2] he used to be in a school for girls . . . the school was closed, and Charles is very lonely in London, but he cuts bread for tea in a beautiful thin fashion. I like to introduce him to 46.

In the meanwhile I read about Dostoevsky's religious philosophy and grow dissatisfied, the idea that when we murder it's because somebody sometime could not accomplish this task in fact, and hereditary. I inherit this instinct

331

and therefore not really guilty, yet he brings at once an opposition that if a child is murdered, he cant do the vengeance, but it is necessary . . .
How is your energy? miely, intelectual Titanus

Your Titania

L.

1 F. W. Pethick-Lawrence (1871–1961) was a Labour M.P.
2 Earlier, on 19th May, James Strachey had told Alix that there were 'practically no servants' in the house.

King's College, Cambridge, Sunday 31st May, 1925

My dearest darling Lydochka,

Yesterday was the final meeting of all the Fellows to make the decision about Kennedy's plans. We sat all day at this and other business, and made speeches to one another. The result was complete triumph for Kennedy! 3 did not vote, 3 voted against him, and 25 voted for him. So much support was most unexpected. Now he can begin to build.

After so long a meeting, I could do no work, but walked about looking where the new buildings would be and so forth, and drank claret in hall. I have now given up my book until term is over; so this morning I worked again at Dennis's egg. I think I have discovered what is true in it and see how to express it correctly – it is very interesting and new and important, but wasn't right as he wrote it. Then I went round to talk with him about it and left him what I had written to think over.

To lunch with my father and mother, found them a little depressed – my father because he is going to retire soon from his office.[1] But I told them that they took after me in having cycles and that it would pass; and after 2½ hours of chatter they were cheered up. My father said he wanted to give you and me a handsome wedding present – what would we like? Subject to what you would say, I said I would like, and I thought you would too, a complete outfit of fine linen for use in the house. What do you say?

To-night I give a small dinner-party – Geoffrey Young (an old friend who was an Eton master when I was a boy), Dennis, Wansbrough (my pupil, the stroke of the University boat who caught crabs), Erskine Childers (lively Irish Trinity undergraduate, son of the one[2] who was shot as a rebel after the Irish rebellion), and Balfour (Molly's nephew whom I promised her to ask).
I enclose a new big Bob instead of the one you have broken

and I kiss you very, very hard

M

1 As Registrary (chief administrator) of the University of Cambridge.
2 Of the same name.

332

(41 Gordon Square), Monday 1st June, 1925

What a sinless day, very few peoples on the streets, perfect for strolling, I walked back and forth to Coliseum, wanted to see my Ninette, of course she is ever so nice, we had tea together (my offer), she studies now with big Stas with enthousiasm and does not linger on big hopes with big Serge, she is very thankful for the training but she also strives for higher ideals, (besides she is 27.) (Do you have a nice Don for me in Cambridge to marriage purpose?) I am very pleased by the offering and choosing of linen compound from your father and you. It is beautifully sensible.

. . .

I also fluctuate with my hand on any soft skin that belongs to you, when you are not intelectual i.e. in the evening.

L.

King's College, Cambridge, Monday 1st June, 1925

My dearest darling,

No letters from you to-day because of Bank Holiday posts, – which is very dull. The day altogether is very dull – even when I sit in my room alone I can smell the Bank Holiday outside.

My party last night was pleasant. Molly's nephew is delightful – with a look of Molly's father in him; I think that he may be full of talent.

Dennis and I have at last come practically to agreement about what is right and tasty in the egg and what not – which is a relief.

. . .

Your bored, needing a jester
M

(41 Gordon Square), Friday 5th June, 1925

Woe, woe, I am such an unhappy person: *5 pounds are lost* running from 46 to 41 the little portmonnai slipped from the books I carried, I stayed a minute inside of 41, realising the misfortune, flew back from 41 to 46 but it was *gone*, someone has taken it from the pavement; in your house Mrs Harland and I searched in vain for it and I know I lost it on the pavement. *Oah oah* I feel so unhappy, my throat is in pains and my eyes are so tearful and sad, why am I such a careless fool, and so wretched for it by now.

Florrie and Teddy gave me their sympathies, Florrie lost the other day 10 pounds, but then found it was 10 shillings only. Florrie mistook pences for dollars.

333

Please, forgive me for this calamity, I cant speak of anything else, and how I wish you would be here.

Your sad wretch
L.

[telegram]   6th June, 1925

12.53 CAMBRIDGE

LPOKOVA 41 GORDON SQUARE LDN =

= BE CONSOLED NOTHING COULD BE MORE UNIMPORTANT IN RESULT AND SINCE THE CAUSE IS IN YOU I AM VERY FOND OF THAT +

(41 Gordon Square), Saturday 6th June, 1925

Miely Maynard, I thank you very much for your 'sweet nature' swift communication. I am mountains better than last night, when I was so disturbed and at midnight fell into exhaustion, the bed did the rest (nyctitropism) I had no dinner, nor to-day as Luba, Grigoriev and I had very late in 41 and fed ourselves with gossip. It seems that all the money they can gain here is to be spent for a week in Paris, as every little hole in Paris always plastered with gold before it's use. As for myself, Grigoriev does not know at all and rather doubtful, when they return, the first week offers not *Boutique Fantasque.*

A new order at the Coliseum: no one is allowed to the dressing room (revenge on Florrie?). Diaghilev denies his influence but he is surely behind the scenes. He looked such a monster that I ran away from him . . . Pat dances in darkness (revenge on Pat?). If I would be Pat I would leave the company at the end of the season and fling a few knives into Serge's reputation.

About 8 o'clock menage Grigoriev were on their feet and poor Luba slipped in the passage with her whole body: a few moments of distress then: 'I'll be English and shall not cry.' I soothed her, saying such slipperings happen to me as often as possible, and then we laughed and walked out together to the taxi.

I kiss your face and other Holy places.
L.

(41 Gordon Square), Sunday 7th June, 1925

Morning was full of mellow perspirations, perhaps your intelect was just as ripe in relation, every little bit of fluff outside in nature helped to bring insides out. I have cooled very much since and concentrated on my tongue-value lavishly. After lunch I dribbled to 46, Vanessa, Duncan and a lady . . . For a little while we were coffenists, Van. had least so we dripped from our cups into hers as she really wanted most; the little scene had plenty of life and humour.

Then I left them to expect my beetle (so called Mim), beetles always run in all directions and very quickly. She was in a hurry, and only talked for 2½ hours, Big Serge is angry with her because she lunched with Pat in Monte Carlo and discussed questions of life, without death. Her husband's [Ashley Dukes'] play is to be performed in New York, Vienna and London . . .
. . .

My intentions at the moment to climb onto the bus, as I have been such a heavy sitter down all the afternoon.

My incurable touches of tenderness for you.
L.

King's College, Cambridge, Sunday 7th June, 1925

My dearest, sweet

I'm rather tired – too much company, coming and going and talking. This is the week-end when Cambridge is full of visitors and I have to attend to them – no work is possible.

Yesterday morning I went to hear Lytton give his lecture before the University on Pope[1] – it was a great success. In the evening I dined with the Vice Chancellor to meet him. To-night I give a dinner party and after that an At Home in his honour.

Kennedy was up yesterday for a meeting with the Committee, Arthur Cole (the one of the opal buttons) was here; Sanger is staying with me; and there are others too; so it is all buzz and fuzz.[2]
. . .

Here is a big bob instead of the one which fell in the Square, and also five little ones. I sympathised so much with your sad letter. It must have been maddening. Yet it is no matter.

I shall be glad now when this term is over. I can't possibly until then concentrate on my book

I kiss you gently
M

1 He was delivering the prestigious Leslie Stephen lecture.
2 I.e. they were barristers like the classic Mr Sergeant Buzfuz in Dickens's *The Pickwick Papers*.

King's College, Cambridge, Monday 8th June, 1925

My dearest darling

They have all gone away – peace and quiet again. At least I thought so, until – just as I was sitting down to write this letter – the Earl of Reading and Lord Bradbury dropt in (they are here to take their honorary degrees to-morrow); and then when they had gone some Frenchman appeared – I don't know his name.

It has been a *beautiful* day – perfect sky and breezes. I sat in the garden in the afternoon and when my eyes closed I did not disturb them.

My party last night was fairly pleasant – 6 to dinner and perhaps 20 came in afterwards; but I don't like the responsibilities of host and, as usual, would have enjoyed it much more if only it had been someone else's party.

To-night I dine with the Wine Committee on another winetasting expedition. I can't concentrate on my book yet, but this evening I have written a short article on a technical financial point – not very suitable for the *Nation*, but I am offering it to Hubert if he cares to have it.

I enclose Mrs Bertie Russell's *Hypatia*[1] for you, not because it is very interesting, but because I like the picture at the beginning which is a portrait of you and me (after I have grown my beard).

But you *must* eat your dinner, although it says on p. 26, 27 of *Hypatia* that the smallness of the feminine appetite is explained because in the savage state only those females survived who could exist on the small scraps which was all that the greedy male allowed to them.

(Where does nyctitropism (see page 000) come from – the Dictionary? its new to me)

Your greedy male
M

1   The sub-title of Dora Russell's book was *Woman and Knowledge*. Apropos of a piece of Chinese porcelain, the author wrote (p. 78) that 'compared with their generous acceptance of instinct our Christian dread of sex and horror of the body are obscene.'

(41 Gordon Square), Tuesday 9th June, 1925

I thank you for the 'unascetic sage' it looks touching, and I marched through *Hypatia* with interest. I find it healthy, even if it lacks poetical literary qualities of Plato; it is written in a elementary fashion for everybody to read, and it plants sympathetic roots in men and women. I cannot believe about the 'greedy males' in such an immense degree, but I laugh a few times about it.

The party last night was very pleasing, Vera and Garia, Vanessa and

Duncan, Adrian did not leave the house till everybody was gone. Vanessa lost her virginity in mouse holes, appearing in a dress à la mode; Duncan performed the operation . . . Next to me sat a beautiful old lady full of cocles. I told her I loved her dress (black embroidered with grey) and she told me her name Adine it was nothing to me in Russian it means only 1. I did not dare to this elderly lady pronounce my odd 'Lopsky' and only said I was a Russian. V. and D. thought her wonderful and an 'aristocrat'.

In fact she is Teddy's aunt and 83 and delicious, the sister of his mother, (who also wore a fame for a remarcable woman). She told Teddy that I was very nice and being Russian probably is the wife of a Russian Ambassador. Rather young for that post I thought, nevertheless flattering.

Sam had a few minutes with me, in the afternoon Winston had a meeting with him tête à tête, for no reason, just chatting, but Sam thinks there must be something in the back of his mind, but cant reach the essence. As for big Serge, Sam advised me to drop Serge for ever, as his ballet was 'veux jeu', his expression was 'if I would be you I would let him go to Hell.'

Now you have your 'honoraris causas' [honorary degrees] for Earls and Lords, do give me one too . . .

L.

P.S. No universities news till to-morrow (a respite).

King's College, Cambridge, Tuesday 9th June, 1925

My dearest pupsik

My mother came in this morning to bring me an anti-baldness mixture which she says is very good (you will have to rub it on) and to tell me that you were dancing at the Coliseum last night! It seems that Sokolova was mis-printed Lokolova by the *Times*, and then another paper went just a little further and put Lopokova. *I* avoid misunderstanding by writing PUPSIK.

To-day has been given up to ceremonies and feasting. In the morning the Degrees – then lunch with the Vice-Chancellor (I enclose the menu) – now in a few minutes a big feast at Trinity. When I got back from the lunch I found a telegram making *me* an Honorary Doctor – of the University of Kiel in Germany; but if it means going in person to receive it, I shall have to refuse.

. . .

After to-day Cambridge is over, so far as I am concerned, for four months; and when I come back I shall be a changed man – at least they will think so, I shan't be really.

Your, completely yours
M

I *know* it is *very* difficult to find a nice case for cigarettes – that is partly the reason why I have never got one. But they do exist, if you go on looking long enough. To-day I went to buy a new tie and ended in getting two of the latest gaudy kinds, which the undergraduates wear, for *you*. But whether they're in good taste I don't yet know.

(41 Gordon Square), Sunday 14th June, 1925

Miely Maynar

. . .

My state of health yet low, but to-morrow with a good lesson I shall revive myself and bring *life* to my body, it is necessary!

Your Russian rabbit
L. (out of running, except for you)

Univercities news:
    Russian humour
        Hygienic coffin
            conversation:
—What coffin do you desire? maple, oak or tin?
—Which is the best?
—All are good, but the tin one is stronger and better for health.

King's College, Cambridge, Sunday 14th June, 1925

My dearest Leningradievna,

I went to the Vice Chancellor this evening and he agrees to appoint me to be the representative of the University at the Leningrad Bicentenary. The dates are Sept 6–14. I think our best plan might be to go from Warsaw direct to Leningrad and then back home by way of Moscow. What distances! Leningrad is nearly as far from Warsaw, as Warsaw is from London! I thought that when one had reached Warsaw one was almost there, but it is another 1000 miles further.

I complained to my mother about my knee. She says I must not drink wine or eat fruit, and she rubbed it with Iodex, which certainly seemed to do it good. I have brought the pot with me, so that you can rub more on – I know you will approve because it is made of Yod. She also says that I must be careful – because bad knees run in the family. One of my aunt's knees are now so bad that she can't walk at all.

M.

On 27th July, 1925, Lydia's nullity decree was made absolute, and on that very afternoon she and Maynard went to the St Pancras Registry Office to give notice that they would be married there on 4th August.

On that day Duncan Grant and Vera Bowen were the witnesses, and a large crowd of curious Londoners greeted the pair as they emerged from the office after the ceremony.

Dramatis Personae

(The distribution of emphasis in this list is explained on page 11.)

Anrep, Boris von (1883–1969). The Russian mosaicist. He made floors for the Tate and National Galleries, Lydia having been his model for Terpsichore in the latter.

Arfa, Hassan The Persian army officer who married the dancer Hilda Bewicke. He wrote an autobiography *Under Five Shahs*. He became a general and later ambassador to Pakistan.

Asquith, Herbert Henry (1852–1928). Liberal Prime Minister 1908–16; created Earl of Oxford and Asquith 1925. He and his second wife, Margot, were Maynard's close friends.

Astafieva, Serafina Alexandrovna (1876–1934). Celebrated Russian dancer and teacher; she was with the Diaghilev company (1909–11) before opening a school in London, where Markova and Dolin were among her pupils.

Bakst, Leon (real name Rosenberg, 1866–1924). Russian painter and designer who was one of the most influential of Diaghilev's collaborators. He became famous for his designs for the ballet *Scheherazade* (1909), which had a revolutionary effect on fashions in dress and interior design.

Barrie, Sir James (Matthew) (1860–1937). Scottish novelist and playwright whose *Peter Pan* was first produced in 1904. His numerous ballerina friends included Lydia. He was already very famous by the time they met, and had recently written the plays *Mary Rose* (1920) and *Shall We Join The Ladies?* (1921).

Barocchi, Randolfo After breaking off her engagement to Heywood Broun, a drama and sports critic, Lydia went through a ceremony of marriage with Barocchi on 22nd October, 1916, in New York State, before he had obtained his decree absolute from his wife, Mary E. Hargreaves. An Italian by birth, Barocchi was Diaghilev's new business manager, having previously been the secretary of an American opera company; the fullest description of him (see, also, p. 25 above) is provided by Beaumont (1940, pp. 115–7) but, given the lapse of time, this is not necessarily entirely accurate; also, Beaumont had found him a 'most engaging

340

and vivid personality', whereas there were others who disliked him heartily. Beaumont sometimes visited the Barocchis in their hotel suite in 1918–19 where, on one occasion, an apparently cheerful Lydia provided cups of cocoa and encouraged her pair of canaries to eat biscuit crumbs from the table; but before Lydia's disappearance he had begun to notice a serious cooling off in their relationship. In a letter of 16th July, 1919, to Diaghilev, Barocchi stated that for a 'few weeks' before her disappearance she had acted totally out of character, so that he had sometimes felt like going away; however, he had preferred to help her to get her divorce 'very peacefully, immediately after the London season, so that we would avoid scandal and dishonour . . . All my life I have never met a more sweet, charming, decent, good and generous woman than L.' Indeed, Barocchi behaved with great dignity throughout. On 4th September, 1923, he wrote to Lydia from Rome (King's Archives) apropos of her wish for a divorce; he suggested that it might be necessary for one of them to go to Reno, though he could not afford to go there himself. The last of his letters to be preserved in the King's Archives came from Rome on 27th December, 1950, when he may have been about 65 to 70 years old; it is not known when he died.

Beaumont, Comte Étienne de (1883–1956). A French patron of the arts (also a painter and jewellery designer), he was an old friend of Diaghilev's whose artistic style he attempted to emulate, even designing some ballets himself. According to Massine (1968, p. 158) he was 'a man of great charm and versatility.' *Les Soirées de Paris* of 1924, in which Lydia danced, was a series of 'evenings of dance, drama, music, painting and poetry' (*ibid*, p. 158) which had been planned, with the help of Massine, as a charitable venture for the assistance of French war widows and Russian refugees.

Bell, Angelica (1918). Daughter of Vanessa Bell and Duncan Grant; she married David Garnett, and published *Deceived with Kindness: a Bloomsbury Childhood* (under her married name) in 1984.

Bell, Clive (1811–1964). Art critic and author; the husband of Vanessa whom he married in 1907; during 1922–25 he often lived in Gordon Square and was also at Charleston.

Bell, Julian (1908–37). Son of Vanessa and Clive Bell; killed in the Spanish civil war.

Bell, Quentin (1910). Son of Vanessa and Clive Bell. Artist, art historian, art critic and author (including a life of Virginia Woolf).

Bell, Vanessa (1879–1961). Née Stephen, sister of Virginia Woolf, wife of Clive Bell. A distinguished painter who commonly worked alongside her life-long companion Duncan Grant, by whom she had a daughter, Angelica. Maynard's Bloomsbury 'mother figure' and confidante before he married Lydia. Despite her

341

overt hostility to Lydia kindness often crept through while she was living in Gordon Square in 1922–25. See *Vanessa Bell* (Spalding, 1983).

Beveridge, Sir William H. (1879–1963). Director of the London School of Economics, 1919–37. Much later, author of the famous 'Beveridge Report' on the social services.

Bewicke, Hilda (?–c.1970). The first British dancer to join Diaghilev, she became a soloist of distinction. Rambert (1972, p. 98) dwells on her extraordinary gift for languages, including Polish and Russian (which she spoke without an accent) as well as Arabic and Persian. Appropriately, she married Hassan Arfa and went to live in Persia.

Bibesco, Princess Elizabeth (1897–1945). The only daughter of H. H. Asquith, she married the Roumanian diplomat Prince Antoine Bibesco in 1919; she wrote stories, plays and poems.

Bowen, Sir Albert Bt (1858–1924). Chairman of the Buenos Aires Great Southern Railway Ltd, he was created a baronet in 1921. Harold Bowen was his younger son.

Bowen, Harold ('Garia', 1896–1959). The younger son of Sir Albert Bowen Bt, he was educated at Harrow and Pembroke College, Cambridge. From 1917 to 1919 he was in the Political Service in Iraq. In 1919 he returned to Cambridge to read oriental languages but did not stay to take a degree; at that time he is believed to have shared rooms with Mountbatten. He married Vera Donnet in 1921. Exceedingly wealthy, he generally led a life of scholarship, writing and leisure from 1921–30, his special interest being Islamic history. He had first studied Russian at Harrow, and later mastered Persian, Turkish, Arabic and several European languages; he was a translator and author of academic books; he wrote many plays, but only one was (unsuccessfully) produced. He was on the staff of Chatham House from 1931–33; after the war he became Reader in Turkish history at the School of Oriental & African Studies. Although he carried his learning very lightly and was happy to associate with a chattering ballerina, yet he (and his wife Vera) were more conventional than Lydia and, as his fascinating unpublished diary for 1923–24 shows, he could not help disapproving of her minor escapades.

Bowen, Vera (1889–1967). Lydia's beloved Vera was the daughter of a wealthy Ukrainian landowner, who owned a town house in Kharkov and a country estate at Yarovka. She was largely brought up by foreign governesses. Her first husband, Victor Donnet, was Swiss; she had met him while she was a university student in Geneva. She soon moved to Paris where in pre-war days she was Rambert's 'dearest companion'; 'She was a woman of the highest intelligence and culture, as well as unique charm, and we forthwith began to meet every day and all day' (Rambert, 1972, p. 80). She had many artist friends and a real knowledge of the theatre (Clarke, 1962, p. 32). She was not only the first to teach Rambert the art of theatrically presenting dances which had been planned in a studio, but also instructed her in the art of dress. She went to London on the outbreak of war, persuading Rambert to follow her. Rambert gave her much choreographic help with her first ballet, *La Pomme d'Or*, 1917, which achieved a remarkable success; her second was *Fêtes Galantes*, 1917; her third, *Ballet Philosophique* 1919, to music by Franck, is denoted by Clarke as possibly the first 'abstract ballet' – the press, though respectful, was 'obviously puzzled' and ballet reference books have always ignored her. The first sign of her association with her future husband, Harold Bowen, came in 1920 with her production of Chekhov's *The Three Sisters*, in a version translated by Harold, then a student at Cambridge. Enchanting though she was, Vera was apt to quarrel with her best friends, as (perhaps justifiably) with Lydia in 1922 in connection with Lydia's production of her ballet *Masquerade*, and with Rambert, at around the same date, when the cause of a break of 'several years' was 'a misunderstanding so trivial that we could hardly believe it could have estranged us for so long.' (Rambert, p. 113). In 1922–25 when Lydia was unmarried, unsure of herself with 'Bloomsbury', and so often unemployed, Vera and Harold provided her with the much-needed security of close friendship, mainly in London but also at their colossal country house, Colworth.

Braithwaite, Richard Bevan (1900). A fellow of King's College from 1924; later professor of moral philosophy at Cambridge.

Brown, Kenneth Everard (1874–1958). Maynard's maternal uncle who founded the highly successful legal firm Kenneth Brown, Baker, Baker.

Browning, Oscar ('O.B.', 1837–1923). A lecturer at King's College from 1880 to 1909; a famous 'character'.

Carrington, Dora Houghton (1892–1932). A painter. Lytton Strachey's companion from 1917, she took her own life soon after his death.

Cecchetti, Enrico (1850–1928). Italian dancer and ballet master (always known as 'Maestro'), was one of the greatest teachers in the history of ballet. In 1918, after a full-time attachment to the Ballets Russes, he decided to settle in London with his wife, and to open a ballet school, which every dancer of note attended. His studio was at 160 Shaftesbury Avenue, where he worked from 9 to 6, his flat being above a tobacconist's in nearby Wardour Street. Beaumont states (1940, p. 176) that 'he conducted the lessons with the discipline and rigour of a drill-sergeant, whistling a set melody to each movement, and emphasizing the time with rigorous taps of his cane on the floor'; although he was very severe, loosing 'a searing spate of mingled Italian and Russian, the precise nature of which it would be unwise even to guess' (p. 177), none of his pupils ever bore him a grudge. He was an unrivalled mime and played the part of Carabosse for the

166th time in *The Sleeping Princess* on 5th January, 1922, to celebrate his appearance in the original production in Petrograd in 1889; even earlier he had been 'a tubby little man with a figure like a peg-top' (p. 173). The Cecchetti Society was founded in London in 1922. Although he made a lot of money from his classes, he decided to leave London for Italy in June 1923 for his health's sake. Clarke (1962, p. 42) reports that more than a hundred of his pupils bade him farewell at Victoria Station and that Lydia was there in a little black turban hat; 'carry on the tradition' Cecchetti urged her. In London Lydia had taken some private lessons with him, in which de Valois sometimes joined (Keynes, ed. 1983, p. 106); in St Petersburg before 1909 she had attended his classes once a week. 'The pupils who had talents he loved and upbraided. His abuse was terrible. All of us he would reduce to tears. But it was a bad sign not to be abused, for that would show that one had no gifts, no possibilities.' (Keynes, ed. 1983, p. 46)

Courtauld, Elizabeth Theresa Frances ('Lil', d. 1931). Née Kelsey, she married Samuel Courtauld in 1901 and had one daughter. Towards the end of her life she was described as 'brisk and grey-haired, given to lawn tennis, trout fishing and camping holidays' and had an appearance to match. She also had a passion for music. Calling herself the London Opera Syndicate, in 1925–27 she spent nearly £50,000 of Sam's money on three international seasons at Covent Garden; and in 1929–30 she booked the Queen's Hall in London six times where, pricing the tickets very low to appeal to ordinary people, she presented the London Symphony Orchestra under the young Malcolm Sargent.

Courtauld, Samuel ('Sam', 1876–1947). A descendant of French Huguenots long-settled in England, in his earlier years he was involved in converting a small family silk firm into a vast concern producing rayon. By 1921, when he became chairman of Courtauld Ltd, the firm owned more than twenty factories in the UK and had ramifications in many parts of the world, including the American Viscose Company. As an art lover he was a slow developer, at first preferring the Royal Academy to the National Gallery, but once he had cultivated his taste he bought French impressionist and post-impressionist works perspicaciously and voraciously, as well as some more modern paintings. In 1923 he made a gift of £50,000 for the purchase of impressionist and post-impressionist paintings for the Tate Gallery. Following Lil's death, he made over the lease of his grand Adam residence, 20 Portman Square, to trustees who would house the Courtauld Institute of Art (the Institute's Gallery is now at Woburn Square). Many of his paintings, which are of astonishingly high quality, are in other public collections. He greatly admired Lydia's dancing (see p. 27 above); and he was the only man to arouse Maynard's jealousy owing to his close friendship with her – though she found him rather too grand for her taste. He always drove fast cars and drove them fast. As Lydia wrote (19th June, 1924), he had 'a happy disposition and a wild desire to succeed.'

Courtauld, Sydney (1902–1954). The only child of Sam and Lil. In 1926 she married the famous politician R. A. Butler. She did not get on with her mother, but loved her father though she stood in awe of him.

Coxon, Dorothy A dancer with Diaghilev.

Croxton, Arthur Manager of the Coliseum from 1912.

Derain, André (1880–1954). Prominent French painter who was closely associated with Diaghilev, e.g. the decor for Massine's *La Boutique Fantasque*.

Diaghilev, Sergei Pavlovich ('Serge' or 'Big Serge', 1872–1929). The Russian impresario, who came to ballet by way of art, opera and theatre, mainly in St Petersburg; his Ballets Russes never performed in Russia, being a product of Western financial aristocracy. Evidently helped by Maynard, Lydia wrote an obituary of her 'Big Serge' for the *Nation*, 31st August, 1929, from which this entry is drawn. From his first performance in Paris in 1909, to his last at Covent Garden in 1929, he carried the burden 'of choosing, displaying and financing as remarkable a combination of work by the greatest artists of the day as any age has known.' Avant-garde composers and artists associated with the world's most famous ballet dancers and choreographers to produce splendid and lavish spectacles which were the representative artistic achievement of his epoch. The special qualities which made all this possible were, first, Diaghilev's authority, which did not always stop short of ruthlessness. Second was his energy, which was always transmitted through a staff who carried out his orders. Third was his courageous faith in his own judgment. Fourth was the combination of lavish spending and financial prudence; he ultimately came to appreciate the patronage of English audiences, whom he had always earlier mocked. Fifth was the cunning with which he combined 'the excellent with the fashionable, the beautiful with the chic, and revolutionary art with the atmosphere of the old regime.' Sixth was his amazing grasp of a young dancer's potential gifts. Last, was 'the personal motive' of his successive attachments to Nijinsky, Massine and Lifar, which led him to celebrate them in the world's capitals. 'He had a big nature, and faults which might not be forgiven in others were in him part of a grand naturalness.'

Dobson, Delia The Cornish first wife of the sculptor and painter Frank Dobson (who remarried in 1926). She was a weaver.

Dobson, Frank (1888–1963). The sculptor who finished a bronze bust of Lydia in 1924; he was also a painter, being responsible for the curtain for the first performance of Walton's *Facade*.

Dolin, Anton ('Pat', 1904–1983). Born Sydney Francis Patrick Chippendall Healy-Kay, he became a renowned British dancer, choreographer and teacher.

Durnford, Sir Walter (1847–1926). Provost of King's College, Cambridge, 1918–26. Assistant master at Eton 1870–99; mayor of Cambridge 1905.

Falk, Oswald Toynbee (1879–1972). Financier. Treasury delegate to the Peace Conference. Maynard's close friend.

Fokine, Mikhail Mikhailovich ('Michel' 1880–1942). The renowned Russian choreographer, who was also a great dancer. During his time with Diaghilev as his chief choreographer (1909–14) he created entirely new styles of expressive ballet. Lydia danced with him in his *Firebird* and *Carnaval* in Paris in 1910. Among his sixty-odd other ballets were *Les Sylphides* and *Petrouchka*.

Fry, Roger Eliot (1866–1934). Artist, art critic, organiser of art exhibitions and historian. A central figure of 'Bloomsbury' and Maynard's close friend, he first attracted attention by the exhibitions of Post-Impressionist paintings which he organised in 1910 and 1912. He became Slade professor of fine art at Cambridge in 1933.

Garnett, David ('Bunny', 1892–1981). Writer. Although younger than the other people usually thought of as composing 'Bloomsbury', he was an important member of their circle and was particularly approved of by Maynard. In 1919 he established a bookshop near Gordon Square.

Gavrilov, Alexander (1892–1959). A Russian dancer who had sometimes partnered Lydia in the Diaghilev ballet. After graduating from the Maryinsky in 1911, he took over some Nijinsky roles.

Genée, Dame Adeline (1878–1970). Born in Denmark, she came to London as a dancer in 1897 where she long reigned at the Empire theatre. A renowned figure in the history of English ballet, she retired as a dancer in 1917 but continued to play a leading part in ballet, being the first president of the Association of Operatic Dancing of Great Britain (later Royal Academy of Dancing) from 1920 to 1954. She was created a DBE in 1950.

Grant, Duncan James Corrowr (1885–1978). The 'emotional lynch-pin' of Bloomsbury (Skidelsky, 1983, p. 424), who had been Maynard's intimate and not so intimate friend for many years in his youth. A celebrated painter, who sometimes designed for the ballet. For over forty years he mainly lived with, and worked alongside, Vanessa Bell, being the father of Angelica Bell.

Grenfell, Edward Charles ('Teddy', 1870–1941). Husband of Florrie. A banker; Director of the Bank of England 1905–40. Later Lord St Just.

Grenfell, Florence ('Florrie', 1888–1971). The tall Florrie prances through Lydia's letters, second only in importance to Vera Bowen. The daughter of a wealthy Scottish business man, Florence Henderson started going regularly to the theatre very early in life. On 21st June, 1911, she attended the first performance of the Diaghilev ballet in London (Buckle, 1979, p. 207), having seen Pavlova at the Palace theatre earlier that afternoon. In 1913 she married the banker E. C. Grenfell who became Conservative M.P. for the City of London, 1922–35. Later she became a close friend of Diaghilev's, entertaining him grandly in her house 4 Cavendish Square and elsewhere. She, like Vera Bowen, gave great support to Lydia in Paris in the summer of 1924. Not being a Bloomsbury figure, she has received scant attention in the literature.

Grigoriev, Serge Leonovich   (1883–1968). Russian dancer and ballet master. As Diaghilev's régisseur (stage manager) for twenty years from 1909, he had a phenomenal memory of the repertoire.

Hargreaves, Mary E.   Barocchi's first wife.

Harland, Mr and Mrs   Maynard's servants at 46 Gordon Square. In a letter to his mother of 2nd September, 1922 Maynard wrote 'we now have a jewel of a cook, and she has a husband who used to be a valet to the nobility' – 'we think of taking him on and dressing him up as a butler.' (King's Archives)

Henderson, Faith Marion Jane   (1889–1979). Wife of Hubert Henderson; she read economics at Newnham College.

Henderson, Hubert Douglas   (1890–1952). Cambridge economist, editor of the *Nation*, 1923–30.

Higgens, Grace   (1904–83). Vanessa Bell's life-long servant who joined her in 1920.

Hill, Archibald Vivian   ('A.V.', 1886–1977). The husband of Maynard's sister Margaret, he was a renowned physiologist who jointly won the Nobel prize for 1922 (awarded in 1923).

Hill, Margaret Neville   (1885–1970). Maynard's sister, wife of A. V. Hill.

Hutchinson, Mary   (1889–1977). Wife of the barrister St John Hutchinson; after about 1914 she was the constant companion of Clive Bell.

Idzikovsky, Stanislas   ('Stas', 1894–1972). The Polish dancer and teacher (always called 'Stas') who often partnered Lydia, e.g. in the Blue Bird *pas de deux* in *Sleeping Beauty*, 1921–22, and in *The Postman*, 1925. Before joining Diaghilev in 1914 he had been taught by Cecchetti and worked in London at the Empire. Although very short and thin, his legs were extraordinarily muscular; indeed, his elevation and technique were universally regarded as prodigious – comparable even to Nijinsky's. Lydia evidently had much affection for him although, like everyone else, she ridiculed him at times.

Karsavina, Tamara Platonovna (1885–1978). One of the greatest dancers in ballet history, excelling in dramatic as well as classical roles. She had her debut at the Maryinsky in 1902. She joined the Diaghilev ballet on its foundation in 1909, becoming its outstanding ballerina. With her second husband, a British diplomat, she left Russia in 1918 to settle in London.

Keynes, Florence Ada (1861–1958). Maynard's mother. Eldest child of Dr John Brown, pastor of Bunyan's Meeting at Bedford. At Newnham College, Cambridge, 1878–80. She was to become very active indeed in public affairs.

Keynes, Geoffrey Langdon (1887–1982). Maynard's younger brother. Surgeon; also bibliographer, book collector and very prolific literary author, best known perhaps as a life-long student and collector of William Blake. His autobiography *The Gates of Memory* was published in 1981.

Keynes, John Neville (1852–1949). Maynard's father. Logician, economist and university administrator. Son of John Keynes, a successful market gardener and Mayor of Salisbury, 1876–77. Lecturer, Cambridge University, 1884–1911; registrary, 1910–25. His two books, *Formal Logic* and *The Scope and Method of Political Economy*, met with much success, the latter having been published very recently in an Italian translation.

Keynes, Margaret Elizabeth (1890–1974). Daughter of Sir George Darwin, she was the wife of Geoffrey; author of *A House by the River: Newnham Grange to Darwin College*, 1976.

Kochno, Boris (1904). He joined Diaghilev in 1923, becoming his friend and secretary; he invented many ballets.

Langdon-Brown, Sir Walter (1870–1946). Maynard's maternal uncle; a well-known consultant physician.

Legat, Nicolai Gustavovich (1869–1937). Russian dancer, ballet master, choreographer and teacher. His many distinguished pupils included Karsavina, Fokine and Nijinsky. He left the USSR for London in 1923, with his wife Nicolayeva; he succeeded Cecchetti as Diaghilev's ballet master.

Lopukhov, Andrei Vasilivich (1898–1947). Lydia's favourite young brother. He graduated from the Imperial School in 1916. A character dancer with the Kirov ballet and a prominent teacher.

Lopukhova, Constanza Karlovna Douglas ('Karl', 'Karlusha', 1860–1942). Lydia's mother. She was of Baltic-Scottish origin, having been born in Estonia; her mother tongue was German and she never learnt to speak Russian well. She was adored by Lydia. She died in Leningrad during the blockade.

Lopukhova, Eugenia (1885–1943). Lydia's elder sister. A well-known dancer, who accompanied Lydia to the United States in 1910, she had graduated from the Imperial Ballet School in 1904. She was awarded the title of Distinguished Artist of the RSFSR.

Lopukhov, Fedor Vasilivich Lydia's father. His father was a lay-server at Tambov 250 miles south-east of Moscow and his mother was a midwife. He was an attendant (an usher) at the Imperial Alexandrinsky Theatre; he loved the theatre and used to recite monologues from classical plays with gusto. It is believed that he died of cancer, perhaps before 1914.

Lopukhov, Fedor (Vasilivich) (1886–1973). Lydia's eldest brother. Dancer, choreographer, teacher and ballet master, he was the most famous member of the Lopukhov family in the Soviet Union. After going to the United States with Lydia in 1910, he rejoined the Maryinsky, remaining there in a general way until 1970, though he was also at the Maly theatre. Though an *avant-garde* choreographer of great celebrity, he was sometimes out of favour and out of work. (See Keynes ed. 1983, pp. 41–2).

Lopukhov, Nicolas Lydia's only brother who was not a dancer. He failed his audition to enter the ballet school and later became an engineer.

Lucas, Frank Laurence ('Peter', 1894–1967). Fellow of King's College and an English don at Cambridge; a prolific writer; his first wife was Topsy.

MacCarthy, Charles Otto Desmond (1877–1952). A Cambridge man who became a literary and dramatic critic. Literary editor of the *New Statesman* from 1920.

MacCarthy, Mary ('Molly', 1882–1953). Wife of Desmond; a writer.

Macaulay, William Herrick (1853–1936) Vice-Provost of King's College, 1918–24.

Maine, Basil Stephen ('Vaz', 'Vasiline', 1894–1972). Lydia's 'platonic lover' who often entertained her in her 'bachelor rooms' by playing the piano, reciting and singing. He was a writer on music and a music critic who wrote eleven books, including an autobiography, *The Best of Me*, 1937, in which he made little of his 'laughing relationship' with Lydia, while admitting that it had enabled him to sun himself for a time on 'Bloomsbury's beach.' He had been an organ scholar of Queens' College, Cambridge. After some time as a school master and organist, he arrived in London as an actor and lived in Chelsea; but he abandoned acting in favour of music. According to the New Grove's *Dictionary* 'his musicianship enabled him to avoid in his speech the unconscious imitation of musical rhythm and cadence.' He was ordained a church of England priest in 1939.

Marshall, Alfred (1842–1924). The famous economist. As professor of political economy, Cambridge, 1885–1908, he was Maynard's revered master, from whom in later years he struggled to free himself. A misogynist who did the women's cause much harm in Cambridge.

Marshall, Mary Paley (1850–1944). Wife of Alfred. One of the first five women students at Cambridge; she was actually allowed to take (informally) the moral Sciences Tripos in 1974, being placed between the first and second classes. She was mainly responsible for *Economics of Industry* (1879), attributed to herself and her husband.

Massine, Leonide Fedorovich (1895–1979). The great Russian dancer, choreographer, ballet master and teacher. After graduating from the Bolshoi School he joined Diaghilev in 1914 as dancer and choreographer, being his great favourite after Nijinsky, whose affair with Diaghilev broke up on Nijinsky's marriage. While still astonishingly young, Massine created many important ballets including *Les Femmes de bonne humeur* (*Good Humoured Ladies*) and *La Boutique Fantasque*, in which he often partnered Lydia, notably in the latter ballet as the Can-Can dancers. He had bandy legs just above the ankles (usually concealed by special trousers) which Diaghilev considered a great defect. Like Lydia, he left Diaghilev in 1921, the two of them then being closely associated in producing minor ballets as items in London variety programmes, and in touring the provinces, when he was sometimes jealous of Lydia's reputation. He invited Lydia to appear in *Les Soirées de Paris* in 1924. As Lydia wrote – 'Massine may have seemed to have got into toils and entanglements, lacerating and imprisoning the bodies of his dancers, from which he could not find an escape for himself or for them, but in this ballet [*Boutique*] he found an escape into the world of unimprisoned emotion.' (Keynes, ed. 1983, p. 209)

Melchior, Carl (1871–1933). A German representative at the Paris Peace Conference, when Maynard contrived to meet him furtively; a partner in the banking firm M. M. Warburg. Maynard was deeply affected by his relationship with this ex-enemy alien, whose Jewishness perhaps attracted him, and he was the subject of his most intimate Memoir – 'Dr Melchior: A Defeated Enemy' – which was published posthumously.

Montagu, Edwin Samuel (1879–1924). Liberal politician and administrator who helped Maynard in his career in very many ways – see Maynard's letter of 16th November, 1924.

Mordkin, Mikhail Mikhailovich (1880–1944). Russian dancer, choreographer, teacher and ballet director, trained at the Bolshoi. On an American tour in 1911–12 he had Lydia and Idzikovsky in his company.

Morrell, Lady Ottoline (1873–1938). A renowned hostess and patroness of the arts both in London and at Garsington, near Oxford. Lydia was apt to be bored by her, despite her spectacular appearance.

Myers, Leopold Hamilton ('Leo') (1881–1944). Writer, philosopher and novelist; a Bloomsbury habitué who had been at Trinity College, Cambridge.

Nemchinova, Vera Nicolayevna (1899–1984). Russian dancer and teacher. Joined Diaghilev in 1915.

Nicolaeva, Nadejda (1889–1971). A Russian dancer who married Legat. She had a ballet school in England.

Nijinska (Nijinskaya), Bronislava Fominitshna (1891–1972). Russian dancer, choreographer, ballet mistress and teacher. Sister of Nijinsky.

Nijinsky, Romola (1891–1978). Nijinsky's Hungarian wife who married him in 1913. She attached herself to Diaghilev's group and, after studying with Cecchetti, managed to join the corps de ballet. Diaghilev broke with Nijinsky following his marriage, when his decline into illness began.

Nijinsky, Vaslav (1888 or 1889–1950). The greatest male dancer of his generation; also a great choreographer responsible for *Apres-midi d'un faun* (which was a *succès de scandale*), *Jeux* and *Le sacre du printemps*. After dancing at the Maryinsky, he became the star performer of Diaghilev's Paris seasons, as well as his idol. He partnered Lydia in *Spectre de la rose* and *Petrushka*. During a subsequent S. American tour he showed increasing signs of being afflicted by the schizophrenia which soon destroyed his mental and physical life; see Lydia's letter of 15th June, 1923.

Pavlova, Anna Pavlovna (1881–1931). Lydia first saw Pavlova dancing in *Giselle* in 1906. In 1907 she created Fokine's *Dying Swan*. She remained attached to the Maryinsky until 1913, but spent most of her time on tours abroad, occasionally with Diaghilev. In 1914 she formed her own company and began her triumphal world tours, London being her home. '. . . Diaghilev led a new movement of culture in the great capitals of the world. Anna Pavlova carried the Muse of the Ballet as Holy Saint of Beauty to high and low to everyone in the world.' From 'Pavlova' by Lydia in Keynes ed. (1983), p. 206.

Picasso, Olga Diaghilev's dancer Khokhlova who married Picasso in 1918.

Picasso, Pablo Ruiz (1881–1973). The celebrated Spanish painter who was closely associated with Diaghilev as a designer – and who married one of his dancers. See Lydia's letter of 16th June, 1924, for the stir caused by his work for the ballet *Mercure* in Paris.

Pigou, Arthur Cecil (1877–1959). Professor of Political Economy, Cambridge, from 1908, and Fellow of King's College.

Polunin, Elizabeth British portraitist of Ballet dancers who also assisted her husband Vladimir.

Polunin, Vladimir (1880–1957). Diaghilev's principal scene painter in London from 1918.

Rambert, Dame Marie ('Mim', 1888–1982). Dancer, teacher and ballet director. Like de Valois, she was one of the great pioneer personalities of British ballet. She was of Polish origin. She was early influenced by Isadora Duncan, but went to Paris, intending to study medicine. After some years with Dalcroze in Switzerland she was seen by Diaghilev who engaged her as Nijinsky's rhythmic adviser for *Le*

Sacre du Printemps (1913). Danced in Diaghilev's corps de ballet and studied with Cecchetti. Having left Diaghilev, it was on Vera Bowen's advice that she went to London in 1914, making her permanent home there. She married the dramatist Ashley Dukes. Her own ballet school was formed in 1920.

Ramsey, Frank (1903–30). Economist and philosopher; a Fellow of King's College, Cambridge.

Raverat, Gwendolen Mary (1885–1957). Daughter of Sir George Darwin, wife of Jacques. Wood engraver and author.

Raverat, Jacques (1885–1925). A painter. A Frenchman who had been mainly educated in England, he married Gwen Darwin in 1911.

Reece, Holroyd A business man who claimed more familiarity with Lydia and Maynard than in fact he possessed.

Robertson, Dennis Holme (1890–1963). A well-known economist. Fellow of Trinity College, Cambridge from 1914. A close friend and collaborator of Maynard's in the 1920s.

Rose, Charles Archibald Walker ('Archie', 1879–1961). Diplomat and business man; expert on China; Maynard taught him economics and he taught Maynard riding.

Ruck, Berta (1878–1978). The popular novelist and short story writer; she was otherwise Mrs Oliver Onions.

Runciman, Steven (1903). The historian; fellow of Trinity College, Cambridge, 1927–38; son of Walter Runciman.

Runciman, Walter (1870–1949). Liberal politician. President of the Board of Trade 1914–16.

Rylands, George Humphrey Wolferstan ('Dadie', 1902). The youngest member of 'core Bloomsbury' in the early post-war years. Scholar of Eton and King's College, Cambridge (where he was later to be a Fellow and English don), he worked temporarily with the Woolfs on their press before leaving to complete his dissertation. Much involved with Cambridge theatrical productions.

Sakharov, Alexandre (1886–1963) and **Clotilde** (1895). Dancers who developed a type of 'abstract mime' which greatly influenced Massine. He was Russian and she was German.

Sanger, Charles Percy (1871–1930). Fellow of Trinity College, Cambridge, 1895–1901; later a barrister and a statistician at University College, London.

Savina, Vera. An English dancer, with a lovely classical style, who joined Diaghilev in 1919. She married Massine, as his first wife in 1921. She toured with

Lydia and Massine in 1922. After the collapse of her marriage she rejoined Diaghilev in 1924. (She is living in retirement in Southwold, Suffolk.)

Sedova, Julie (1880–1969). Russian–French dancer and teacher.

Sheppard, John Tressider (1881–1968). Classicist. Fellow of King's College, Cambridge, from 1906 and lecturer from 1908. Well known in the university for his production of Greek plays.

Shove, Gerald Frank (1887–1947). Cambridge economist. Fellow of King's College from 1926.

Sickert, Thérèse (1884–1944). Née Lessore. She married Sickert as his third wife (her second husband) in 1926, but had earlier lived with him. She was the artist-daughter of a French artist-father.

Sickert, Walter Richard (1860–1942). English painter of figure compositions and urban scenes; also etcher, writer and art critic, and active in artists' associations. His second wife died in 1920. He was delighted to be elected ARA in 1924, although he was later to resign from the Royal Academy. Maynard was an important patron and Lydia treated him most affectionately; he was devoted to them both.

Sitwell, Osbert (1892–1969). Son of the cantankerous Sir George Sitwell, during the period covered by these letters he was living with his younger brother, Sacheverell, at 2 Carlyle Square, where he may have been responsible for introducing Maynard and Lydia. Poet, essayist, novelist, writer of short stories, autobiographer, etc; an eager, if snobbish, host.

Sitwell, Sacheverell (1897–1988). Prolific author, poet and art connoisseur.

Slavinsky, Taddeus (Tadeo) (1901–45). Polish-born dancer who first joined Diaghilev in 1921. Danced in Vera Bowen's *Masquerade*.

Sneddon, Mrs. The cook at 41 Gordon Square who was abruptly dismissed in 1924.

Sokolova, Lydia ('Hilda', 1896–1974). Born Hilda Munnings, she was the first English girl to join Diaghilev's ballet in 1913; during her time with the Ballets Russes, from 1913–22 and 1923–9, she created many roles. She and Woizikovsky, with whom she lived after leaving her husband, worked with Lydia and Massine in 1922–23.

Spessiva (Spessivtseva), Olga Alexandrova (1895). One of the greatest classical ballerinas of all time, she joined the Maryinsky in 1913; she went to the U.S. with Diaghilev's company in the war and was a guest ballerina in the *Sleeping Princess* in 1921–22. She finally left the U.S.S.R. in 1923.

Sprott, Walter John Herbert ('Sebastian', 1897–1971). Psychologist and sociologist who left Cambridge for Nottingham University in 1925. Maynard's young friend from his old way of life until Lydia captured his universe.

Sraffa, Piero (1898–1983). The celebrated left-wing Italian economist who finally settled permanently in Cambridge in 1927, after earlier visits there; Maynard assisted him to overcome the obstructiveness of the immigration authorities.

Stephen, Adrian Leslie (1883–1948). Virginia Woolf's brother; temporarily separated from his wife, he lodged at the same house as Lydia, 41 Gordon Square, while training as a psycho-analyst.

Stephen, Karin Elizabeth Conn (1889–1953). Adrian's American wife who had distinguished herself at Newnham College, Cambridge. Though deaf and sometimes sad, she was a psycho-analyst.

Stoll, Sir Oswald (1866–1942). The great impresario was chairman of the Coliseum and had many other theatrical interests.

Strachey, James (1887–1967). Younger brother of Lytton. Psychoanalyst and translator of Freud's collected works. Like Lydia, he lodged at 41 Gordon Square.

Strachey, Lady (Jane) (1840–1928). Mother of Lytton and nine other surviving children.

Strachey, Giles Lytton (1880–1932). Critic and biographer: Maynard's old Cambridge friend.

Strachey, Marjorie (1882–1964). The youngest of Lytton's five sisters; sad and exhibitionist; a teacher and author.

Strachey, Oliver (1874–1960). Historian and civil servant; the sixth member of the Strachey family.

Strachey, Rachel ('Ray', 1887–1940). Second wife of Oliver, sister of Karin Stephen. Author; active in public work.

Tchernicheva, Lubov (Luba) Pavlova (1890–1976). Russian dancer. Married Grigoriev in 1909 and joined the Diaghilev company.

Trefilova, Vera Alexandrovna (1875–1943). Russian dancer from the Maryinsky, whose final performance with Diaghilev was in the *Sleeping Princess*. She danced with Massine, who was 20 years her junior, in London in 1924.

Valois, Dame Ninette de ('Ninnie', 1898). Irish dancer, choreographer, teacher and ballet director who founded the Royal Ballet. Trained by Cecchetti. Worked with Lydia and Massine in 1922. With Diaghilev's company 1923–5. Lydia's close friend.

Vladimiroff, Pierre (1893–1970). Russian dancer. He had the chief male role in Diaghilev's *Sleeping Princess* in 1921–22.

Waley, Arthur David (1889–1966). Austere half-member of 'Bloomsbury' who lived in Gordon Square with Beryl de Zoete and worked at the British Museum. Well known for his translations from the Chinese and Japanese.

Wallas, Graham (1858–1932). Author and teacher of political science at the London School of Economics.

Walston, Sir Charles (1856–1927). Fellow of King's College, reader in classical archaeology at Cambridge.

Weller, Ruby (d. 1987) Lifelong and much appreciated servant of the Keynes' at Tilton; she was married to Edgar.

Wittgenstein, Ludwig Josef Johann (1889–1951). The famous philosopher. Born in Vienna, he first came to Cambridge in 1912. He was a recluse and Maynard was one of the few who knew him well.

Woizikovsky, Leon (1897 or 1899–1975). Polish dancer and ballet master. Trained by Cecchetti. Joined Diaghilev in 1916 becoming one of his outstanding character dancers. He and his friend Sokolova worked with Lydia and Massine in 1922–23 and then returned to Diaghilev.

Woolf, Leonard Sidney (1880–1969). After leaving the Ceylon civil service, he married Virginia Stephen in 1912. Founded the Hogarth Press 1917; literary editor of the *Nation* 1923–30; a socialist and expert on international affairs. Author, including novelist.

Woolf, (Adeline) Virginia (1882–1941). Née Stephen. The novelist, critic, biographer etc., whose published diaries have ensured her immortality. She sometimes had very poor mental health and committed suicide after several much earlier attempts. While she had a poor appreciation of Lydia as a newcomer to 'Bloomsbury', she later changed her mind.

Zoete, Beryl de (1877–1962). Life-long companion of Arthur Waley; expert on far eastern dance.

Key to First Names and Nicknames

ADRIAN Stephen	KARLUSHA (KARL) Lydia's mother
ALIX Strachey	LEON Massine or Woizikovsky
ANGELICA Bell	LEONARD Woolf
ANGUS Davidson	LIL Courtauld
ARCHIE Rose	L.G. Lloyd George
ARTHUR Waley	LUDMILLA Nicolaeva
BASIL Maine	LYTTON Strachey
BERTA Ruck	MAESTRO Cecchetti
BORIS Anrep or Kochno	MARGARET Hill or Keynes
BUNNY David Garnett	MARGOT Asquith
CHRISTABEL Lady Aberconway	MARJORIE Strachey
CLIVE Bell	MARY Hutchinson
COLEBOX Lady Colefax	MIM Marie Rambert
DADIE George Rylands	MOLLY MacCarthy
DENNIS D. H. Robertson	MURIEL Gore
DESMOND MacCarthy	NINETTE (NINNIE) de Valois
DOBBY Frank Dobson	OSBERT Sitwell
DUNCAN Grant	OSWALD Stoll
ELIZABETH Princess Bibesco	PAT Anton Dolin
FAITH Henderson	PETER F. L. Lucas
FLORRIE Grenfell	QUENTIN Bell
GARIA Harold Bowen	RAY Strachey
GEOFFREY Keynes	RICHARD Braithwaite
GRACE Higgens	ROGER Fry
HASSAN Arfa	RUBY Weller
HELEN Anrep	SACHEVERELL Sitwell
HETTY King	SAM Courtauld
HILDA Sokolova or Bewicke	SEBASTIAN W. J. H. Sprott
HUBERT Henderson	SERGE (BIG SERGE) Diaghilev
JACK Hutchinson	STAS Idzikovsky
JULIAN Bell	SYDNEY Courtauld
KARIN Stephen	TEDDY Edward Grenfell

Key to First Names and Nicknames

Select Bibliography

Beaumont, C. W. *The Diaghilev Ballet in London*. Putnam, 1940.
Beaumont, C. W. *Bookseller at the Ballet*. Beaumont, 1975.
Bell, Anne Olivier, ed. *The Diary of Virginia Woolf*, Vols. I to V. Penguin Books, 1977 to 1985.
Bell, Q., *et al. Charleston: Past & Present*. The Hogarth Press, 1987.
Buckle, R. *Diaghilev*. Weidenfeld and Nicolson, 1979.
Buckle, R. ed. *Dancing for Diaghilev: The Memoirs of Lydia Sokolova*. Murray, 1960.
Clarke, Mary, *Dancers of Mercury: The Story of Ballet Rambert*. Black, 1962.
Dolin, A. *Ballet Go Round*. Michael Joseph, 1938.
Grigoriev, S. L. *The Diaghilev Ballet: 1909–29*. Trans. and ed. by Vera Bowen, Constable, 1953.
Harrod, R. F. *The Life of John Maynard Keynes*. Macmillan, 1951.
Haskell, A. L. *Balletomania*. Gollancz, 1934.
Holroyd, M. *Lytton Strachey: A Biography*, 1967–68. Penguin Books, 1971.
Karsavina, Tamara. *Theatre Street*. Dance Books Ltd, 1930.
Keynes, J. M. *The Collected Writings*. Thirty volumes, Macmillan, 1971 to 1987.
Keynes, M. ed. *Essays on John Maynard Keynes*. Cambridge University Press, 1975.
Keynes M. ed. *Lydia Lopokova*. Weidenfeld and Nicolson, 1983.
Maine, B. *The Best of Me: A Study in Autobiography*. Hutchinson, 1937.
Massine, L. *My Life in Ballet*. Macmillan, 1978.
Meisel, P. and Kendrick, W. eds. *Bloomsbury/Freud: The Letters of James and Alix Strachey, 1924–25*. Chatto and Windus, 1986.
Moggridge, D. E. *John Maynard Keynes*. Penguin Modern Masters, 1976.
Nicolson, N. ed. *The Letters of Virginia Woolf*. Vol. III. Hogarth Press, 1977.
Rambert, Marie. *Quicksilver: An Autobiography*. Macmillan, 1972.
Sitwell, O. *Laughter in the Next Room*. Macmillan, 1949.
Skidelsky, R. *John Maynard Keynes*. Vol. I 1883–1920. Macmillan, 1983.
Skidelsky, R. 'The Wooing of Lydia.' 1986 (unpublished lecture).
Spalding, Frances. *Vanessa Bell*. Macmillan, 1983.
Wilkinson, L. P. *A Century of King's*. King's College, Cambridge, 1980.

Index

Index

Index